Contents

Preface and Acknowledgments

Perhaps this book is not the result of a sheer accident, yet it is still the outcome of an initially unforeseen project. Nine years ago, while conducting a course on the Mexican Revolution at Bar-Ilan University, I explained to my students in a very general way how the word "revolution" had assumed a political meaning sometime during the early modern period as a metaphor borrowed from the language of astronomy. I based this explanation on data found in several trustworthy dictionaries and encyclopedias, and it appeared at the time as though my students were satisfied with the presentation. But somehow my own curiosity as to the circumstances that changed the word's meaning was aroused. As I began to read specific studies that had tried to answer the question, the fog surrounding the penetration of the term into the political language of Italy, France and England (these turned out quite early to be the crucial polities) would not clear up. Scholars, even when they indicated some of the major texts relevant to the politicization of "revolution," seemed to remain indecisive on where exactly it came from, what was the connection of the new term with ongoing political events, or when precisely it assumed a sense of unidirectional political change.

The first paper I ventured to write dealt with the emergence of the epithet "American Revolution." I then went back, however, to earlier stages of the political history of the word, an effort which resulted in a string of five articles. Two of them dealt with the beginnings of the term in Italy; one each attempted to cover its entrance to the political discourse of France and England; the fifth dealt with its presence in seventeenth century English astrology. These articles, albeit substantially expanded, correspond with chapters one, two, three, four and eight. I would like to take this opportunity to again thank the editors and anonymous referees of the *Journal of American Studies* (1993), *History of European Ideas* (1994), *History* (1995), *Journal of the History of Ideas* (1995), *Rinascimento* (1995) and *Historical Reflections* (1997) for sponsoring my raw ideas and at the same time forcing me to rephrase and elucidate them. The other parts of the book were written last, appearing here for the first time.

Once I had enlarged my aim and decided to cover the place of "revolution" in political discourse throughout the entire early modern centuries, I began an extended search for a variety of works believed to contain matters relevant to the subject. In practical terms it necessitated shorter and longer visits to research centers in Europe and America, in addition to what was available to me in my own country (Israel). I thank the staff of the following libraries, where my requests were handled considerately and efficiently. They include the British Library in London, the Bibliothèque Nationale in Paris, the New York Public Library, the Folger Shakespeare Library and the Library of Congress in Washington, the National Library of Canada in Ottawa, the National Library in Prague, the Biblioteca Nazionale Marciana in Venice and the National Library in Jerusalem. Much needed help was given to me at the stage of converting the manuscript into a printed text. I am beholden to my dear friend of many years, Joan Lessing, for patiently amending my syntax and style; my thanks go also to Isabelle Klebanow, who skillfully prepared the typesetting. Unless otherwise indicated, translations of passages from Italian and French are my own. In citations in the original from sources in these languages, as well as from English sources, I kept the spelling of the time. It creates inconsistencies, but it hopefully helps to retain an authentic flavor of the expressions.

Introduction

This study is intended as a contribution to the history of political discourse. It will attempt to put together a succinct and reasoned survey of the route through which a new word entered the political vocabulary of western Europe (and by extension, modern Western culture). Before the fifth decade of the seventeenth century hardly any European writer employed the word "revolution" in the straightforward, obvious political sense it later attained (with the exception of a few Italian authors, who merely reflected a tenuous and almost imperceptible local vernacular tradition). But less than a century and a half afterwards, on the eve of the assault on the Bastille and other epoch-making events in France, this word had become not just a vital part of political language, but to a certain extent also a slogan, a banner-word for those advocating thoroughgoing changes in the structure of government. Of course, as it became synonymous with faith and hope to some, it aroused hate and fear in others. People were soon going to die for or against it. Moreover, it expanded its lexical forms. Very soon one was called a "revolutionary" ("révolutionnaire"). As early as September 1790 Mirabeau said that he was accused of being "un conspirateur" and a "contre-révolutionnaire." A new expression that was minted at about the same time reinforced the status of "revolution." This was the phrase "ancien régime." It came to mean the abolished past, whereas "revolution" signified the new age.[1] Therefore, the period of its transition from a non-political word to a conclusively integrated political term, would appear as that long stage of gestation in which it gathered incipient, tentative senses and meanings. This period, roughly stretching from 1640 to 1790, might be considered to encompass the early history of "revolution."

Words, maintained Ludwig Wittgenstein, are everything. The meaning man ascribes to words governs his actions and conditions his social behavior. The classification of words according to certain criteria of hierarchy and propriety is thus an expression of the innermost sensibilities of a given society. Consequently, to remove a word from a language and to replace it with a new one might indicate a change in human outlook or perception. Similar judgments on the significance of words and their replacements have been pronounced, of course, in previous ages. Back in the late seventeenth century George Savile, Marquess of Halifax, wrote:

> The World has of late years never been without some extraordinary *Word* to furnish the Coffee-Houses and fill the Pamphlets. Sometimes it is a *new* one invented, and sometimes an *old* one revived. They are usually fitted to some present purpose, with intentions as differing as the various designs several parties have, either to delude the People or to expose their Adversaries.[2]

He believed, however, that these new words were of short duration; becoming fashionable, and being repeated often for a period of time by everybody, then losing their attractiveness and being replaced in their turn.

But we might consider a contrasting case, one more in congruence with our study. What if a new word endures? What if it becomes an integral part of conventional language? What if it turns into a highly important, emotionally charged political term? Would we not be right to postulate that in this case the regular process of semantic change had coalesced at some point with the history of ideas? Does not the use of the new word reflect a new and widely distributed attitude in society, or to be more specific, did not the use of a new term to denote the violent capture of power in the state, reveal a growing belief that in certain circumstances this kind of action was right and proper? Considering it from this point of view, the conversion of the word "revolution" from its earlier meaning of circling motion to a term essential to our political discourse, can in itself be regarded as a "revolutionary" occurrence within the framework of early modern Europe's intellectual development.

We will return to the stage at which the word began to expand its meanings. At this point let us examine the end results and consider the various definitions "revolution" had taken following its final incorporation into the language of politics. The basic definition of the term might be phrased as *an overthrow of a government of a state by force*. However, this limited-sense definition has been frequently challenged by yet another originally seventeenth century phrase - "coup d'état," which would suggest that the mere upset of a government by extra-legal means falls short of the high notion we believe "revolution" should carry. The second definition therefore underscores the *sudden and fundamental change effected in the system of a government*. Here the weight is on the outcome of the transfer of power from one ruling apparatus to another, something that might entirely change the character of a regime, or reflect the replacement of one social group by another in the holding of power in the state. But beyond these two definitions, crucial as they are to our manner of understanding of political matters, there is an equally important usage of the word in political discourse in the broad and loose sense of "change," particularly change that in the speaker's view has an uncommon significance and great consequences. In this last lax and arbitrary manner of use, "revolution" might refer to a change consisting of a single event, and it might embrace changes that took shape through a long, extended development. Hence such expressions as the "Roosevelt Revolution" (in reference to measures undertaken by the American president to deal with the economic slump of the 1930s), the "Islamic Revolution" or an almost contradiction in terms such as the "democratic revolution" (to argue the consequences of a law allowing the enlargement of the electorate in a given polity).[3] In fact, this manner of usage of the word has become so preponderant that it is employed in the context of spheres of action that are far removed from politics. Thus we speak of the "scientific revolution," the "industrial revolution," the "computer revolution" or the "revolution" in any subject, theme and business, including babies' swaddling-bands. In all of these phrases the term actually functions as a rhetorical device. It adds a dramatic significance to the changes that took place within the context of the subject examined. Therefore, to the previous two definitions we might add a third one: "Revolution" - *a word employed rhetorically to magnify the importance of a given or desired change.*

The concern that the word should not be used arbitrarily to suit the speaker's own political aims surfaced as soon as it attained its final meaning. In 1797, when the young emigré François René

Chateaubriand completed his first work in England, *Essai sur les révolutions*, he took pains to explain what it meant to him:

> By the word revolution I understand only a total change of government of a people, be it from a monarchy to a republic, or from a republic to a monarchy. Thus any state that succumbs to foreign arms, any mere change of dynasty, any civil war that does not bring meaningful alterations in society, any partial change in a nation momentarily in revolt, I do not consider as revolutions.[4]

This characterization was formulated, of course, under the overwhelming impression of the changes effected by the French Revolution. Therefore, when Chateaubriand set forth the events in Western history up until 1789 that he considered true political revolutions, he listed only twelve instances, seven of which belonged to modern times. These last were (roughly in his own words) the Florentine republic, that of the Swiss, the commotions in France in 1358 during the reign of John the Good, the revolt of the League just before the accession of Henry IV, the break of the United Provinces from Spanish domination, the misfortunes of England during the reign of Charles I and the formation of the United States of America as a free nation. From the perspective of the late 1990s these choices might be challenged, but it is clear that they were meant to illustrate events where the issue of monarchy versus republic weighed on the scales, and admittedly up until 1789 historically important events of this nature were rare and uncommon. It is significant that Chateaubriand did not include in his list the unseating of James II in 1688, the first major event in modern history that was quickly named a "revolution," apparently because it involved no basic change of regime.

There is yet another relevance to Chateaubriand's insistence on the correct meaning of "revolution." Indirectly, it is a recognition that until his time Western political discourse lacked a common word to express the idea of fundamental political change through forcible means. And perhaps, given the premise that the term took a long time to consolidate its status, that would also mean that the idea itself was, until about 1789, either dormant or repressed; this at least is an hypothesis that this study will carefully consider. In any case, it is incontestable that the arsenal of political terms of ancient Greece and Rome, to which our current political discourse is still largely indebted, fell short of suggesting a viable phrase to denote the idea of revolution. Greek authors, such as Aristotle, used the words *stasis* and *metabolé politeion* in reference to a violent coup followed by a change of constitution. Otherwise an overthrow of a political regime was called by Thucydides *neoterismos*, whereas Livy employed in Latin the expression *res novae*.[5] It is especially with this last term that the idea of political change was given a negative flavor as something instigated by a desire of innovation for its own sake.

Thus, although so many important political terms that we use are plainly derived from the discourse of classical antiquity, and were used then in a sense not far removed from the modern one (e.g., "democracy," "oligarchy," "monarchy," "republic," "dictator"), the term chosen to impress the notion of violent seizure of power and change of regime is based on a relatively new word.[6] *Revolutio*, a derivation of the past participle form (*revolutus*) of the verb *revolvo* (to roll backwards), is a Neo-Latin word which means circling motion. It does not occur in classical Latin literature, but early in the fifth century St. Augustine already employed it in the sense of a cycle of time.[7] As we shall see in the next chapter, "revolutio" needed almost one thousand years to acquire a political meaning, and that came about merely as a result of experimentation with the vernacular Italian form of the word - *rivoluzione*. The political term "revolution" is therefore a creation of the early modern centuries. Of popular origins, employing the image of circling motion as a metaphor for political turnover and change, it actually stayed in limbo, as if in a period of incubation, for three hundred years before making its real bid to be a political term of rank.

It is important to stress that this development of an entirely new political idiom in the early modern era is not a unique case. Two other terms of crucial significance were launched around the same time, which might help us to understand better the problems involved with the proliferation of the term "revolution," since their emergence raises comparable and corresponding questions. These two are the words "state" and "sovereignty." Like "revolution" they have lexically a Latin parentage, but were not used in antiquity in the political sense which they later attained. Like "revolution," also, they joined the political vocabulary of the early modern period on the basis of meanings they were given in vernacular languages.

The political meaning of the word "state" is perhaps best remembered to students of Renaissance political literature from the opening sentence of Machiavelli's *The Prince*: "All the states, all the governments that have had and still have authority over men, are states and are either republics or principalities" ["Tutti gli stati, tutti e' dominii che hanno avuto e hanno imperio sopra gli uomini, sono stati e sono o repubbliche o principati"]. Machiavelli defined the term here in its modern sense as any political body of people occupying a fixed territory and organized under one government. There was a need of course in the early sixteenth century for a term that would express the inclusive idea of an organized political body, whatever its particular form of government. Classical antiquity somehow neglected to answer that need. Terms such as *polis, civitas, respublica, regnum,* evidently failed to satisfy the Renaissance quest for a broader and at the same time communicable idiom, and one that would equally apply to the variety of political organizations in Italy and the rest of Europe. At about the same time that Machiavelli wrote *The Prince,* the other great Florentine political author, Francesco Guicciardini, furnished for the same term a definition that cynically highlighted the arbitrary nature of political power: "The state and [political] authority are nothing else than violent sway over citizens, disguised in a few cases by some pretense of honesty" ["Non è altro lo stato e lo imperio che una violenza sopra e' suditi, palliata in alcuni con qualche titulo di onestà"].[8]

Nevertheless, although Machiavelli and Guicciardini left us splendid definitions, they certainly were not the first to imbue *stato* with a political sense. This meaning of the word in Italian is already attested to by a variety of Florentine authors throughout the fifteenth century. In his sermons Savonarola, among other uses, warned, for example, those who opposed "questo stato di Firenze."[9] Before him the term is found in the vocabulary of Vespasiano da Bisticci's political biographies.[10] In fact, it is already present in Alberti's *Della famiglia* (1435), and even in the language of a very early fifteenth century history of Florence by Goro Dati. He too speaks of "lo stato di Firenze," and in one place, explaining the Roman republican inspiration of his contemporary Florentine government, he refers to Julius Caesar, who had "destroyed that State and the popular regime" ["guastò quello Stato, e'l reggimento populare"].[11] Finally, as we go further back to the closing years of the fourteenth century, we find handy examples, demonstrating both the popular origins of the term and the lexical frame of mind that impelled the shift towards a political meaning. For the year 1386 the *Cronica volgare di un anonimo fiorentino* describes a revolt in Naples against Queen

Margaret, where the crowd went on shouting: "Viva il buono istato e muoiano le gabelle" ["Long live the good state and death to excise taxes"]. And in Siena in 1393 the cry is: "Viva il popolo e'l buono istato."[12] Clearly, the Latin word *status*, as related to one's social and political standing, position or condition, had become in the vernacular, and as used in popular speech, a term denoting the power structure that underlay one's political standing.

Traces of the new meaning of *stato* can also be gathered in the histories of the Villani brothers, written in the middle of the fourteenth century.[13] This is significant because the Villanis are our main source showing the early use of *rivoluzione* as a political term. The evidence would thus imply that both words shifted meaning at about the same time. It is also appropriate to add that the two words would be associated almost from the start in the expression *rivoluzione di stato* (later also in the early uses in English and French; "revolution of state," "révolution d'état") to distinguish the use of the term in political discourse from its use in the sense of motion. But the parallel aspects of the histories of the two words are not confined to their origins as popular expressions in the Italian vernacular. As we shall see, "revolution," when taken from Italy to France and England, would be employed specifically for its rhetorical potential. So too were later employments of the word "state," especially when examined in relation to the emergent ideology of princely absolutism. The best known work in this respect is Giovanni Botero's *Della ragione di stato* (1589), where the first sentence almost says it all: "The state amounts to firm domination over peoples, and reason of state is knowledge of the proper means to establish, maintain and extend a domination of this kind." We have advanced here beyond the definitions of Machiavelli and Guicciardini. In Botero's handling of the term "state" is a pliable rhetorical device to argue a complete, unrestricted authority of the ruler over his subjects.

To seek out, however, even more prominent examples demonstrating the rhetorical bearing of "state" on the theory of absolutism we should go to France. The political sense of the word came to France from Italy. As late as 1549 Robert Estienne's French-Latin dictionary contained many illustrations for the word *estat*, making it synonymous with condition, situation and grade, and also tying it with *république*, but it did not yet endow it with a political meaning. This took place in the second half of the sixteenth century, as can easily be seen in the works of Montaigne and others.

Then, in the early seventeenth century, the usage of the word turned remarkably absolutist. In Pierre Charron's *De la sagesse* (1601) the inspiration clearly comes from Botero: "L'estat, c'est à dire, la domination," and he goes on to explain that without the state human society could not exist, thus bestowing on the state a dimension of inviolability.[14] Some three decades later Gabriel Naudé, also inspired by Botero's concept of "reason of state," coined the phrase *coup d'état*. Gradually, this figure of speech would come to mean any violent, quick seizure of power, especially a military takeover. But in Naudé's definition a *coup d'état* is a violent act undertaken by the ruler himself, irrespective of the laws, in order to reassert his authority over his subjects. Indeed, if the state is defined as essentially domination, then the person in charge of the state would be justified in using any act to maintain his full share of power. This rhetorical tradition stands behind Louis XIV's famous utterance: "L'état c'est moi." Years later the Sun King's claims to absolutism would be bolstered with semi-theological arguments. But this saying, for which he is so well remembered, actually belongs to the early stage of his reign. Apparently, it was declared in 1665, during an impromptu reply to the *parlement* of Paris.[15] At that stage no other term but "state" could emit a persuasive resonance, emphatically asserting that the king had no restrictions and was, in fact, the law.

It must be acknowledged that the word "state" proliferated not just because it offered a synthetic and comprehensive term covering all forms of bodies politic. Nor was it only the rhetorical potential of the term, which is the facile way of exploiting it in arguments legitimizing the supreme power of the ruler, that expanded its use. Considered from the broadest perspective, "state" and some other political terms ("revolution" included) were adopted in the sixteenth and seventeenth centuries, because, with the Reformation, the political history of western Europe turned unusually volatile. Germany, the Netherlands, France, England and other countries experienced extended periods of internal divisions, culminating in revolts and long and bloody civil wars. In these circumstances "state" became also a rhetorical antidote to political disunity. We might consider briefly the other new political term that was catapulted to the forefront by the nature of these developments - the word "sovereignty." In this case the comparison with "revolution" is not the Italian vernacular popular origin, as was the case with "state," but rather the circumstances in which it was launched. "Sovereignty" emerged in a polity in a state of turmoil and quickly fitted into the discourse of other places, in a way comparable with that which introduced "revolution" in the 1640s.

"Sovereignty" (*souveraineté*) is of French origin, a word fashioned very likely from the Neo-Latin *superanus*, which meant being above or dominant. Its real entrance into political discourse at a rather late stage was the well-known accomplishment of Jean Bodin, who in his *Six livres de la république* (1576) defined the term as "the most high, absolute, and perpetual power" ["la puissance absolue et perpetuelle d'une république"]. To Bodin sovereignty meant the supreme power of the state over its citizens, unrestrained by law. He maintained that to avoid anarchy there could be only one high authority whom the people must obey. That the term he had chosen to represent this idea consisted of a French vernacular word was conceded by him in a roundabout way in the 1586 Latin translation of his work, done by himself, where he rendered *sourveraineté* as *majestas*. Besides, *souveraineté* was then employed also by several Huguenot pamphleteers, some of whom even used it shortly before Bodin, though in a slightly different sense.[16] It would appear that we have here a case of an old word in the vernacular that suddenly, under the strain of the disturbed political conditions of the French Religious Wars, was given a new definition and brought in as a rhetorical weapon to an ongoing political debate. The adjective of the same word had served Brunetto Latini as early as the second half of the thirteenth century in reference to God ("Nostre Soverain Père"), and also in reference to Plato and Aristotle ("soverain philosophe").[17] In the early fifteenth century Christine de Pisan made similar uses of this word, but also related it to the authority of a king ("telle souveraineté, c'est assavoir majesté royal...").[18] By the sixteenth century, even before the outbreak of the civil wars (1562), the sense of the word had turned political. In his aforementioned dictionary of 1549 Robert Estienne, among other examples, translated "souverain puissance, et dont on ne peult appeler" as *imperium summum*. Bodin, therefore, built on a long standing French lexical tradition. His success in having his own definition of "sovereignty" accepted in France and elsewhere was due to the wide circulation of his book, to his being recognized as a political theorist of stature, and to the support his use of the term gave the trend towards royal absolutism throughout western Europe. In England in 1628, Sir Edward Coke rejected the expression "sovereign power" as "no parliamentary word."[19] But eventually the parliamentary opposition to the Stuarts came to appreciate the rhetorical and argumentative value of the term. On the threshold of the Civil War "sovereignty" was claimed also on behalf of parliament.

As previously suggested, the cases of "state" and "sovereignty" carry lessons that should help us as we chart the route of "revolution." The clear evidence that the two terms originated from words in the vernacular should lead us to consider the plausibility that "revolution" too began that way, i.e., not really from the Latin *revolutio* but from the Italian *rivoluzione*. Moreover, in both cases, particularly that of "sovereignty," we see words that for a very long time had carried borderline, circumstantial political meanings, until they suddenly acquired a pivotal role. Finally, in both cases we can easily appreciate the rhetorical leverage, that is, the potential of the new term to help sway opinion in the direction advocated by the user. There is, however, one substantial difference. Whereas "state" and "sovereignty," once entered into political discourse, were settled there for good, "revolution" would face an inhospitable reception. Having entered, it would withstand threats of being thrown out. During an unusual length of time it would be bypassed by many important writers. Or else, its significance would be tarnished by attempts of deliberate adulterations. Why it happened so should not be hard to comprehend. In contrast with "state" and "sovereignty" which essentially helped to reinforce an existing power structure, "revolution" had to swim upstream against the current. It had to overcome the timidity to use a new term of a suggestive import in polities which had basically conservative social and political makeups.

These problems, affecting the historical emergence of "revolution," inevitably complicated and apparently impeded the attempts to compose learned outlines of its history. To this day there is really no comprehensive study of this subject in English. Despite the vast scholarly interest of the past three decades in the history of political discourse, the number of papers on "revolution" is small. One may astonishingly discover, for example, that a collection of fifteen articles on the languages of political theory in early modern Europe, published just over a decade ago, had nothing at all to say on this particular term.[20] As contended, this might be no accident. It is rather a combined result of the problems mentioned above and the disorganized state of the sources. The fact that the term was not fully espoused until well into the second half of the eighteenth century, meant that up until then no major work on politics employed the word in a determined, sustained and conclusive manner. Therefore, in order to reconstruct its entrance into the language of politics, we must rely on infrequent occurrences of the word in writings of diverse character such as histories, memoirs, diaries, pamphlets, recorded speeches, letters, articles in periodicals, dictionaries and (last but not least) astrological almanacs. Yet another seed of difficulty is the fact that most of those who pioneered the use of the term were writers of lesser stature, whereas among recognized authorities there was often reluctance to use it, or even an outright rejection. The result is that not a little of what was written on the early history of "revolution" in the twentieth century relied on speculation. It is only once we realize the nature of the difficulties and the unsatisfactory state of research on the subject that we can forgive such a great historian as R. G. Collingwood for erroneously maintaining (in 1942), without giving his source, that "The word 'revolution' was borrowed towards the end of the seventeenth century by the vocabulary of politics from the vocabulary of literary criticism."[21]

At present, strictly speaking, there is but one printed work approaching a book-length study on our subject; a monograph in German by Karl Griewank.[22] Although first published in 1955, it was actually based on the state of research before World War II and failed to point out the essential mid-seventeenth century texts. Still, Griewank's interpretation carried weight with many scholars; it was practically adopted, for example, by Hannah Arendt in her widely-read *On Revolution* (1963).[23] In contrast, Arthur Hatto's paper, published in 1948, did not conceal the author's sense of fogginess with respect to the origins of the term, but at the same time had some sound observations and suggested points for further research.[24] Eventually, a number of other papers appeared, concentrating on the entrance of "revolution" to the political discourses of individual countries as England and France. These will be appraised later on in the appropriate chapters.

Perhaps the most trustworthy summary of the established literature on the early history of "revolution" is in the article that Felix Gilbert contributed in 1973 to the *Dictionary of the History of Ideas*. Though aware of the fact that *rivoluzione* had a political meaning as early as the fourteenth century, Gilbert, following Griewank, insisted that the term gained its own particular physiognomy in the course of the sixteenth century. The reason for this, he felt, was the appearance of the word in the title of Copernicus's *De revolutionibus orbium coelestium* (1543), combined with a contemporary sense that a term denoting the orbital movements of the planets could be aptly applied to designate political movements on earth. However, as we shall see, this trend of interpretation lacks real foundation. Although the sixteenth century saw the medieval concept of a stable society destroyed, and although both chiliastic expectations unleashed by the Reformation and notions of a better civil society as revived by the humanists seemingly promoted an outlook more favorable towards political transition and change, there simply is no serious data to connect these developments with the word "revolution."[25] And yet Gilbert apparently took it for granted that the term at that time descended to our worldly political parlance from heaven, that is, from the uses it had in astronomy (and astrology), while retaining something of the original meaning of the parent Latin verb *revolvo*, to roll back.[26]

According to Gilbert, this sense of the word was still embodied in the epithet "Glorious Revolution," given to the events of 1688, since contemporaries arguably saw in it a return to the true old constitution of England and as such a closed cycle. In actuality, however, there is evidence to demonstrate that "revolution" (without "glorious") was employed in 1688 before any constitutional problem had even been addressed or envisioned, and as we shall see, the complexities and dilemmas which bore on the use and meaning of the term in the last quarter of the seventeenth century were of a different kind. But there is more at stake here than just a debate over the precise meaning of the term. Gilbert neglected to notice the question of the *politics* involving the use of "revolution," that is the evidence that the term was employed as a rhetorical device to sustain a political standpoint. For example, while acknowledging the substantial presence of the term in titles of popular French works on history during the first half of the eighteenth century, he merely pointed out that the term was becoming fashionable, overlooking the possibility that its use in a broad and imprecise meaning might have expressed a tendency to sterilize "revolution" of dangerous, subversive semantic implications.

As contended, the most crucial difficulty in reconstructing the early history of "revolution" consists in gaining a clearer picture of its vernacular Italian antecedents. This too would hopefully settle accounts with the notion that the term was acquired from the language of astronomy/astrology. The first chapter of this study thus surveys the place of the twin words *rivoluzione/rivolgimento* in the writings of

Italian historians and political authors from the fourteenth to the early seventeenth century. It develops the argument that *rivoluzione* first established a political meaning as a Florentine slang and then maintained, during some three hundred years, an almost subterranean existence before being recognized and given a conclusive lexical definition. Chapter two takes the theme of the emergence of the term in Italy in the mid-1640s and 1650s. It stresses the contributions of historians of a second rank such as Luca Assarino, Alessandro Giraffi, Majolino Bisaccioni and Girolamo Brusoni, and tries to assess to what extent their new use of the term came in reaction to the climate of pervasive crisis which then permeated European politics. Chapters three and four then follow the term as it was taken from Italy and penetrated the political discourse of France and England at about the same time. As we shall see, the advent of the new meaning in both countries did not proceed without signs of resistance to its use, including cases of maladaptation, evasion, aloofness and even outright rejection. And yet there should not be any doubt that the years of the Fronde in France and the years that followed the setting up of the Commonwealth in England saw the beginning of a new terminology. At this stage of the discussion it would suffice to say that the word was then put to use even by the greatest political personalities of each country, Cardinal Mazarin in France and Oliver Cromwell in England. The first employed it innovatively in his correspondence; the second exploited it brilliantly (from a political rhetoric point of view) in his speech of 22 January 1655.

Chapter five deals with the term in Louis XIV's absolutist France and England of the Restoration. There is an undeniable question associated with the limited diffusion of "revolution" in the political language of both countries in the generation that followed 1660: why a term that had already achieved an incipient measure of use was at that stage noticeably discarded? To perceive that this was so we need no more than examine the works of the greatest writers of that time; Molière, Racine, Bishop Bossuet and Mme de Sévigné in France, and the later works of Milton or the language of Dryden in England. Of course, a complete eradication was impossible, and so we still encounter exceptional cases in a late work of Hobbes, or in Locke and Sidney, enough to tell us that they knew of the political use of the word. The case is otherwise with William Temple, and after the storm of the Exclusion Crisis (1679-81) the frequency of use of the term in England somewhat accelerated, as might be seen in the writings of Nalson, Halifax and Burnet. Still, against all odds, real gains for "revolution" were then scored in France. Two French authors of outstanding political memoirs employed the term in an almost sustained manner. They were the comte de Modène and Cardinal Retz (although the latter would be published only in 1717). Also, the term was given in France (ahead of England) a lexical definition; it was used tendentiously in the popular historiography of the 1670s and 1680s, and it appeared in the polemical writings of French Huguenots, primarily Pierre Bayle's. All of this set the stage for the great gain of 1688, as related to the ousting of James II of England. Chapter six follows therefore the battle of words that hammered out for "revolution" a semantic answer to the usurpation by William of Orange of the British throne. As mentioned, it took a considerable length of time for the epithet "Glorious Revolution" to consolidate. In fact, this seems to have taken place after the controversy surrounding Dr. Henry Sacheverell's trial (1709-10). In France in the meantime a new brand of historiography took shape, commonly known as "Histoires des Révolutions." Unabashedly partisan, strongly committed to the tenets of absolutism (at least in its early phases), it actually made "revolution" synonymous with political change in its broadest sense, that is, change of a cataclysmic nature, which man can neither control nor benefit from.

  Therefore, although the Enlightenment already acquired "revolution" as a word that fully belonged to the language of politics, it encountered considerable difficulty in making good use of it. Chapter seven takes an overview of the term in the writings of the eighteenth century *philosophes*. It demonstrates the gap that existed between the use of the word by early and later authors of that period; for example, Montesquieu who saw in "revolutions" something peculiar to despotic states, and Rousseau, who in rare instances employed the term in the context of a great change which one hoped for. Similar uses, indeed visions of a "revolution" that would deliver Europe from the anguish of inequality and injustice, are found in the writings of the abbé Raynal and Linguet. And yet, there is not enough evidence to suggest that the Enlightenment, a movement claiming that change and progress would be achieved by the effects of reason rather than by the might of force, bestowed on "revolution" a fully modern sense. This is confirmed also when we consider the use of the term by eighteenth century British political authors, such as Hume and the early writings of Priestley. It would appear that in England the word was mainly used in reference to the events of 1688, thus explaining the Glorious Revolution as an extraordinary episode, one of a kind and the only instance permissible for changing a government by violent means. According to this view all other revolutions were messy experiences of turmoil and destruction, violent political ruptures rather than planned performances to achieve a better political system.

What finally changed the sense, place and stature of the word was the independence of the United States and the repercussions it brought about in European intellectual circles, especially in France. Chapter eight follows the minting of the phrase the "American Revolution," a rhetorical formula that was completely missing in 1776, but emerged in the early 1780s following an exchange between Raynal and Thomas Paine, and an important pamphlet by the English philosopher Richard Price. Chapter nine then surveys the manner in which this epithet rebounded and influenced political discourse in Europe on the eve of the great upheaval in France. As we shall see, the "American Revolution" infused a new blood in the language and ideas of such harbingers of 1789 as Condorcet, Mably, Mirabeau and Brissot. The diffusion of the new sense of the word is revealed in the casual recording by Arthur Young, who on 17 October 1787 during his travels in France entered in his diary: "Dined today with a party, whose conversation was entirely political... One opinion pervaded the whole company, that they are on the eve of some great revolution in the government." He then summarized the explanations offered at the dinner as to why a revolution was unavoidable. He mentioned the financial crisis, the lack of true political leaders in the government, the weak character of the king, the pleasure-craving style of life at the court, and "a strong leaven of liberty, increasing every hour since the American revolution."[27] Thus, two years before events in France turned towards violence, we get an indication that indeed a political idiom was being circulated in a manner which painted it with new bright colors. "Revolution" was being equated with liberty. For better or for worse, rhetorical invention was again at work, harnessed to bring about real political change.

Chapter One

The Antecedents:
Rivoluzione (*Rivolgimento*)

The purpose of this chapter is to trace the linguistic and conceptual tradition, stretching from the fourteenth century on, which prepared the term "revolution" for its central role in modern political discourse. As we shall see, in contrast with English and French (where "revolution" could at best on rare occasions evoke the notion of change), Italian contained the word from the fourteenth century on, also in a clear sense of seizure of power through violent means. Thus, what took place in the seventeenth century, when the word was all of a sudden advanced by a group of Italian historians to the foreground of political discourse, should actually be considered a resurrection of an old tradition. As such it demonstrates how a sense of a word can linger on for a very long time, until suddenly new circumstances endow it with an imperative vitality. Rather than an invention, the case of "revolution" should be seen therefore as one of a portentous renovation.

By way of introduction let us recall that at the end of the thirteenth century Italian literary language generally speaking, and Italian political discourse particularly, were still in the stage of formation. Then, around the end of the first quarter of the fourteenth century, with Dante's *Commedia* making its impact felt, the Tuscan dialect asserted itself as the leading idiom in vernacular literature. This development has a bearing also on our subject, since *rivoluzione* appears to be a contribution of Tuscan, specifically Florentine authors. It is important to stress, however, that the term is not found in early Florentine histories in the vernacular, such as the works of Ricordano Malespini and Dino Campagni.[1] Yet the reason for that is certainly not the lack of opportunity. Rather the contrary is the case. The political reality portrayed by these two authors is one of turmoil and lack of stability, including frequent violent changes of government in Florence and elsewhere in Italy.

What terms do fourteenth century authors employ with respect to political change? Classical Latin had transmitted to Italian several words – *coniuratio, seditio, tumultus, rebellio*, all quite adequate to describe political strife also in the setting of communal and seignorial governments of the late Middle Ages. But contemporaries used the Italian forms of these words infrequently, and sometimes they refashioned them in suggestive ways. Thus, for example, from Malespini onwards we find the form *rubellazione* for *ribellione*. The impression is that at this stage political discourse in the vernacular is heavily saturated with colloquialisms, a trend further underscored by a tendency to write the same term in different ways. In any case, the words more frequently employed in the fourteenth century in reference to political turmoil are *romore, novità* and *trattato*. To express the idea of a popular uprising, the first, reverberating with the notions of noise and commotion, is preferred to *tumulto*. The second, not unlike the classical Latin *res novae*, denotes the altered conditions produced by a change of government, and at the same time hints at its unusual and unwanted nature. The third, which commonly has the meaning of contract as well as written composition, is employed in the context of politics to indicate a secret scheme or plan, hence a plot, a conspiracy.[2]

This terminology was bolstered at about the middle of the fourteenth century with *rivoluzione*. The innovators were the two most important Florentine historians of the time, Giovanni Villani and his brother and continuator Matteo.[3] Their use of the term catches the modern reader off guard, a point that will be examined later on. But there is no mistake as to what is meant by it. Describing a failed attempt of political exiles to capture the government of Florence in 1323, Giovanni Villani details how they formed a conspiracy with some nobles inside the city. Accompanied by hundreds of men, they approached the walls. Next the citizens, alerted to the danger from the outside and the possible betrayal from within, rushed with arms to the walls and by their presence there demonstrated that the city was well defended, which then resulted in the departure of the attackers. Thus, he concludes, by the grace of God the city was rescued from "great danger and revolution" ["grande pericolo e rivoluzione"], adding that the intention of the conspirators was to overthrow the executive committee of the priors and the Ordinances of Justice, which had restricted the power of the nobles, and to "subvert all the peaceful state of the city" ["tutto il pacifico stato della città sovertere"].[4]

Giovanni uses the term both in the singular, in reference to a specific change of government, and in the plural, as changes that happen during times of political unrest. Thus he speaks of "great mutations and diverse revolutions" ["grandi mutamenti e diverse rivoluzioni"] that affected Florence in the early 1340s because of the disagreements among its citizens.[5] Overall, in his application *rivoluzione* signifies several things; either a general political unrest, a popular uprising or the end result of an extralegal overturn of government. In this last sense *rivoluzione* also carries an intimation of something beyond human control, a notion which might be contrasted, for example, with the choice of words of Giovanni's contemporary, the Roman "popular tribune" Cola di Rienzo, who declared in 1347 that his intention was to work for "reformation and renewal of justice and liberty" ["riformamento e rinovamento della giustizia et della libertà"].[6] Of course, Cola's terminology betrayed an indebtedness to ancient Roman discourse that plainly differed from Giovanni Villani's colloquialism.

A similar employment of *rivoluzione* is found in Matteo Villani. Referring to a popular uprising and change of form of government that took place in Siena in 1355, while emperor elect Charles of Luxemburg stayed in the city, he speaks of "the sudden revolution accomplished by the citizens of Siena, who had overthrown and knocked down their old government" ["la subita revoluzione fatta per gli cittadini di Siena d'havere disfatto, e abattuto il loro antico reggimento"]. Shortly afterwards he terms a series of attempts of popular insurrections in Lucca, Pisa and Siena as "the revolutions, and dangerous novelties" ["le revoluzioni, e gravi novità"]. But when he uses the term to describe conditions in the kingdom of France, it is clear from the context that the word also stands for confusion and disorder.[7]

In the histories of both Villani brothers two other words, closely related to *rivoluzione* in derivation and meaning, are employed – *rivolgimento* and *rivoltura*. As the first word they signify extralegal political change, though they are also given related meanings, such as movements of rebellion and turning, politically, from one side to the other.[8] Semantically, all three words are considered a derivation from the Latin verb *revolvo* (to roll backwards), though as mentioned in the introduction *rivoluzione* is obviously a vernacular form of the Neo-Latin word *revolutio* (circling motion). It was only natural, therefore, that from the twelfth century on, as western Europe became better acquainted with ancient astronomy and astrology, mostly through translations from the Arabic, this word, *revolutio*, would begin to serve as the conveyor of several notions. To begin with, it referred to the circling movement of the planets, but in addition to that also the time that corresponded to the completion of these gyratory movements, and by extension, the time measured by any cyclical phenomena, such as the day, the month and the year.

Given its connection with the idea of cyclical beginnings and ends, and its use in a discourse where the planets were believed to influence human existence, it was the opinion of Arthur Hatto that at some point, perhaps early in the fourteenth century, *rivoluzione* had been borrowed from astrology and given a new, political meaning. He was confident that eventually an appropriate contemporary quotation, linking the word both to astrology and politics, would be found; but he apparently gave up an attempt to search for it himself.[9] His supposition is quite plausible. Indeed, in the second half of the thirteenth century Italian astrologers, like Guido Bonatti and Pietro de Abano, became famous for the assertive manner in which they practiced their art. Their bold forecasts could have been matched by an inventive language and new metaphors, or could have tempted others to transpose astrological terms into the language of politics. In the words of an important modern commentator, Bonatti believed that "all that happens below the orbit of the moon is linked by strict determinism to the revolutions of the celestial bodies."[10] Still, it is difficult to locate a passage that would indicate a shift of the meaning of the word from motion to politics. In Bonatti's huge tract on astrology in Latin (although its title is *De astronomia*), divided into ten parts, the fourth is entitled *De revolutionibus*. It explains with the utmost care and detail what the revolutions of the planets consist of, and how they are to be measured and interpreted. A correct interpretation, vows Bonatti, should yield the secrets of what would occur in a coming year for good or for bad, including the fates of kings and governments. But it is clear that his "revolutions" are the key to the foreknowledge of almost everything, not merely political events.[11] De Abano's standard handling of the term in his 1293 translation of Abraham ibn Ezra is to associate it with the concept of time, e.g., *revolutio anni, revolutiones annorum mundi*.[12] In this both he and Bonatti seem to maintain a formulation established with the early translation to Latin of the Arab astrologer Albumasar (Abu Mashar Jafar ibn Muhammad; 787-886) in the twelfth century. As for non-astrological texts, the word *revolutio* is apparently missing from the Latin chronicle of Bonatti's contemporary, Salimbene de Adam, whose language is quite flexible in addition to his interest in astrology.[13]

A search for the word in late thirteenth century political and cosmographical texts in the vernacular yields likewise a slight harvest. Brunetto Latini's encyclopedic work *Li livres dou trésor*, although written in French, was completed in Florence in about 1266, shortly after he returned from a long stay in northern Europe. Here the words employed for the movements of the planets are "cercle," "course" and "chemin," and the author's endorsement of astrological lore is expressed by his assertion that the comet of 1264 signified the "shake-ups of kingdoms or death of a great lord" ["remuemens de regnes u mort de grant signor"]. In the last section of this work Latini deals with politics, "the noblest and highest science." Still, the word "revolution" is absent throughout.[14] We do find it, however, in the cosmography of Ristoro d'Arezzo, *Della composizione del mondo*, written in 1282. He too refers to circling motions with words like "cerchio," "giro," "orbi" and "movimento circolare," but we also encounter clusters of "rivoluzioni," related to either movement, course of motion or time, and not to the concept of change or to politics.[15] Actually, Ristoro comes close to providing us with the sought after formulation. This occurs at the end of his book, where his cosmography turns to astrology. In his universe "everything is turning and moving" ["tutto volgere e muovere"], and the movement of heaven is given as the source of the constant changes on earth. Nevertheless, the term he employs is simply "movimento," not the "revoluzione del cielo" which he uses elsewhere.[16] In a similar vein, with respect to recurrence and meaning, we find the word in Dante. It appears only in *Il convivio*, his unfinished treatise on the universe and knowledge, and has the sense of a full circling motion around a fixed point as related to the stars.[17]

Perhaps the most suitable candidate to have given us an evidence of an expanding meaning of *rivoluzione*, is the astrologer Francesco Stabili, better known as Cecco d'Ascoli, who was burned alive in

Florence in 1327 on the charge of heresy. In his Latin astrological texts the word has its place; it is even employed in passages where he maintains that the circling motion of a planet has a controlling effect on the fate of things below.[18] But it does not appear in his major work in the vernacular, the long poem *L'Acerba*, which describes the forces of nature in a sort of allegoric-didactic manner. Although the whole work is saturated with astrological ideas and abounds with examples equating circular movement with control, the words employed there for the motion of the stars are just "giro," "cerchio."[19]

This apparent discernment in the use of *rivoluzione* is noticed also in the language of Giovanni Villani. In addition to his use of the word in a political sense, he frequently relates to comets and other astrological subjects, besides leaving us a detailed account of Cecco d'Ascoli's case. He dedicates a long chapter to the conjunction of Saturn, Jupiter and Mars in the sign of Aquarius in 1345, where it is said to presage "great commutations of kingdoms and of peoples, the death of a king and transfers of dominions" ["grandi commutazioni de' regni e di popoli, e morte di re, e traslazioni di signorie"].[20] Here, however, and in other places where astrological matters are discussed, the word *rivoluzione* is not employed. Given the associations of his subject and the fact that he has a grasp of the political meaning, this is contrary to one's expectations. But it raises the possibility that he does not regard the term as a metaphor derived from astrology.

Therefore, we might look as well for an alternative explanation of the political sense of the term. A clue to that can be found in yet another passage of Giovanni Villani. Describing events of the year 1328, he tells of the death of Castruccio Castracani, the famous warrior and lord of Lucca. On his death bed, Castruccio allegedly said to his close friends:

> 'I am about to die, and once I am gone you will witness a downfall,' [said] in his vulgar Lucchese tongue, which means in a more broad vernacular: 'you will see a revolution,' or else in a Lucchese saying 'you will see the world pass away'. ['Io mi veggo morire, e morto me, vedrete disasseroccato,' in suo volgare lucchese, che viene a dire in più aperto volgare: 'vedrete rivoluzione,' ovvero in sentenzia lucchese, 'vedrai mondo andare'].[21]

Here we have *rivoluzione* in yet another sense – a change of circumstances for the worse. But the quotation also indicates that the word is considered an informal or colloquial expression, which in turn should set us thinking about its source in terms of a vernacular semantic development. As stated above, the word we encounter in the histories of the Villani brothers has its parallel in the forms *rivolgimento* and *rivoltura*. These words, like others which were used in an alternative form, such as *mutazione/mutamento*, derive from the same verb. In the case of *rivoluzione/rivolgimento* the verb is *rivolgere*, denoting to turn, to turn over, to overturn and some other related meanings. Significantly, this verb is used by early fourteenth century authors to describe changes in politics. Dino Compagni, who ends his *Cronica* with a reproof to the faction that had taken power in Florence, promising the offenders that Emperor Henry VII would punish them, utters vehemently: "Ora vi si ricomincia il mondo a rivolgere adosso" ["Now the world is beginning again to turn over you"]. And if this example is still highly metaphorical in its imagery, then by the time we get to Giovanni Villani the phrasing has become appreciatively more precise. Telling of an attempt to unseat the government of Siena in 1324, he writes that the conspiracy was undertaken "per rivolgere lo stato della terra ["in order to turn over the government of the city"]. Here, as we see, not only *rivolgere* is used in the context of politics, but the word *stato* has been added and given the meaning of government, a development that is seen in other contemporary sources.[22] From this point it is only one step more to the language employed by Matteo Villani when he writes on the failed attempt of the Doge of Venice, Marino Faliero, to take control of the government from the Council of Ten in 1355. Faliero, who was subsequently tried and beheaded, is said by Matteo to have aimed at: "il rivolgimento dello stato di quella città" ["the revolution of the state of that city"].[23]

If we accept the view that *rivoluzione/rivolgimento* is derived from a semantic development of the same verb, *rivolgere*, we can at least bypass the difficulties of the assumption that *rivoluzione* is a metaphor borrowed from astrology, for which, as we saw, definite documentary evidence is still lacking. Either way, the terminology occasionally employed by the Villani brothers barely penetrated the writings of their own generation and the next one. Although a sixteenth century authority on the language of Boccaccio saw fit to note that the author of the *Decameron* had used the term *rivolgimento* in one of his letters, it is equally significant that neither this word nor *rivoluzione* appear in his major work.[24] Other collections of stories of the second half of the fourteenth century equally avoid the words. They are missing in

Ser Giovanni's *Il pecorone*, Franco Sacchetti's *Trecentonovelle*, Giovanni Gherardi da Prato's *Il paradiso degli Alberti* and Sercambi's *Il novelliere*. The same goes for Fazio degli Uberti's long poem *Il dittamondo*.

Among Florentine authors of chronicles in the generation that followed the Villani brothers it is somewhat different, but only slightly so. We do not find the terms in the short anonymous chronicle that covers the years 1301 to 1379, nor in several eyewitness accounts of the Ciompi revolt of 1378.[25] But Marchionne Stefani, the most outstanding historian of that generation, does employ on a rare occasion "rivolgimento dello stato" in reference to uprisings and change of government that took place in Florence in 1383.[26] The terms is missing, however, in the *Memorie storiche* of Nado da Montecatini, covering the years 1374 to 1398. But we encounter it in the *Cronica volgare* (formerly attributed to Piero Minerbetti), where we read of a "grandissima discordia e rivolgimento dello istato" that took place in Siena in 1388 and of "grandi rivolgimenti" in the towns of Sicily in 1392.[27] And yet the term is not repeated in the chronicles of Giovanni Morelli and Jacopo Salviati that cover the first decade of the fifteenth century.

To sum up, the impression is that the terminological innovation of the Villanis had failed to reach the political language of the next generation. Although the chroniclers of the second half of the fourteenth century continued to employ the traditional terms *romore*, *novità* and *trattato*, and also enhanced the political meaning of the word *stato*, sometimes in combination with the twin terms *mutazione/mutamento*, on the whole they avoided *rivoluzione* and *rivolgimento*. The use of these two words apparently entered a period of subterranean existence, which only the rare evidence of singular, infrequent employments separated from complete disappearance.

How can this be explained? To paraphrase the famous sixteenth century author Baldassare Castiglione, some words get worn-out, lose their charm and fall into disuse, while others grow in appreciation until time catches up with them in their turn. Castiglione thought that had Petrarca and Boccaccio returned from the dead to live and write, they would not have used many of the words which abounded in their works. In this he echoed ideas expressed by Renaissance students of the nature of language since Dante, who had subscribed in the *Convivio* to similar views, including the observation that "Latin is permanent and incorruptible, whereas the vernacular is not stable and

corruptible."[28]   Still, in the case of *rivoluzione/rivolgimento* a well
defined historical development helped to decide the outcome, at least
in the short run. This was the advent of humanism. We have a
circumstantial indication for this from Filippo Villani, the son of
Matteo. At about the turn of the century, assessing the importance of
the works of his uncle and father, he found great fault with their
language and narrowed their value as historians to merely collecting
facts worthy to be remembered so that eventually more talented
writers could render their books in a polished style. Filippo, who had
become a full-fledged classicist, looked down on the vernacular and
admired Boccaccio for employing Latin only in his later work. As for
political discourse, the man to follow, according to Filippo, was
Coluccio Salutati, the chancellor of the republic of Florence for thirty
years (1375-1406), and "the greatest imitator of the ancients," who
fashioned his style, of course, on the language of Cicero.[29]

Under the weight of the new norms of literary esthetics and
rhetorics, even champions of the vernacular were bound to expurgate
their discourse and unload terms that sounded like half-baked
colloquialisms. The best known and most influential accounts of
Florentine history in the Quattrocento were written by Leonardo Bruni
and Giovanni Francesco Poggio Bracciolini, but in Latin and in a
language charged with terms associated with ancient republican
Rome.[30]   Major accounts in *volgare* also reflected these canons of
humanist writing. Gregorio Dati, for example, covering the history of
Florence from 1380 to 1405, has been found by a foremost modern
authority to lack "an adequate politico-historical terminology" and yet
to anticipate in many ways the reasoning of later Renaissance
historians.[31]   The twin words *rivoluzione/rivolgimento* are missing
from his vocabulary. On the other hand, Giovanni Cavalcanti, who
left us the only contemporary detailed account of the expulsion and
return of Cosimo de' Medici (1433-34), allowed himself on a rare
occasion to refer to "tanti rivolgimenti di Romagna," by which, it
seems, not just extralegal political changes were meant but rather
general and widespread disturbances.[32]   In comparison with these
works of Dati and Cavalcanti, the *Ricordi storici* of Filippo Rinuccini
retained much of the outlook of the Trecento, and of its vocabulary as
well, though without making use of *rivoluzione*.[33]

By the mid-1430s, however, humanist culture was coming to terms
with the vernacular.   The two outstanding examples of this
development are Matteo Palmieri's *Della vita civile* and Leon Battista

Alberti's *Della famiglia*. In both works one finds a political terminology that discards colloquialisms in favor of clearer, more precise, and at the same time rather eloquent expressions. Thus Palmieri, in a well known passage where he discusses the fate of societies whose members stray from values contributing to the common good, employs formulations as "terminare lo stato di quella città" ["end of the government of that city"], "ruinato lo stato" ["the state having been ruined"] and "l'estremo disfacimento della republica" ["the utmost disintegration of the republic"]; whereas Alberti has: "perturbazioni di stati, eversioni di republiche" ["confusions of states, destructions of republics"].[34] Needless to say, this manner of rhetoric has no place for either *rivoluzione* or *rivolgimento*. But as a matter of fact neither of these words occur in the language of such a popular contemporary preacher as Bernardino da Siena, who, when touching upon the subject of forcible change of government, uses "mutamento di stato."[35]

During the next two generations humanist eloquence continued to shape literary style in the vernacular. It is important to remember, however, that even at this stage major texts on politics were more likely to be written in Latin, as was the case of the works of Francesco Patrizzi and Bartolommeo Platina. Therefore, it would appear that the non-gyrational meaning of the word *rivoluzione* perhaps continued to be used in conversation, although it is extremely difficult to demonstrate this with concrete evidence. For example, in his famous commentary on Dante, written in the 1470's, Cristoforo Landino employs the word, though not in a political sense,[36] but it is not found in the texts of non-learned diarists such as Luca Landucci and Bartolomeo Masi.[37] And yet, as we approach the 1490s we come upon evidence that the term is still alive. In the collection of biographies of famous men by Vespasiano da Bisticci it is used twice in the same paragraph in a passage describing Florentine politics in 1434, following the capture of power by Cosimo de' Medici.[38]

Vespasiano's *Vite* were written when Florence was becoming attentive to the moral preachings of Savonarola. To claim that the enhanced visibility of *rivoluzione* at the end of the Quattrocento was due to the prophecies of doom of the Dominican friar would perhaps appear rather tenuous. Nevertheless, next to the Villani brothers, Savonarola is possibly the most influential user of the term, and the one who gave it a measure of ingrained status in political discourse. After the commencement of the invasion of Italy by Charles VIII of

France and the banishment of Piero de' Medici in November 1494, Savonarola began calling on the citizens of Florence to effect a complete change in their system of government, to join politics and morality, civil and religious societies. It is significant, therefore, that he employed *rivoluzione* in the context of this campaign. We find it in his "Outline of the Revelations" of 1495, where he writes of predictions he had made some years before and divulged only to his close followers so as not to cause a public scandal. Among those were predictions on the deaths of Pope Innocent VIII and Lorenzo de' Medici, and "the revolution of the State of Florence, which I said would be when the King of France will be in Pisa." This formulation is repeated with a slight change in the next paragraph. Here "the revolution of the Florentine State" is something that he contemplates in awe, since on the one hand it might be the fulfillment of his vision of a sword hovering over the city and much blood spread around, while on the other hand it might still turn out that God would save Florence if its people would repent their bad ways.[39] The term returns once again in the last paragraph, where he mentions yet another vision, of the "revolution of the Church."[40]

We find the word also in his sermons, as in the one given on 19 December 1494, where he recommends reforming the city government along the lines of Venice, reminding his listeners that that city never experienced "the dissensions and revolutions that had happened here to you in former times."[41] The term is missing from his great cycles of preachings on themes from the Psalms and the prophets Amos and Zechariah, which belong to the years 1495 and 1496; here he employs "mutazione," and also "rinnovazione." But we should not doubt that the "revolution" Savonarola had predicted to his followers would take place upon the coming of the king of France was remembered a very long time afterwards. As late as 1530, Girolamo Benivieni, a friend of Pico della Mirandola and a follower of Savonarola in his early manhood, addressed a long letter to Clement VII, urging the Pope, that now that the republic set up in 1527 had been crushed, he endow Florence with a government fitting its traditions. In this letter Benivieni revered Savonarola as one of the greatest persons Christianity had produced since Christ himself. He reminded the Pope of the friar's prophecies, which in his opinion had largely come through, and specifically recalled the prediction Savonarola had made to his close followers back in 1491 on "the revolution of the state of Florence." Benivieni wrote that he was not present personally when

Savonarola had spoken of "the above mentioned revolution," but he remembered some of the persons who were there and the man who conveyed to him the friar's words.[42] This evidence, that the term *rivoluzione* passed in Florence in the early 1490s from mouth to mouth, is quite important.[43] It warrants the assumption that Florentine political writers of that period were familiar with it, and that their use or non-use of the term was not a consequence of lack of acquaintance. This is relevant of course to Machiavelli. It is very unlikely that he missed hearing of the usage given to the term by Savonarola. Besides, as an author of a history of Florence, he could not have missed it in the works of Giovanni and Matteo Villani, which figured prominently among his sources. Nevertheless, although in the short introduction to his *Istorie fiorentine* he tells us that the main axis of his history is the series of political breakdowns which the republic had experienced since its early existence, the terms he uses are "civili discordie" ["civil strife"], "intrinseche inimicizie" ["internal enmity"] and "divisioni" ["divisions"]. In all his works possibly the only place he uses the word is in the last chapter of the *Prince*, where he refers to "tante revoluzioni di Italia" ["so many revolutions of Italy"]. Here, however, the sense of the word is not strictly political. It rather carries the notion of general disturbances, change of circumstances or a series of changes for the worse. Otherwise, Machiavelli employs "mutazioni dello stato," "alterazioni" and "variazioni de' governi," but by using these he is hardly an innovator.[44] Therefore, given the premise that he is familiar with the political sense of *rivoluzione*, it is hard to escape a conclusion that Machiavelli avoids the word intentionally, probably because he and others consider it too coarse, lacking refinement, or below the standard of an acceptable literary vocabulary.

It is not much different with Francesco Guicciardini. We find the term used some half a dozen times in his first work, *Storie fiorentine*, written in 1509. For example, it is employed in the first chapter for the events which saw the banishment and return of Cosimo de' Medici in 1433-34; and in the second chapter where he mentions the fear of a revolution following the death of Cosimo's son, Piero the Gouty, in 1469; and in chapter twenty-three, as he assesses the accomplishments of an outgoing Signoria in 1498.[45] This work of Guicciardini's, composed when he was in his twenties, is distinguished by its lively style and succinct colloquial and popular expressions, which, by the way, are easily communicable to the modern reader. But afterwards his style became more formal, as would befit a papal administrator, statesman and diplomat. *Rivoluzione* is absent from his essays on government and from his great masterpiece, *Storia d'Italia*, the only work of his that was published at the time (although two decades after his death). This is comprehensible in light of his wish to write a work that would meet the standards of a classical history in the humanist sense.[46] But the term neither exists in his second history of Florence, written about 1527 and left unfinished. At the opening of this work Guicciardini examines Florence's experience in 1343 under the shortlived rule of the Duke of Athens. He argues that, because the latter had adopted tyrannical methods, he was chased out by the common action of all parties, and since then the city never again consented to relinquish control over its own government. It is clear that Guicciardini's discussion of these events is based on materials taken from Giovanni Villani, who, while dealing with them in his twelfth book, employed the term *rivoluzione* several times. Guicciardini, however, dubs them "grandissimi disordini" and "divisioni."[47]

Thus, by avoiding the term, both Machiavelli and Guicciardini supply us with clues on the status of *rivoluzione*. Accordingly, in the early part of the sixteenth century, it is a word that belongs to the lowest level in the hierarchy of terms denoting political breakdown; something of an old Florentine slang, unfit for use in a true literary text. The occurrence of the term in major works on history and politics in the next few decades seems to corroborate this view. Its use is extremely rare and the handful of examples that we come across tend to point to the Florentine derivation. Apparently, the term does not exist in the writings of Machiavelli's friend, Francesco Vettori, nor in Castiglione's *Il cortigiano*. Yet another prominent author of that generation, Pietro Bembo, master of the Ciceronian style, employs in his officially commissioned history of Venice "mutazione di stato" (as do Vettori and Castiglione). But the young Niccolo Guicciardini, nephew of Francesco, writing, in about 1518, a short essay on the Medici political ascendency, refers to the seven years after the fall of Piero de' Medici in 1494 as a period of "great revolutions and troubles" ["grandissime revoluzioni et travagli"]. In an oration in honor of Cardinal Giulio de' Medici, given in 1522, Alessandro de' Pazzi mentions "many revolutions and many banishments" ["molte rivoluzioni, e molti confinamenti"] that had taken place in Florence prior to the arrangements introduced by

Cosimo de' Medici in 1434. In Iacopo Nardi's history of Florence, written two decades later, we find "la rivoluzione dello stato dell'anno 1494," when the Medicis were banished, and "la presente rivoluzione," for 1512, when they came back. As for Nardi, born in 1476, it is appropriate to recall that in his youth he had been a follower of Savonarola.[48]

A Florentine historian who belongs to the next generation, Benedetto Varchi (born 1503), refers to Tommaso Soderini, who in 1527 "joined with all his heart against the Medicis in favor of liberty before and after the revolution of Friday" ["innanzi e poi al venerdi della revoluzione s'addirò vivamente contra i Medici in favore della libertà"]. He employs the term once again when speaking of "la rivoluzione di Genova" in 1528, and also uses "rivolgimento dello stato;" this last phrase is used when he tells of Machiavelli's thoughts just before his death to destroy the manuscript of the *Prince*. Varchi, it should be mentioned, was an enthusiast of the Florentine vernacular of the fourteenth century. He revived the use of some old words, for example *romore*. The same relish for the old vernacular marks the works of Annibal Caro, who employs *rivoluzione* when announcing the news about the seemingly successful conspiracy and uprising of Count Gianluigi de' Fieschi in Genoa in 1547. But apparently this is the only time Caro uses the word in his well known collection of over 800 letters.[49]

For all its rarity, it was still easier for historians to use the term, since they dealt with concrete events, pointedly addressed to and evaluated, than for authors of tracts on politics, who dealt with abstractions. Therefore, one can understand why *rivoluzione* is completely absent from this class of literature. It is missing from Gasparo Contarini's famous essay on the government of Venice, which in any case was originally composed in Latin. But it is likewise missing in another renowned work on Venice by Donato Giannotti. A secretary of the Florentine government during the last republican phase (1527-30) and later an exile, Giannotti is perhaps the outstanding political theorist of that time who least hid his revolutionary convictions. His ideas, moreover, fitted well with the use of the word. For him, as he wrote in 1552, an uprising for liberty was basically an attack against tyranny in an attempt to return things back to the state they were in before oppression had become prevalent. This kind of action could reasonably be expressed through a metaphor that envisioned political change as a wheel revolving backwards to its starting point. Giannotti, however, also considered a case where prior to tyranny government had not been well ordered. In this case one actually had to construct an entirely new form of government, which would be able to resist corruption and disallow a descent to a second tyranny. But the term that Giannotti employs is "mutare lo stato," and his word for introducing new mechanisms to the government is "rifomare."[50]   Neither he, nor Bartolomeo Cavalcanti, another Florentine exile and author of a discourse on the different kinds of republics, have use for *rivoluzione*. On the other end of the political spectrum is Bernardo Segni, a loyal servant of Duke Cosimo, to whom he dedicated his translation of Aristotle's *Politics* to Italian in 1548. Book five of this work contains the famous analysis of revolutions. Segni, however, employs here terms as "sedizione," "tumulto" and "discordia."   His generic term for the main subject at hand is "mutamento di stato."[51]

On the background of this political vocabulary, the language of Sebastiano Erizzo in his *Discorsi dei governi civili* is unusual. This short essay was first published in 1555 together with the above mentioned work of Cavalcanti.[52]   Erizzo, a Venetian senator and a member of the powerful committee of ten, was also a scholar of wide intellectual interests. Besides a work on ancient Roman medals, he translated to Italian Plato's dialogues, wrote on the poetry of Petrarca and composed a well known collection of short stories, *Le sei giornate*. His short tract on government is an early work, published when he was thirty, which may account for the daring terminology. Right at the opening Erizzo suggests that the "revolution of human affairs" ["rivolgimento delle cose humane"], is an existential truth and can offer a preliminary answer to the question of why great states and empires do not last forever. He then refers to "tanti rivolgimenti e mutamenti di stati e di governi," thus equating the meaning of *rivolgimento* with political change proper. Erizzo paraphrases Plato's and Aristotle's ideas on the inevitable changes which affect all forms of government, and he draws on Polybius' theory of the cycle that causes the sixfold political structures to alter one into another (monarchy to tyranny, aristocracy to oligarchy, democracy to anarchy).   This theme had been taken earlier by a number of Renaissance political theorists, notably by Machiavelli in the second chapter of the first book of the *Discorsi*. Machiavelli, however, spoke of the circle ["il cerchio"] in which all republics moved as they underwent changes of regime. Articulating the same idea, Erizzo uses instead "the revolution of the Republics as if in a circle" ["il rivolgimento delle Republiche quasi in un cerchio"]. He employs the verb "rivolgere" in the sense of change, and uses "rivolgimento" to elaborate on the differences between Plato and Aristotle. The latter, he writes, objected to Plato's idea that everything in this world "admits change in a certain revolution of time, according to the rotation of heaven." ["receva mutazione con un certo rivolgimento di tempo, secondo il girare de' cieli"].[53] Elsewhere he maintains that for Plato the power and emotion of the soul make a circular movement "in imitation of the revolution of the universe" ["ad imitazione del rivolgimento dell'universo"].[54]

The terminology employed by Erizzo is not repeated in major Italian histories and political tracts of the second half of the sixteenth century. We get only conventional terms in *Del governo, dei regni et delle republiche*, edited in 1561 by the prolific Venetian author and publisher Francesco Sansovino. This book has descriptions of the constitutions of eighteen states, old and contemporary, written by the editor and others, including a translation of More's *Utopia* by Ortensio Lando. The same goes for the history of western Europe since the Peace of Cambrai (1529) by Lodovico Guicciardini, another nephew of Francesco's and an author much acclaimed at the time. For him the revolt in Naples against the Spanish viceroy Pedro de Toledo and the Fieschi conspiracy in Genoa, both happening in 1547, are "two accidents and tumults of importance" ["due accidenti e tumulti di momento"].[55] In 1565, the same year that Guicciardini's book appeared in Venice, the history of the revolt of the barons against Ferrante I of Naples (1485-87) by Camillo Porzio was published in Rome. Here too *rivoluzione* is missing, as it is apparently lacking in Giovanni Battista Adriani's huge volume on the history of his own time, covering the years 1536 to 1573. A distinguished Florentine, Adriani opens his work with an observation on how a long series of wars and foreign invasions had affected the governments of Italy, so that there was no state, kingdom or principality "that had not felt a great movement or made to change" ["che non habbia sentito gran movimento, o fatto mutazione"]. He claims that among the main factors that cause political disorder are the nature of the peoples and the ambitions of the rulers, but first of all "the continuous revolving of the Heavens" ["il continuo girar del Cielo"]. Yet *rivoluzione* is not a term he uses.[56]

Towards the end of the sixteenth century the vocabulary of Italian historians and political authors came under the influence of new factors. Inside their own country rigidly enforced stability encouraged expressions of support for princely absolutism. We find testimonies of this new state of mind in such works as Giovanni Botero's *Della ragione di stato* (1589) and Giambattista Guarini's *Trattato della politica libertà* (1600). To these authors the term *rivoluzione* seemed out of place, probably not anymore because of semantic considerations, but in view of the fact that it did not carry a censure of those who challenged the ruler's supreme authority. In Botero's *Delle relazioni universali*, dealing with events all over the world, the revolt of the Dutch people against Philip II is emphatically presented as *ribellione*, an act of transgression against a legitimate ruler, which had been preceded with an offense against true religion.[57] The connection between the reformation of religion and rebellion was stressed also in such masterpieces as Paolo Sarpi's *Historia del concilio tridentino* (1619) and Henrico Caterino Davila's *Historia delle guerre civili di Francia* (1630). In Davila's opening paragraph we find, however, the word "rivolutione," though in the sense of a winding course of events.[58] Paolo Paruta, the Venetian writer who belongs to the generation just before Sarpi and Davila, still sticks, in his history of Venice, to a Ciceronian terminology, as would befit a continuator of Bembo. But in his *Della perfezione della vita politica* (1579), where he too discusses the cycle of the six forms of governments, he considers Roman history from the banishment of King Tarquin to the establishment of Caesar's single-person rule as an example of such a politico-historical cycle. He sees it as a proof of the existence of "all these various revolvings" ["tutti questi varij ravolgimenti"][59]

A host of other Italian political theorists likewise dealt at the turn of the sixteenth century (and after) with the issues of civil strife and breakdowns of government, among them Felice Figliucci, Giovanni Antonio Palazzo, Ludovico Zuccolo, Ludovico Settala and Fabio Albergati.[60] Seemingly, not one of them considered *rivoluzione* a useful terminological aid. Ciro Spontone, however, is an exception. In his tract on government, published in Verona in 1600, the word is first employed in a political sense when he mentions the influence of the planets on things below. Then, much further on into the work, he has a chapter on the "causes of the revolution of a state" ["le cagioni della revolutione d'uno stato"]. He divides them into external and internal causes, of which "the internal revolution is of two kinds" ["la revolutione interna è di due sorti"]; either it is a non-violent one that afterwards uses violence tyrannically, or it is one carried by unrestrained violence from the very start. This use of the term is not reiterated enough to endow it a definite significance. But at least, when contrasted with his use of the word "sedition," it appears that "revolution" is an attempt to take power which had been successfully carried through and produced a new government.[61]

If authors with a conformist political bent usually declined to use the term, neither did it enter the parlance of those few who dared to criticize. Traiano Boccalini, champion of political freedom in his *Ragguagli di Parnaso* (1612) and author of the anti-Spanish *Pietra del paragone politico* (1615), is a good illustration. His style is quite facile, verging on journalism, and much of what he writes is tinged with irony, but his political terminology is rather conventional. Yet another adversary of the Spanish presence in Italy, Tommaso Campanella, actually had to conform much of his political writing to his existential conditions during almost three decades of being incarcerated in Naples. His *Aforismi politici* (written about 1602), a major text of his, in the opinion of a modern authority, does not have *rivoluzione*, although considerable attention is given there to the theme of political collapse and transformation. Campanella could have established a connection with the term also in his writings on astrology, but it is absent there too, in spite of his attributing to the movement of the planets above the power to change governments below.[62] In contrast with Campanella, Giordano Bruno employs the word in his main works, particularly in *Degli heroici furori*, where he develops his pantheistic view of the universe. But the context of *rivoluzione* there is cosmological and devoid of a political sense.[63]

Given this predominant absence of the term just before and after the year 1600, we might wonder what had become of the limited, though noticeable semantic tradition, sponsored by Savonarola, the young Francesco Guicciardini, Nardi and Varchi. The answer is twofold: First, when we search hard we can still come up with examples demonstrating the use of the political sense of the word in the works of less important writers;[64] second, we have indications that the word is still employed in conversation or in popular colloquial expressions at the same time that it is barred from literary endeavors. The re-publication of the history of Milan by Bernardino Corio affords a good example. Corio, who died about 1519, had not used the term in the title or text of his work when it first came out in Milan in 1503. But when Giovanni Maria Bonelli reprinted the book in Venice in 1554, he added an announcement on the title page that it also contained "the accidents and the revolutions of almost all of Italy and of many provinces and kingdoms of the world" ["gli accidenti, e le revolutioni di quasi tutta l'Italia, e di molti provincie, e regni del mondo"]. Yet another example is found in *De l'historia di Siena* by Orlando Malavolti, published in Venice in 1599. The author of this work had died in 1596. He had not used *rivoluzione* in his text, and cannot be held accountable for the fact that the three separate indices of the three parts of this volume contain entries under this word. Thus, while Malavolti had termed an uprising against the Medici in Florence in 1527 a "grandissimo tumulto," the man who arranged the index to this posthumous publication termed it "Revolutione di Firenze."[65] In both cases, that of Corio and that of the posthumous book of Malavolti, we encounter printers, rather than authors, advancing the use of the term.

In the end perhaps it did not greatly matter, as the word underwent a major change of status in 1612 with the appearance of the famous Florentine dictionary of the Italian language, the *Vocabolario degli accademici della Crusca*. To some extent the development was anticipated. Although the term was not included in Alberto Acharisio's *Vocabolario, grammatica, et orthographia de la lingua volgare* (1543), it appeared in the forms of *rivolgimento/ravolgimento* in Francesco Alunno's *Della fabrica del mondo* (1584), where the Latin equivalent was given as *perturbatio, commotio, desidium*. It is also of interest to observe that by the end of the century the political sense of the Italian words began to penetrate other European languages through dictionaries. In John Florio's famous Italian-English dictionary, *A World of Words* (1598), the following entry is found:

> *Rivolgimento*, a revolving, a revolution, a turning and tossing up and downe. Also a winding or cranking in and out. Also a cunning tricke or winding shift. Also a revolt, a revolting or rebellion.[66]

In the equally famous *Tesoro de la lengua castellana, o española* by Sebastián de Covarrubias Orozco, which first came out in Madrid in 1611, the word "rebolución" is given as a noun of the verb "revolver" and its meaning is shortly indicated as "alteración."

Printed in Venice, the dictionary of the Accademia della Crusca, a product of years of collective efforts of Florentine scholars, was based primarily on texts in the vernacular of the fourteenth century. Here *revoluzione, rivolgimento, rivoltura* and *rivoluzione* were all given separate entries, and the meanings ascribed to them emphasized the political sense, with illustrations supplied from the histories of Giovanni and Matteo Villani. Thus we find *"Revoluzione. Rivolgimento.* Ed e più proprio degli stati, che d'altro" ["And it is more appropriate for states, than for anything else"]. And an even more concise definition: *"Rivoltura.* Rivoluzione, rivolgimento, mutazion di stato." These definitions stayed the same in the second edition, which came out in Venice in 1623.

The *Vocabolario*, exercising a tremendous influence on later Italian lexicography, prepared the term for its new role in political discourse. But we should not entertain an idea that this now happened overnight. In 1628 a work by Ottavio Sammarco, *Delle mutazioni de' regni*, appeared in Naples, which merited enough interest to be reprinted in Venice and Turin in the following year. The term *rivoluzione* is completely absent from this book; but it says something about the ensuing shift in the European political vocabulary that when this book came out in London in 1731 in an English translation, it carried the title, *A treatise concerning revolutions in kingdoms*, and the word "revolution" replaced therein other terms, such as *mutazioni, cambiamenti, ribellioni*, and *congiure*, to denote violent political changes.

Still, from the second decade of the seventeenth century we encounter other signals. In Alessandro Campiglia's history of the reign of Henry IV of France there is a passage explaining the link between changes of religion and political upheavals. If a society moves away from its old religion, he asserts ingenuously, it is bound to add "to the revolution of the ritual... the revolution of the state" ["al rivolgimento del culto... la rivolutione dello stato"].[67] Giorgio Tomasi's history of Hungary which was published in Venice in 1621 carried the title, *Delle guerre et rivolgimenti del regno d'Ungaria*.[68] In 1629 Agostino Mascardi saw fit to put in the mouth of one of the protagonists of his masterpiece on the 1547 Fieschi conspiracy the expression – "una turbulenta rivoluzione."[69] Alessandro Goracci, who completed in 1636 the history of his small town Borgo di San Sepolcro, employed the term some half a dozen times within the space of twelve pages.[70] By 1642 we find Majolino Bisaccioni speaking about the "infection of the revolutions" ["contagio delle rivoluzioni"], and in the same year Alessandro Zilioli employed the term several times in his survey of European history since 1600, using, for example, the phrase "unconcealed signs of new revolutions" ["segni non occulti di nuove rivoluzioni"].[71] The road was thus seemingly being paved for the term to move to the center.

Let us now recapitulate the ups and downs of *rivoluzione* as a political term from the fourteenth to the seventeenth century. To begin with, what we find is a substantive of the verb *rivolgere*, from which are also derived the parallel words *rivolgimento*, *rivoltura*. *Rivoluzione* had of course another, earlier meaning, that which signified circling motions, but although the parent Neo-Latin word of that sense, *revolutio*, played its part in medieval astrological parlance, we do not encounter evidence demonstrating an unequivocal association between the astrological and the political senses. Actually, the first time that we encounter the term in the political sense in the writings of Giovanni and Matteo Villani it already carries a finite, self-understood meaning, and is handled by these writers accordingly. This should allow us to believe that *rivoluzione* is a Florentine colloquial expression. As we have seen, the political terminology of the fourteenth century contained many colloquialisms (with *romore*, *novità* and *trattato* heading the list). *Rivoluzione/rivolgimento* belongs to this list, but it is less frequently used. Even in the language of the Villani brothers it trails behind *mutazione/mutamento*, which is really the main generic term employed to express political change and transformation and the foremost word used by Italian authors throughout the whole period under review.

The advent of humanist culture in the years immediately following the generation of the Villani brothers, exercised an adverse effect on the status of *rivoluzione*. As a term extraneous to the vocabulary of ancient rhetorics, it was excluded from humanist writings on history and politics. But this does not mean that the use of the word in a political sense died out. Very likely, it receded to the level of a term used in informal language, though the impression is that even at this level it may have declined. As we have also seen, at the end of the fifteenth century Savonarola again raised the visibility of the word. From then on we find more Florentine writers who employ the term, although on rare occasions. Moreover, in the second half of the sixteenth century we encounter signs indicating that the word is alive again in informal speech. The publication of the *Vocabolario* in

1612, finally gave it the legitimacy it needed. As we shall see, what happened next was due to a combination of two main factors: First, the early seventeenth century's deliberate free manner of writing; second, the uprisings and civil wars which affected western Europe in the 1640s. Events and a new writing style thus encouraged historians and political commentators to enliven their language and epithets. In this climate and circumstances, *rivoluzione*, a long repressed political term, came into new life.

Chapter Two

Italian Historians and the Emergence of "Revolution"

Although the penetration of the term "revolution" into European political discourse in the mid-seventeenth century has attracted the attention of some scholars, no real attempt has been made to relate this development to the so-called "general crisis" which took place at that time. Also lacking, however, is an assessment of the contributions of contemporary Italian authors to the emergence of the new terminology. These, as we are going to see, are important, because they seem to establish that Italian historians and political commentators were the first, and perhaps the only group of writers, to observe the crisis from the widest point of view as an all-embracing European phenomenon. They also indicate that Italians preceded all others in applying the new word to the series of uprisings and civil wars that affected various parts of Europe in the 1640s. This, one might say, could hardly have been otherwise, given the fact that the word already had an accepted political sense in the Italian language. But it is critical to realize that Italian authors arrived at that stage to "revolution" in their search for new metaphors to account for the widespread cases of political instability. In doing this they ended up influencing the adoption of the new term into other European languages.[1]

As observed in the preceding chapter, during the 1630s and early 1640s *rivoluzioni* seemed to appear with more frequency in the writings of some Italian historians. Admittedly, this new trend is not easily detected and even more difficult to explain, because the new word merely joins, here and there, older terms, without yet establishing a clear dominance or distinction. Besides being possibly related to psychological pressures, provoked by the miseries of the never ending Thirty Years War, perhaps the occurrences of this and other terms are connected with new currents in the writing of history, wherein the Renaissance humanist canons, emphasizing adherence to ancient classical models, began to give way to a manner of writing which allowed more freedom of language. This new versatility also stressed the historian's access to information and his experience in politics, war, diplomacy or administration as assets that would allow him a better grasp of his theme.[2]

As we shall see, much of the literature that came to employ the new term dealt with contemporary events. It would be overly convenient to claim that this enlargement of political vocabulary had been inspired from the start by the series of revolts which shook the foundations of European monarchies beginning in 1640. But certainly the acute and generalized nature of the crisis could not but have its impact. Following years of continued wars, contemporaries witnessed the tottering of the mighty Spanish monarchy, shaken by revolts in Catalonia and Portugal in 1640. Two years later the long civil war in England began. In 1647 Sicily and Naples burst into revolt against Spain, and shortly afterwards France succumbed to prolonged political agitation (1648-1652). Italian historians, observing and documenting these events, felt a need not only to offer explanations, but presumably also to update their relevant terminology.

The quality of the new historiography might be illustrated with a look at the personality and style of Ferrante Pallavicino. In his short creative life, mostly lived in Venice, Pallavicino achieved tremendous fame, in Italy and beyond, on the merit of his scandalous satires; and he paid for his irreverence towards the powerful and the church, when he was murdered in 1644, aged only twenty-eight. Among his works there was one of an innovative historiographical character, *Successi del mondo dell'anno MDCXXXVI*, which came out in Venice in 1638. Here he attempted to present an overall survey of events in Europe in the year 1636. The author moved in his description from Spain to Turkey and from Italy to Germany and Poland, recording battles, revolts, and even instances of outbursts of religious fervor. Although "revolution" did not figure among the terms he used, the work is of relevance to our theme. In its scope and perspective it prefigures similar attempts at recording contemporary affairs that will soon be coming from the pens of other Venetian authors, among them Zilioli, Siri, Birago, Bisaccioni, Gualdo and Brusoni, in whose works "revolution" will already have a role to play. As for Pallavicino, he at least reveals the new concerns and dilemmas facing the historian. These are discussed in his short opening address to the reader. Gone are the humanist ideals of emulating the styles of Livy and Tacitus, and even Machiavelli's and Guicciardini's concerns about the teachings of history and its use as a laboratory to study man's behavior and his ability to control his destiny. Pallavicino's main interest was how to please; what style and language to employ, which themes should be emphasized, how to deploy the sources so as to retain the attention of the readers. Naturally, this flexibility with regards to the means, allowed a new approach with respect to the choice of words and terms.

While it is not an easy task to determine when, where and why Italian authors first began to move the word *rivoluzione* to the forefront, it would appear that the aforementioned group of Venetian historians had something to do with it from the very start. At the end of the preceding chapter mention was made of a colorful expression employing the term in a work of 1642 by Majolino Bisaccioni. Two years later Vittorio Siri used it in the first volume of his famous *Il mercurio*. In addition to these two authors, Alessandro Zilioli used it, albeit sporadically, in his survey of the history of Europe since 1600. As mentioned, in his second volume, published 1642, we find the term several times. In Zilioli's third and last volume, published posthumously in 1646, a description of the constitution of Genoa and its sanguine political history ends with: "quasi sempre si ricorda i Genovesi esser stati travagliati da sedizioni e rivoluzioni domestiche."[3] ["The Genoese are almost always remembered as having been afflicted by seditions and domestic revolutions"]. But as it happened, the presence, visibility and status of the word underwent a dramatic turn in the 1640s in a rather unusual and striking way. A series of monographs came out on the revolts of Catalonia, Portugal, Palermo and Naples, where for the first time use was made of the term in a political sense in the title of the work. The four works are: Luca Assarino, *Delle rivoluzioni di Catalogna* (Genoa, 1644); Giovanni Battista Birago Avogadro, *Historia delle rivoluzioni del regno di Portogallo* (Geneva, 1646); Alessandro Giraffi, *Le rivoluzioni di Napoli* (Venice, 1647); and Placido Reina, *Delle rivoluzioni della città di Palermo* (Verona, 1649).

If only because of the innovation of incorporating *rivoluzioni* into their titles, these books must have given a decisive push to the diffusion of the term. Added to this is the fact that the first and third works were quite successful, enjoying several printings. Assarino's was reprinted in Bologna (1645), and later, in an enlarged form, again in Genoa (1647) and Bologna (1648). Giraffi's was quickly reprinted in 1648 in Padua, Geneva, Ferrara and La Gaeta and appeared in 1650 in London in an English translation. Also important was the typography of the title pages of the four books. *Rivoluzioni* was printed here in block capital letters on the entire width of the page, an undisguised attempt to incite the inquisitiveness of the reader. The visual aspect of these books had thus a touch of sensationalism. In fact, if one raises the question of why the term *rivoluzioni* was appropriated and made use of in such a manner by authors and printers, perhaps the answer is that it had been considered effective in helping to sell the books.

Essentially, what we have here is a commercial literary device, not so much a conscious breakthrough in the practice of political discourse. Indeed, a survey of the text of the four works reveals that the authors employed the new term sparingly and erratically, preferring in most instances conventional words relevant to political violence. In the case of Birago Avogadro's work it is also clear that the term *rivoluzioni* was not endorsed by the author. The Geneva publication of 1646 was actually a pirated reprint of his *Historia del regno di Portogallo*, first published in Venice and Lyon in 1644. In a later work Birago admitted this, declaring that he only recognized as his the Venice edition. In the others, he claimed, many changes were made against his wishes and without his knowledge. He complained of the addition of "many barbarous words" and "intolerable mistakes."[4]

It is not inconceivable that the Geneva printer of Birago's book got the idea for a new heading from the title of Assarino's work, which by 1646 had already gone through its second printing. It is from Assarino therefore that we might gather clues providing an explanation for the innovation.[5] A resident of Genoa (though he had been born in the famous Peruvian mining town Potosi), Assarino had a stormy life as a soldier before he successfully turned to writing novels in his late twenties.[6] *Delle rivoluzioni di Catalogna*, published when he was forty-two, was his first venture into the field of history. He tells us this in the introduction, adding that in contrast with other writers on political events, who base their works mainly on "the announcements in the newspapers," he constructed his story from documents composed by some of the principal leaders of the revolt.

He does not specify how these sources came into his hands, nor whether they contained the new term *rivoluzioni*. It is more likely, however, that the word surfaced at the time in Genoa in conversations touching on the events in Catalonia, or that Assarino simply sought to have a resounding title for his first work in the field of history, than that he had encountered the term in Catalan sources. In an unusual note inserted after the first chapter he apologized to the reader for his tendency to employ words as "fate," "destiny" and the like. It is quite probably that "revolutions" too was incorporated because of this admitted inclination of the author to use expressions suggesting the fatalistic nature of human existence.[7]

If this was his motive, then Assarino might also have justified his choice as a paraphrase on Copernicus's *De revolutionibus orbium coelestium* (1543), a work that returned to the forefront in the first decades of the seventeenth century with the resurgence of the controversy between heliocentrists and champions of the old cosmology. He could have been aware as well of the recent use made of *rivoluzioni* in works by Zilioli and Bisaccioni, and should have known the definitions of the term in the dictionary of the Accademia della Crusca. Still, it is not easy to say what Assarino exactly meant by the term; he hardly used it in his text. Towards the end of his introduction he stressed that the occurrences he was going to describe were not of the nature of great historical events such as destructions of kingdoms, the fall of mighty rulers or horrible defeats of armies. Rather, he wrote, it was the story of seemingly insignificant acts, first undertaken by simple people, to which were added suspicions and religious pretenses, until finally they resulted in uprisings, civil wars and "mutazioni di Dominio" ["mutations of government"].

Assarino's book was not the only contemporary piece to cover the Catalan revolt. Late in 1645, only one year after Assarino, Francisco Manuel de Melo had his *Historia de los movimientos y separación de Cataluña* published in Portugal. Although completed in Lisbon, where the author was at the time imprisoned on the charge of manslaughter, this book was written in Spanish, and in a lively inspired style. An author of other distinguished works, Melo had been a career military officer and served in 1640 under the Marquis of Vélez, commanding the forces charged with the suppression of the Catalans. He had therefore a firsthand acquaintance with the revolt and is said to have undertaken the writing of its history by order of King Philip IV of Spain. Following the separation of Portugal from

Spain at the end of 1640, however, he came under suspicion in Madrid, lost his military commission and was briefly arrested. Eventually, he went back to Portugal, where, as mentioned, he soon got back into trouble.[8] His book on the Catalans displayed nevertheless an understanding of the reasons which had motivated the insurrectionists, and, surprisingly, employed the word "rebolución" in the sense of a violent popular uprising. It is indeed intriguing to speculate whether Melo was aware in 1645 of the existence of Assarino's book and its title, and borrowed the word from there, or whether his use of the term simply reflected an independent penetration of the political sense into Spanish discourse, which might well be the case. In any event, his use of "rebolución" must be considered highly experimental in view of his standard employment of other, more conventional terms ("sedición," "tumulto," "rumor," "movimiento," "alboroto").[9]

As with Assarino, so too Giraffi and Reina did not employ the term *rivoluzioni* abundantly in their texts. Giraffi's work covered the ten days in July 1647, which witnessed the Masaniello revolt in Naples. If that affair has passed into history as the first modern "revolution" it is certainly due to this author, who wrote hastily and had his book printed before the end of that year. His contribution also consisted of employing the term in the singular and infusing it with a time dimension. Thus, the ten days that saw Masaniello's rise to power and death are referred to as "tempo di detta revoluzione."[10] On the other hand, Reina's work on Palermo was written from the standpoint of a foregone condemnation, an attitude which reflected on his use of terminology. The author, a son of Messina, the rival of Palermo, and a town that had remained loyal to Spain, speaks of "le brutte, e vituperose rivoluzioni di Palermo" ["the ugly and abusive revolutions of Palermo"], which are a proof that the citizens of that city are "ribelli di cuori" ["true rebels"]. At one point, he is even willing to cast this approach in words that turn it into a far reaching generalization. All legal experts, he says, hold that "the revolutions, and popular tumults similar to those of Palermo, are crimes... rebellions of the most horrible and detestable kind that have been in the world."[11]

With regard to these works of Giraffi and Reina we may repeat the question: Was the word *rivoluzioni* actually heard in 1647 in either Sicily or Naples, or do we have it in the titles of the two books because the authors or printers felt it appropriate to take advantage of the recent literary innovation of Assarino? As for Palermo, among a group of contemporary accounts of the revolt only Reina employed *rivoluzioni*.[12] In a second book, published over a dozen years later, he returned to the events of 1647-48, but avoided the term *rivoluzioni*; nor do we encounter the term in letters exchanged at the time between the king of Spain and his officials charged with quelling the revolt.[13]

The case is different, however, with regards to Naples. Here the uprising, in spite of the death of Masaniello, went on unabated for almost ten months. It aroused great interest outside of Italy, particularly in France, which was then at war with Spain and supported the still obstinate Catalans. At the very end of 1647 the Duke of Guise came to Naples as supreme commander of the forces resisting the Spaniards. He was supposed to act as emissary of the king of France, but actually tried to consolidate his own independent government. A regime inspired by the Dutch republican model was experimented with, but quickly gave way to a test of the "Venetian" model. By April 1648, however, when he was defeated and the revolt finally crushed, Guise was no more than a military dictator. In the meantime, orders and laws were issued, manifestoes proclaimed and more books, in addition to that of Giraffi, composed by eyewitnesses. What do these sources tell us on the status of the term "revolution" during the revolt?

Giuseppe Donzelli, a Neapolitan noble, versed in the sciences and a fervid republican, published in February 1648, still before the failure of the revolt, a book entitled *Partenope liberata*. It was dedicated to the Duke of Guise and defended "the heroic resolution made by the people of Naples to deliver themselves and all of the kingdom from the unwanted yoke of the Spaniards." With one or two exceptions, Donzelli does not use the term *rivoluzione*. It is not related in any way to his arguments that Naples possessed true republican political traditions, nor does it appear in the text of several manifestoes that he included in his book.[14] His choice of terms for the revolt are rather "sollevazione," "tumulti populari" and "publiche turbulenze." Similar terms, especially "sollevazione," are used by Gabriele Tontoli, who also published his book in 1648, but shortly after the subjugation of the city, expressing his joy over the demise of the revolt. Like Giraffi, Tontoli deals mainly with the Masaniello phase. He argues that at least at that stage it was a "Sollevazione Fedele;" that is, a popular uprising motivated by the unsupportable burden of mounting taxes, but not a rebellion against the rule and sovereignty of the king of

Spain. On the background of this view, his use of *rivolutioni* in a few places does not add to the significance of the term. Rather than a label for the whole affair, it continues to carry here the old sense of popular commotions and the like, violent but politically aimless.[15] It is otherwise in the work of Agostino Nicolai, *Historia o vero narrazione giornale dell'ultime rivoluzioni della città e regno di Napoli*. This book was printed in Amsterdam in 1660, but both author and publisher explained that the manuscript had been written in Naples at the very time of the events. The claim is credible, and it is also possible that the title had been decided upon shortly before the publication. Nicolai, however, employs the term also in his text. In a manner reminiscent of Giraffi, he speaks of this or that day "della rivoluzione," and mentions "un altra rivoluzione gia successa in Napoli" ["another revolution that had taken place in Naples"], referring (though his date is wrong) to the uprising in 1547 in reaction to Viceroy Pedro de Toledo's establishing of the Inquisition. In yet another place he writes that some learned people in Naples believed that Masaniello was sent by heaven, being an "instrument of divine vengeance in these revolutions." But in the final account even in this book the term lags far behind "sollevazione."[16]

Official documents that came out during the revolt likewise eschewed the term. It is apparently missing from the texts of over two hundred laws, orders and declarations issued by the rebels' governments from October 1647 to April 1648.[17] On the other hand, in his book Nicolai gives the long text of an accord between representatives of the people of Naples and the Spanish viceroy, Duke of Arcos, reached on 7 September 1647. The fifth clause of this document promises a pardon for all the "romori, rivoluzioni, commovimenti" that had happened until that day, although they implied "sedizioni e ribellioni," because the people claimed that they took part in them only to defend their privileges and while they were still shouting "long live the King of Spain." Here the placing of "rivoluzioni" near "romori" speaks for itself; it cannot mean more than commotions or disturbances.[18] The term was also used by one, Vincenzio de' Medici, an agent of the Grand Duke of Tuscany, in letters reporting to his master on conditions in Naples and the south. Even before the outburst, in a letter of 18 June 1647, writing on the uprising in Palermo, he calls it "la rivoluzione," and goes on to speak of anxieties in Naples lest its people were about to "far rivoluzione come Palermo." Then, on 13 July, he announces that "Sunday, the seventh of this month, the revolution has begun" ["Domenica 7 stante, cominciò la rivoluzione"], and he adds words in praise of Masaniello as a leader. But we should not jump to the conclusion that these phrases amount to a conclusive terminological or conceptual endorsement of the word. In subsequent letters, where he again uses the word, it is in the sense of riots and disturbances. The Archbishop of Naples, Cardinal Filomarino, employs the word in a letter to Rome, dated 19 July 1647.[19] In all these sources, however, *sollevazione* is regularly preferred to *rivoluzione* as an all-embracing label for the events. This permits the inference that, although the new term was showing signs of advancing in circulation, its subsequent singling out as a word that resounded with references to Masaniello and Naples, apparently emanated primarily from the title of Giraffi's book, the earliest and most successful account of the revolt.

That *rivoluzioni* was considered a literary innovation can be suggested also from clear and indirect signs of objection to it. In 1649, for example, Agostino Inveges, concluding the preface to the first volume of his huge history of Palermo, came out against historians who employ "pretty descriptions, capricious metaphors, scheming admonitions, or other ornaments allowed to poets and academicians." Possibly with Reina's book in mind, he called himself an *annalista* of the old style.[20]

A similar attitude is revealed in the works of Birago Avogadro. This prolific author, who (as mentioned) had *rivoluzioni* introduced in 1646 to the title of one of his pirated works, virtually banned the term from the series of political histories published in the late 1640s and early 1650s. A clergyman of sorts and with an impetuous personality, Birago offended Vittorio Siri in 1648 by publishing a survey of Europe in the year 1642 which he called *Mercurio veridico*, an undisguised slight of the latter's *Mercurio*, whose second volume appeared that same year. The affront was answered by Siri in 1653 with a whole book that enumerated Birogo's mistakes and charged him with dishonesty.[21] Neither author employed in these books *rivoluzioni*, in spite of Siri's use of it in 1644, although their subjects easily lent themselves to an association with the term.

Birago's position was particularly interesting because there are indications that he was avoiding the term although people around him were taking it up. Thus, in his *Historia africana*, published in Venice in 1651, the index includes an entry "Rivoluzioni dell' Africa." But the section on the page that corresponds to the entry is subtitled

"Causa delle sedizioni nell' Africa," and "rivoluzioni" is nowhere to be found in the text.[22] A year later, again in Venice, a small volume on the English civil war, translated by Birago from Latin to Italian, came out. Here again, although the outline of the English political system and of English political history is quite knowledgeable, other terms rather than *rivoluzioni* are employed. When we turn to the short introduction, written not by Birago but by publisher Giovanni Maria Turrini, the subject of the book is summed up thus: "These pages describe the origins... of one of the greatest revolutions of State that the centuries could produce."[23]

Birago's real test, however, came with his next book, *Delle historie memorabili che contiene le sollevazioni di stato de' nostri tempi*, also published in Venice by Turrini, in 1653. Here all the main European uprisings, revolts and civil wars of the past thirteen years were narrated, but none was labelled *rivoluzione*. In addition to *sollevazioni*, he also employed *sedizioni*, *tumulti*, *moti*, *rumori*, *turbolenze* and of course *ribellioni*. In one passage, however, where he saw fit to abandon the straight narrative in order to theorize on the phenomenon of widespread revolts, we find a clue to his non-use of the new terminology.

Popular revolts, he writes echoing Bisaccioni's words of 1642, are contagious diseases ("morbi contagiosi") of which the pestiferous poison passes from place to place in a manner that not even distance, different climates or customs can impede. People in one place are emulating what other people do elsewhere through the force of example. It is, therefore, man's evil nature and his proclivity to imitate which is at the core of the series of uprisings that Europe had experienced, rather than fatal, heavenly decreed causes. Those who really understand these matters, he continues, laugh at the opinion of those who attribute the causes to the power of the stars: "They want the uprisings of peoples to be the results of the bearing of some star on that part of the world in which they happen, and [they believe] that certain heavenly constellations have power to incite the spirits of the inhabitants of a country to seditions, tumults and revolutions."[24]

It is in this passage, possibly the only place where he employs *rivoluzioni* in the sense of uprisings and popular revolts, that Birago's objection to the term becomes comprehensible. Its use is wrong not just in view of it being a recent literary innovation and therefore unnecessary from the standpoint of semantic purity, but because it hints at the possible innocence of rebels, suggesting indirectly that their revolt is a fatal event, the effect of the (revolutions of the) stars on men.

While Birago must be seen as a true die-hard, other major Venetian historians of his generation likewise had difficulty with the new term. Galeazzo Gualdo Priorato is a good example. A professional soldier in his youth, he could brag even after he had become an established author: "As for the manner of my writing it is the same that I have always used, rude and unpolished." One might expect that this attitude would have encouraged Gualdo to incorporate into his vocabulary new terms. Indeed, he apparently never rejected *rivoluzioni*, but it took some time until he came to exploit it. In his massive three-volume history of the latter part of the Thirty Years War, which he completed in 1650, he covered such events as the Masaniello revolt in Naples, the execution of Charles I in England and the French Fronde, but stuck to the traditional vocabulary.[25] His *Histoire des révolutions et mouvements de Naples*, however, which appeared in Paris in 1654, is apparently the first book in French to have the term in its title. The Italian text of this work has never been published. The distinctive manner in which the word *révolutions* is printed on the title page is probably the responsibility of the publisher, Simeon Piget, who had acquired the rights to the book. In his text Gualdo employed the term very sparingly. Still, writing a work which carried the story of the events in Naples beyond the stage covered by Giraffi's book of 1647, he perhaps felt comfortable to opt for the same epithet.

The year after, Gualdo's *Historia delle revoluzioni di Francia*, an account of the Fronde and its aftermath, appeared in Venice. Here the typographical display of the word in the title page is somewhat inhibited, although the book's title is repeated at the head of all the verso pages. But as *rivoluzioni* is almost entirely missing from the text, Gualdo's choice of words for destabilized political situations clearly remained traditional. Only in the opening sentence of his preface, addressed to the reader, do we come upon a significant expression, as can be gathered also from the contemporary English translation: "Amongst those changes which the vicissitudes of Worldly things hath in this our Age produced, I believe there are none either worthy to be remembered, or that can better satisfy our Curiosities, than a clear knowledge of the late Revolutions in France."[26] Here, it would seem, we have one of the first examples of the term "revolutions" used in the approach to history as an account of great changes, the rise and decline of kingdoms, the fall of dynasties and the like. As we shall see, in the last decade of the seventeenth century this point of view would produce the genre of *Histoires des Révolutions*, with which French authors would gain many readers. As for Gualdo, although we find *rivoluzioni* in some later works of his, it never amounts to more than a second-choice term.

The case of Bisaccioni is different. Prolific and somewhat pretentious, not unlike Birago, Siri and Gualdo, he was nevertheless much older, having been born in 1583. As we saw, he had employed the word *rivoluzioni*, albeit sparsely, even before the appearance of the works of Assarino, Giraffi and Reina. We have to look hard for the term in his history of the Thirty Years War, published by Turrini in Venice in 1653. In the previous year, however, his *Historia delle guerre civili di questi ultimi tempi*, covering, like Birago's book of a similar title, the uprisings in western Europe during the past twelve years, to which Bisaccioni added also chapters on eastern Europe and the Turkish empire, was printed in Venice. In this successful work, which earned a fourth edition by 1655, the new term stars from the start. The opening key passage merits being cited at some length:

> But if any work on history should benefit a Prince, that one, in my opinion, should be most useful which describes the revolutions or violent agitations among peoples. I know well that the most important exploit of a ruler is the conduct of war, but because today few Princes deal with it themselves, in fact almost all of them carry it on by means of procurators, as if they are involved in litigation, delegating command over their armies to Captains and Generals... that is why, I say, I consider the other subject of history, that which examines the government of peoples, to be indispensable to the Prince, especially since one does not tire much in it. The revolutions of the peoples are for the most part the results of bad government by ministers. Hence it is then that I decided to write on many revolts of peoples that have happened during my lifetime, which reasonably may be named Earthquakes of State.[27]

It is not insignificant that Bisaccioni here suggests the study of revolutions as an essential theme of the history of government and politics. To the question, what causes revolutions, he has a quick answer. Revolutions, he writes, are mainly the result of bad administration by appointed ministers. He may have in mind the cases of Olivares in Spain and Mazarin in France. But elsewhere in the book he considers also other causes. When he comes to the revolt of Naples in 1647, which he regards as one of the most memorable *commozioni popolari* (but elsewhere he also calls it *rivoluzione*) that has ever happened anywhere, he declares that he is writing on that event with more pleasure, because he did not see anybody attempting to consider its true origins. Almost everybody, he adds, saw in it a mere accident, devoid of any preceding causes. He therefore repeats his intention, not just to narrate the events, but to help those who rule understand that they should always examine all the factors which might change the state of affairs.[28]

In the case of Masaniello's Naples he believes that the hidden cause was lack of sensitivity and practical judgment on the part of the Spanish authorities. He is more pronounced with regard to the "rivoluzione dell' Inghilterra", which resulted in the execution of Charles I and the founding of "la nuova Repubblica." In England, he thinks, the revolution was the result of arbitrary changes in religion since the times of Henry VIII, which reflected a lack of piety and tyrannical inclinations on the part of that king and his successors. The outcome was a revolution, and it should serve as a warning to rulers everywhere. Once religious customs become lax and corrupted, the effects are like those of an ulcer in a healthy body, and a kingdom is heading toward its ruin. Otherwise a political body should endure, "since the form of dominion can never change unless preceded by the corruption of religion, or customs, or by perpetration of cruel inhuman acts."[29]

Bisaccioni, Siri, Gualdo and Birago were known representatives of an acclaimed generation of Venetian historians. They achieved recognition in the 1640s and maintained it during the next decade. We have an interesting literary piece, a dialogue, probably composed in the early 1650s by Giovanni Francesco Loredano, purporting to be a conversation between one, Henrico, and the soul of the writer Ferrante Pallavicino, who had been dead since 1644. The soul asks Henrico about developments since its demise, including in the field of historiography. It is answered with witty remarks that confirm, however, the prestige then accorded to the four aforesaid authors. As mentioned earlier, Pallavicino died just as the new term *rivoluzioni* was starting to gather momentum; but it is still absent from his own work. One of his last satires had as a theme the disgrace and fall of the man who had long ruled Spain, the Count Duke of Olivares. Pallavicino refers in this work to the revolts of Catalonia and Portugal against Spain, but the term he uses for both is *ribellione*.[30]

Some ten years afterwards, in the imaginary conversation with Pallavicino's soul, we do find the new terminology – *rivoluzioni*. The soul listens to a description of the crises in the Spanish empire in the late 1640s, when to the rebellions of Catalonia and Portugal were added those of Sicily and Naples, and defeats in Flanders and Germany. The question of how Spain managed to rise again is then answered with an explanation that she sowed disagreements, envy and strife among other nations. Thus she succeeded in dividing France, and "ha fatto nascere rivoluzioni ne i popoli" ["caused revolutions to happen among the peoples"]. In like manner Spain overcame "le rivoluzioni di Napoli." It employed deceit, gave vain promises to the common people, courted the support of the nobility and used any pretext to have the revolt's leaders executed. England, which is discussed next, is then censured for having fought, defeated, imprisoned and executed its own king, and for its people's determination to "vivere in Repubblica" ["to live in a Republic"]. Later in the discussion the term *rivoluzioni* returns in connection with the rebellion of the Cossacks in Poland. Henrico explains that the worst menace to the ruling princes came not from foreign enemies, but from "intestine wars," that is from their own subjects' conspiring and turning openly against them. Pallavicino, astounded by the extent of wars and distress that had come to afflict the world in the years following his death, utters in desperation: "In conclusion, this is a furious century."[31]

From this imaginary conversation with the soul of Pallavicino, it is natural to move to the writings of Girolamo Brusoni.[32] An author of works on literary themes as well as on history and politics, Brusoni had come to Venice in the early 1640s as a very young man and befriended Pallavicino. Later, he wrote a short biography of his comrade, which was included in the latter's posthumous edition of selected works. In 1656 Turrini published Brusoni's *Guerre d'Italia*, a survey of the political history of the wars of northern Italy from 1635 onwards. This volume was labelled by the publisher "the sixth part of the *Historie Memorabili* of Zilioli," the fourth and fifth parts (in addition to Zilioli's own three) having been written by Bisaccioni and Birago respectively and published by Turrini shortly before. In this first significant work of his in history, Brusoni barely shows familiarity with the new terminology, alluding at one point to "si strane rivoluzioni di Stato, e di Fortuna" ["so strange revolutions of state and of fortune"], though in most instances he employs other terms. His vocabulary, however, is marked with an updated versatility in his next work, published in 1659, *Varie osservazioni sopra le Relazioni Universali di Giovanni Botero nelle quali si toccano le rivoluzioni di stato delle più principali monarchie dell'universo succedute a nostri tempi.* Here, although the old terminology is far from being discarded, one falls upon a number of suggestive formulations.

The term *rivoluzioni* appears in the sense of great changes in the fortunes of a huge empire during a course of time, in the sense of territorial losses and gains of a certain dynasty in a period of some decades, and as changes in government and religion that may result from long and widespread wars. Brusoni also uses the term when he comes to give an interpretation of contemporary England. As with Bisaccioni, he sees the origins of the civil war in changes that took place as far back as the reign of Henry VIII. In his view it was not so much religion, but rather government that was the issue. Henry VIII and his successors reduced the authority of parliament, turning it into not much more than an advisory council to the king. This treatment was further aggravated by Charles I when he decreed new taxes, a matter always regarded as a prerogative of parliament. The reaction, continues Brusoni, produced: "the first movements towards the revolutions of Great Britain, from which proceeded the change of Royal to Popular Government; which having been gradually returned by Cromwell back to the old form of regime, is still maintained with a greater authority than any king had ever possessed in that Island."[33]

Here, it seems, *rivoluzioni* stands not only for the first great change in government from regal to popular, but for the whole "circular motion" which saw absolute personal political power destroyed and then returned to the forefront in another manner. Brusoni, as if to tell us that this is what he meant here by *rivoluzioni*, reiterates the stages of the process. In England, he sums up, the execution of Charles I extinguished royal authority in order to substitute for it "una Repubblica popolare," which then adopted as its head a "Protettore" ["Protector"], who destroyed all of its reasons for existence by assuming an authority superior to that which the king had exercised before.

With Brusoni's work of 1659 on the *rivoluzioni di stato* the small wave of publications begun by Assarino in 1644 might be said to have reached a conclusion. Brusoni continued to use the term in later works, but he did so sparingly, the word being apparently employed again interchangeably with *sollevazioni* and others.[34] It is particularly interesting to note that Assarino, who had been the first to come up with the innovation, discarded the term completely in his massive *Delle guerre e successi d'Italia* of 1665 (covering the period 1613 to 1630). Also in the famous history of Venice by Battista Nanni (published in two volumes 1662-86) the term hardly exists and its significance is in any case underplayed.[35] Perhaps the only Italian author of consequence who continues in the 1660s to press on with the term is Gregorio Leti. In his case, however, personality and circumstances might explain the choice of vocabulary. Having matured in the years when the term *rivoluzioni* was being popularized, Leti must have felt perhaps less constricted than other authors in using it because he was then residing and publishing in Protestant Geneva, where he could criticize papal government and other Italian authorities with relative freedom. In his *Dialoghi politici* of 1666 the events of 1647 in Naples are again and again referred to as "tempo delle rivoluzioni di Masaniello." The outcome of this tagging procedure is not only to impose the term on the events, but to paint the whole historical experience with glowing colors.[36]

But in fact Leti goes further than just confirming an historical epithet. His two speakers in these dialogues consider the phenomenon of revolutions as they discuss diverse issues touching on the nature of politics. Thus, when they approach the question whether politics are governed by divine predestination, the opinion of those who believe that "God was resolved on punishing Spain by means of the revolutions of Naples and Catalonia" is rejected with a sarcastic remark. The question of the behavior of different social groups during revolutions is also addressed, and it is pointed out that in Naples the local nobility, hated by its own people, suffered more material damages than even the Spanish authorities. Furthermore, it is observed that during times of revolution subjects compel their rulers to act against their own will: "In the time of the revolutions of Milan, Sicily and Naples, the Catholic king was seen forced to concede many privileges in order to oblige the people to put down their arms, which showed the prudence of the king and the foolishness of the people." Leti here almost commends the king for his careful assessment of the situation and his clever policy of appeasement, but indirectly he hints at his own support of the revolutions.[37]

We may now recapitulate the preceding findings on the shifts in meaning of the term "revolution." As we have seen, in Italy its early attainment of a political meaning had little to do with the belief that circular motions of the stars influence events on earth. The political sense of the word was rather inaugurated as a colloquial development, which penetrated to chronicles of the Villani brothers and somehow survived in Renaissance vernacular literature on history and politics, particularly that of Florence. The dictionary of the Accademia della Crusca reflected these origins of the term. Nevertheless, during the first four decades of the seventeenth century hardly any Italian historian employed the word as a viable political term, except in a very few cases. This changed in the 1640s, when a climate of instability created by a series of widespread revolts and civil wars challenged authors of works on politics to come forward with new metaphors. Thus, *rivoluzioni* was resurrected and given a sensational display by Assarino, and then Giraffi, Reina and others. Essentially, it was a literary gimmick, also designed to sell the authors' books.

No wonder therefore that the innovation evoked resentment from those who, like Birago, felt that *rivoluzioni* resounded with inevitability and fatality and absolved the rebels of blame. Others evinced their disapproval by simply shunning the term. Nevertheless, some well known historians and political commentators reacted positively and annexed it to their vocabulary, as Bisaccioni and Brusoni, or as with Gualdo Priorato, incorporated it into the titles of their works. Still, almost all these Italian authors who accepted *rivoluzioni* used it in addition to older more conventional terms. Moreover, updating their vocabulary did not mean that they came to appreciate or champion the idea of a political revolution. With the possible exception of Gregorio Leti, these authors were conservatives who tended to stress the harmful consequences of any attempt to overthrow by force a constituted authority.

This attitude might explain why in the 1660s "revolution" fell into relative disuse, a drift which coincided with the coming back of stability and the gradual emergence of absolutism all over western Europe. Simultaneously, Italian historians and political authors were then quickly losing the stature that had made their works acceptable in other European countries at mid-century in either the original language or in translation.[38]

This brings us finally to the question of Italian influence on the adoption of the term "revolution" into other European languages. It is an intricate issue, which will return to occupy us in the next two chapters. At this point, however, it is safe to say that prior to the publication of the *rivoluzioni* books by Assarino and others, no work on politics in western Europe employed the word in its title. Moreover, it is difficult to find examples outside Italy where the word was previously used in political discourse; and in those few that are found the word is mostly used as a borrowed metaphor, and by authors such as the French Henry, Duke of Rohan and Gabriel Naudé, who were deeply immersed in Italian language and culture.

The first political essay in England to carry the word in its title was Anthony Ascham's *Of the Confusions and Revolutions of Governments*, first published in 1648. In 1649 Robert Mentet de Salmonet's *Histoire des troubles de la Grande Bretagne* appeared in Paris, and employed "révolutions" several times in its introductory essay. As we shall see, from then on the use of the term slowly proliferates, in spite of opposition to its use, and it is easier to find more and more examples in the political literature of Cromwell's England and the French *Fronde*. If indeed the penetration of the term to England and France was influenced by the Italian publications of the 1640s, then clearly the Italian examples bore fruit even before the translation of Giraffi's work into English in 1650 by James Howell, and certainly before the publication in Paris in 1654 of Gualdo's work on the revolution of Naples. Furthermore, it is inconceivable that the works of Assarino and Giraffi had not come to the attention of men of letters in England and France in a very short time. Therefore, the employment of the term in the two countries in the late 1640s must have been encouraged, if not inspired, by the Italian innovations. Nevertheless, even if this assumption is correct, one should not neglect to point out that the fact that both England and France were then undergoing political crises was of major importance. Thus, authors in these two nations, who began to employ the term "revolution," did so in order to sort out, or influence, political issues in their own lands.

Chapter Three

How "Revolution" Came to France

When and how did the term "revolution" enter French political discourse? It was the opinion of Jean Marie Goulemot, in a study published about thirty years ago, that the most decisive development in promoting the use of the word "révolution" in French, in a political sense, should be found in the reactions to the dethronement of James II of England in 1688.[1] He conceded that "revolution" belonged to the language of politics even before that date, but in his view it had heretofore lacked a precise meaning. In spite of some of his own findings, which indicated, for example, that the word appeared in Renaudot's weekly *Gazette* as early as 1649 (though in reference to Scotland), he felt confident in writing that there was no use of it during the Fronde.[2] Not long ago, Goulemot's study still served Keith Michael Baker as a launching pad for a discussion of the political sense of the word in the seventeenth and eighteenth centuries.[3] Recent studies of the political literature of the Fronde abstained from examining whether the word exercised any role in that great mass of propaganda.[4]

It is the aim of this chapter to show, however, that the years of the Fronde (1648-1653) coincided with the penetration of the word "revolution" into French political discourse, and that the new meanings of the word were instigated from the outside, as well as being responses to internal developments. It will also be attempted to show here that the acceptance of the new political sense was incomplete, and the reasons for this. It is this aspect of the usage of "revolution" which explains why the status of the new term continued unsettled during the next several decades.

We might start with a concise examination of the relevant terms employed in France during the three generations prior to the Fronde. "Révolution" is completely missing from Bodin's *Republic* (1576); there the preferred word is "changement," and every state is deemed disposed to eventual decline and breakdown, due to "the diversity of human affairs, which are inconstant and uncertain" ["la variété des choses humaines, qui sont muables et incertaines"]. Similar terms are employed in another famous essay of that time, François de la Noue's *Discours politiques et militaires* (1587). In addition to "changement" both he and Bodin employ "altération," "mutation," "ruine," "accident." In the case of La Noue, however, the absence of "révolution" is perhaps more noticeable to the eye of a modern reader, since he adds to his list of factors endangering the stability of a state astrological and cyclical elements. Thus, in his mind the duration and fate of a political entity is also determined by the periodic movements of the planets and a certain allotment of time granted to it by divine providence.[5] The historian Estienne Pasquier, author of the ten volume *Recherches de la France* (1561-1621), has likewise no use for the term. For example, when he writes on Etienne Marcel's revolutionary initiative of 1357 to force the royal government to relinquish direct power to the Estates General, he designates it "la réformation de l'état."[6] Montaigne also eschews "révolution." He deals with the fate of government in his essay "On Vanity," first published in 1588. Rome, he writes, had been fatally destined by the stars to serve as a model of all that a state can endure, the good and the bad. But he does not believe that one has to look to the sky, like the astrologers, in order to find clues of an approaching political storm. There is nothing like innovation, says Montaigne, to cause tension in a state, and besides, "the preservation of states is something that probably surpasses our intelligence."[7]

Given these examples from late sixteenth century French political discourse, what are the semantic uses of the word "revolution" at that time? It had been employed in French since the twelfth century in reference to the movement of the planets. By the thirteenth it also began to suggest the measure of time of a given cycle, most frequently the year, imagined as a span of time made up of the turning of the seasons.[8] It is exactly in this form, "l'an révolu," a completed year, that we find it in Robert Estienne's French and Latin dictionary of 1549, and again in Jean Nicot's dictionary of 1573. In the *Mémoires-Journaux* of Pierre de l'Estoile, which cover the years

1574-1611, the expression is "la révolution de l'année."[9] Yet another mode of use of the word emanates from the *Centuries*, the famous rhymed collection of astrological prophecies by Michel de Nostredame, first published in 1555. In the preface, addressed to his newborn son, the author employs the term half a dozen times. He begins by speaking of "Astronomiques révolutions," but later has the word in quite suggestive formulations, phrased in symbolic language, as "où le grand Dieu éternel viendra parachever la révolution" ["where the eternal mighty God will come to complete the revolution"].[10] Considering the great popularity of the *Centuries*, it is probable that its text had a bearing on the changing sense of the word. In any case, the astrological base is evident in the phrase "la révolution de la nativité," by which was meant the destiny of a person at his birth as interpreted from the position of the stars.[11] These nuances, however, fell short of altering the meaning of the word.

This can also be seen when we examine the use of the word in the writings of one of Bodin's contemporaries, the humanist scholar, historian and political theorist, Loys Le Roy. He does not employ it in an early short tract on political upheavals resulting out of religious tensions, although he subscribes therein to the notion that every change in the world below is determined by the movements of the celestial bodies above.[12] In another tract, defending the principles of strong royal government and the personality of Henry III, he defines "sédition" and other terms related to attempts to undermine a state, and maintains that they all lead to "mutations pernicieuses."[13] But in his translation of and commentary on Aristotle's *Politics* the word is introduced in relation to Plato's concept of the "greate yeare," that is the completed course of all the heavenly bodies, "when the seven planets, and other fixed stars come back again to their fixed places, and represent to us the same nature that was in the beginning of the World." In this sense, "revolution" approaches the meaning of a predetermined beginning and end, and Le Roy even comes close to using it in reference to a political entity, when he writes that "a Towne hath the revolution and the time of the continuance thereof prefixed, as well as the life of a man."[14] Even more so in his most famous work, *De la vicissitude ou variété des choses en l'universe*, first published in 1575, two years before his death. Here the main subject is change, both in the physical world and in human affairs, and Le Roy has not only "les révolutions et l'influence des planetes" and "la révolution du grand an," but also speaks of "la révolution naturelle des polices." With this he means, in a manner reminding of the Venetian author Sebastiano Erizzo, one generation before him, the circle in which the forms of government alternate from monarchy to tyranny, aristocracy to oligarchy and democracy to mob rule.[15]

Shortly afterwards, however, we begin to encounter the word in the sense of change. In Pierre Charron's celebrated essay, *De la sagesse* (1601), there is a whole chapter surveying the different "accidents" that can befall a state. He enumerates and explains one by one the terms "conjuration," "trahison," "émotion populaire," "faction," "sédition," "trouble," "guerre civile," "rébellion." Throughout this discussion the word "révolution" is absent. But just prior to this we encounter the expression "dangereuse révolution des choses humaines" ["dangerous revolution of human affairs"].[16] Evidently the word is about to expand its meaning, though it is not yet a part of political discourse.

The word's meaning in the early decades of the seventeenth century did not alter much, and even the use in the sense of sudden, unforeseen or fatal change in the moral and social order appeared to remain extremely rare. We do not find it in the massive memoirs of the Duke of Sully which came out in 1638, neither in Pierre d'Avity's *Le monde*, a description of the regions and states of Europe, Africa and America (and their governments), which first appeared in 1637 and was reprinted several times thereafter, nor in the political works of Jean Silhon, secretary of Cardinal Richelieu. But in the important tract of Cardin Le Bret, a staunch supporter of royal absolutism, one encounters a use of the word in reference to changes in political fortune, and the expression "révolution de fortune" is found elsewhere.[17] Granted that the word was showing signs of becoming more acceptable in refined discourse, the definitions given in 1636 in Philibert Monet's French and Latin dictionary still come as a great surprise. He defines the word in four contexts: First in the sense of a circle, "Révolution, contour, tournoiement;" second as "Révolution des astres;" third in the sense of change, "Révolution, mutation, changement;" and fourth in the political sense, "Révolution d'état," to which the matching Latin translation is "Publicae rei commutatio, conversio, -onis."[18] Invariably, entries in dictionaries trail the new meanings of words by an appreciable lag of time. In this case we have a rather unusual reversal of the order. It is quite probable, however, that Monet took the political definition from the only dictionary which at that time carried one, the *Vocabolario* of Florence's Accademia della Crusca (1612; second edition 1623).

One year before the publication of Monet's dictionary the term had been employed by the Duke of Rohan in the short dedication, addressed to Cardinal Richelieu, which preceded his essay on European politics, *De l'intérest des princes et états de la Chrestienté*. The word was not repeated in the body of the essay, and apparently is missing from other political writings of Rohan's. But in the dedication to Richelieu of 1635 it is used twice: First in the singular and in a general sense of change, "la Révolution des affaires de ce monde;" then in the plural, but with a more specific political meaning, "voyant tous les jours tant de Révolutions Estrangeres devant mes yeux" ["seeing every day so many Foreign Revolutions in front of my eyes"]. It is not easy to say whether we have here a real breakthrough in the use of a political term, although its presence, twice, in a short text that opens an important essay on politics cannot be overlooked.

In 1639 "révolution(s)" appeared four times in the text of another remarkable political essay - Gabriel Naudé's *Considérations politiques sur les coups d'estat*. This innovative work was published in Rome in an extremely limited number of copies. Therefore, what influence it had at the time of publication was at most related to the author's concept of "coup d'éstat." By this term Naudé understood "daring and extraordinary actions that Princes are constrained to carry out in difficult situations." He gave many examples drawn from history, illustrating self-protective violent acts by rulers to reassert their authority; his foremost example with regard to France was the St. Bartholomew's massacre of 1572. A firm believer in absolute monarchy, Naudé had nothing to do with the modern concept of revolution. Still, his handling of the term showed an advance when compared with that of Rohan. He equated "révolutions des Estats" with the death of empires, which invariably caused changes in laws, religion and public order. He pointed to the extraordinary ability of Luther and Calvin, who had used only language and their pens to cause "grandes révolutions." In another place, he told of Muhammad, the prophet of Islam, who employed an astrologer to predict "une grande révolution" both in religion and in the government, so that people would be prepared to accept his preaching. It may be, however, that Naudé's long stay in Italy, where his book was written, partly influenced his experimentation with the word.[19]

In 1643 we find the term in the preface of an influential work, the *Histoire de France* by François-Eudes de Mezeray. In this case, however, we are in a far better position to judge. When finally completed, Mezeray's history consisted of three huge folios, of over one thousand pages each, covering events from ancient times to the Peace of Vevins (1598). Of these, the first volume came out in 1643, the second in 1646, on the threshold of the Fronde, and the third in 1651, at its climax. As we shall see, there is a huge advance in the use, meaning and rhetorical manipulation of the term in the third volume in comparison with the first two. In the preface Mezeray announces his aim to recount "l'Histoire entière de cette Monarchie, ses guerres et au dedans et au dehors, ses révolutions, les conseils de ses Princes, les moeurs de ses Peuples, ses Coustumes et ses Loix,..." The employment of the term in the plural form in this context amounts to nearly identifying "révolutions" with historical change itself. Later in the first volume he has the term in the singular in the heading of a paragraph on the end of the kingdom of the Goths in Italy, which is also given an entry in the index, and he refers to the Norman conquest of England in 1066 as "la révolution de l'Estat." We also find the word in the second volume; for example, in reference to the unstable government of Genoa, or as he treats Charles VIII's 1494 invasion of Italy.[20] Although other terms are used by Mezeray in a standard manner, it seems that for him, even before the Fronde, "révolution" is a word with application to the writing on history and politics.

These two first volumes of his history brought Mezeray fame and, in 1649, election to the Académie Française. Granting that it might seem far-fetched at first glance, it is from the point of view of this institution that we can glean an understanding of the issues then involving the proliferation of the new sense of "revolution." An outgrowth of a circle of literati who used to meet informally in Paris, the Académie was organized by Richelieu in 1634 and given the status of an official body, charged with overseeing French grammar, spelling, vocabulary and rhetoric. Among its founding members were Jean Chapelain, now mostly remembered for his attack on Corneille's *Le Cid* in 1637, and Valentin Conrart, who became the first "perpetual" secretary. To complete their number to forty, the original group was joined by such eminent writers as the essayist Guez de Balzac; the poet, famous also for his model letters, Vincent Voiture; and the grammarian Claude Favre de Vaugelas.

From the start the Académie undertook the compilation of a dictionary, a project that was meant to protect the French language from lewd expressions and vulgar colloquialisms, and establish an authoritative meaning and usage of words. The preference was for anything marked with a clear provenance from classical Latin or the works of the acclaimed French masters of the sixteenth century. The word "révolution" had really neither this nor that, and certainly not in its new political sense. But the new meaning must have been objectionable to most members of the Académie also on other grounds. Being part of a body that was backed by persons who inculcated in France the norms of monarchical absolutism, it was hardly conceivable that the *académiciens* would encourage the use of a term that dealt with political change as something fatal or predestined, thereby lessening the blame that would fall upon those who dared oppose their ruler.

When the *Dictionnaire* was finally published it contained, of course, a twofold definition of the word "révolution" in both its gyrational and political meanings. But this took place only in 1694 and after two other well received dictionaries, by Pierre Richelet (1680) and Antoine Furetière (1690), had acknowledged the political sense of the word. In their own writings founding members of the Académie, such as Balzac and Voiture, did not employ the term; nor was it included among the words discussed by Vaugelas in his *Remarques sur la langue française* (1647).[21]   Yet another rising authority, Gilles Ménage, who was about to inherit Vaugelas' place as a leading linguist (though not his seat at the Académie), did not place the word in his *Les origines de la langue française* (1650), where he hastens nevertheless to explain the background of an even more recent term – "FRONDEURS.   Nom de party en ce derniers troubles de l'année 1649" ["Name of a faction in these latest troubles of the year 1649"].[22] In 1656 Ménage edited the writings of his friend Jean François Sarrazin, who had died two years before. Among the last works that Sarrazin wrote were essays on historical themes, where the issue of gaining political power through violence frequently came under discussion. But Sarrazin, who ended his life as a clown of the Prince of Conti, an aristocrat deeply involved in the Fronde, did not employ the term "revolution."[23]

This apparent absence of "revolution" from works of leading French writers on the eve of the Fronde, is even more significant in light of the fact that exactly at that time, as detailed in the previous chapter, the term was given a new kind of exposure in Italy. Of the several works which carried in their titles the word "revolution," the one that generated most interest was *Le rivoluzioni di Napoli* by Alessandro Giraffi, narrating the story of the ten days in July 1647 that saw the rise to power and demise of Masaniello. It is also appropriate to add that the events in Naples exercised an influence on the Fronde right from the start. In his *Journal*, Jean Vallier reported on the first great popular demonstrations in Paris in January 1648, where the crowd called for a repeal of recently imposed taxes and higher rents, employing "seditious words, quite punishable in other times." Battista Nanni, then Venetian ambassador to France, saw fit to mention that the shout "Napoli! Napoli!" was heard several times.[24]

We should not imagine, however, that "revolution" was included among the "seditious words." When Renaudot's *Gazette*, France's official weekly news bulletin, first informed on the uprising in Naples, it printed the text of a report sent over from there on 11 July 1647, where the affair was called "grand soulèvement" and "cette émotion." From here on the *Gazette* gave regular weekly coverage of the progression of events in Naples, but neglected to use "révolution." Rather than this word, the terms employed were "la sédition," "mouvements," "troubles," "grand tumulte," "désordre." Only in his first issue of 1648, where he gave a general survey of political conditions in Europe at the beginning of the new year, Renaudot suddenly opined: "... la révolution de Naples, elle soit de telle conséquence qu'aucun autre progrez des années precedentes ne scauroit l'égaler." ["... the revolution of Naples, it might be of such consequence that no other development of recent years could equal its importance"]. Even here, however, the use of the word might have been the result of inadvertence, aided by the linkage, in the same sentence, with "conséquence" and "progrès," because Renaudot hardly used it again; although on 8 February 1648 he referred to Masaniello's uprising of July 1647, "que commença la révolution des affaires de Naples."

This is a scant harvest, and it raises the possibility that Renaudot, although aware of the new political sense of "revolution," found it inappropriate for his tasks. An indirect confirmation might be gleaned, many months later, from a special issue of 19 April 1652, where he described a recent palace revolt in the court of the young Ottoman sultan, Mehmed IV. Writing on this affair in an undisguised jovial mood, Renaudot styled it "la nouvelle révolution" that took

place in the court of Constantinople, evidently having in mind the
revolt of the Janissaries in 1648 which resulted in the murder of
Sultan Ibrahim. He justified the use of the new term in this particular
instance by telling his readers that the affairs of the Ottoman empire
were as mutable as the crescent, the symbol of its might, which
changes shape from night to night. For this reason, he continued, he
found it "more fitting to give to that which happened the title of
revolution rather than that of [revolution] of State, which signifies
consolidation and consistency" ["plus à propos de donner le titre de
révolution à ce qui se fait que celui d'Estat, qui signifie affermissment
& consistance"].[25]

   Renaudot's predicament   in using "revolution" with regards to
Naples, should be compared with the employment of the term by
others. In his memoirs, we find the Duke of Guise commenting that
when he prepared in December 1647 to go from Rome to Naples,
everybody told him that "the revolutions of Naples had already calmed
down" ["les révolutions de Naples étoient apaisées"].[26]   This was
written, of course, years later, and cannot be taken as evidence that the
same words were employed at the time. But we have as well a
contemporary source, surprisingly phrased by the very person who
then ran the government of France, Cardinal Mazarin himself.

   Born and educated in Rome, Mazarin certainly had a grasp of the
political sense of "revolution" in Italian. Apparently, he did not use
the word in his correspondence in French prior to the revolt of Naples.
But in a memorandum of the king, dated 15 November 1647, which
was most probably authored by Mazarin himself, the word does appear
in the plural form ("les nouvelles révolutions arrivées à Naples") as
French aims and policies regarding Naples are carefully detailed.
Shortly afterwards, in a letter of 25 November to his ambassador at
the Vatican, the marquis de Fontenay, Mazarin warned not to waste
efforts, in spite of ongoing peace negotiations with Spain, in order to
make France "profit as much as we could wish from this revolution"
["... de profiter, autant que nous le pouvons désirer, de cette
révolution"]. Later still, on 22 February 1648, he instructed his
ambassador to Naples to work for the unity of all the Neapolitans,
because on that depended the outcome of the revolt, repeating that that
was the most important thing, "whichever revolution they are going to
take concerning the form of government" ["quelque révolution qu'ils
prennent pour la forme de gouvernement"]. In this case the word is
employed not in the sense of violent seizure of power, but as an act

that decides between a possible republican or monarchical government. The ambassador, Bernard du Plessis-Besançon, used the term in a letter dated 1 May 1648, referring to news on the "latest revolutions of Naples" ["dernières révolutions de Naples"]. Then, in his reply to Besançon of 4 September 1648, Mazarin again employed the term, this time in the clearest political sense. He wrote there that the capture of Salerno from the Spaniards was not a victory decisive enough "to bring about a general revolution of the kingdom" ["pour causer une révolution générale du royaume"][27]

Both Mazarin and Besançon use "revolution," however, as an extraordinary, exceptional term. Other, conventional terms serve them as a matter of routine. Still, it may well be that men of government, at least when they exchanged confidential letters, were more willing to use the word's new meaning than "professional" writers. The correspondence of Valentin Conrart affords an uncommon opportunity to see how a man of learning reacted to the term. In 1647 and 1648 he exchanged numerous letters with the art historian André Felibien in Rome, reporting to him on the political climate at home, offering his views on events in Italy and asking for help in procuring Italian books. Conrart referred frequently to the Neapolitan revolt. He wanted to know more about it, and seemed to believe that its success would benefit France. In none of the references did he employ "revolution," but in his letter of 31 July 1648, he mentioned to Felibien that he was in possession of a copy of a Geneva edition of Giraffi's book and wanted to have the original Venice edition as well. Even here, however, he merely cited the Italian title of the work. Only in his letter of 30 October 1648, where he acknowledged to Felibien receiving the Venice edition, did Conrart refer to "the account of the first ten days of the revolutions of Naples" ["la relation des dix premières journées des révolutions de Naples"]. Otherwise the term is completely missing from his letters, many of which also contain references to the escalating political crisis at home.[28]

A somewhat similar attitude can be seen in the numerous letters written by Jean Chapelain to the Dutch scholar Nicolas Heinsius. At the time of the Masaniello uprising, the latter happened to be staying in Naples. Chapelain refers several times to the revolt. Nevertheless, with two exceptions (the second time its political sense is really half-baked), he does not employ "revolution," not even while deploring the destiny of France during the Fronde.[29] Therefore, in the case of both Conrart and Chapelain it is not a lack of awareness of the new meaning, but an unwillingness to use it that explains the attachment to the traditional vocabulary.

From the previous examples, showing the use of the term in private or confidential expressions, we now move to a completely different arena – one that is public and demands high eloquence and utmost decorum, since it involves the presence of the sovereign himself. Omer Talon, advocate general of the *parlement* of Paris, included in his memoirs, written almost as a diary, the texts of his addresses in the *lits du justice*, or formal sessions of registration of royal edicts. The one he gave in January 1648 in the presence of the young Louis XIV and his mother, the queen-regent, is actually considered a landmark; there, for the first time, complaints about the weight of taxes, the poverty of the peasants and the extreme misery of all Frenchmen were publicly aired. In this memorable speech Talon did not employ the word "révolution." But it exists in his address of 24 October 1648, given on the occasion of the registration of important royal concessions, following the first violent stage of the Fronde. Here he asserts that the good or bad fortune of great states is reckoned not only from the position of the stars at the time of their foundation, "but it is also measured by the great mutations and notable revolutions which they experience" ["mais même se mesurent par les grandes mutations et les révolutions notables qui s'y rencontrent"]. Interestingly, although the word has here a political meaning, its impact is mellowed by the underlying astrological supposition.

The term returns in the text of yet another speech by Talon, which he was about to deliver on 1 April 1649, though it did not materialize. Here it is just "the ages and revolutions of past centuries" ["les periodes et les révolutions de siècles passés"]. Significantly, Talon does not employ the word in his address on behalf of the *parlement* to the queen-regent on 2 February 1651, although he assures her that "these troubles and agitations" do not aim at changing the government or undermining the monarchy, but only at bringing about a better order. In his speech of 7 September 1651, he rejects the astrological interpretation of the fate of states, and tells the king that all depends on the good or bad administration of the ruler. Here too "revolution" is missing, but the impression is that Talon is aware of its new sense, which he avoids so as not to add fuel to the exciting political issues which he tackles.[30]

We may now consider the *Mazarinades*, that mass of thousands of pamphlets and posters, representing all currents of public opinion, which animated the Fronde. As this avalanche of printed literature mostly evaded royal censorship and generally carried no name of author, one would expect to find there a considerable number of instances demonstrating the expanding usage of the new meaning of "revolution." This, however, is not quite the case. When a thorough search for the word in the five thousand odd documented *Mazarinades* is conducted, it will most likely show that "revolution" never captured the imagination of the pamphleteers; but even so, the word was still employed enough times in its new meaning to suggest that the term was gradually penetrating political discourse.[31]

The difficulty of using the term is indirectly reflected, early in 1649, in dozens of pamphlets composed under the impression of the execution of Charles I and the conversion of England from a monarchy to a commonwealth. All of this literature, almost without exception, is strongly in sympathy with the deceased monarch. Some pieces even go as far as calling for a united action of European rulers to return England to the dead king's son. Some writers tie these events with instances of revolt elsewhere in recent years. One, for example, believes that the world is living in a deplorable age, in which sovereigns are bound to lose their authority and "see their Kingdoms transformed into Republics" ["voir leurs Royames se métamorphoser en des Républiques"].[32] But the word "revolution" is not used in these short tracts, and neither, in fact, in the majority of the pamphlets of the year 1649, which deal with political issues in France. Many of these contain fierce and fiery attacks against Mazarin, though not on the monarchy as a model of government. Conditions in France are termed "guerre civile," "troubles" or "mouvements," and only on very rare occasions, as in a pamphlet, for example, distinguished by its satirical bent, one falls upon the expression "dans les troubles, dans les désordres, ou dans les révolutions des Estats."[33] The same is true for the numerous *Mazarinades* in verse, where the language used is usually designed to fit the popular taste. But even in this genre it is possible to come upon a clear example, illustrating that the term is in a sort of an intrusive stage. The following passage comes after its author had protested against the insincerity of ministers appointed by kings to carry on governments and deplored the changing nature of politics and life:

Depuis le commencement de nations,
Les frequentes révolutions,
Ont produit mille changemens,
Par les grands boulversemens,
Des Républiquies & Monarchies
Qui ont esté anéanties,
Par les folles passsions des hommes,
Qui regnent au siècle où nous sommes.[34]

This of course is mainly playing with a new word. But we also find a few examples where the term is exploited rhetorically in a political discourse. It is used in the short "Advice to the Queen upon the Conference of Rueil" of March 1649. This piece is attributed to the abbé de Chambon, who counsels the queen-regent to appease her enraged subjects. "It appears Madame," he writes, "that for thirty years heaven has conspired the ruin of all the Monarchies. This is why it is necessary to carefully avoid that which might give room to such fatal revolutions." In this case the mode of use shows an ability to exploit the new meaning for the sake of rhetorical resonance and force of argument. The term, therefore, is employed again by this author in the last paragraph, where the queen is urged to make concessions:

Beware lest the famished people will rightfully lose the respect it owes to Your Majesty; and beware also that these revolutions, so wonderful and so harmful to so many kingdoms, will not complete their course to the detriment of yours, if you will not give it soon the peace, putting an end to all these wars, domestic and foreign.[35]

In the preceding examples the word is still linked to its old astrological context. Indeed, the writer is utilizing the two senses of the word to gain intensity and persuasiveness for his argument. This play on double meaning could also be handled in a humorous or clownish manner. In a tract of 1649 we find the expression "Maudite révolution!" ["Damnable revolution!"] exclaimed half in jest in reference to the Prince of Condé, who in the opinion of the writer had turned from a great national hero into an oppressor of the people. Better still, in January 1651 a piece written in words filled with florid imagery and ridiculing the pretensions of the Duchess of Longueville contained the utterance: "last year 1650, year of revolution, of liberty and of Jubilee" ["l'année dernière 1650, année de révolution, de liberté et de Jubilé"][36] It is quite transparent that the order of the words in the old expression "révolution de l'année" had been reversed, thus casting the term in its new political meaning while still hinting at its astrological source. In 1652 two tracts, apparently written by Jacques Mengau, an author of an astrological dictionary, employed the term in their titles in an undisguised allusion to the new political sense. One was called *Révolution imperiale de Louis XIV*, by which the astrological horoscope of the young king was meant, and the other – *Cistème général ou révolution du monde, contenante tout ce qui doit arriver en France la presente année 1652*. In both, the author pretended to follow the predictions of Michel de Nostredame and did not use the term in the body of his text.

In the important call of the assembly of the nobility in Paris to convoke the Estates General, issued late in February 1651, the term is already handled in a strictly political sense. Here the queen-regent is told that disorders in all parts of the kingdom "make us reasonably fear some deterioration or strange revolution" ["nous fait appréhender avec raison quelque decadence ou révolution estrange"]. And again, several paragraphs later, the nobles reiterate that they cannot hold back their demand for an Estates General "in the fear that they all have of a revolution which will destroy them within a public collapse" ["dans l'appréhension qu'ils ont tous d'une révolution qui les anéantiroit dans la ruine publique"]. In yet another tract, probably from 1652, the term is employed to make a comprehensive political observation: "Strange révolutions have taken place in all the States of the world" ["Il y a eu d'estranges révolutions dans tous les Estats de la terre"].[37]

More examples are encountered. We find the expression "funestes révolutions dans l'Estat" ["fatal revolutions in the State"] employed rhetorically in a royalist pamphlet of 1651 attempting to dissuade the leaders of the town of Bordeaux from cooperating with the Prince of Condé.[38] It is likewise used in an anti-royalist leaflet of 1652, where "tragiques révolutions de Estats" are claimed to be the consequence of governments where rulers exceed their legal authority.[39] In the same year also the Duke of Guise, who had just returned to France after a period in Spanish captivity, used the term as he accused Mazarin of treachery, declaring that his work in Naples had been wholly carried out according to the king's orders. In his manifesto the expression "les révolutions de l'Estat" apparently referred to the Fronde itself in its widest sense.[40] But the vast majority of the *Mazarinades* avoided "révolution." Even writers acclaimed for their ability to deal with the political issues in an imaginative, forceful and persuasive manner, such as Claude Dubosc de Montandré and the one hiding behind the pen name Sieur de Sandricourt, failed to appreciate the value of the new term. Still, given the fact that in two of the documents cited above the term is employed twice, one is inclined to suppose that it is not by sheer accident or that it might reflect a deliberate choice on the part of the authors. In other words, we might consider the possibility that the diffusion of the new meaning owed much to an intentional and pioneering use of the term by certain authors, even as they faced the negative attitude of the vast majority.

That appears to be the case of Robert Mentet de Salmonet. The learned son of a distinguished Scottish family, he moved to France in 1633 and converted to Roman Catholicism. Eventually he became the protégé of the Coadjutor of the Archbishop of Paris, the future Cardinal de Retz, who gave him a canonry in the cathedral. He was well known to Ménage, who like him was then a protégé of Retz, and was acquainted with such writers as Chapelain, Guez de Balzac and Naudé. Conrart held him in high regard.[41]

Salmonet's history of the English civil war was given permission to be published in July 1648; the first printing was completed ten months later, in May 1649. Entitled *Histoire des troubles de Grand' Bretagne*, it was dedicated by the author to his benefactor Retz, who had supported the venture. Actually, only the first six books, covering the years 1639 to 1646, came out in this first printing. The entire work in twelve books, ending with the trial and execution of Charles I, appeared only in 1661. By then the author had died, but a note to the readers, seemingly added by Ménage, announced that Salmonet himself had prepared and corrected the second part which was printed without any changes. We might add in passing that the work made an impression in literary circles right from its first partial printing, and was deemed significant enough to merit translation into English in 1735. As for the word "revolution," although missing in the title, it appears already in the first sentence of the dedication, then several times in the introduction ["Avant-propos"], and again at the very end of book twelve in a sort of epilogue that brings the work to an end. Apparently the word is not employed in the text of books one through eleven, which would suggest that Salmonet adopted the term shortly before May 1649, when he composed the dedication and introduction.

Therefore, the cluster of examples which we encounter here appears to be an attempt to pioneer the use of a new terminology.

In his dedication to Retz, Salmonet labels his work "the History of the strangest revolution that ever happened in the world" ["l'Histoire de la plus estrange révolution qui soit jamais arrivée dans le monde"]. In the introduction he first uses the word in its old sense ("la révolution des années;" "la révolution de siècles"); then he moves to experiment with the new political meaning. This introduction is actually a short essay containing the author's views on human nature, particularly man's innate tendency to disobey and revolt. Men are wicked, murderous, deceitful, hateful to God, rebellious toward their fathers and mothers. They live in society merely for the sake of personal gains and in order to establish positions of superiority one upon the other. This is why human history is a record of man's quarrels and conflicts. Employing Biblical aphorisms and powerful imagery, Salmonet then moves to characterize his own age. It is one of the worst, an "age of iron" overwhelmed by wars and destruction. "It is famous for the great and strange revolutions that have happened in it" ["Tousjours est-il fameux pour les grandes et estranges révolutions qui y sont arrivées"]; it is a time marked by easy usurpations of kingly government, when princes are humiliated and even put to death, and subjects dare to charge their sovereign before a tribunal. Revolts have been frequent both in Europe and elsewhere. "But of all the revolutions that have happened in this age, that of Great Britain is the most remarkable, the most surprising and the most fatal in all its circumstances."

Salmonet's view of the causes of the English Revolution is given in the epilogue at the end of book twelve. Though it was first published in 1661, this text had been composed much earlier, probably not later than January 1653, when the author had to leave Paris following the arrest of Retz. All who want to understand "this fatal revolution of Great Britain" ["cette funeste révolution de la Grand' Bretagne"], wrote Salmonet, have to take cognizance of the fact that it happened not under an arbitrary ruler such as was Henry VIII, but during the reign of Charles I, "the best of all the kings that ever swayed the sceptre either in Scotland or England." He observed the same phenomenon in ancient history; for example, in Rome where commotions took place during the humane reign of Titus and not under the vicious rule of Caligula. This, in his view, demonstrated that revolutions are more than anything the outcome of man's rebellious, yet deceitful and cowardly nature; man surrenders to repression and is ungrateful to those who treat him well. But "the extraordinary revolution, the history whereof we are finishing" ["l'estrange révolution dont nous achevons l'histoire"], should also teach meaningful lessons: First, that those who separate from the Roman Catholic Church inherit bad religion and political confusion; second, that those who forswear obedience to their legitimate rulers always end in misery and ruin.[42]

Salmonet's pioneering use of "revolution" presents nevertheless a riddle. Somehow it is unfitting that a foreigner, although one with a remarkable command of the language, would undertake the introduction of such a crucial political term. Moreover, it is odd that he ventured it even though great masters of French, with some of whom he had personal acquaintance, remained adverse to the term. One wonders, therefore, whether he was encouraged by his benefactor Retz, who, as we shall see, had his own separate record of using "revolution." This possibility is not lessened by Salmonet's tendency to paint the term in the darkest colors. For him "revolution" is either God's punishment or the horrid result of rebellion, which is in turn an illegitimate attempt to effect changes in government against the will of a king, "who is the deputy of God." Both senses of the term are reflected in the manner that Salmonet employed it at the opening of a very rare tract that he penned early in 1652 in honor of the exiled Charles II. Since Retz obviously instigated the writing of this piece, and also added to it a short introductory note attesting to the quality and truthfulness of its contents, it is almost impossible to dissociate him from Salmonet's "ceste révolution si funeste, arrivée dans vos Royaumes" ["this revolution, so fatal, that had taken place in your Kingdoms"], which all of Europe had witnessed with despair.[43] The impression is that the tract meant not just to console and strengthen the spirit of the young monarch in exile, but also to exculpate Retz from accusations that he admired Cromwell and his system of government. Therefore, the term refers here to an experience which is extremely painful, devastating and completely discredited. But as we shall see next, "revolution" could also be used to justify violent political change as rightful and due.

This perception of the term is found in the third volume of the history of France by Mezeray. We observed earlier that in the first two volumes, antedating the Fronde, Mezeray had already employed the word to express notions concerning the end and the beginning of political existence. In the third volume, published in 1651, the use of the word is more frequent and carried out with enhanced assurance. For example, we find Mezeray putting in the mouth of one speaker the phrase: "all things were made subject to revolution,... according to the pleasure of Divine Providence" ["toutes choses estoient sujettes à révolution,... selon qu'il plaist à la Providence Divine"].[44] This must be one of the earliest versions of an expression that would become an eighteenth century cliché. But the really new sense with which Mezeray endows the term takes shape when he employs it while treating concrete political emergencies. Describing the uprising of Paris and other towns early in 1589 against Henry III, he writes of the arrival of the Duke of Mayenne to the capital, where the crowd, overflowing with feelings of support for the League, offered him the crown. Mayenne refused, and Mezeray justifies his action, explaining that to have accepted could have alienated other great nobles, who meant to help Mayenne without becoming his subjects. Then he adds the following comment: "The main authors of this great revolution did not appear disposed to submit themselves to a Duke after having shaken the yoke of a King, but imagined that they could form a Democracy in the mold of that of the Swiss, whom they called the most happy people in Christendom."[45] Irrespective of the accuracy of this statement, it is quite striking in terms of the developing political discourse. In Mezeray's new formulation here we have a "grande révolution" in order to "former une Démocratie."

The term returns shortly afterwards as the narrative follows the uprisings of supporters of the League in several French towns. This time the anachronism appears blatant, since the word is ascribed to none other than the political theorist Jean Bodin. According to Mezeray, Bodin, a royal advocate in Laôn, first abstained from backing the insurgents only to meet demands that he be removed from office and his property confiscated. In order to extricate himself Bodin addressed the crowd and adhered to their cause, declaring that "the uprising of so many towns should never be termed a rebellion, but a revolution; that it was just against a King who was perfidious and a hypocrite, and that destiny itself seemed to authorize it."[46]

Mezeray then makes Bodin explain that as there are climacteric periods in the life of individuals, so in the life-span of kingdoms. Therefore, the reign of Henry III, being the 63rd in number since that of Faramond, signals the death of the French monarchy. In fact, this idea fitted well with beliefs during Henry III's time. It is found in La

Noue's essay which alluded, however, not to a "révolution" but a "mutation."[47]   Still, it is very unlikely that Bodin had used "révolution" in a straightforward political sense.[48]   This must be Mezeray's own formulation, which, by juxtaposing "rebellion" and "revolution," sharpened the new meaning of the term; in contrast to an attempt at a violent and illegal change of government, Mezeray postulated one which was lawful and within the rights of the subjects. Mezeray's subsequent fall from grace was due to these kinds of utterances (and others on religion).   Although he retained his seat at the Académie, after the Fronde his pension was reduced and later canceled, and a younger historian was commissioned to replace his history of France with a new version.[49]

We may now proceed to an examination of the leading Frondeur, Cardinal Retz, and his use of "revolution." His memoirs reveal Retz as an exceptional student of politics and perhaps the boldest examiner of the dynamics of revolution during the *ancien régime*. In addition, Retz made there innovative uses of the term, describing in one often quoted passage "la révolution des Etats" as an event that demanded from its main actors the most acute awareness to changing circumstances in order to exploit opportunities at the critical moment.[50] But the memoirs were written during the 1670s, and not published until 1717; they could not have contributed to the use of the term while it was coming into existence. We cannot glean from the memoirs anything conclusive about Retz's employment of "revolution" during the Fronde.   Retz had, however, a long association with the political sense of the word.   As a young man he had adapted a work in Italian by Agostino Mascardi on the 1547 Fieschi conspiracy in Genoa, giving it a French version: *La conjuration de Fiesque*.   This was probably done around 1639, following his first visit to Italy (and not when he was eighteen as claimed in his memoirs), but it was printed only in 1665.   The likelihood that the phrase "révolution des Etats" which appeared there had been part of the original manuscript is strengthened by the fact that Mascardi had already used the word in an unmistakably political meaning, though on a rare occasion.   Also, the same phrase, "révolution des Etats" was used by Retz in a sermon preached on 4 November 1646 in the presence of the queen-regent.[51]

We have alluded earlier to Retz's probable bearing on the important employment of "revolution" by Salmonet.   But the twelve pamphlets that Retz himself authored during the Fronde, as given in his collected works, apparently bypass the term. In yet another piece, addressed to the king and attacking Mazarin's alliance with Cromwell, he used the phrase "sans attendre la révolution de l'Angleterre," meaning the eventual fall of Cromwell and his supporters.[52] But this was penned in October 1657 from exile in Italy. As for the Fronde years, we have to go to his letters for an expression such as "the revolutions, which are but too common" ["les révolutions, qui ne sont que trop ordinaire"]; or search for it in a pamphlet merely attributed to him, said to have been written by Retz against his own party, where he ended thus: "There is no example of a revolution that one does not have to dread from a people so cruelly mistreated."[53] The record of Retz with regard to the use of "revolution" thus presents a dilemma. It would appear that the personality most qualified to employ the term during the Fronde actually handled it in the most circumspect manner.

Ironically, the man whom Retz strove to ruin left clear evidence that he knew of Retz's association with the term. We have already seen Cardinal Mazarin employing "revolution" in 1648 in his correspondence on the affairs of Naples. We might add that Mazarin had not used the word in the instructions to his emissary to England two years earlier, although "the troubles" that tormented that country worried him and he was concerned lest "a republic will be formed."[54] On April 10, 1651, however, while exiled in Brühl, near Cologne, he wrote to the queen, inveighing expressly against Retz. He accused his rival of hostility to the monarchy and fomenting the idea of a republic among the people. He charged Retz as well with being an admirer of Cromwell, citing Ménage as a hearing witness. But worst of all, Retz, according to Mazarin, ordered one of his men at the start of the Fronde "to write and print all the revolutions of England" ["faire écrire et imprimer toutes les révolutions d'Angleterre"], and this was done so that everyone could be familiar with the method of bringing down a monarchy.[55]

Whether justified or not with respect to Retz, Mazarin's accusations were an unfair judgment of Mentet de Salmonet and his work. As we have seen, that book defended from beginning to end the values of royal absolutism. Perhaps Mazarin, embittered by his temporary exile, was carried away by the vague recollection that the word "revolution" had figured prominently in the book, and concluded that its interpretive bent as well was politically sinister. Be that as it may, Mazarin's own correspondence of the next years contains various instances of the use of "revolution," although the term always retains a secondary or even tertiary status in his political discourse. He uses expressions such as "la révolution de nos affaires," "une révolution générale dans la ville," "une révolution advantageuse," "une révolution entièrement favorable," "quelque grande et dangereuse révolution" and more.[56] In 1655 he employed the word in a letter to his ambassador in London, Antoine de Bordeaux. With this we move slightly beyond the chronological boundaries of the Fronde, but we can easily sense a marked advance in Mazarin's use of the word in contrast with his phrasing of 1648. This quotation is from a letter that had been intercepted by agents of the Protectorate government, translated to English and delivered to Secretary John Thurloe, head of the intelligence department. Although the writer's name is missing, there should be no doubt as to his identity, since he mentions receiving a letter from his brother, a member of the "consistory" of cardinals in Rome. This, therefore, is Mazarin's answer, dated 3 March 1655, to the ambassador, who requested permission to return:

> [Y]our business will not be done so soon as you expected, since your island doth dispose itself to become suddenly the theatre of the new and dreadful revolutions. As for the commotions of France, they never happen but once in an age; and if you will recall your memory upon our histories, you will find this to be truth; but England is not so stable and constant;… and I do not admire at the presages of those novelties and commotions in that island, and at this conjecture, the government of that state being put on them by their force and violence; and it is impossible it can subsist without some notable change and revolution.[57]

Reassessing the preceding quotations and passages of French writers, what do they tell us about the early use of the word "revolution" as a political term? To begin with, they seem to indicate the existence of a slight trend, even prior to the Fronde, associating the word with the idea of political transformation. It is difficult, however, to say whether this alone would have led to anything significant. But the coming of the Fronde, coupled with a prevailing climate of political crisis in western Europe in the late 1640s, gave "revolution" a better prospect. As Frenchmen experienced unrest at home, following closely upon news of the revolt in Naples against Spain and being astounded by the execution of Charles I and the emergence of the Commonwealth government in England, political substances were suddenly appearing frail, temporary and changeable.

This allowed room for a new term, one that would combine a metaphoric sense with a dramatic undertone. The choice of "revolution" was also boosted by a series of books in Italian, particularly Giraffi's, which displayed prominently the word in their titles.

Still, what finally ensued may perhaps indicate the difficulties as a word climbs up the hierarchy of terms. Rather than being easily accepted and quickly diffused by the barrage of *Mazarinades*, "révolution" found only a handful of promoters. Bearing in mind the subsequent sensational career of the term, this is at first sight hard to grasp and even harder to explain. Certainly, the term had a subversive undertone, since it suggested a *fait accompli* and something beyond the control of men. As such it contradicted the tenets of monarchical absolutism. But after all the Fronde was, if anything, a huge wave of protest against the growing power of the monarchy. Yet even so, merely a scant number of writers recognized the rhetorical and argumentative potentials of the word. The resistance would continue after the Fronde, and the employment of "revolution" would remain infrequent and haphazard for another full generation. It is only by acknowledging the existence of this opposition to the term that we can explain why it is missing from lengthy contemporary accounts of the Fronde such as the *Journal* of Olivier Lefevre d'Ormesson and that of Jean Vallier, or the letters of Guy Patin; why Cyrano de Bergerac, known for his fantastic imagination and comical inventions, declined to use it in his *Mazarinades*, as did the novelist Paul Scarron, whose level of lewdness in his tirades against Mazarin suggested that he might be willing to employ any word under the sun; or, to mention a much more serious anti-Mazarin author, why it is absent from the works of Claude Joly.

On the other hand, there can be no denial that during the Fronde "revolution" made its first decisive strides into French political discourse. Although it does not seem to have done so in the radical, regenerating sense that characterized the word after 1789, it began to assume a clear political meaning. This is attested to not only by the growing number of relevant examples but equally by evidence that the term is being given new definitions. For Salmonet it served as the dire consequence of rebellion; for Mezeray it was the opposite of rebellion, a lawful and justified uprising; Mazarin, however, contrasted it with commotions, which never result in a change of regime, and saw it as something peculiar to unstable monarchies. His approach was already close to that of Montesquieu, who, as we shall see, in a well known passage of the *Esprit des lois* (V, 11) would furnish a comparable definition.

One important peculiarity of words and their meanings is that once said (or written) they cannot be unsaid. We are unable to wipe the senses of words out of our minds, and at a certain point we again employ even those expressions we never really sanctioned. The post-Fronde subsistence of "revolution" may well fit this condition. The following are random examples, but they are as good illustrations as any other. In January 1653 Jacques Dupuy, a friend of Chapelain's, wrote to Nicolas Heinsius that Cardinal Retz was in prison and did not stand a chance of gaining his freedom "sans quelque grande révolution dans l'estat."[58] In the next year (as told in the previous chapter) an enterprising Parisian publisher, Simeon Piget, brought out Gualdo's *Histoire des révolutions et mouvemens de Naples*, where the term appeared in large capital letters on the full width of the title page; this was the first book in French to feature the word in its title.[59] England, then under the Protectorate, caused Frenchmen in the late 1650s to recall the term. Antoine de Bordeaux, still Mazarin's ambassador in London, employed "révolution" many times in his reports on the events leading up to the Restoration.[60] In 1659 Charles de Saint-Evremont, then a soldier and a writer, used the term in a subsequently famous letter to the marquis de Créqui, where he charged Mazarin with making undue concessions to Spain in the Peace of the Pyrenees. In his opinion, the memory of the Fronde's past disturbances hampered Mazarin as a statesman because it made him fear new revolutions ["rappelloient dans son esprits les desordres passées et luy faisoient appréhender des révolutions nouvelles"].[61] With the discovery of this letter two years later, Saint-Evremont hastened to leave France for exile in England, dying there in 1703. At about the time he left, however, the man he feared, Louis XIV himself, used the term in his memoirs. The king mentioned a number of times the events of the Fronde, employing the terms "désordres domestiques," "factions," "troubles," "confusion." The word we seek appeared only once. It comes in his memoirs of the year 1662, appropriately as he mentioned the arrangement he made with Retz after the death of Mazarin. As long as Mazarin was alive, wrote the king, Retz only expected to return through "des intrigues ou de révolutions de la cour."[62] How fitting an expression for a man who believed himself the incarnation of the state. For the king the use of "revolution" was admissible in reference to a minor affair such as a court intrigue. Other uses of "revolution" in a political sense were obviously incorrect.

Chapter Four

"Revolution" in the English Revolution

Admittedly, the heading of this chapter consists of an anachronistic play on words. The "English Revolution" is a term gradually devised by modern historians; first by the French François Guizot in his *Histoire de la révolution d'Angleterre* (1826), then by Samuel Rawson Gardiner, who in 1889 coined the phrase "Puritan Revolution" to distinguish it from the Glorious Revolution of 1688; finally by twentieth century historians, who meant to express by this term the wide ranging changes – political, economic, social, religious, ideological – that took place in England from 1640 to 1660.[1] Contemporaries employed other terms for the events, terms which basically reflected their concern for principles of legitimate government. Thus the "(Great) Rebellion," proclaimed by supporters of the royal cause, was balanced by the "Interregnum" and by the matter of fact "Civil War." During the 1640s we find men employing a variety of words and verbal constructions to characterize their political situation. The times are called "turbulent" and conditions are dubbed "civil distractions." As early as 1642 one member of Parliament declared: "We are at the very brink of combustion and confusion." In 1645 James Howell, that virtuoso of words, lamented the destruction brought about by the civil war with the following lush imagery: "And when I consider further the distractions, the tossings, the turmoilings, and the tumblings of other regions round about me, as well as my own, I conclude also, that kingdoms and states, and cities, and all bodies politick, are subject to convulsions, to calentures, and consumptions, as well as the frail bodies of men, and must have an evacuation for their corrupt humours..."[2]

Howell's political terminology of 1645, and that of his contemporaries, was as yet devoid of the word "revolution;" although we do find him warning the common people of England to avoid "novelties and Utopian reformations."[3] But although we would have to wait two centuries to have the word applied to the years 1640 to 1660 by modern historians, we should not fail to perceive that it made its first decisive stride into English political discourse during a twelve-year period beginning in 1648. Already then some persons began to employ the word (mostly in the plural form) in reference to political events in England. While they stopped short of forging from it a viable historical label, they at least managed to include it in an array of other words denoting political instability.

In the past four decades a number of studies have focused on the penetration of the term "revolution" to seventeenth century English political discourse, of which the contributions by Vernon F. Snow, Melvin Lasky and Christopher Hill are outstanding.[4] Snow identified leading examples employing the new term, but he hesitated to decide whether by 1688 "revolution" had established a political meaning completely dissociated from its previous astronomical sense of circular motion of the stars. Lasky pointed out the variety of sources that contributed, in the first half of the seventeenth century, to fashion "revolution" as a metaphor for change. He credited especially James Howell and Marchamont Nedham with accomplishing the twist toward a political meaning, but he felt that "revolution" still remained associated with "the principle of circularity, not of linear progress", which explains that "the events of 1648-49 failed to be given the definitive name of revolution in their own epoch because they were not a return to a previous regime."[5] It is exactly this point, the transition to a modern sense of one-directional political change, on which Hill centered. Employing passages already used by Snow and Lasky, and adding many more examples, Hill concluded that a decisive shift in the meaning of "revolution" had occurred well before 1688.

Our purpose here is to pursue the change of meaning of "revolution" from a different angle. Rather than just aiming at finding when or how "revolution" came to signify unidirectional forcible political change, we are going to focus on the politics of its usage, and especially on the way the development of the new meaning of the term takes shape as a rhetorical device in debate.

In fact the sense of the word as change had been there from the very start. As early as the fourteenth century Chaucer employed the word for the circular motion of the stars, speaking of "heavenish revolucioun," but at the same time coined the phrase "Thurgh change and revolucioun" in his translation of the *Roman de la Rose*. This meaning of the word echoes early in the seventeenth century in Shakespeare's *Hamlet*, where, in the graveyard scene, the Danish prince, seeing a grave digger throwing up a human skull, exclaims: "Here's fine revolution, if we had the trick to see't" (Act V, scene I, 88). Yet the use of the word in the sense of change remained rare and extraneous to political discourse. We do not find Shakespeare's contemporaries, neither Francis Bacon nor Walter Raleigh, employing "revolution" when dealing with the subject of political change. Thomas Browne, however, in the middle of the third decade of the century, pointed toward the meaning which the word would assume, when he wrote: "because the glory of one State depends upon the ruine of another, there is a revolution and vicissitude in their greatness."[6]

How can we account therefore for the fact that within a generation after Browne's writing of *Religio medici* "revolution" acquired unambiguous political meaning? Actually, the answer to that is not very complicated. Once the rhetorical value of the word had been recognized and appreciated, it became only natural that it should be exploited, sometimes in an opportunistic manner, to support a variety of political arguments. The English political debate of the 1640s, emanating from an unprecedented constitutional crisis, encouraged, of course, such a development. But as we shall see, the fact that the change of meaning as related to discourse and rhetoric was triggered from the outside was also important.

We may already at this stage of the discussion take a stand in the contention between Hill, Lasky and Snow. Hill is right; the change of meaning took place before 1688, and in fact before 1660. Indeed, given the large number of examples that we have, the discrepancy in interpretation among scholars is in itself an indication of a hidden source of difficulty. Even after 1660 the word "revolution" in the sense of a change of government by violent means, is employed by some, while it is avoided or actually rejected, by others. Moreover, those who avoid the word are perhaps the majority and will remain so until 1688. But we have to go back to 1648 to understand the nature of the problem.

Hill has shown how the crisis of the 1640s influenced a shift in the use and meaning of "revolution." He found instances in sermons preached before Parliament from 1644 to 1648 in which the word came together with "change," and also noticed similar phrases in astrological literature of those years.[7] But a decisive turn can be claimed to have really taken place when the new meaning of the term had been introduced to political writing. As it turns out, for this to happen ongoing semantic tendencies in England were not enough. Some example and legitimation was needed from abroad. This, apparently, was supplied by the books in Italian, conveying the term *rivoluzioni* in their titles, on the revolts in Catalonia (1640), Portugal (1640), Sicily (1647) and Naples (1647), particularly the two by Assarino and Giraffi which gained a relatively large circulation since they were reprinted several times. Is it conceivable that either of these two books, or possibly both, failed to impress contemporary English literati?

As yet there is no proof of the influence of these books by direct contemporary reference. Nevertheless, Snow felt confident enough to write that the first English author who employed "revolutions" in the title of his work incorporated it from Giraffi. Lasky did not deal with this specific issue; and Hill, while implying an influence of the Italian works, seemed to by-pass the question, maintaining that by then the sense of "revolutions" as popular revolts was common.[8] As we have seen, this is not so. The works which appeared in Italy in the 1640s with "rivoluzioni" in their titles really renewed, in a rather sensational manner, a long neglected political meaning of the word, and influenced other Italian authors, as Majolino Bisaccioni, Galeazzo Gualdo Priorato and Girolamo Brusoni, to employ it. Furthermore, the unusual titles of the books aroused interest outside Italy, as in France, where Valentin Conrart was urging, in 1648, André Félibien in Rome to send him Giraffi's original Venice edition. As for England, Giraffi's work would appear in London in translation in 1650. But as will be made clear later on, we have reason to believe that the translator, James Howell, was in possession of the book perhaps two years earlier.

Relevant to the new meaning of the term is its place in a short treatise on "the birth, increase and decay of monarchies," which was printed in London in 1648. It was written by an unknown gentleman, identified only as P. D. In this work the revolts in the Spanish empire are branded "popular commotions" and that of Naples is described in some detail. England's system of "composed Monarchical Government" is found by the author to be the best that was ever invented, despite "our civil distractions." Though the work is an inquiry into the theme of transformation of government, the term "revolution" is employed only once: "it is impossible for the greatest Princes, or Statesmen to prevent the change and revolutions of Common-weales and Monarchies, by their wisdom, policy, valour, and the power of their men of warre, if the day of their ruine, appointed by the secret counsell of God, be come." Significantly, "revolutions" here means God decreed political changes, which no human interference is able to halt.[9]

A same or similar meaning is conveyed by the term in the title of the tract that Anthony Ascham published in 1648, *A Discourse Wherein is Examined What is Particularly Lawfull During the Confusions and Revolutions of Government.* A Cambridge King's College fellow who had taken the side of Parliament in the civil war, Ascham wrote in order to persuade Englishmen to transfer allegiance to the new government. He regarded the coming of a new political power into being an act of providence, and in this sense a "revolution."[10] No other word then employed to convey the notion of alteration of government suggested inevitability, fate and an inexorable movement in a predestined direction. Ascham thus sought out "revolution" as a word that, unlike "rebellion" and others, would not evoke an idea of illegitimacy and would balance "confusion" and other similar words with a slight nuance of a sense of a *fait accompli.* Familiarity with the Italian works on the revolts of either Catalonia or Naples must have given him the idea to introduce the term to the title of his treatise. Indeed, in 1649, when the book was republished in an expanded version, the title was changed to *Of the Confusions and Revolutions of Governments,* a change that was matched in the design of the new title page, where the new sensational term was displayed in an even more conspicuous manner.[11]

In the text of his work Ascham employed "revolution" both in the singular and plural forms, though sparingly and almost always together with "confusion(s)." He did not use the term, however, when discussing changes from one regime to another. Indeed, he tried to convince his readers that from a point of view of subordinates it should make little difference to them which form of government existed. Be it a monarchy, aristocracy or democracy, any type of government had the right to enact laws, collect taxes, judge of life and death and make war and peace. Therefore, once the impact of the newness of a changed government wore off, there should not have been reasons to reject its rule. The essential point about revolutions, to paraphrase Ascham's argument, was not the political change that they brought, but the fact that they took place and were the work of the inscrutable wisdom of heaven. Those who doubted whether they might submit to a commonwealth government should recall worse times, when Englishmen had to switch their allegiance again and again to a new ruler in breach of their oath to the one deposed, such as during the Wars of the Roses: "There I see true confusions and revolutions in Government," he declared in the preface. In the opening chapter he again took up the subject, reminded the reader of the atrocities of Richard III, and concluded: "Yet notwithstanding, particular men (according to the calamity of those times) were by oath and allegiance forc't to submit to this Injustice; which after another bloody Warre had its change, and after 24 years confusions and revolutions ended peaceably in the person of Henry the Seventh."[12]

As it happened, in the interval between the first printing of Ascham's book and the appearance of the second, expanded, edition, far-reaching political events took place in England. On 17 August 1648 Cromwell defeated the Scots at Preston, practically bringing to an end the second civil war. In November the so-called Treaty of Newport between Charles I and Parliament collapsed, as the king was seized by the army. Next came Pride's Purge (6 December 1648), which, through the expulsion of most members, left Parliament under army control, thus making possible the decision of the remaining members (Rump Parliament) to try the king. This led to the actual trial, the execution (30 January 1649) and the change of regime from monarchy to republic, known as the Commonwealth. In the face of these events, one might wonder whether they marked Ascham's usage of "revolution" in the second edition or whether his launching of the term was reflected in contemporary discussions of the events.

Admittedly, one encounters in these critical months instances in which the term is given an obvious political meaning, or is even exploited rhetorically for a political purpose. Matthew Barker said in a sermon delivered 25 October 1648: "The Lord knows what revolutions and changes we may see before the next monthly fast." Earlier that month a declaration written in Edinburgh as a response to those who sided with the king, opened thus: "As the only wise God is pleased to exercise his people, and carry on his work in these kingdoms with many strange revolutions of providence."[13] But these examples (perhaps a few more are yet to be uncovered), establish only a remote link with Ascham. The impression is that more than just a few months was needed for the innovation to have its impact, and so it may be that Ascham's own decision to bring "revolution" to the center of the title of his book in its second edition is indeed the best evidence that ties the new term with the events.

This interpretation adds confirmation from another angle. Ascham's ideas aroused controversy. He was attacked by the royalist Oxford theologian Robert Sanderson, who charged him with "Encouraging of daring and ambitious Spirits to attempt continuall Innovations, with this Confidence, that if they can by anie waies (how unjust so ever) possess themselves of the Supreme Power, they ought to be submitted unto." Yet another pamphlet came from the pen of Henry Hammond, the former chaplain of the deceased Charles I. Both Sanderson and Hammond declined to use the word "revolution;" and Ascham, in his replies, similarly abstained from the term, though he substantially radicalized his opinions, maintaining in his answer to Hammond that a ruler might not be allowed to continue in office once he downgraded the "people's wellbeing" and favored his own.[14] On the other hand, a reference to Ascham seems to be in a tract by Matthew Wren, son of the Bishop of Ely, who wrote of the world being "full of both books and pamphlets," designed "to treat of the most general causes of those strange revolutions we have seen."[15]

Ascham was assassinated in Madrid the day after he arrived there, in June 1650, as resident envoy of the Commonwealth. Among his six assailants, all refugee English royalists, one was in the retinue of Sir Edward Hyde (later Earl of Clarendon), then present in Madrid as ambassador of the defeated government. Hyde, the future lord chancellor of Charles II and author of the famous history of the civil war, saw fit to leave Spain. At their trial the assassins justified their act by claiming that Ascham had "particularly fomented the death of the King, and the change of government," and that he had come to Spain "to seduce and deceive by a book of his, which was found among his papers."[16] Actually, Ascham had anticipated the charge. At the end of the 1649 preface to his book he added a note reminding the reader that the first edition had been published long before the king's trial and execution. It therefore never intended to "point at that which it could not then by any means see." Still, the impression is that *Of the Confusions and Revolutions of Governments* made

Ascham both famous and notorious. We should not doubt that part of the notoriety proceeded from the unusual and unorthodox term that he had introduced into the title.

Other political thinkers must have been aware of Ascham's terminological innovation almost from the start. Clarendon, for example, who met Thomas Hobbes in Paris on his way back from Spain, might have given him details on the affair. In any case, Hobbes later wrote in his autobiography that he returned in 1652 to England after Clarendon had set exiled Prince Charles against him, and because he remembered the fates of Ascham and Dorislaus (another Commonwealth emissary, murdered by royalists in Holland). John Milton knew Ascham well, since as secretary to the new government he wrote his letter of credentials to the court of Spain. If these three authorities, belonging to either side of the political spectrum, took a negative attitude towards "revolution" as a political term, it was certainly not because they had been unaware of the innovation right from the start.[17] Yet another political author who responded to Ascham was Robert Filmer. He found Ascham a theorist of importance, enough to mention him twice, together with Grotius, Selden and Hobbes, in an essay of 1652. The heading of the essay, "Observations Upon Aristotle's Politiques Touching Forms of Government Together with Directions for Obedience to Governours in Dangerous and Doubtful Times," is in itself an echo of the central issue raised in Ascham's tract. Filmer's conclusion is diametrically opposed to Ascham's. Equally significant, he completely refrains from employing "revolution." Rather he prefers "transgressions of government," or "alteration and change." In an essay of 1648, Filmer too had spoken of "these distracted times."[18]

Marchamont Nedham, the man who in a manner of speaking succeeded Ascham as apologist of the Commonwealth government, also might be said to have followed Ascham's example in the use of "revolution." After having spent some years at Oxford, Nedham became, in 1643, an editor of an anti-royalist news sheet. His writings displayed a wide breadth of knowledge, and he tackled political issues in a clear style, which is easily communicable to a present day reader. On the merit of his essays Nedham should have been remembered as one of the early champions of modern democracy, but a thorough assessment of his entire career reveals him as no more than a brilliant literary drudge. From 1647 he became a royal propagandist, serving as editor of the weekly *Mercurius Pragmaticus* until 1649. After the execution of Charles I he again changed sides, becoming the Commonwealth's chief hired writer and from 1650 until March 1660 editor of the semi-official weekly news bulletin *Mercurius Politicus.* He would change sides once more after the Resotration.[19]

Prior to 1650 "revolutions" are absent from Nedham's vocabulary; in a pro-royalist poem which he wrote in 1648 he speaks of "accidents of state... the like no age e'er knew."[20] But in his first pro-Commonwealth essay the term already has a role to play. The aim of Nedham here was to convince of the "necessity of a submission to the present government," exactly as Ascham's aim had been. Similarly, he begins by declaring that "Governments have their Revolutions and fatall periods." He compares changes in the from of government to "those rapid Hurricanoes of fatall necessity" and claims that "It is the weight of Sinne which causeth those fatall Circumvolutions in the vast frame of the World." God leaves men to pursue their lusts, but takes retribution by eventually destroying the mightiest governments. The term returns as he contends that "the Power of the Sword is, and ever hath been, the Foundation of all Titles to Government." This, too, is proven by the history of states and empires "in their Rise and Revolutions." Significantly, he does not employ the term in later parts of the essay, in which the advantages of "a Free-State, above a Kingly Government" are discussed.[21]

Nedham introduced the term to his writings in the *Mercurius Politicus.* But considering his opportunities of employing the word in numerous editorials of obvious political bent, the actual number of examples is quite small. The impression is that "revolution" was espoused by him as a term of a limited context.[22] Late in 1652, however, he used it in a preface to a work of John Selden that he had translated from the Latin. Here he claimed that "the Soveraigntie of the Seas flowing about this Island" has in all times been held by the British Empire, "both before the old Roman Invasion and since, under every Revolution, down to the present Age."[23] Here "revolution" seems to mean any change of government effected through the use of force, such as the Anglo-Saxon invasions of the fifth century, the Norman conquest of 1066, and the victory of Henry VII at Bosworth Field in 1485. All the same, his short essay of 1654 marks a certain shift in meaning. This essay sought to defend Cromwell's setting up of the Protectorate in December 1653. Nedham here went beyond all bounds to argue the supposed elective and democratic nature of the new constitution. He began by claiming that it is the making of divine providence; "so it affords abundant cause of praise and thanksgiving, that those great Changes and Revolutions which have been in the midst of us, have not engaged us in blood among our selves, nor exposed us for a prey and spoil to the Common Enemy... which the Lord himself hath owned by many glorious Deliverances in the behalf of our Nation." Afterwards, he equated "the many great changes of Affairs and revolutions of Government" with "the Occasions of our Change into a Free-State or Commonwealth."[24] Here again the process of political change, which brought about a different kind of government, was conceived as heavenly inspired.

By this time Nedham was only one of many who experimented with the term. In the early 1650s the new meaning of the word began to permeate the language of politics. Hill has given some dozen examples for those years, in which a variety of writers employ "revolution" in diverse senses. The word stands for change in cosmic, global, or continental European dimensions, as change in national political circumstances, as change in the most personal, intimate sense, and as a word expressing the idea of a certain change to come.[25] Still, it is one thing to fall upon a passage phrased in polished, sophisticated language such as William Sancroft's (many years later archbishop of Canterbury), "that Alterations and Revolutions in Kingdoms are the rods with which God scourges miscarrying Princes...,"[26] and yet another is to observe how the new term penetrates daily political conversation or how it is employed in response to political events as they take shape.

The setting up of the Protectorate affords such an opportunity. The editor of *Great Britain's Post* reported to his readers on the events, including the remonstrance of members of Parliament following their sudden dissolution of 12 December 1653:

> On the midst of this great *change* and *Revolution*, Give me leave (I beseech you) *once more* to usher in, and act the Tragicomedy of this unexpected *Catastrophe*. O admirable constitutions! from whose rare Architecture, proceeds so excellent a *Basis*, essentially necessary to the very Being of these Nations; unto whose protecting Sanctions, we owe the Beauty, and Order of our present Enjoyments. I shall not be copious in my first Center; but descend to the Effects of this *Revolution* to wit;

Here follows a description of the Parliament's resigning of power into Cromwell's hands, his appointment of a council of army officers, and their drawing up a constitutional document, whereby Cromwell was to share power as Lord Protector with a twenty-one-member council of state.[27]

The term "revolution" is employed twice in the quoted passage, first in association with "tragicomedy" and "catastrophe," then in relation to its immediate effects as summarized by the writer. In the first instance "revolution" is as if made to be the outcome of a narrative development of a drama. But the writer's choice of calling this drama a tragicomedy and not a tragedy, is apparently a deliberate attempt at ambiguity. Rather than making his "revolution" an unmistakable catastrophe, which is the reversal of fortune at the end of a tragedy, he hints at its farcical nature as the comic end that undoes tragedy in a tragicomedy. Evidently, we have here a person who is displeased with the setting up of the Protectorate but is careful not to spell out his opposition. This interpretation fits with his words on the "admirable constitutions," which again are cast in a certain ambiguity and perhaps said in irony. In any case, his second use of "revolution" is comparatively straightforward and plain. This time it is not only given in the singular form and has a clear one-directional sense, but it is used in connection with the change in the form of government, and not with the transfer of political power.

One month after the writing of the quotation discussed above a new editor of *The Politique Informer* found it necessary to tell his readers that "the Gentleman that formerly writ this Pamphlet" had been imprisoned and replaced for his daring to vent his opinions on recent events. He therefore had for his predecessor and for others a piece of advice: "But give me leave to tell him, the Revolutions and Changes which this Commonwealth hath sustained, ought not to be questioned by every Subject; for private men, who know little of, or converse little with state transactions and affairs, are not competent Judges, when the observation of the letter of the Law is of a dangerous and threatening import to publique safety."[28]

On the background of this use of "revolution" in the popular press, it is not unexpected, yet still quite startling to find Cromwell himself employing the word. This comes in his speech of 4 July 1653 to the newly nominated Barebone Parliament. Comparing the years of the civil war to "those strange windings and turnings of providence," he exulted in their outcome "in this revolution of affairs, and issues of those successes God was pleased to give this nation." He then enumerated the important changes that had taken place. They consisted of "bringing the state of this government to the name, at least, of a commonwealth... the King removed, and brought to justice, and many great ones with him, the House of Peers laid aside; the House of Commons itself, the representatives of the people of England, winnowed, sifted and brought to a handful, as you may very well remember."[29]

The term does not occur in Cromwell's next two speeches, both pronounced during September 1654. But his fourth, delivered 22 January 1655, to his first Protectorate Parliament, which he was about to dissolve, is singularly full of illustrations:

> And I say this, not only to this assembly, but to the World, that that man liveth not, that can come to me, and charge me that I have in these great Revolutions made necessities. I challenge even all that fear God. And as God has said, "My glory I will not give unto another," Let men take heed, and be twice advised, how they call his Revolutions, the things of God, and his working of things from one Period to another, how I say, they call them necessities of men's creation, for by so doing, they do vilify and lessen works of God,... And God knows what he will do with men when they shall call His Revolutions humane Designs, and so detract from his Glory, when they have not been fore-cast, but sudden Providences in things.

Cromwell revealed the source which had inspired him to use the term, when he mentioned in his speech "a Book, entitled, *A True State of the Case of the Common-wealth*, published in January 1653[4]." That was Nedham's essay which had defended the setting up of the Protectorate. In any case, Cromwell alone drew the apocalyptic tone. In his handling of the term, "revolutions" completely transcended politics. Yet on further consideration , it appears that we might face here an early version of a "revolution" being enshrined by its own author, who thus feigns to dissociate himself from the charge that he craves power. Another utterance of the Protector, toward the end of the speech, suggests that this is the case, as he fulminates: "They that shall attribute to this or that person the contrivances and production of those mighty things God hath wrought in the midst of us, and that they have not been the revolutions of Christ himself, upon whose Shoulders the Government is laid, they speak against God, and they fall under his hand without a Mediator."[30]

We may now examine the contribution of James Howell to the usage of "revolution." Lasky believed that Howell's are the central texts to be considered and that they coined the modern ideological idiom. Snow and Hill at least implied the priority of Howell, when they accepted his date of the letter in his *Epistolae Ho-Eliane*, in which he combined the meaning of revolution as a circular movement with its new meaning of insurrection and popular revolt.[31]   In this letter, purportedly sent to the Earl of Dorset, Howell said: "And now my Lord, to take all nations in a lump, I think God Almighty hath a quarrel lately with all Man-kind, and given the reines to the ill Spirit to compass the whole earth, for within these twelve years there have the strangest revolutions, and horridest things happen'd not only in Europe but all the world over, that have befallen man-kind, I dare boldly say, since Adam fell, in so short a revolution of time."[32]

Howell marked this letter "20 January 1646[7]." But the date is clearly incorrect, given the fact that he referred to the revolt in Naples, which broke out only in July 1647. Indeed, considering that towards the end of the letter he mentions that peace had been concluded between Holland and Spain, the date of composition cannot be before sometime in 1648. By then Howell was probably in possession of Giraffi's *Le rivoluzioni di Napoli*, the book he translated and printed in 1650 as *An Exact Historie of the Late Revolutions in Naples*. Neither in the preface to this translation, nor in *The Second Part of Massaniello* (1652), which is his own composition, does Howell make proficient use of the new term. But his range of expression is different in *Parthenopoeia* (1654), a history of the Kingdom of Naples, partly written by him and partly translated. Here, in his "Epistle to the Reader," Howell begins by introducing Naples as a "Politicall Instrument so often out of tune, having had forty popular *Revolutions* in less than four hundred years, yet none that brought a *Ruine* with it." He then goes on to give a succinct description of "this last Revolution in the year 1647," which besides its striking use of the term in a modern sense, brings alive the personality and meteoric career of Masaniello and the legendary, romantic qualities of the events. This text of Howell's was written at a time when "revolution" had already found many practitioners. Yet Lasky is right in assigning it an importance of its own.

In contrast with Ascham, Nedham, and Cromwell, Howell tends to a more secular meaning of "revolution." His understanding of the term is clearly affected by his profound knowledge of Italian. Moreover, as he was the author of dictionaries, including one of simultaneous English-French-Italian-Spanish, it stands to reason that he was familiar with the political definition given to *revoluzione* in the famous dictionary of the Accademia della Crusca.[33] In any case, when he published, in 1655, a short treatise in dialogue on the proper government of England, his grasp of the term again was made clear. This booklet, in the form of a dialogue between two Englishmen, one of whom had been travelling abroad, reflected Howell's personal views. A monarchist by conviction, he had become nevertheless an admirer of Cromwell as a ruler and a man of strong character, and dedicated the work to him. Addressing his hero with lavish praise, he suggested that Cromwell act as "Charles Martell in the mighty Revolution in France, when he introduced the second race of Kings."

Throughout this work, Howell berated the Long Parliament, justified its dissolution, and indeed claimed that parliaments were not an essential part of the English political tradition. He employed the term "revolution" both in the singular and the plural. The returning traveler refers to "this mighty revolution," by which he means "a kinde of *transposition* of all things in point of government, that England may be said to be but the *Anagram* of what she was." Elsewhere, the traveler is asked: "what doe they say abroad of these late revolutions in England?" And the answer is: "They say that the English are a sturdy, terrible and stout people, that the power and wealth of this Island was never discovered so much before both by Land and Sea, that the true stroke of governing this Nation was never hit upon till now."[34]

In these instances Howell is consistent in his view of the English "revolution(s)." Although his phrasing in the first quotation is somewhat ambiguous, in the final reckoning he endorsed here "revolution" in its new, linear meaning. This indeed is a problematic interpretation, given his well known conservative political outlook; but it seems that what Howell really wants to say is that England is new not because of different governing institutions but because of effective political leadership. He never hides his belief that monarchy is almost always the best type of government, for England as well. But then in his mind Cromwell is ruling England in nearly monarchical fashion and better than the kings who preceded him. The new ruler, therefore, his manner and quality of government, is the basis for the newness of the revolution.

Shortly after the Restoration, Howell, newly appointed as Charles II's royal historiographer, was accused by Sir Roger L'Estrange of having been a supporter of the Commonwealth and of having encouraged Cromwell to crown himself. Of course, L'Estrange made use of passages from the above mentioned dedication in Howell's *Sober Inspections*.[35] But long before that attack the booklet merited an answer from a different direction. This was Nedham's *The Excellencie of a Free-state* (1656). Alarmed by Howell's advice to Cromwell "to lay aside Parliaments," and also by what he termed Howell's plea for an "absolute monarchy," Nedham composed his most elaborate defense of democracy. He marshaled examples from both ancient and modern history to argue the merits of a government by the people. In his words, "nothing will satisfie for all the Blood and Treasure that had been spilt and spent, make England a glorious Commonwealth, and stop the mouths of all gainsayers, but a due and orderly succession of the Supreme Authority in the hands of the Peoples Representatives."

From the point of view of the permeation of "revolution" within the political language of the Protectorate, it is quite astonishing to find that the two major practitioners of the term, Nedham and Howell, were at odds. Equally surprising, however, is to discover that in Nedham's treatise "revolution" had a changed meaning. He employed the word several times but mostly in the sense of rotation of government in a democracy, not in the sense of capture of power and change in the form of a regime. The periodic rotation of men charged with political office is also what he meant by "revolution" in the following quotation:

> And since a revolution of Government in the Peoples hands, has ever been the only means to make Governours accountable, and prevent the inconveniences of Tyranny, Distractions, Misery; therefore for this and those other reasons fore-going, we may conclude, That a Free-State, or Government by the People, settled in due and orderly succession of their supreme Assemblies, is far more excellent every way, than any other form whatsoever.[36]

There may be an explanation for that. Nedham's early use of "revolution" had been inspired by Ascham, who had meant by the word something akin to heavenly ordained crises in polities. Yet during his years of serving the Commonwealth as a hired pen Nedham became close to John Milton. He identified with Milton's republicanism, and was possibly also influenced by his style and choice of terms. Milton, however, rejected Ascham's innovation. We find the word in his poetry, though not in a political sense, and never in his pamphlets in defense of the Commonwealth. In *The History of Britain* (1671), "revolution" appears in the opening passage and the last sentence; but its meanings there are related to time and to a disaster repeating itself. On the basis of this evidence Lasky concluded that with respect to "revolution" Milton's vocabulary was at best transitional, but is it not more likely that this rather tardy employment of the word in his prose was an attempt once more to register his disavowal of its new political meaning?[37]

A somewhat similar implicit manner of rejection of the political meaning of "revolution" is found in Hobbes. In 1650 his *De corpore politico: or the elements of law, moral and politick; with discourses upon several heads, as of the law of nature, oaths and covenants, severall kind of government, with the changes and revolutions of them* was printed in London. We know from the "To the Reader" of this book that Hobbes, then in France, was not connected with this publishing venture. The employment here of "changes and revolutions" must therefore be an initiative of the printer, who had received the manuscript from a friend of the author and responded thus to the budding terminological trend in England. In the text of this work, which includes a full chapter on rebellion, Hobbes employed this last word and "sedition," or constructions such as "to dissolve into civil war," "aptitude to dissolution," "distraction" – never "revolution." Still, in 1652 Hobbes's French friend, Samuel Sorbier, brought out in France a translation in which the title ended, as in the English edition, with "les diverses sortes de gouvernemens; leur changemens et leur révolutions."

In the same year Hobbes's greatest work on politics, *Leviathan*, appeared in London, this time with his full cooperation. He added to it a postscript ("A review and conclusion"), which was clearly intended to help make his peace with the Commonwealth and secure his return to England. The line of reasoning he took there was close to that which Ascham had argued, and in the last paragraph he employed "revolution of states," a term entirely missing from his text previously. But even so, he really managed to endow the phrase with an ambiguous meaning, so that it is difficult to say whether "revolution" here relates to politics or astrology.[38] Finally, in *Behemoth*, published in 1679 though written some ten years earlier, in the penultimate paragraph, Hobbes referred to the restoration of 1660 thus: "I have seen in this revolution a circular motion of the sovereign power through two usurpers, from the late King to his son." Is this use of the term in reference to a concrete historical event a recognition on the part of Hobbes that "revolution" has a political sense or just a reiteration of his view that the proper meaning of the word is circular motion?

Yet another prominent political thinker reacted ambiguously to "revolution" – the author of *Oceana*, James Harrington. All of his works (unless posthumous) were published between 1656 and 1660, when the new meaning of the term was gaining currency. There should not be any doubt that he was aware of the development, but the word is seldom employed in the hundreds of pages of his political prose, apparently no more than three times. Moreover, with one exception he used the term to convey an idea of circularity or rotation, as he described methods to replace magistrates in a commonwealth by means of re-election at regular intervals.[39] When in need of terms signifying a breakdown of government, Harrington employed "disorder," "corruption and dissolution," "change," "alteration," "state of civil war," and of course "ruin of the balance," his own term, expressing his view that those who possess the balance of property in a state must inevitably possess sovereignty. Thus, according to Harrington, when most property is held in the hands of a group inadequately sharing in the government, the result is political disturbance. Bearing these views in mind, we may more fully appreciate his use of "revolution" in the following passage from *The Prerogative of Popular Government* (1658):

> Property comes to have being before empire or government two ways, either by natural or violent revolution. Natural revolution happeneth from within, or by commerce, as when a government erected upon one balance, that for example of a nobility or a clergy, through the decay of their estates comes to alter unto another balance; which alteration in the root of property leaves all unto confusion, or produceth a new branch or government according to the kind or nature of the root. Violent revolution happeneth from without, or by arms, as when upon conquest there follows confiscation.[40]

We have here a unique passage where "revolution" was given a distinct modern meaning, as Harrington's "natural revolution" situated the term within the context of the interplay of the social and economic forces that bear on politics. Yet Harrington never repeated the performance. We do not find the term in his substantial essay of the following year, *The Art of Law-giving* (1659). Here it is absent, in spite of numerous opportunities afforded by the nature of the discussion and his selecting Masaniello, leader of the Neapolitan *rivoluzione* of 1647, as a prototype of "government against the balance" in the form of anarchy. In the final account it appears that to Harrington as to Milton and Hobbes, the legitimacy of the political meaning of the word was at best doubtful.

Oddly, exactly at the same time Harrington was wavering with regard to the use of "revolution," the term became even more visible than before. During the twenty months that separated the death of Cromwell and the Restoration, the word began for some reason to crop up almost anywhere. Possibly this had to do with the pervasive sense of political transitoriness that took hold of contemporaries. Still, it should not be overlooked. Hill has given us a cluster of examples from the years 1659-1660, which are in themselves enough to prove the point; but there are more. Reporting on Cromwell's death, the *Mercurius Politicus* referred to the date, 3 September 1658, as "a day, which after so many strange Revolutions of Providence, high Contradictions, and wicked conspiracies of unreasonable men, he lived once again to see."[41] Soon after the fall of Richard Cromwell in May 1659, the event was termed in a letter of a highly ranked naval officer "this late greate Revolution and change of the whole Civill Government of these Nations."[42] At the very end of that year a report sent from Ireland was published, again in the *Mercurius Politicus*, informing that "Great Revolutions have fallen amongst us; Dublin has declared for the Parliament, and is now in quiet possession of those that are friends thereunto."[43] As mentioned at the end of the last chapter, in the reports sent from London by the French ambassador, Antoine de Bordeaux, to Cardinal Mazarin one finds the word at least half a dozen times between November 1659 and May 1660. Even Milton was apparently once carried away. In his State Papers there is a 1659 letter to the King of Denmark where he allowed "a Revolution of this government" to slip in.[44] Christopher Harvey, who on 11 March 1660 completed a postscript to a treatise on rebellion, which he had composed sixteen years before and from which the term was absent, remarked: "how great Revolutions have been seen to all the world in the publick affairs of these Nations since that time."[45] In a new 1659 edition of John Florio's Italian-English dictionary, we may notice an early lexicographic acknowledgement of the new meaning. It comes in the English-Italian part compiled by Giovanni Torriani: "*A Revolution*, rivolutione, mutatione." This was indeed an advance, because Edward Phillips's authoritative dictionary that came out in 1658 carried only a definition of the word in its gyratory sense.[46]

Confirming indications come from astrological literature of these years. The celebrated William Lilly, always committed to the cause of the Commonwealth, assured his readers that there is nothing like the astrological method to discover "the fatall Mutations of Kingdoms, the Grand Revolutions of Empires and Dominions,..." For the year 1658 he predicted "various and unusual Changes, Actions, Revolutions in all or most of the Nations of Europe."[47] For 1659 William Andrews opened his predictions by reminding his readers "That the publique mutations, and admirable revolutions of Empires, Countreys, Kingdoms, Cities, and the general accidents of this World" are foreseen by the motions of the planets, comets, eclipses and the like.[48] For 1660 *The Bloody Almanach* announced the foretelling of "the strange *Catastrophes, Changes,* and *Revolutions*, that will befall most Princes, States, and *Commonwealths* throughout Europe."[49] George Wharton, the royalist astrologer, blessed heaven in 1660 after "our late twenty years Confusion..., at this happy, and (by many, almost) unexpected Revolution of Government; viz. of turning from *Anarchy*, to the most Natural of all Governments, *Monarchy*."[50] Perhaps the best proof for the visibility of "revolution" on the eve of the Restoration is the fact that the double meaning of the word now allowed room for jokes. Thus goes the first proposition in an anonymous short pamphlet of 1659: "Whether it be not convenient that the doctrine of Copernicus, who held that the world turns round, should be established by act of Parliament, which our late changes, alterations, and revolutions, in part have verified.[51]

It should not come as a surprise then that "revolution" plays a role at least in the rhetoric of the debate which preceded the Restoration. The term appears in a letter sent by officers from London to General Monck's forces in Scotland.[52] While it does not occur in Monck's letter of reply, he is supposed to have made effective use of it in a speech to the principal citizens of London at Guildhall in February 1660. Unleashing himself against the old Rump Parliament, the general remarked: "You are Witnesses Gentlemen that in this fatal Revolution of our Kingdoms, the most unjust, and most wicked, and most violent Actions, have been authorised by the popular Fury of a silly Multitude."[53]

Charles II, about to take advantage of the opportunity to return, also found it necessary to employ the term. To put it bluntly, the monarchy, putting on a façade of appeasement, broadened its vocabulary, so as to communicate better with its subjects, perhaps even cajole and blandish them. We find the term in four out of five letters and declarations, all issued by the king from Breda on 14 April 1660. In the famous Declaration of Breda, addressed to all his subjects, the king mentions "the continued distractions of so many years, and so many and great revolutions." In a letter to the members of the House of Commons, he has "mistakes and mis-understandings which have produced and contributed to inconveniences which were not intended; and after so many revolutions." In a letter to the Lord Mayor and Aldermen of London the reference is to "these great revolutions which of late have happened in that our kingdom to the wonder and amazement of all the world," by which the king actually has in mind the "publick manifestations of their affection to us in the City of London." Finally, in the letter to General Monck "revolutions" are claimed to carry a moral lesson: "You have been your selves witnesses of so many revolutions, and have had so much experience, how far any Power and Authority that is only assumed by Passion and appetite, and not supported by Justice, is from providing for the happiness and peace of the people."[54]

The employment of "revolutions" in these documents was deliberate. This is so not only because we have here four carefully phrased pieces of evidence; rather it gains support from the fact that once the king had returned the term disappears from the royal vocabulary. Afterwards there will be an attempt to stress "rebellion," not the ambiguous "revolution." Admittedly, a complete eradication was not possible, and thus, in the few cases that we encounter the word in the early 1660s, it was given a pejorative characterization. For example, in April 1661, the day before Charles II's coronation, one of the king's loyal subjects reminded him of the past "many Sad and Destructive Revolutions;" quite a shift from the king's own "great revolutions" of the previous year.[55]

In the same year James Howell published a collection of short political pamphlets entitled *Twelve Several Treatises of the Late Revolutions in These Three Kingdoms.* "Revolutions" was printed here in large capital letters on the entire width of the title page. But the tracts were selected mostly from the material Howell had published in the 1640s, that is, before he began to use the term.[56] And there was something more to it. Apparently, the same printer re-issued the book, still in 1661, with a different title, from which "revolutions" was dropped – *Divers Historicall Discourses of the Late Popular Insurrections in Great Britain and Ireland.* Although Howell continued to employ the word on a rare occasion in the early 1660s, the right tone in those years was better displayed by his opponent, Roger L'Estrange, who as licenser held an effective censorship on the popular press. In L'Estrange's *A Memento* (1662), one of the first political essays on the civil war and the Commonwealth written after the Restoration, "revolution" is not to be seen. Those subjects of Charles I who had teamed up against him are said by the author to have used "Armed *violence* to *invade* the *Sovereignty,* and to improve a *loose* and *popular Sedition,* into a *regular Rebellion.*"[57]

As argued in this chapter, to understand how "revolution" penetrated English political discourse we have to realize that its new meaning aroused opposition. This was not a case of slow diffusion due to lack of exposure. Rather the contrary is true. We have enough evidence to show that shortly after Ascham had published his *Confusions and Revolutions of Governments* everybody who had to know did. But to those who supported or opposed the term it mattered little whether "revolution" would mean a change back to a previous form of government, or a forward change to a new form. Royalists objected to the term because it relieved the rebels of responsibility, suggesting, given its associations, that changes of government are heavenly inspired, fatal and inevitable. Supporters of the Commonwealth could accept it, and precisely for the same reasons. This basic division with regard to the innovation became blurred at times because of other concerns, such as critical stylistic attitudes toward anything that lacked the sanctity of classical literature, or a refusal to accept an *à la mode* term imported from Italy.

Still, the word quickly began to permeate the language of the 1650s and at the same time broadened its perimeter of contexts, nuances and meanings. On the eve of the Restoration it had gained such a level of pervasiveness that the returning monarchy saw it as a term useful to its efforts toward ingratiation. However, immediately after the Restoration the monarchy's attitude would reverse and reflect once more the original opposition to the term. Somehow, these premises continued to bear on the status of "revolution" until 1688.

Chapter Five

Endurance in the Absolutist Decades

As argued in the concluding part of the last chapter, although it was showing some signs of proliferating towards the end of the Protectorate and given prominence in proclamations issued by the returning monarchy, the term "revolution" was very soon afterwards noticeably discarded. The aim of this chapter is to review the status of the term in the two countries, England and France, during the following three decades, that is, the entire period of the Restoration (1660-88), which roughly corresponded with the height of Louis XIV's monarchy in France. In both countries the political climate during much of this time had something in common as it reflected responses to high handed policies from above, designed to curb potential sources of opposition, identified as religious nonconformism. In England these policies were shaped in the Clarendon Code (1661-65) and the Test Act (1673), both aiming at restricting public offices to followers of the established church. In France, on the other hand, the first to experience the brunt of royal displeasure were the *dévots* inside the Catholic Church, such as the Jansenists, but by the late 1660s French Protestants began to feel the pressure and a tide was mounting, which eventually led to the revocation of the Edict of Nantes (1685) and the exodus of some 250,000 Huguenots. The two countries, therefore, experienced as polities a period permeated with an atmosphere of threats and intimidations, which affected people psychologically and in their behavior. On the one hand this impelled political writers to tone down their language. On the other hand we might seriously consider the possibility that the use of political terminology during these decades proceeded from a tacit understanding that language had been a factor in pitting men against each other in the preceding upheavals, and that future conflicts might be avoided by suppressing language or controlling its meaning.[1] Circumstances were not auspicious, therefore, for a new word that implied the demise of an existing political order. In both England and France at least the superficial impression that one gets from reading the sources is that "revolution" made no advance at all. The term is used here and there, but usually in an exceptional manner. It is more likely to be found in literary works in a loose or ambiguous sense of change, than in avowed political texts. Still, if one makes a comparison between the two countries, the word might have been under more exclusionist pressures in England than in France. In England, for example, with one or two exceptions, no book published during the Restoration carried "revolution" in its title.[2] Moreover, in contrast with France, no English dictionary of that time gave the word a political definition.[3]

A convenient way of explaining the status of the term during these decades would be to contend that it was denied the distinction of being considered politically correct by contemporaries. This explanation, of course, runs the risk of sounding anachronistic as it employs a recent idiom to interpret the working of the minds of men over three hundred years ago, men who had to grapple with quite dissimilar problems. But in as much as banning a word or a label today as politically incorrect means exercising censure over rhetoric, so in the seventeenth century the bypassing of "revolution" after it had made an initial entrance to political discourse meant at least a rhetorical surrender. This having been said, an important qualifying remark is in order. Even though the term was not employed by most authors, some writers still felt it was the right word to use.

In England the abandoning of "revolution" was signaled in the long speech that the new Lord Chancellor, Edward Hyde, soon to become Earl of Clarendon, delivered to both houses of Parliament on 29 August 1660. Though he had been familiar with the political sense since its introduction to English discourse by Ascham, and also associated with its employment in the royal proclamations issued from Breda on 14 April 1660, he now declined to use "revolution," although he offered his listeners nothing less than an astrological interpretation of English politics of the past twenty years:

Let us not be too much ashamed, as if what has been done amiss, proceeded from the humor and the temper, and the nature of our Nation. The astrologers have made us a fair excuse, and I truly hope a true one; all the motions of these last Twenty years have been unnatural, and have proceeded from the evil influence of a malignant Star; and let us not much despise the influence of the Stars. And the same Astrologers assure us, that the malignity of that Star is expired; the good *genius* of this Kingdom is become Superior, and has mastered that malignity, and our good old Stars govern us again.[4]

Would it not have been more straightforward and rhetorically more effective for Clarendon to phrase his politico-astrological argument with a claim that "the revolutions of a malignant star" were responsible for the "unnatural revolutions of the last twenty years"? Yet he preferred "motions" instead. In fact, he continued to bypass the term even much later in his important works written in exile. Apparently, it is not used in his long critique of Hobbes's *Leviathan*, completed in France in 1673 and published in England three years later. In his famous *History of the Rebellion*, where he incorporated the text of the Declaration of Breda and Charles II's letter to General Monck of 14 April 1660, the word "revolution" rarely appears in his own text.[5]

If Clarendon's avoidance of the term in that passage from his speech of August 1660 amounts to just one example, then an examination of a longer body of literature, consisting of writings of the main English astrologers of that time, would confirm the same impression. We have seen how on the eve of the Restoration astrologers too shed the timidity with respect to the new political meaning of "revolution." But in the 1660s the old semantics seemed to return. For example, in 1662 a book containing 150 nativities, or short astrological biographies of famous Europeans, among them many important political leaders such as Richelieu, Mazarin, Cromwell and various kings, was published. It was written by John Gadbury, a protegé of the veteran royalist astrologer George Wharton. Nowhere in this book can the word "revolution" be found carrying a political meaning, although it is employed in some places in an astrological context. When Gadbury discussed Cromwell's activities in the years 1650-51, he remarked: "and the Revolutional Figures of those two years, most singularly fortunate in all things as to his particular interest." He also included a nativity of Masaniello, where he saw fit to mention "Mr. Howell's History of him." Therefore, there should be no doubt that he was familiar with the political sense. Henry Coley, a disciple of William Lilly's, was inclined to drop the word altogether, and John Partridge, who began to publish almanacs in 1678, employed it only in an astrological context. Lilly himself, signing on 25 September 1679 the preface for his penultimate issue of *Merlini Anglici Ephemeris*, revealed traces of the language of the late 1650s with his reminder that "the several Configurations of the Planets, Prodigies, Conjunctions, Eclipses, Comets, and other natural and supernatural Apparitions" help discover "the Grand Revolutions of Empires and Dominions." But John Holwell omitted any use of the term in a political sense both in his short prophecy on the comet of 1677 and in his *Catastrophe Mundi: or Europe's many Mutations until the Year 1701*, published in 1682. This non-political use of the word by astrologers continued throughout the Restoration. Ironically, even if Gadbury used the expression "this Revolution 1688" in his almanac predicting the events for that year, he only meant it in the astrological, time revolving sense.[6]

In comparison with astrologers, some English diarists, authors of memoirs and historians of the 1660s and the 1670s were somewhat less constrained with the term. Hill has cited from over a dozen works, where the use of "revolution," although sporadic, approached a modern sense. Among the authors he mentioned were the diarists Pepys and Evelyn, Bishop Thomas Sprat and the historian Henry Stubbe. But equally important is Hill's observation that old Cromwellians used the word when they discussed politics in private. It fits well with the hypothesis advanced here that the political sense of the word, although remembered, was largely bypassed or suppressed.[7] The following two examples from the late 1660s are especially indicative because they come from works on politics which at the time gained large audiences through repeated editions and translations. In the opening passages of his classic, *The Present State of the Ottoman Empire*, first printed in 1668, Paul Rycaut used the term in a context which brought to light the full extent of the new sense:

> But there must be yet certain Rules in every Government, which are the foundations and pillars of it; not subject to the alteration of time or any other accident; and so essential to it that they admit of no change, untill the whole model of Politie suffer a Convulsion and be shaken to some other form; which is either affected by the new laws of a Conqueror, or by intestine and civil revolutions.

Rycaut's phrasing recalls Harrington's passage of 1658, cited in the last chapter, on the "natural or violent revolution." The difference, however, is that Harrington used the term to explain the change of government as a result of the rise of a new social group, whereas Rycaut employs it to illustrate what might cause a fundamental constitutional change. We meet the word again in this context in Edward Chamberlayne's *Angliae Notitiae, or the Present State of England*, first published in 1669. In this work, which by 1684 had its fifteenth edition, the author explained and held up his countrymen's attachment to a monarchical form of government. Even in the last "revolution," he claimed, when men and the devil worked hard to change the monarchy into a democracy, the distinctive political inclination of the nation finally convinced most Englishmen to recall their exiled king.[8]

The evidence supplied in the writings of Sir William Temple, England's renowned ambassador to the Netherlands, is more remarkable than the previous examples. Here is an author who used the term repeatedly, though not at the expense of the older terminology, even as he held a liaison with the royal government. In his essay on the origins and nature of government, written in 1672 and first published in 1680, Temple employed "changes and revolution of States" right from the start. For a writer that subscribed to the view that government was founded on personal authority and not on a contract between the ruler and his subjects, this was particularly bold semantics. Later in that essay he dealt with the factors that made governments stable in either a monarchy or a commonwealth. He imagined all governments to have the shape of a pyramid, whose base is "the consent of the people, or the greatest or strongest part of them." When that consent eroded, either because the monarch heeded more to the interest of particular men contrary to those of the people, or because a government supported by the people came to reflect the interest of the persons who shared in it – a government was in danger of being overthrown. Consequently, "any man may deduce from it the causes of the several revolutions we may find upon record to have happened in the governments of the world." The essay ended with a discussion of "the two freshest examples... the revolutions of England in the year sixty, and of Holland in seventy two." In yet another essay, "Of Popular Discontents," written later in the 1670s, Temple explored the theme of political instability as a product of man's nature, that is his "certain restlessness of mind and thought." This flaw, he argued, afflicted man in his private life, but was also at the bottom of "the factions, seditions, convulsions and fatal revolutions" that have at one time or another damaged most of the governments in the world. The same or comparable phrasing returned in several other places of the essay, most conspicuously in his interpretation of "those long miseries, and fatal revolutions of the Crown and nation, between 1641 and 1660, when his Majesty's happy restoration seemed to have given a final period to all new commotions or revolutions in this kingdom."[9]

Compared with Temple, other English political theorists of the 1670s displayed an awkward refrain from the term, even when their sympathies were far removed from an emerging Tory ideology. Henry Neville, Harrington's friend and follower, used the term rarely in his 1675 translation of the works of Machiavelli. In one place, for example, he rendered the Italian "presono speranza di potere innovare le cose," as "began to hold up their heads, and hope for a revolution." Moreover, in a supposed letter of Machiavelli to Zanobius Buondelmonte (appended at the end of the volume), which was really Neville's own composition, he made the Florentine theorist say: "Having lived in an Age when our poor Country and Government have suffered more changes and revolutions, than ever did perhaps befall any people in so short a time..."[10] And yet, in his *Plato redivivus*, a dialogue published in 1681, where he contrived to express some republican ideas, the term is almost entirely missing, in spite of the many opportunities afforded by the nature of the discussion. Indeed, here its absence is particularly significant since in the foreword to the work it is stated that "whosoever sets himself to study politicks, must do it by reading History, and observing in it the several turns and Revolutions of Government."[11]

The same holds for Andrew Marvell, Milton's assistant during the last years of the Protectorate, whose long pamphlet decrying the attempts "to make our Monarchy Absolute," created a sensation in 1677 and provoked the government to offer a reward for the discovering of the identity of the author. If he used the word it was certainly unrepresentative of his choice of terms.[12] On the other hand, the young Gilbert Burnet who published in 1679 the first part of *The History of the Reformation of the Church of England*, told his readers in the first sentence of his preface: "There is no part of History better received than the Account of great Changes, and Revolutions of States and Governments, in which the Variety of unlooked for Accidents and Events, both entertains the Reader and improves him." And he too then generally refrained from making use of the word in his text.

The two most important authors on politics of those years, whose writings conform with this pattern of use of "revolution," were of course John Locke and Algernon Sidney. Both the *Two Treatises on Civil Government* and the *Discourses Concerning Government* were written as rebuttals of Robert Filmer's *Patriarcha* (first printed in 1680). Both furnished arguments allowing the use of force against a coercive monarchical government, and both remained for that reason unpublished until after 1688. In both, however, the term "revolution" appears as a great exception. Locke used it twice towards the final part of the second treatise as he explained that not every minor breach of the contract between the ruler and the ruled was a sufficient excuse for the people to force a change in the government. In this connection he mentioned "the many revolutions... in this kingdom in this and former ages," carefully noting that with all the changes they had introduced these revolutions never turned England away from its model of mixed monarchy of king, lords and commons.[13] In contrast, Sidney defended the idea of revolution as an inherent right of the governed throughout. This right, he claimed, should be recognized since "All human Constitutions are subject to corruption, and must perish unless timely renew'd." Men should have the right to innovate and perfect matters in politics in the same manner that they had changed and advanced their technology, invented printing and the like. If the forefathers of a nation were so ignorant as to set up a bad political system, why should it not be altered by later generations? While formulating these ideas, however, and berating all forms of tyranny, Sidney used terms such as "rebellion," "civil war," "tumults," "sedition." Only on a very rare occasion did he refer to "the Authors of great Revolutions," who conspire to kill the tyrant in order to thus dismantle the entire system of a tyranny.[14]

What holds for major authors as Locke and Sidney applies as well to the pamphlets issued from both ends of the political spectrum during the imaginary Popish Plot (1678) and the Exclusion Crisis (1679-83). The term "revolution" is missing from the speeches of the Earl of Shaftesbury as printed at the time.[15] Dryden used it rarely in *Absalom and Achitophel* (1681-82), and not quite in an obvious political sense. Elkanah Settle, who began writing for Shaftesbury and then changed sides, also neglected the term. So did John Somers in *A Brief History of the Succession* (1681) and John Northleigh in *The Parallel* (1682).

All of this negative evidence raises a question; how are we to explain that some thirty years after authors of considerable influence such as Ascham, Nedham and Howell had introduced "revolution" to the rhetorical arsenal of English political debate the term was still at best lingering in a limbo?   Moreover, this question should be considered in the light of the positive data, sporadic as they were, demonstrating its use in an almost full modern sense of unidirectional political change accomplished through violent means.   As already suggested, the answer is that the term was consciously avoided; that it was not considered during the Restoration as politically correct. Indeed, it is nearly inconceivable that professional pamphleteers of the early 1680s, master practitioners of persuasive words and political discourse, remained unaware of it.   Therefore, if they neglected to employ the term it was done out of choice. Perhaps Cromwell's use of it in his speech of January 1655, when he applauded "the revolutions of Christ himself," did cast a long shadow.   As Cromwell's personality became, after 1660, the object of intense visible dislike and loathing, so perhaps the term he once used acquired in most people's minds an association with subversion.

Unless we find a contemporary source directly addressing this question, the validity of the answer would remain hypothetical. But in the meantime it might gain more plausibility through an observation of the passionate concern for correct terminology on the side of those who championed the royal prerogatives.   One of the earliest spokesmen for this camp was Henry Foulis, whose long diatribe of 1662, attacking Roman Catholics and Protestant dissenters alike, so delighted the royalists that copies of it were chained to desks in churches and public places so it could be read by all.   Foulis called dissenters "Conditional Subjects," because they were not obedient to their king (obviously not in matters of religion).   As he was sub-rector of Lincoln College, his abundant use of "rebellion" and "treason" must be indicative of political and discursive trends at the time in Oxford. He did not employ "revolution" in his tract of 1662, nor, as far as could be ascertained, in his much longer *The History of Romish Treasons and Usurpations*, completed in 1666 and printed posthumously in 1671. In the first work, however, the term appears in a passage enclosed in quotation marks, which thus makes it a phrase that seemingly belongs to the discourse of the author's adversary:

"'Contzenus saith, these Revolutions must be done moderately, and with abundance of cunning'."[16] Here therefore the word belongs to the pretended conspiratorial language of the enemies.

But the real personifier of militant royalist discourse during the Restoration was Robert L'Estrange. Although he had been publishing broadsides calling for the returning of the monarchy since the autumn of 1659, his rewards began to come only three years later. First he was given a commission to seize seditious literature, and then, on 15 August 1663, appointed to the office of "surveyor of the imprimery" as conceived by the new Licensing Act. This post gave him considerable control over printers and publishers; it may have been his own personal achievement that until 1688, except once, no English book carried the word "revolution" in its title. Besides exercising censorship, L'Estrange put his writing skills at the service of the monarchy. It came to a high point in the years 1681-1687, when he published *The Observator*, a political newspaper, appearing about twice a week on a densely printed folio sheet, written in the form of a dialogue. The ferocious Tory verbosity of this publication is characterized by its author's propensity to detect seditions and plots on almost every corner and by his upholding of the principle that kings are God's trustees. The word "revolution" is never found in *The Observator*, but one wonders whether it had not crossed L'Estrange's mind in February 1685, when, following the death of Charles II, he rejoiced over "the Peaceable Devolution of the Crown, upon our most Gracious Sovereign, the Illustrious Successor to his Late Sacred Majesty."[17]

The important duty of an Englishman to express himself with correct political terms was stressed by L'Estrange time and time again. Here it is how it comes out in a conversation he made his speakers carry in the issue of 4 March 1685:

> Trimmer: I have wonder'd many a time within my self, as I have been thinking of our *Late Troubles* -
> Observator: (The *Late Rebellion*, thou mean'st.)
> Trim.: How it was Possible of men of Those Times –
> Obs.: (The *Conspirators*, That is.)
> Trim.: To Run-Down Charles the First. –
> Obs.: (Prethee Frame thy mouth to a little Loyal English once; and call it *Murdering* their most *Gracious Sovereign*, that *Blessed Martyr*.)

In a discourse where the old term "troubles" was not considered as complying enough with the requisites of "Loyal English," there was no place for "revolution." In fact, this same message was delivered in one way or another by other agents of the Restoration power structure. A decree issued in July 1683 by the convocation of the University of Oxford listed twenty-seven condemnable political propositions and the names of the authors who had endorsed them, among them the *Vindiciae contra tyrannos*, Hobbes, Milton, the Jesuits and the Quakers. First to be condemned was the idea that all civil authority was derived originally from the people; then came rejections of the notions that there was a contract between the king and his subjects, that lawful rulers could become tyrants and forfeit their rights, that the theory of the state of nature had any base and that there existed natural rights of men and a retention of these rights by men entering society. All books containing such ideas were deemed to corrupt the minds, "stir up Seditions and Tumults, overthrow States and Kingdoms and lead to Rebellion, Murder of Princes, and Atheism itself."[18] During the same month the trial of William Russell took place, accused of attempting with others to launch "war and rebellion" in the nation, which is the "most horrible treasons." Nowhere in this trial was the term "revolution" made use of, although both the prosecutor and the presiding lord chief justice availed themselves of all the words in the English language relative to the idea of unseating a government by force. The terminology used during Sidney's trial in November was the same. An undeniable semantic urge of a clear political bent ran throughout to portray the acts and intentions ascribed to the accused with words of unquestionable meaning as to the severity and punishability of the pretended crimes. Two years later, when the Duke of Monmouth spoke his last words as he was standing on the scaffold, expressing his sorrow for *"invading* the Kingdom," one of the four clergymen present interfered in a retort: "Give it the *true* Name, Sir, and call it Rebellion."[19]

*   *

At first sight the shift from England to the continent does not open new vistas. There is nothing to indicate, for example, that "revolution" meant anything to such great political theorists as Spinoza and Pufendorf; and in both cases the main reason must have been a reliance on Latin as a vehicle of their thoughts.[20] But to follow the trail of the term on the continent means essentially to trace its growing use in French. This is so because the last third of the seventeenth century witnessed not only the political and military ascendency of France but also the proliferation and wide influence of French letters. By 1685 Bayle could call French a "transcendental" European language. What Italian had meant for European culture in the Renaissance, and was still contending to be in the early decades of the century, French now uncontestedly stood for.

Even in French, however, were one to undertake a survey of the works of major authors written between the years 1660 and 1688, one is bound to discover that "revolution" is mostly distinguished by its absence. Pascal's *Pensées*, written about 1660, and containing many observations on history and politics, does not have it. Bishop Bossuet, active as a renowned preacher and a writer throughout this period, used it only on the rarest occasions. We find, for example, the phrase "les fatales révolutions des monarchies" in his eulogy of Henrietta Maria, queen consort of Charles I, who died in 1669, or at the head of a chapter in his famous *Discours sur l'histoire universelle* (1681), which affirmed that "The revolutions of empires are ruled by providence, and serve to humiliate the princes." But when we take into consideration Bossuet's vast literary production this is less than a pittance. Actually, it raises the question whether the regular absence of the term in his text does not amount to a contention that the word should not be given a political sense. In 1688 when he published the *Histoire de variations des eglises protestantes*, Bossuet could not have been unaware of a work on a similar subject by Varillas, with "revolutions" in its title, which had begun to appear two years earlier and aroused a lot of attention. And yet he bypassed the term even now, and continued to do so also in his additions to the original work, which were written in the early 1690s in answer to French Protestant authors.[21] The same impression is confirmed by Mme de Sévigné's letters, some 1600 in number and written from the late 1640s to the early 1690s. One has to look hard to find there a trace of the word, although the letters cover almost any subject worth discussing.[22]

In the France of Louis XIV, therefore, as in Restoration England, "revolution" was not accepted as politically correct. To come upon the word in a contemporary essay on politics is something of a semantic event. Not that it is a completely exasperating and fruitless search however, because at some point even an ordinarily circumspect author may lose his attention and succumb to the alluring flare of the

word. Thus Jean François Senault, one of the favorite preachers at the
court, in a work filled with flattery to the king and his government, in
apparently just one place concluded that history also taught men of
"les diverses révolutions des Monarchies." Paul Hay, who wrote a
general description of France that displeased the king and earned him
two weeks in the Bastille, referred to the "révolutions" that England
had undergone because its kings neglected to keep an adequate
number of fortified positions. The Jesuit poet and essayist Pierre
Lemoyne, however, used the word three times in a single page. This
came deep into his tract on the art of ruling, where incidentally he
espoused some critical views on the high pretenses of royal
absolutism, remarking that real sovereignty belongs to God alone.
Indeed, his employment of "revolution" came in this connection.
Bringing up the Biblical story of the split of the kingdom of Israel
after the death of Solomon because of the foolishness of his son
Rehoboam, he argued that it was God's wish that this event should be
recorded for posterity and serve to instruct monarchs; first, that they
should care for their subjects in a fatherly manner, and secondly, that
they should be warned that "the revolutions and the changes of States,
are not quite games of chance,..." ["les révolutions & les changemens
des Estats, ne sont pas des jeux de la fortune,..."]. Here the rhetorical
implications of the use of the word resembled some of the examples
which had been improvised during the Fronde.[23]

In fact, the Fronde might be a key to an understanding of both the
absence and endurance of "revolution" in French in the 1660s and the
1670s. Its absence might be tied to the threatening flare that the word
was given in the Fronde; its endurance is related to colloquial patterns
adopted by persons who had been immersed in the politics of the
Fronde, and who later wrote memoirs of their experience. The
memoirs of the Duke of La Rochefoucauld, who had fought on the
side of the princes Condé and Conti and was wounded, began
appearing in 1662 in truncated, incorrect and furtive editions. The
term does not really fit in his polished style and is used very rarely.
But even so it made a difference, because in 1680 Richelet borrowed a
quotation from him to illustrate the new meaning of the word in his
dictionary: "Ils s'assurerent contre tout ce qui pouvoit arriver dans une
révolution comme celle que les menaçoit" ["They secured themselves
against all that could happen in a *revolution* as that which threatened
them"]. The Duke of Guise, would-be liberator of Naples, whose
memoirs were first published in 1668, also used the term very

infrequently. So did Françoise de Motteville, companion and confidant of Anne of Austria, Louis XIV's mother and regent during the Fronde. Motteville's memoirs were written in the 1670s. She apparently bypassed the term in the body of her text, but her short preface ended with a praise to the queen she had served in these words: "I fear not to affirm, that in the midst of all the Revolutions with which France was shocked, and amidst her greatest Triumphs, this Princess always appeared the same."[24]

The best example is of course the memoirs of Cardinal Retz, written in the 1670s, and dealing mainly with the years of the Fronde. As already mentioned in a previous chapter, Retz now used the term repeatedly, though still as a special word, whose frequency is less than such terms as "guerre civile" and "émotion."[25] In some respects his use is comparable to that of William Temple, since both authors actually experimented with the term while trying to explain the revolutionary phenomenon. But in Retz's case the word looms higher. Here it is employed to sustain a view on politics consolidated through personal experience. The following passage supplies an outstanding example, as phrased in an English translation that came out just six years after the first French edition:

> The Cause of the Drowsiness in People that are in a suffering State, is the Continuance of the Evil, which works upon their Fancy, and makes them believe that it will never cease. But as soon as they find any room to hope, which always happens when the evil is come to a certain Point, they are in such a Surprize, such a Joy, and such Transports, that they are of a sudden carried to further Extream, and instead of looking upon Revolutions as impossible, they become easy in their Eyes; and that Disposition, without any other help, is sometimes able to bring those Revolutions about. It is what we have experienc'd and felt in our last Revolution.[26]

This passage, whereby Retz introduced his reader to the first uprising of the Fronde, is strikingly modern in outlook, irrespective of the underlying Machiavellian cynicism, precisely because of its grasp of the open, unrestricted nature of the political process. When first published in 1717, some four decades after the death of the author, this kind of discourse was still shocking enough, which might explain the huge success of the work and its repeated printings. But the belated publication precluded that Retz would influence the new meaning of "revolution" in the pre-1688 years. This is the reason why the most decisive work to appear in France in this respect must be the memoirs of the comte de Modène, *Histoire des révolutions de la ville et du royaume de Naples.* It was published in Paris in three small volumes in the years 1665-67, with a second edition in 1668.

Modène had been the main adviser of the Duke of Guise in Naples. He also distinguished himself as a military commander in combats against the Spaniards. Mazarin, who held Guise in somewhat low esteem, was worried about Modène's influence on the duke, and called him, apparently just because of that, a "frivolous man of wicked inclinations" (in a letter where he referred to the whole Neapolitan affair as "cette révolution").[27] From the portrayal of Modène in the history of the Neapolitan revolution by Agostino Nicolai we know, however, that he was a man who commanded respect for his education, wisdom and courage. But there was a basis to Mazarin's concern that Modène might counsel the duke to form a republic in Naples and declare himself its protector, so that he could eventually change it to a monarchy, perhaps with a government similar to that of the House of Orange in Holland. Ultimately the relations between Modène and the duke became strained. He was arrested on Guise's orders, faced a death sentence on a charge of negligence, and was saved only by the falling of Naples back in the hands of Spain. The Spaniards then prolonged his imprisonment, letting him return to France in 1650.

The work that Modène began publishing fifteen years later did not match fully the category of memoirs, since it covered also the story of Naples under the rule of Spain, and then dealt with the Masaniello uprising and the prolongation of the revolt at the head of the Prince of Massa and Gennaro Agnese, prior to the arrival of the Duke of Guise. Thus, about half of the book chronicled events in which the author had not participated or witnessed at close range. Furthermore, even when he told his own story, Modène tended to use a third person form of address, perhaps in an effort to display an historian's measure of objectivity. From the start, however, he referred to the Neapolitan experience of the years 1647-48 as "une soudaine et grande Révolution." He explained that he wrote in order to unravel the secret motives of the revolution, and stated confidently that other historians who had touched the same subject almost always favored this or that side, and so tended to neglect "les causes et mêmes les événemens de cette Révolution,…" On the other hand, he argued, those who were interested in politics should be able to benefit by the case of Naples.

Specifically, they would be able to see and appreciate how the least failure of policy on the part of either the Spanish ministers, the Neapolitan nobility or the people of Naples could cause the loss of a whole state.[28]

These aims, announced in a short prefatory note to the reader, are then pursued throughout the work. The result is a truly remarkable piece of historical writing, combining detailed descriptions with analyses and assessments. Modène examines the attitude of Rome towards the revolt, the eagerness of France to exploit it, and the strength of the Spanish argument that all monarchs should cooperate in putting it down lest it become a shocking example against the bindings and essence of royal government. Though not an outright partisan of any side, he lets the reader feel his sympathy for the people of Naples, who in his mind, whatever were their final political aims, rose bravely against oppression. Other books, he writes, told of the great havoc and the bloodshed unleashed by the participants in the revolt. He therefore insists that those who burned the homes of hated tax collectors consumed everything by the fires, even jewelry and sacks full of money, saving only devotional paintings. They did not loot, and they aimed particularly at those who had exploited the state. The people acted therefore in a fury that was not quite a senseless, uncontrollable violence. Had the nobility joined them in the first stages, "the revolution of Naples could have been similar to that of Portugal, where the Spaniards were driven out with so little difficulty."[29]

After narrating Masaniello's murder, which ended the first phase of the revolt, Modène goes on to consider the stature of the man, his role at the time and his historical significance in retrospect. Here the word "revolution" is used again several times as an all-inclusive term. Many, he writes, who were astounded by the tempestuous quality of the events and watched with disbelief how a plain fishmonger suddenly acted as if he were a great monarch, could not but conclude that "this revolution was a downright and simple result of the judgments of God" to punish the Spaniards and the local nobles for their inhumanity and avarice. But as for himself he clearly tends towards a secular, God free interpretation of the causes of the revolution. He is of the opinion that the general uprising of the people in Naples resulted from worsening economic conditions, which intensified everybody's discontent. Masaniello, who had his own private reasons for hating the Spaniards, was driven mainly by a desire for vengeance. Modène thinks that once at the head of the people Masaniello was aided with the advice of persons of political experience. He also observes that during his short meteoric career Masaniello never spoke of separating Naples from Spain.

The last chapter of the work is again an assessment, this time of the later phases. Modène passes judgment on the conduct of the Duke of Guise, on Gennaro Agnese and on the chief Spanish commander, Don Juan of Austria, without avoiding the issue of his own conduct and mistakes. He opens this chapter however with remarks on the phenomenon of revolutions; how it is better understood in light of the events in Naples. "It is certain," he asserts, "that bravery, prudence and chance are the three principal factors of these favorable events which change the face of the universe, and of these revolutions which make the scepters pass from one dynasty to another, or that turn a monarchical state to a republic or a republic to a monarchy" ["Il est certain que la valeur, la prudence et la fortune, sont les trois prinicpales causes de ces heureux événemens, qui changent la face de l'Universe, et de ces révolutions qui font passer les Sceptres d'une maison dans une autre, ou qui d'un Etat monarchique en font un républicain, ou d'une république une monarchie"]. In his mind, this was plainly demonstrated in Naples, where time and again it was proven that chance and bravery are not enough where prudence is lacking. In fact, Modène's ideas here on the nature of revolution recall similar notions of Retz.[30]

It is not easy to estimate the influence of Modène's work. The book was considered important enough to merit a short review in the year old *Journal des Savants*; given the title of the work, the journal was forced to print the word "révolutions" for the first time, but the reviewer still employed the phrase "ces troubles des Naples."[31] The title of Modène's book perhaps inspired the heading of *Révolutions d'Angleterre depuis la mort du Protecteur Olivier jusques au rétablissement du Roy*, which appeared in Paris in 1670. This book contained material left over by Mazarin's ambassador to England, Antoine de Bordeaux. But Bordeaux had died in September 1660, one month after his return to France and the title of this posthumous book was probably devised by the publisher. In the same year François Bernier's *Histoire de la dernière révolution des estats du Grand Mogul* was also printed in Paris. In this case the author was alive, and the book enjoyed a great deal of success; it was translated into English in 1671 and into Italian in 1675. Although not in the titles, the word "revolution" also figured in books published around that time by Ferdinand de Galardi, a Spaniard, apparently, who ran some diplomatic missions on behalf of France. In his case, however, it is almost certain that the term was borrowed from the text of Lemoyne.[32]

The modest influence of Modène's book might also be judged from another unexpected connection. According to trustworthy evidence, Modène had a long liaison, both before and after his sojourn in Naples, with the actress Madeleine Béjart. The two had a daughter, who was eighteen years old in 1662, when she married the playwright Molière.[33] In Molière's plays, however, the term apparently does not appear, with the exception of the tragedy-ballet *Psyche*, performed before the king in January 1671. There the word is employed (lines 611-617) in a context which seemingly relates to the ups and downs that one encounters in one's personal life, and which might be overcome by one's strength of character. But Molière's play on words is so artfully ambivalent that the passage can also be taken as a promise to the king that he would be able to subdue all (political) revolutions:

Tous les révolutions
Où nous peut exposer la fortune inhumaine,
La perte de grandeurs, les persécutions,
La poison de l'envie, et les traits de la haine,
N'ont rien que ne puissent sans peine
Braver les résolutions
D'une âme où la raison est un peu souveraine;

Corneille, older than Molière and adhering to strict classical norms and vocabulary, does not include even that. Racine on the other hand employed the term in an obvious political sense in his prose. But that was done in 1692, when much of the pressure barring its use had gone. In Louis XIV's France there was no room of course for a dramatic work treating the abuse of political power (Racine's *Esther* being perhaps an exception). It is no surprise therefore that the only French play of that time that took politics lightly was composed in England by the exiled Saint-Everemont. This author, as previously noted, had used the term in 1659, but in his comedy, *Sir Politick Would-Be* (1665), "revolution" is missing. Mme de La Fayette, however, author of the first great French novel, used it twice in her biography of Princess Henriette, Charles II's sister who died in France. Here it was used first in the plural of "grandes révolutions," alluding to the political history of England in the seventeenth century, then in the singular "une révolution quasi aussi prompte" ["as though a very quick revolution"], in reference to the restoration of 1660.[34] This work was written in the 1670s, though published only in 1720. Here and there the word crops up in interesting contexts in writings of other non-political authors. For example, in 1680 Richard Simon referred in the opening of the preface to his pioneering book on textual criticism of the Old Testament to "les diverses révolutions du texte Hebreu de la Bible depuis Moyse jusqu'à nostre temps" ["the various revolutions of the Hebrew text of the Bible from Moses to our own time"].[35]   Half a dozen years later in one of his maxims-observations of *Les caractères ou les moeurs de ce siècle* Jean de la Bruyère spoke of the "revolutions" of fashion.[36] These last two examples belong however to a time when the term was registering some advances.

To appreciate the obstacles standing in the way of "revolution" from yet another angle, one should take a glance at French books teaching the rules of a proper style and the correct meaning and use of words. A spate of these books came off the presses between 1675 and 1695, penned by such masters of language as Gilles Ménage (who had been familiar with "revolution" since the Fronde), the Jesuit priest Dominique Bouhours and others. None, however, mentioned the new term; Ménage dealt, for example, with the modes of employing "Réforme, réformation," whereas Bouhours suggested "se soulever" as a word to be employed in relation to "une révolte générale."[37] With this background, it must have taken some courage and a good deal of independence of mind for Pierre Richetet to give the word a political definition in his *Dictionnaire françois*, published in two volumes in Geneva in 1680.   This was the first French methodical dictionary, illustrating its definitions with quotations from recognized literary authorities, mostly of the seventeenth century.   Richelet gave "Révolution" two explanations: the first was "Tour & retour, cours & suite," with quotations taken from his friend, the translator Ablancourt; the second went, "Trouble, désordre & changement," substantiated with the quotation, already cited, from the memoirs of La Rochefoucauld.   The explanation of the political sense was preceded by an asterisk, indicating that that use of the word was in a figurative manner. This first lexicographical daring probably inspired Antoine Furetière, who as a churchman and a member of the Académie since 1662 might be looked upon as less suitable for the part, although he was also the first French novelist to develop the *roman bourgeois* and a friend of Racine and Molière. We know from his definition in the first part of the entry, that which supplied the gyratory sense of the word, that it was written in 1682 ["en cette année 1682"]. Then followed the second sense:

> Révolution, se dit aussi des changements extraordinaires qui arrivent dans le monde. Il n'y a point d'Estats qui n'ayent été sujets à des grandes *révolutions*, à des decadences. Les plus grands Princes ont eu des *révolutions* en leur fortunes. La mort d'Alexandre causa une grande révolution dans ces Estats. [Revolution also refers to extraordinary changes that happen in the world. There is no State that was never exposed to great *revolutions*, to downfalls. The greatest Princes have had *revolutions* in their fortunes. The death of Alexander caused a great revolution in his States."]

Furetière got a royal permit to print his dictionary as early as 1684. But his project aroused strong opposition in the Academy, whose members, still working on their own perennial enterprise, excluded him from further participation in their meetings and appealed to the courts. The result was that Furetière's *Dictionnaire universel*, long announced and awaited, was finally printed in Holland in three large volumes only in 1690, two years after the death of the author.[38]

Needless to say, the acceptance of the political sense by two leading French lexicographers would have its long term impact. But during the 1680s "revolution" was given a push forward apart from that. It came to play a role in the debate which pitted French Catholic and Protestant authors against each other. Louis XIV's absolutism had been aided from the start by an outpouring of apologetic literature of varied stripes. Within this milieu, a number of historians, seeking the favors of the king and being accorded with them, produced books designed to sustain a claim for a strong, unopposed monarchical government. Among them we find authors such as the Archbishop of Paris, Harduin de Péréfixe, the abbé de Saint-Real, and the tutor of the Dauphin, whose election to the Académie in 1676 was supported by Bossuet, Geraud de Cordemoy. Yet the two authors who earned most of the attention of the public were Louis Maimbourg, a member of the Jesuit order, and the master teller of historical anecdotes, Antoine de Varillas. Maimbourg, the older of the two, had been occupied since the early 1670s with writing a series of works which covered cleavages through the history of Christianity. They dealt with the

Arian heresy, the Iconoclastic controversy, the fall of the Carolingian empire, the Crusades, the rise of Lutheranism, then Calvinism, and finally the history of the League during the French Religious Wars. In some of these works Maimbourg took the liberty of introducing the theme at hand by using the new term. He called the Crusades "tant de grandes révolutions," whereas the Lutheran Reformation was referred to as "cette grande révolution."[39] In his last work, that on the League, published in 1683, he censured French Catholics for having refused allegiance to their legitimate king, Henry IV, on the grounds that he was a Protestant. He thus demonstrated that he placed the obligatory submission to the royal dignity above his concern for the true religion. No wonder that within a year of its publication this book was translated into English at Charles II's request to help sustain the right of his brother, a Catholic, to succeed him in a country with a Protestant majority.

Maimbourg's *Histoire du Calvinisme*, which appeared in 1682, denounced Calvin and his followers as "the most furious and terrible of all the enemies France had ever had." Actually, the book had an immediate political purpose; it helped consolidate a dense climate of opinions in favor of the repeal of the Edict of Nantes. It is noteworthy, however, that in this work "révolution" is hard to find. Maimbourg rather associated Calvinism with "rébellion," "révolte" and "sédition." Proving to be his most controversial opus, this work was answered within a year by at least six Protestant tracts, of which the important one was the *Critique générale de l'Histoire du Calvinisme de M. Maimbourg* by Pierre Bayle. It was printed in Amsterdam, still in 1682, and although employing against Maimbourg mainly facts, arguments and a sense of irony, enraged him so much that he went on to obtain a royal order to have it burned in public, an act which was performed in Paris in March 1683. Bayle too generally declined to use the word "revolution" in his polemics. But in one place, charging Maimbourg that his attitude toward the Huguenots was completely biased, he asked whether the same biases should not have led him to justify the Jesuits with regard to their activities in China and Japan, even though, in order to achieve their ends, they exploited all the opportunities offered by "les révolutions des États."[40]

But as for Bayle, we have evidence showing that in spite of his reluctance to use the term in politico-denominational polemics, he had been aware of the political sense all along. In his first influential work, on the comet of the year 1680, which dealt particularly with the relationship of astrology to politics and history, Bayle already spoke of those who pretended to know "at which times should take place the great revolutions" ["en quel temps doivent arriver les grandes révolutions"]. He censured the sixteenth century Huguenot commander and historian, François de La Noue, for having written that France was "on the eve of an unfortunate revolution" ["à la veille d'une facheuse révolution"], on the basis of superstitious ideas such as the belief in the evil effects of comets and eclipses. Of course, La Noue never used the term "revolution." That was Bayle's phrasing, probably adopted from the seventeenth century historian Mezeray, to whom he referred several times. In yet another place of this work Bayle argued emphatically that "the revolutions that must happen in the world" ["les révolutions qui doivent arriver dans le monde"] were caused not by the stars in heaven, but by the terrestrial stars of whom the poets sang, namely princes and rulers, their manner of government and clash of interests.[41]

Both Bayle's *Pensées diverses* (on the comet) and his answer to Maimbourg were published after he had left France for Holland, following the suppression of the Calvinist academy of Sedan in 1681, where he had been teaching. Based in Rotterdam, he, in March 1684, launched a tremendously successful monthly publication. This journal, called *Nouvelles de la République des Lettres*, consisted of reviews of books on almost any subject, entirely written by himself. The venture ran for exactly three years and must be considered one of the greatest pioneering examples of freedom of speech in early modern times. Here the term "revolution" appeared infrequently and was applied by Bayle equally to sudden political and religious changes.[42] Early in 1686, however, and not really as a result of Bayle's initiative, the term began to draw considerable attention due to the publication of the first volume of Antoine de Varillas's *Histoire des révolutions arrivées dans l'Europe en matière de religion*. By this time Varillas had been publishing historical narratives for some three decades, never demonstrating an appreciable concern for the new term. His decision to have it included in the title of his book did not mean, in the given context, that he was about to change his accustomed discourse, but rather that he resolved to carry his arguments to extremes. In the introduction he stated quite frankly that his aim was to attack the Protestants from the side of politics. He would show, he wrote, that all those who since before the Lutheran

Reformation had preached against Catholicism, had been really stirred up by human and even criminal motives, and that those who supported them and fought on their behalf meant "to incite in all the countries of Europe revolutions, which would give them opportunity or pretext to usurp them" ["pour exciter dans toutes les contrées de l'Europe des révolutions, qui leur donnassent occasion ou prétexte de les usurper"]. In his review Bayle cited these words of Varillas verbatim as the keynote of the whole work.[43]

The shift that now placed the word at the center of the politico-denominational debate did not end with that. In the ninth book of the second volume of his work Varillas dealt with the Reformation in England. Naturally, he attacked the views of Gilbert Burnet, author of the most recent work on the subject. The latter, residing at that time in Holland, was quick to answer. His *Reflections on Mr. Varillas's History of the Revolutions that have happened in Europe in Matters of Religion* appeared in Amsterdam still in 1686 and had a simultaneous edition in French. During the next year Varillas retorted, and in 1688 Burnet published his response to the rebuttal, again in English and French. Although the two authors mostly strove to downgrade the credibility of the other side and not really to flaunt the word "revolution," the mere fact that the term appeared in the titles of all of these books/pamphlets kept it in high public relief throughout the years 1686-88. Moreover, in all these works "revolutions" belonged to the sphere of politics. The term stood clearly for political breakdowns that happened as a result of religious ferment.[44]

In the midst of this politicizing trend, the word was employed once again in the ongoing debates in the sense of a change that is not controlled by man but decreed from heaven. Pierre Jurieu, who like Bayle had been a teacher at the academy of Sedan, also left for Rotterdam in 1681. For a time the two remained close, but eventually their relations became strained. Both reacted in writing to the revocation of the Edict of Nantes in October 1685 and the resulting French Protestant exodus. Bayle denounced bitterly the coercive bent which the Roman Church always allowed itself when dealing with the Protestants. He used invectives and a condemning language against Louis XIV, but essentially called for an end to the use of force in matters of religious conscience. On the other hand, Jurieu saw in the act perpetrated by the French king a breach of contract which might rightly justify a revolt. Furthermore, not subscribing as Bayle did, to the idea of religious tolerance, he attacked the Roman Church as the empire of the Antichrist and interpreted the current persecutions of the Protestants as a prelude to an approaching age of Christian unity. His chiliastic frame of mind, he explained, was based on an historical analysis of the unfolding of Christianity from its beginnings up to the Reformation. Then he added: "After this, I considered the present posture of the World, and it seem'd to me, as if all things were prepared for some great *Revolution*. 'Tis as easy with God to work in one moment, and without preceding disposition, as to take time and prepare the matter... For example, the *Fall of* Paganism by the preaching of the Gospel, and the conversion of the Heathen World, was a great Revolution."[45]

These ideas were expressed and published early in 1686, about the same time as Varillas's *Histoire des révolutions* aroused indignation in Protestant circles. In his journal Bayle promptly rejected Jurieu's "grande révolution" as an oddity. Later, he would accuse his former friend of misleading the exiles with unfounded, imaginary promises of an unnatural deliverance. Bayle was much more receptive to works such as Elie Merlat's *Traité du pouvoir absolu des souverains*, which came out in 1685, shortly before the Revocation, with an intent to instruct French Protestants how to face their ruler even when he was exceeding his power. Merlat had no promises for a "revolution." He employed the term rarely, at one spot in reference to English history from Charles I (and Cromwell) to Charles II's restoration. Basically, he counseled non-resistance. In his review of this book Bayle seemed to second the author. He too felt that sovereign power was absolute, at least in matters secular; otherwise kingdoms and states would be unstable forever. But three years afterwards, on 12 October 1688, when he wrote to a friend on the naval expedition that had just left Holland on its way to England, his spirit was on an uplift. He began by stating confidently that people were about to witness "quelque grand Événement," and then referred to those who had endured so much in recent years, and who were still ready to suffer while they expected "ces grandes Révolutions." Thus, although it was man-made and would perhaps usher in just an earthly reinforcement of the Protestant camp, not a heavenly deliverance, the envisioned unseating of James II was for Bayle too an event apt to be designated with the new expression.[46]

*   *

At this juncture we too might cross the channel. Given the terms and the extent of the discussion, there is room for a separate examination of the place and use of "revolution" in England in the years just prior to 1688. As we have seen, English litterateurs of the early 1680s still largely avoided the word, although, as argued, they were acutely aware of the political sense. For example, in her only political play, *The Roundheads*, staged in 1682, Aphra Behn completely bypassed the term. But in the "Dedicatory Epistle" to the same play, addressed to Henry Fitz-Roy, Duke of Grafton, she drew a very convincing, sinister and modern image of a "peevish *Politician*, testy with *Age*, *Disease*, miscarried *Plots*, disappointed *Revolutions*, envious of *Power*, and of *Monarchy*, and mad with *Zeal* for *Change* and *Reformation*."[47] In Sir Bulstrode Whitelocke's *Memorials of the English Affairs*, which appeared posthumously, also in 1682, the term is likewise hard to find. But in the short preface the publisher saw fit to assure the reader that given the important posts which Whitelocke had filled in the years up until 1660, "throughout all the Revolutions,… few mysteries of State could be to him very Secret." These examples might suggest that by the 1680s the term was already heard in England in casual talks or used by people inside and outside the literary circles, and yet still consciously avoided by professional writers for reasons of lexical decorum. Dryden, the foremost literary figure of the decade, provides a case for corroboration. It was Dryden who produced the beautiful translation of Maimbourg's *Histoire de la Ligue*, which was published in London in 1684. In one of the opening passages of that work the new term turned up, and was duly translated by Dryden as "revolutions altogether contrary to those which were expected." But in the long postscript which he appended to the translation, actually a forceful rebuttal of all those, in England and France, who had attempted to lessen the rights of the monarchy, Dryden emphasized "rebellion," "subversion" and "murther of the late king," never once employing "revolution."[48]

Indeed, this postscript is a prime example of a consolidating Tory ideology, phrased in the politically correct rhetoric, namely the "Loyal English" which L'Estrange never tired to expound. For that reason it is more than a small surprise to discover that another Tory spokesman, John Nalson, allowed himself the liberty to breach the semantic constraint. The case, however, is far from simple. Eager to win favors from the crown, Nalson published in 1677 and 1678 some five pamphlets, all sustaining the royal prerogatives in state and church. His efforts got noticed by L'Estrange, and the two corresponded, the latter advising Nalson not to inflate the issue of a danger of a Catholic plot, because the result might be an equally dangerous Protestant reaction: "for it was under that pretence that they broke in upon the Government in the late Rebellion."[49] L'Estrange, still holding on to his office of licenser, apparently helped Nalson in expediting the printing of his texts and took the right to edit them here and there. In one of his letters he seemed to refer to Nalson's *The Common Interest of King and People*. In this tract, debunking the English republican experience of 1648-60, Nalson in a very rare spot argued that in a republic "Property is always left to the mercy of perpetual changes and revolutions of Faction."[50]

His connection with L'Estrange and the fact that he essentially avoided the term in his early writings, hardly prepare the reader for the use that Nalson does with "revolution" in the introductory essays to the two folio volumes of his main work as an historian, consisting of collections of documents of the civil war. Published in 1682 and 1683, these were meant as a royalist answer to Rushworth's *Historical Collections*, then in process of publication. Nalson was given free access to repositories of state papers and amassed a huge quantity of copied documents, but was able to print only two tomes, covering the years 1639 to the end of 1641, before his death in 1686. Absent from the edited documents, the term is made use of right from the start of the long introduction to the first volume. To begin with, Nalson refers to "great Transactions and Revolutions of States and Kingdoms;" then, in a general sense, to "the Revolutions of this Nation;" and shortly afterwards, having mentioned the work of Rushworth, to "the late Revolutions in these Kingdoms." Further on in the introduction comes the main argument: The conflict between Parliament and Charles I was really the work of a sinister faction that deliberately exploited the issue of "Popery," both in order to accuse their enemies of being tainted with it and to alienate the common people from their legitimate ruler. "By this," says Nalson, "they prepared them for those dreadful Revolutions which afterwards happened, and made even the most Horrid Rebellion that ever was in England, appear a Sacred War,..." And before he ends this introduction, he reassures the reader of his wish "that this True Account of the late Dreadful Revolutions, may in some measure Contribute to the Peace and Happiness of this Nation."[51]

The introduction to the second volume, though shorter, is similarly sprinkled with uses of the term. Here Nalson begins by bringing back to memory the "lowering Times of Popular Fury, the Dismal Events of Civil Rage, Unnatural Rebellions, and unexemplified Revolutions." He is waging a battle against those who in former ages had attempted to delude men by "Pretensions of Liberty of the People, Redress of Grievances and Reformation," and against those who are still trying to do so in his very own time. To all of them history could tell how the attempts invariably ended in tragedies of bloodshed and destruction. But the English experience is even more instructive than that of others, because "among all the Famous Revolutions which have happened in the World, no Age or Story is able to parallel those dreadful Overturnings which happened in these Nations of England, Scotland and Ireland." Although he is employing the word in the already familiar sense of the greatest calamity which might befall upon a given polity, Nalson is actually endowing it with an added meaning. His is not just a repeat of the language of Ascham or Salmonet. Here "revolution" is completely man-made; it is a political enterprise (or adventure) having little to do with theological considerations. According to Nalson, not only the first decision of Parliament to raise an army and go to war against Charles I, but also the final aim, to alter the form of government, had all been from the start the plan of a cleverly cunning faction that knew the art of twisting public opinion to its side. This gives him permission to claim that "the succeeding Revolution had been long under Deliberation." Later on, he proudly asserts his duty both as a loyal subject and a historian "to detect and expose the Artifices and Methods, which occasioned those dreadful and detestable Revolutions, and the entire Subversion of the whole Frame of the Government both Civil and Ecclesiastical."[52]

An appreciation of the effect of its rhetorical bent probably explains why Nalson decided to disregard L'Estrange's ban on "revolution." The latter eschewed the term so as not to muddle the case that resistance to a lawful government was rebellion. Nalson on the other hand, perhaps also in an effort to signal his independence, tried to innovate by using the term in the sense of the worst case of rebellion. Although this interpretation is of a somewhat speculative nature, given the fact that he did not use the term extensively in subsequent pamphlets, the forceful and repetitious use of the word in the two introductions really speaks for itself.[53] Apparently, no other Tory pamphleteer even came close to that manner of use of "revolution." But the issue of which words should be used could not have been far from the minds of those concerned with the supervision of the proper contents of political discourse. Early in the reign of James II, for example, an instruction came out ordering young divines of the established church not to speak on "the Affairs of the State and Government," where indirectly also the correct terms to be used were designated.[54] Still, the hectic and tense climate which lasted throughout the three years that followed the repression of the Monmouth uprising in July 1685, must have made "revolution" more accessible to the minds of Englishmen. If we do not have enough printed testimony for that, the explanation is perhaps to be sought in the effectiveness of both public censorship and self-censorship.

For that reason the utterance of George Savile, Marquess of Halifax, in his pamphlet of 1687 is so significant. Savile had been a close counselor of Charles II, and his advice was also sought during the first months of the reign of James II, that is until October 1685, when his name was struck out of the royal council after he objected to the repeal of the Test Act. Earlier that year he wrote *The Character of a Trimmer*, a pamphlet that was printed without his name in April 1688; the title was suggested by the "Trimmer" in L'Estrange's *The Observator*. One of Savile's more weighty arguments in this tract was that in conducting government rulers should also consider men's passions, not just their duties. Although here he employed the phrase "in all Changes and Revolutions," it carried a very general sense and should not be given any consequential importance. But his use of the word in *A Letter to a Dissenter*, published without name or license in mid-1687, is a different matter. Here Savile attempted to persuade the Protestant dissenters not to abandon the Anglican majority and not to rally to the side of James II. This shift was quite possible after the king's first Declaration of Indulgence of April 1687, establishing freedom of worship. The tenor of Savile's tract was in opposition to the government to the point of casting insincerity on the motives behind its religious policies. Towards the end he came up with this threat/promise addressed to the dissenters: "you act very unskilfully against your visible Interest, if you throw away the Advantages, of which you can hardly fail in the next probable Revolution."[55]

Here "revolution," obviously chosen as a rhetorical alternative to "rebellion," was employed in the sense of a certain fundamental change in the government, soon to happen as an upshot of a given state of national politics. One cannot underestimate the significance of an expression of this nature, and in a piece which circulated in perhaps thousands of copies through the mail. Actually, we have a contemporary reaction to this phrase of Savile's; it appears in a sort of a political diary written at that time, though published only several decades later. In April 1688, after the second Declaration of Indulgence had been issued, the anonymous diarist inserted its text together with an excerpt from Savile's pamphlet, and then added his own comment with this unusual phrase: "The next probable Revolution is the Thing which shocks me mightily, therefore I fear some design against his Majesty. – Nay, troth, 'tis a very suspicious Thing, pray God preserve him from all his open and secret Enemies shall be my daily Prayer."[56]

As one can clearly see, in the mind of a faithful English subject the mere use of the term in reference to current politics was enough in 1688 to raise a sense of bewilderment. What then about a not so faithful subject of James's, and a man of outstanding political and intellectual distinction? Gilbert Burnet passed those years out of England, mostly in Holland, where he became a close advisor of William of Orange and his wife Mary. As detailed above, at that time he engaged in the well publicized controversy with the French historian Varillas, where the word "revolution" starred in the titles of the long pamphlets of both men. But in his numerous sermons and tracts that dealt with the English political issues of the moment, Burnet very seldom included the word. In a rare breach of this self-imposed restriction in 1687 he used the expression "if another Revolution of Affairs should again give them Authority set about it." It referred to a possible regaining of power by the Church of England and somewhat resembled Savile's employment of the term in that same year, although on a much lower level of threat. Burnet was, however, less discreet in "A Meditation," a short memorandum, later found among his papers, written on the eve of the sailing of the impending expedition to England, intended also as his last words in case of a defeat. Here the language is different: "Nor was I at all wrought on by any ambitious or coveteous prospect of raising my own fortunes by contributing to procure a Revolution in England." He was joining the Prince of Orange, he wrote, to save England from "Popery and Tyranny," and he believed that his actions were not inconsistent with his views on "non-resistance."[57] At exactly the same time, in England as well, the word, not yet proclaimed in public, served well in private to indicate in the briefest manner what was taking place. On 29 November 1688 John Evelyn entered in his diary: "The Papists in offices lay down their Commissions & flie; Universal Consternation amongst them: it looks like a Revolution."[58]

Chapter Six

From 1688 to the "Glorious Revolution"

The events of 1688 finally gained for "revolution" a ticket of admission. This is as true for England as it is for France, although in each country the use of the term in political discourse would be marked in the next several decades by somewhat distinct nuances of meaning.[1] In France, as we shall see later in this chapter, the sense of the word would be strongly influenced by a peculiar genre of historiography, known as *Histoires des Révolutions.* On the other hand, in England the word apparently took off from the start as a direct result of the significance of the 1688 experience and its impact on the minds of actors and bystanders. The press being, in effect, free for a time, hundreds of pamphlets were printed in the winter and spring months of 1688-89, informing the public of the changes that took place and debating the various issues relevant to the need to reform the government. In a preface to an early collection of dozens of these pamphlets, the publisher told the readers that they should not doubt its usefulness as it contained an account of "the greatest Revolutions that have been known in many Ages."[2] Although the use of the term strikes one as haphazard in the material printed during the first months, it seems to have expanded quickly, so that the word became a prevalent epithet still before the end of the year 1689. One comes then upon expressions such as "this Great and Extraordinary Revolution," "that stupendous Revolution," "the wonderful Revolution," "the miraculous Revolution," and also "the strange Revolution"; actually, a good number of these, whereas it is yet hard to find anyone calling it "the glorious Revolution."[3]

Most of the pamphlets of 1689 were of course anonymous, but some carried the name of an author, and those printed by James Welwood, White Kennett and Edward Stephens indicated in their titles that the "revolution" was their subject. The time was also propitious for a reprinting of Ascham's tract of 1648-49, the first English essay on political "revolutions," although its title was now slightly changed to suit the new circumstances.[4] There is no doubt that the cumulative result of all of this literature was to make "revolution" for the first time the name adopted for a historical event by its very own agents. This raises, however, the question of meaning; what did the word signify to those who now openly employed it? Not long ago one student of 1688 wrote that his countrymen could not have meant by it "the violent overthrow of authority" and that they rather employed it "in the sense of the revolution of a wheel turning to a former state."[5] According to this view, the epithet "revolution" reflected the Whig interpretation of English history, which claimed that there was an ancient constitution of a mixed or limited monarchy, one that James II defied and that William of Orange restored. It should be noted of course that even within this framework "revolution" came close to an overthrow of a government, because whatever William of Orange was supposed to restore he actually accomplished it through the use of force. But in addition, there is good reason to think that those who used the term at the time were not particularly concerned with the theory of the ancient constitution. We have only to take a glance at the Bill of Rights to verify that the events of 1688 were not justified as a constitutional restoration, but as a necessary action, also perceived as heavenly inspired, to rescue England from popery and arbitrary power. Toward these ends, presumably, force could be defensibly employed as well. Indeed, that "revolution" was essentially the overthrow of a government by force is implied by several writers active in the early months of 1689; for example, the author who compared the dethronement and execution of Charles I to the unseating of James II, seeing in the first an outrageous and in the second a praiseworthy procedure: "And truly the Causes and Occasions of these two great Revolutions in 48 and 88, were not more distant than their Designs and ends; the first intending the Subversion, and the latter the Establishment and Preservation of the best and purest Religion in the World."[6]

It should not be doubted, therefore, that the crucial new visibility of "revolution" meant the acceptance of both the term and its modern meaning of a unidirectional change of government through force. Even a staunch objector to the political meaning such as Dryden was now forced, ironically, to follow the trend in an essay of 1692 where he lamented his declining fortune "since the revolution."[7] But at the same time one must concede that the victory was not a sweeping one. In many pamphlets printed in 1689 the word is still absent. Certain authors would continue to bypass the term even in the next years, especially non-jurors, that is the beneficed clergy of the Anglican church who refused to swear allegiance to William and Mary. It is typically missing from the works of Jeremy Collier.[8] Moreover, "revolution" is not yet to be found in the important official documents such as the Declaration of the Prince of Orange, explaining his reasons for invading England; neither in the Bill of Rights, the blueprint for the new form of government.

   Given this predicament, it is of interest to inquire whether the new visibility of the term was just a spontaneous discharge of a word with a new meaning, which political circumstances had turned more fashionable, or whether it was the product of a more calculated, deliberate approach, one which singled out the term as a rhetorical weapon, appropriate to serve the needs of the victorious camp. On 23 December 1688, only five days after Prince William's coming to London, Gilbert Burnet preached a sermon before him at the chapel of St. James's Palace. It has been recently argued, though not on the basis of the innovative use of "revolution," that this sermon really set the path that Williamite propaganda would follow for the rest of the reign.[9] Burnet justified here the change of government by claiming that William's invasion had been favored by God. As mentioned at the end of the last chapter, Burnet had used the term in private on the eve of his sailing to England, although he avoided it in a short pamphlet, which he published in Holland at about the same time, calling upon Englishmen "to defend their religion, lives and liberties."[10] Therefore, it cannot be by chance that in his St. James's Palace sermon he began thus:

> Things do sometimes speak, and Times call aloud;...so that amasing concurrence of Providences, which have conspired to hatch and bring forth, and perfect this extraordinary Revolution, would lead one very naturally to use these words, even tho we had no such Verse in Scripture; for we have before us a work that seems to our selves a Dream, and will appear to Posterity a Fiction.

Using the word intentionally also in its older sense ("the Revolution of Day and Night"), he returned later in the sermon to the political term and to the providential essence of all abrupt changes in the course of human history: "When Revolutions happen, that carry so many characters of the Attributes of God on them." Further on in the sermon he reminded his listeners also of "the Criminal Excesses of the year Sixty, and how that great Revolution," coming after internal wars and frequent changes of government, was so unsuccessful.[11] Revolutions, therefore, could be either bad or good; it all depended on whether or not they and their operators merited the sponsorship of heaven. In his next sermon, preached before the House of Commons on 31 January 1689, Burnet emphasized this point. Arguing that a nation could never succeed if it had not God on its side, he added: "You see such revolutions, and such disappointments in all humane Councils,...that I hope this will make you for ever consider of what importance the blessing of God is to the success of every undertaking." And towards the end of the sermon he returned again to this theme, using a highly expressive phrasing:

> You who saw the state of things three months ago, could never have thought that so total a revolution could have been brought about so easily, as if it had been only the shifting of Scenes. These are speaking Instances to let you see of what consequences it is to a Nation to have the Lord for its Lord.[12]

Burnet's language reminds one of Cromwell's speech of 1655, where the Lord Protector exploded with "the revolutions of Christ himself." Here and there the claimed godly responsibility for political change promoted the use of the new rhetoric; although in Burnet's case the phrasing seemed to allow somewhat more initiative and control over the events to men. Still, there was more to Burnet's use of the term than just scoring with it the providential nature of William's victory. Very early in 1689 he published a short tract, *An Enquiry to the Measures of Submission to the Supreme Authority*. It had been written apparently in Holland, which explains why "revolution" was missing here, and raised, among other issues, the question whether Englishmen might disregard the oath of allegiance which they had sworn to James II. Right after the coronation of William and Mary, when it turned out that many clergymen refused to swear allegiance to the new monarchs, Burnet hastily wrote "A Pastoral Letter" to the clergy of his own diocese, exhorting them to give a good example to the people and take the oath. This was written on 15 May 1689 and published immediately. It pursued a line of argument not far removed from the one adopted by Ascham in 1648-49, namely that when a king, following a violent change of government, was accepted in fact as the new ruler, allegiance was due to him. Burnet went back to the Old Testament, where "we clearly see that after any Revolution that happened" the people acquiesced to the government of a new king. So too "Primitive Christians understood this to be the Doctrine of Christ," for they respected Roman governments "notwithstanding all the revolutions of the Empire." Therefore, unless they would be permitted to transfer their allegiance from bad rulers that had fallen to new ones, men would be fated "in every Revolution to perish."[13]

Conceivably, the use of the new term now served a purpose of Burnet. It made it possible for him not to dub the unseating of the former king "rebellion." This comes through also in an exchange of letters between James Welwood, a physician, friend of Thomas Burnet and an admirer of his brother Gilbert, and John March, vicar of Newcastle upon Tyne. On 30 January 1689 March preached a sermon on the theme of passive obedience and non-resistance, where, according to Welwood, he treated Gilbert Burnet in the rudest manner, and where the invasion and the behavior it drew out from the English nobility "were scandaliz'd with the name of *Rebellion.*" In letters exchanged during the month of February, and published in April, Welwood argued that all the wars of the Protestants in Europe since the Reformation were fought for the same religious and civil grounds "that appear in the great Revolution of England, at this day," in disregard with the principle of passive obedience. He was particularly offended, he wrote in his last letter to March, to hear "a glorious and unparallel'd Deliverance branded in the Pulpit with the infamous names of *Rebellion, Damnation*, and the like,... You seem'd to me in inveighing against a Revolution wherein the Finger of God was so visible, to act much in parallel with those of old, who dar'd to attribute the stupendous Effects of Omnipotence to a base Influence." In his answers March avoided "revolution." His sermon, he wrote, was in accordance with the doctrines of the Church of England against rebellion. Passive obedience and non-resistance derived from Christ's own words, and he never meant to say anything that would reflect on the Prince of Orange. Besides, he preached in the same vein on January 30th, it being the day of the execution of Charles I. "If the times be changed," he concluded, "Thruth is not, and English Ministers of all Men ought not to be time servers."[14]

This exchange of Welwood and March, and Burnet's pastoral letter of 15 May 1689, are also important because they set up the boundaries of a debate that would continue for the next two decades – the legality of the events of 1688 from the point of view of the Anglican High Church doctrine of non-resistance.   It really gained wide public interest very early in 1691 when William Sherlock, who until recently had abstained from taking the oath, swore allegiance to William and Mary and published an apologetic tract, *The Case of Allegiance Due to Sovereign Powers*.   As a work of a very well known and resolute defender of the principle of passive obedience throughout the 1680s, Sherlock's tract aroused great interest.   It had six editions within one year, and was answered by non-jurors, the author's former allies, and by other critics, who suspected Sherlock of sheer opportunism, given his promotion to the Deanery of St. Paul's Cathedral after he had taken the oath.   His arguments, it must be recognized, were not devoid of plain casuistry.   On the one hand he continued to defend the traditional doctrine of non-resistance of the Church of England.   On the other hand he now ascribed to the church the teaching: "That all Sovereign Princes receive their Powers and Authority from God; and therefore every Prince, who is settled in the Throne, is to be obeyed and reverenced as God's Minister, and not to be resisted; which directs us what to do in all Revolutions of Government, when once they come to a Settlement."[15]

For Sherlock 1688 was "no *Rebellion*, no *Resistance*, but only *Non-Assistance*, which may be very innocent."   Therefore, the events of that year also qualified as a "Revolution."   He introduced the term in the last paragraph of his preface, claiming that once Englishmen were convinced of "their Duty to swear Allegiance to the present Government,…it becomes altogether needless to debate the Legality of the late Revolution"; he then continued to make use of the term throughout the tract.   Both his argument and his use of the term were reminiscent of Ascham's case of 1648-49, with the important difference that in this instance not a republican but a royal government was defended, which turned "revolution" into a rhetorical device employed in the context of confirming the divine right of kings.   The incongruity was noticed by his critics.   One of them, Tim Wilson, a clergyman, who actually held views not far removed from those of Sherlock's, charged him with implying that God placed some princes on the throne though they had no right to it. Wilson admitted, however, resistance to rulers who oppressed their subjects, though without hiding his feeling that "this Revolution hath confounded the wisdom of the wise." His own conception of 1688 was that "the late Revolution is God's just Judgment and Punishment on the Papists, and all Oppressors that joined with them."[16]

Samuel Johnson was more than anything mordant. Johnson had been perhaps the most radical Anglican divine of his time; he argued against unconditional obedience since the early 1680s. He ridiculed Sherlock for accepting the new government on the basis of flimsy theological considerations and not on the basis of its approval by Parliament, the consent of the nation and the approbation of all Protestants on the continent. "The Doctor," he snapped at Sherlock with a biting irony, "has gone hand in hand with Providence since the Revolution." In yet another tract, published in 1692, Johnson chided the entire higher Anglican clergy for denying that crowns and royal titles were the people's gift. "This Revolution," he wrote, "had almost stunny'd the Hierarchy, and was so cross to their Pulpit – Doctrines of Passive Obedience, Unalterable Succession, Indefeasibleness and Unaccountableness of Princes, and the rest of their Jargon."[17]

The echoes of the debate between Sherlock and his critics quickly reverberated abroad. On 22 January 1691 Bayle wrote to a friend that although he had not seen Sherlock's tract, it was explained to him that the latter asserted that "the present Revolution has extraordinary divine features and aims" so that he could continue to deny that kings were dependent on their peoples.[18] Apparently, in the first years following 1688 the term "Revolution" was used in arguments made more freely by those who considered the event the work of providence, than by those who justified it by charging James II with trampling on the "original contract" or by subscribing to a Whig interpretation of English political history. The most important expression of this last view was contained in James Tyrrell's *Bibliotheca Politica*, a massive work, divided into thirteen dialogues and published in parts between 1692 and 1694. A long time friend of Locke, Tyrrell stressed the concept of the "ancient constitution," the supposedly primeval existence of a binding English parliamentary constitutional system. He referred to "the late Revolution" in the long subtitle of his work, but neglected to employ the term in the dialogues. There, a modified Lockean reasoning prevailed; that the Commons were always represented in Parliament, that resistance to a supreme power by a whole nation was justified in a last extremity, and that upon the throne being vacated it was the right of the subjects to appoint a new king.[19]

Although the defense of the "Revolution" tended from the start to be associated with a specific, non-generic, exclusively English concept of political change, by 1692 one could happen upon expressions which reflected an awareness of the comparative aspect of the revolution phenomenon. For example, we find authors referring to "the time of any great Revolutions," or to "such kind of Revolutions."[20] But more important perhaps was the nascent disposition of some writers, even at that early stage, to take account of England's overall improved circumstances and speak of "the late Revolution of Government" which had "carried along with it so many Blessings to the Nations." In April of the same year, when the exiled James II published a "Declaration" from France, announcing his intention to reconquer England with the aid of French troops, he too claimed that "many of our subjects were cheated into the late Revolution;" he was answered with the comment that "Revolutions are and will be bloody, and chargeable, and therefore one Revolution is enough for one Age." By 1695, the willingness to judge 1688 on the merits of its outcome, namely the extension of equal civil rights and religious freedom to all Protestant Englishmen, brought one author to speak of "the direct fruits of the revolution." Clearly, the assessment of the importance of the event on the basis of the tangible changes it had brought, tended to become as meaningful as the debate over the question whether it had been legally warranted or not.[21]

The next significant step in re-interpreting 1688 came, it would seem, in 1697 with the signing of the Treaty of Ryswick. Here, after years of war, Louis XIV acknowledged William III as King of England, also promising not to help his enemies. It amounted to a tacit approval of the manner by which William ascended the English throne. Shortly before the signing of the treaty, James II addressed two memoranda to the envoys at Ryswick, where he asserted his rights and warned against signing a treaty with the man who had usurped his kingdom. These circumstances encouraged the writing of a number of apologetical rebuttals.[22] In contrast with the past, they were now distinguished by a preference to defend 1688 with secular, legal and political arguments. This came through especially in *The Revolution Vindicated*, a tract apparently written by Burnet, although also worked by others. It introduced a new formulation, highly reminiscent of the language of Algernon Sidney:

> That the greatest and wisest nations, and the best of men of all ages, have reckon'd it not only lawful for the People, under the most absolute Governments, to do themselves Justice in the case of Oppression, but have thought the doing it a Duty incumbent upon them, and which they ow'd to themselves and their Posterity: And the chief Instruments of the great Revolutions of Changes that have happen'd in the World from Slavery to Liberty, having been ever considered as Heroes sent by God Almighty from time to time, for the Redemption of Man from Misery in this World, they were accordingly honour'd and respected while they lived, and their Memories have been and will be in veneration by all Posterity.

Thus, by resorting finally to the simple idea of the right of the oppressed to rise, 1688 was enveloped in new rhetoric. The author then justified the revolution also on the grounds that it meant to amend the breaking of the original contract between the kings and the people of England, a contract that had always been in existence, that had prescribed a mixed government of king, lords and commons, and which James II had contravened. He also assailed the concept of non-resistance, since it "must needs render all Power absolute, and such Power being too strong for human Nature, will degenerate into Tyranny." Anything, even rebellion, was preferable to tyranny. "These are," he concluded, "the Principles upon which the late Revolution was carry'd on."[23]

The Revolution Vindicated should be supplemented by *A Memorial Drawn by King William's Special Direction.* This too was probably written by Burnet, revised by others and said to have been inspected by William III himself. It was intended as an answer to the aforementioned James II's memoranda offered to the negotiating envoys at Ryswick, but subsequently not made use of when it was decided that it would only add importance to the reclamations of the deposed monarch. Here the tone assumed was one of self-assured sovereignty. The author did not even allow himself "to enter into the Discussion of the Lawfulness of the Revolution." He hastened, however, to inform his readers of James II's irresponsible and lawless conduct, and that "Nothing was done in the Progress of the whole Revolution, but that which he made inevitable by some Act or other of his own." He then affirmed that 1688 had been a one-time experience: "A Revolution so brought about, carries in it no Precedent against the Security of Government, or the Peace of Mankind." Excluding a possible similar misconduct by some future ruler, the unseating of James II was an exceptional event, not to be repeated. Therefore, the current monarch rejected James II's insinuation of "Revolutions that may happen hereafter." And he concluded:

> There is no great Reason to think, that these Nations, which have been in all past times so careful to preserve their Laws and Liberties, should at any time hereafter come to lose all Regard to them so entirely, as not to maintain a Revolution, which has secured them from imminent Ruin, and has given their Constitution such a Confirmation, and such Explanations, as the Injustice and Violence of the former Reign had made necessary.[24]

Although the two pamphlets, ascribed to Burnet (and others), were first published only in 1704 and 1707, it is clear, as maintained by J.P. Kenyon, that they reflected political rhetoric and beliefs of the Whig establishment since the second half of the 1690s. The confident, self-assured interpretation of the revolution that was given here, based entirely on secular political arguments, was actually an early version of a new Whig political canon, later to be further embellished by Daniel Defoe, and in the famous pamphlet *Vox Populi Vox Dei* (1709-10). Indeed, some fiery passages in the last document would consist of lines taken directly from *The Revolution Vindicated* of 1697. As we shall see, this new manner of looking at 1688 is tied to the epithet – the "Glorious Revolution." In fact, the expression can be found already in a short tract of 1698, and it is noteworthy that the revolution is depicted there as the work of "all true lovers of their country," just as in another tract of the same year it is called "the Work of the People of England."[25] According to this new trend of the late 1690s, the "Revolution" was not anymore an event that men could scrutinize and fathom only with difficulty. Yes, it was still considered a unique occurrence, but one that now could be rationally analyzed and explained. Authors of pamphlets, just before and after 1700 began to refer more to the "causes," "motives" and also to "the Principles of the Revolution." Even an author who wrote in opposition to the new trend, namely against the view that revolutions were an antidote to tyranny, now countered it with reasoned arguments based on historical precedents. This writer dwelt much on the "Revolutions of Government in Greece and Rome," which usually began with "the Tyranny of the People, yet they generally concluded in that of a single person." That was for him too the case of England under the early Stuarts. First appeared the Puritans, still during the latter years of Elizabeth I. Then, "under several Denominations," they became numerous and added to their religious programs "Republican Principles of Government." Finally, they overthrew the constitution, "and according to the usual course of such Revolutions, did introduce a Tyranny, first of the People, and then of a single person."[26] This, of course, was already the budding language of a modern conservative.

Other indications at that time also contributed to an impression that with the years since 1688 the term "revolution" had not just been fully accepted, but had finally taken in people's minds the notion of a change of government by force devoid of any super-natural contexts. In 1697 "a Tragi-Comedy" entitled *Timoleon: or the Revolution* was printed in London. It used the personality of the fourth century B.C. Corinthian general, who had defeated the Carthaginians and demolished tyrannical governments in Greek Sicily, to depict an image of a political hero, the rescuer of his people, comparable with William III.[27] In 1702 we find very interesting remarks on our subject in the preface to John Kersey's *A New English Dictionary*. Extolling the merits of his own work in comparison with other dictionaries, he cited bad definitions of words in Cole's *English Dictionary*, adding this: "Neither are Mr. Cole's Expositions always proper, or pertinent, particularly, of the Word *Revolution*, which he only defines to be a *turning round to the first point*, but this Term, which simply denotes a *whirling round*, is us'd in Astronomy for a certain course of the Planets, Time, etc. and in common acceptation, for some notable change, especially of Government." Therefore, Kersey's own definition ran thus: "A Revolution (i.e. whirling about) *a certain course of the planets, time* etc. or *a change of government*."

Everything considered, this was a very modest lexicographical attempt, but at least a beginning. Nathan Bailey, whose *Dictionarium Britannicum* (1730) was to be the most successful English wordbook of the eighteenth century, would have several definitions for the gyrational meaning of the word, but just this for the political: "Revolution [in *Politicks*] a great Turn or Change of Government." He added, however, a new term: "Revolutioners, those who approved of the great Turn of Affairs, after the Abdication of King James." One should note nevertheless that those "revolutioners," so defined, were *post factum* revolutionaries, not radicals committed to political violence. But as observed above, there was undeniable new freedom in the use of the term at the beginning of the eighteenth century. For example, when he died in 1706, John Evelyn, the diarist, even had it inscribed in the epitaph on his grave: "Living in an age of extraordinary events & revolutions he learn't (as himself asserted) this truth which pursuant to his intention is here declared, that all is vanity which is not honest, & that there's no solid Wisdom but in real Piety."[28]   In 1707 Jonathan Swift used it in his famous satire, "Predictions for the year 1708 by Isaac Bickerstaff," where he made fun of the veteran astrologer John Partridge. Swift ended this piece with a mock account of his own supposed conversion to astrology:

> I was once of the opinion with those who despise all Predictions from the stars, till, in the year 1686, a man of quality shewed me written in his album, that the most learned astronomer, Captain Hally, assured him he would never believe anything of the stars influence, if there were not a great Revolution in England in the year 1688.[29]

Here we have a curious reversal of the sequence of association and meanings. By the time he wrote this work, the political sense of the term had become a commonplace, and Swift could, therefore, make a political revolution the cornerstone of someone's supposed belief in the efficacy of the revolutions of the stars. In terms of one metaphor leading to another, this association was the exact opposite of the one used by Howell and others over fifty years earlier, when the political sense made its first strides.

Presumably, the permeation of the term within the broadest range of English discourse proceeded now in a rush. Still, its continued emplacement at the hub of the political debate throughout the first two decades of the eighteenth century endowed it with a significance apart. The structure and details of this debate were sketched out by J.P. Kenyon in 1977, in a work that used for its title, *Revolution Principles*, one of the more striking expressions that marked the disagreements.[30] The background was clear enough. The compromise settlement of government that followed 1688 left ample latitude to either Whigs or Tories to claim that it matched their separate political beliefs, even though these beliefs were quite different. For most Tories political authority was a gift from God and it passed from one ruler to another through hereditary succession. Though they accepted the limitations on royal power endorsed by the settlement, Tories favored restrictions of the rights of non-Anglicans and supported the Anglican High Church revival of the 1690s with its passionate attempts to suffuse the concepts of state and church. The Whigs, on the other hand, saw in the settlement a proof of their theories on the ancient constitution, the original contract, or even the more radical idea that government originated with and should be watched over by the people. They tended to isolate politics from religion, and although they were supported now by most dissenters, they also got assistance from a wing of established clergymen, known as the Low Church. As long as William III, a Calvinist, was on the throne, the temptation to engage in a full-blown debate remained inhibited. But with the accession of Queen Anne in 1702, the prospects of Tories and High Church defenders of passive obedience became brighter, and they soon made their voice heard. The War of the Spanish Succession (1701-14), in which England was heavily involved, probably served as an indirect factor of restraint on internal squabbles and thwarted meaningful Tory gains.

The High Church speakers did not deny anymore that the revolution had been a salutary and beneficial turn of events, in as much, at least, as it saved the traditional principles governing relations of state and church. According to Offspring Blackall, Bishop of Exeter, speaking on 8 March 1708 in front of the queen, "all Revolutions are brought about by the Working and Permission of God." It followed that the 1688 revolution could not be taken as a contradiction of the view that rulers had absolute and unlimited authority, accountable only to God, although that authority might be lodged, as in England, in the crown, lords and commons. What Tories objected to were the ideas that Whig radicals formulated on the basis of 1688, and which James Drake in 1705 explained as "what some at present dignify with a new name, and call *Revolution Principles*; a sort of principles that will justify all the rebellions, treasons and conspiracies that have ever been, or ever shall be raised or formed..."[31] Drake was reacting to the writings of Whig journalists such as John Tutchin, who though inveighing against the High Church faction, maintained that Queen Anne's authority was based on the consent of the people and not on hereditary rights. To Tutchin, "Revolution Principles" did not imply, of course, a call for a new uprising but rather a way of asserting that the settlement of 1688 conformed with "the ancient constitution of this realm," or with the customs and practices that had always characterized English politics. Both Drake and Tutchin at times overstated their cases, and both eventually sustained legal prosecution. By the second half of the first decade of the century, in addition to Blackall and Drake, the Tory camp benefited from the contributions of the non-juror, eventually turned a journalist, the preacher John Leslie, already famous for his attacks on the dissenters, Dr. Henry Sacheverell, and Francis Atterbury, later to be Bishop of Rochester and an advocate of a Jacobite restoration. On the Whig side Daniel Defoe was active through his journal, *The Review*, and also a talented pamphleteer, the young John Shute, later made Baron Barrington. Yet another relatively young controversialist, who unexpectedly joined the Whig side, was Benjamin Hoadly, rector of London's St. Peter's Poor. Since 1705 he had acquired a name for himself as a leader of the Low Churchmen, maintaining in his preachings that, upon theological grounds, the duty of subjects was to obey rulers who governed for the good of their people. This brought him into collision with the High Church Party, upholders of the divine authority of magistrates, following which Hoadly published in 1709 *The Foundation of the Present Government Defended.* At the end of this tract, where he challenged Blackall's views in the sermon of 8 March 1708, Hoadly went directly to the example of 1688. It took place, he claimed, since almost the entire English people thought they were facing "Universal Ruine." For that reason some persons of the highest rank, including churchmen, "invited over a Prince with armed Men, to awe their Legal King, and force him into a Compliance." When William of Orange landed, he continued, many joined him, even Anglican bishops and the current sovereign, Queen Anne. "A Revolution succeeded" to which "we owe the present Felicity of a Glorious and Beneficial Reign." The manner in which Englishmen acted towards James II, he concluded, amounted to "a National Guilt" in even a fuller sense than the execution of Charles I. Without the "Consequences of this Rebellion," England would never have achieved its present success. Therefore, it was time to recognize that "Resistance" by a whole nation did not merit the name of rebellion.[32]

Hoadly was immediately answered by a pamphlet entitled *The Revolution No Rebellion.* Its anonymous author of course challenged Hoadly's facts. No one, he claimed, invited an invasion in 1688, and William and Mary climbed the throne following James II's abdication "and not upon any Deprivation of him for Male-Administration." But what really appalled the critic was Hoadly's manner of claiming that resistance justified an uprising, which amounted to an endeavor "to prove the Revolution a Rebellion." He felt that over that issue alone Hoadly should have been legally prosecuted, and added in the way of an afterthought: "by your thus making Revolution and Rebellion stand for the same thing, I am instructed what some Men mean, when they say, they are of Revolution Principles."[33] On his part Hoadly did not remain silent. In a broadsheet ascribed to him the recent Tory full acceptance of the "Revolution" was contended as but a ploy to allow further attacks on the supporters of the settlement of 1688 by falsely accusing them of hiding republican or antimonarchial principles.[34]

But at that stage attention had shifted to another person. On 5 November 1709, the twenty-first anniversary of William of Orange's landing at Torbay and the hundred and fourth anniversary of the failure of the Gunpowder Plot, Dr. Henry Sacheverell preached a sermon at St. Paul's before the Lord Mayor of London, attacking "False Brethren," that is dissenters, and all those who abused toleration. Quickly printed, the sermon started a commotion that revealed widespread, narrow-minded, underlying political sentiments. It would witness mob attacks on meeting houses of Presbyterians, and would drive the Whigs out of the government within a few months and make them lose their parliamentary majority. Besides his insinuations against religious opponents, Sacheverell upheld what for him was the great principle of English government, namely "the utter Illegality of Resistance upon any Pretense whatsoever." That brought him to refer to 1688, "the Revolution of this day," and deny that it demonstrated the lawfulness of resistance, since Parliament had supposedly accepted William of Orange as king "upon no other Title, but that of the Vacancy of the Throne."[35] The Whig government, dismayed by the huge sales of the printed sermon and concerned lest it encourage a Tory attempt to make the Pretender succeed Queen Anne, decided to impeach Sacheverell before Parliament. The first and most important charge against him stated that in his sermon he "doth suggest and maintain, That the Necessary Means us'd to bring about the said Happy Revolution, were Odious and Unjustifiable: That his Late Majesty in his Declaration disclaimed the least Imputation of Resistance; and that to Impute Resistance to the said Revolution, is to cast Black and Odious Colours upon his Late Majesty and the said Revolution."[36]

The four months consumed by the Sacheverell trial (December 1709 – March 1710) carried the debate over the validity and meaning of the

Revolution of 1688 to its peak. It was intensely discussed by the press and in a sudden flood of pamphlets, in addition to printed versions of the arguments put forward by the Whig "managers" in the House of Commons who were charged with the prosecution, and the opinions voiced in the House of Lords, where the verdict and sentence were pronounced. The Doctor was supported by the Tories, apparently most of the Anglican clergy, the University of Oxford, many members of the professions and even craftsmen and a good part of London's poor. Faced with this formidable socio-political array, the Whigs tended to tone down their language, so as not to give room to charges that their conception of the Revolution was tinged with antimonarchial ideas. Robert Walpole, the future prime minister and one of the managers of the impeachment in the House of Commons, almost apologized when he spoke of the "commendable resistance used at the Revolution," and added that it was otherwise illegal, inexcusable and unforeseen. It could never be contemplated "but when an utter subversion of the laws of the realm threaten the whole frame of a constitution."[37] Only one of the managers interpreted resistance in 1688 in terms of the people asserting their power, after the "Original Contract" binding them with the monarchy had been broken.[38] One of the surest indictments of Sacheverell came, however, from the elderly Gilbert Burnet. Speaking in the House of Lords, he mentioned his own part in the Revolution, claiming that non-resistance was made an Anglican doctrine only after the Restoration; and then finished thus:

> Yet since Resistance was used in the Revolution, and that the late King [William III] invited all the Subjects to join with him, which was in them certainly Resistance; and since the Lawfulness of the Revolution is so much controverted, the condemning all Resistance in such a crude and general Terms is certainly Condemning the Revolution.[39]

What finally diluted the vehemence of the controversy was Sacheverell's eventual about-face. First his defender in the House of Commons, Simon Harcourt, denied that there had been resistance in 1688 in a constitutional sense, because only James II was defied whereas English sovereignty consisted of king, lords and commons. Then he conceded that the Revolution was indeed an exception, but that Sacheverell, preaching on non-resistance as a general principle, could not be convicted for declining to elaborate on the exception to the rule. The Doctor himself then followed this line and admitted in his final defense: "I neither expressly applied my doctrine of non-resistance to the case of the Revolution, nor had the least thoughts of including the Revolution under my general assertion."[40] It was probably said with an eye to a light sentence or even an acquittal, and was indeed rewarded by the Lords, who anyway were narrowly divided. Sacheverell was only suspended from preaching for three years and his sermons were ordered burned. The Whigs came out of the contest with a Pyrrhic victory. The crucial place of the Revolution in the constitution had been acknowledged, but at the cost of public opinion swaying against them, which soon convinced the queen to throw them out of office. According to a contemporary commentator, the queen saw during the trial that those managing the prosecution "advanced Positions derogatory from the Royal Prerogative; set up the Revolution if not above, at least on the same Level with the hereditary Right."[41] Only the divisions among the Tories in the next four years, and then the Hanoverian succession in 1714 and the failure of the Jacobite rebellion in 1715, would return the party of the "Revolution Principles" to power, and then keep it there throughout the first half of the century.

But during the Sacheverell affair yet another addition to Whig "revolution" rhetoric made its mark. It consisted of a pamphlet openly asserting that political power ultimately belonged to the people – *Vox Populi Vox Dei: or True Maxims of Government*. It was first published in 1709, apparently before the Doctor had delivered his sermon, and then republished six more times in 1710, with a much extended text. In the third edition, where the anonymous author challenged "the great champion, Dr. Sacheverell, or any Jacobite in Great Britain to answer this Book," the title changed to *The Judgment of Whole Kingdoms and Nations concerning the Rights, Powers and Prerogatives of Kings and the Rights, Privileges and Properties of the People*. Under this heading it would be also reprinted twice in America on the eve of independence. These later editions ascribed the authorship to Lord Somers, one of the principal Whig leaders, framer of the 1689 Bill of Rights and author of several political tracts. But as Kenyon has argued, this attribution is doubtful, considering the passages borrowed or plagiarized from others and the fact that Somers's authorship lacked contemporary support. [42]

What distinguished this tract was not so much the core of ideas, but the vociferous and boasting manner in which they were enunciated. The author delved into the Old Testament, European history and the history of England since the Saxons to demonstrate that government proceeded from the people. However, he reserved special efforts to fight the doctrine of passive obedience, "a treasonable, slavish, and pernicious Doctrine," which took away from the people all their civil rights, including the right of self-defense, and gave kings absolute authority, thus making "all the Revolutions and changes of Kings, that have been in England, damnable Rebellions and Usurpations." Not just 1688, but also 1485, the invasion and victory of Henry VII over Richard III, demonstrated the power of the people, since in both the new kings were made "by virtue of Acts of Parliament (while the next Heir was living)." He then hurled at his opponents this rhetorical bravado:

> Now, what say ye for your selves, all ye Patrons, Preachers, and furious Maintainers of the slavish Doctrine of absolute Passive Obedience to the Will and Pleasure of the Prince, that a Bill of Indictment for High Treason should not be preferred against you, for making all our Revolution Kings Usurpers and Rebels; and all that have proceeded from them Usurpers (which yet never failed of a constant Succession) by denying the Power of the People, who made those Revolutions and Changes of Government, and who have made and confirmed the late Revolution in all the succeeding Parliaments? This Revolution King, with Lords and Commons in Parliament assembled, who did alter the Succession from the House of Savoy to the House of Hannover, were the whole Legislative Authority of the Nation: Deny this if you Dare.[43]

As a matter of fact, during the four years which separated the Sacheverell trial and Queen Anne's death "Revolution" kept on being unabatedly a central issue in inter-party debates. Tories, now that they were in power, went so far as to accuse "Revolution Whigs" of intending to set up a republic. Whigs were concerned lest the Tories would back out of the Hanoverian succession and have the Catholic Pretender follow his half sister. The fear of Catholicism was real enough for Gilbert Burnet to return to the public arena and reassert the soundness of "Revolution Principles." On this issue he was answered ironically in 1713 by George Sewell "to give us an entire and complete set of Revolution Principles, that we may be better informed what they are; as also to direct us in the use of them, that we may apply them to all cases and incidents which may happen."[44] In fact, Burnet was by now an exception. At this stage clergymen, both High and Low Church, stayed somewhat out of the scuffle. The debate was entrusted to the hands of professional writers, deliberately employed to convey the views of their political patrons. Actually, they added very little with respect to new ideas and interpretations. But they handled the term in a more facile manner, associating it with new metaphors and with contemporary circumstances. This can easily be seen from the following passage of Jonathan Swift, printed on 3 May 1711 in *The Examiner*. It was his first year of activity in the service of the new Tory ministry, and he accomplished his task combining wild imagination with satire and innuendoes:

> But further, what could be more consistent with the *Whigish* Notion of a *Revolution-Principle*, than to bring in the *Pretender*? A *Revolution Principle*, as their Writings and Discourses have taught us to define it, is a Principle perpetually disposing Men to *Revolutions*: this is suitable to the famous saying of a great *Whig, That the more Revolutions the better*, which how odd a Maxim so ever in Appearance, I take to be the true Characteristick of the Party.
>
> A Dog loves to turn round often; yet after certain *Revolutions*, he lies down to *Rest*, But Heads, under the Domination of the *Moon*, are for perpetual *Changes*, and perpetual *Revolutions*: Besides, the Whigs owe all their Wealth to *Wars* and *Revolutions*; like the Girl at *Batholomew*-Fair, who gets a Penny by turning round a Hundred Times, with Swords in her Hands.[45]

Inventive imagery and up-to-date phrasing came forth, however, also from the other side. In a tract of 1714, *The Revolution and Anti-Revolution Principles Stated and Compared*, probably written by John Shute, the labels Whigs and Tories were conveniently changed to "Revolutionists" and "Anti-Revolutionists." These last were ridiculed by the author because "they have no way to prove their point except by supposing, that Men like Mushrooms rise out of the Earth, a few sitting on Thrones with Crowns on their Heads, and Scepters in their Hands; all others lying prostrate on the Ground, with Saddles on their Backs, Bridles in their Mouths, Chains on their Hand and Feet, and marked differently..." He explained the basic views of the "Revolutionists" in a Lockean manner, namely that they "can never be suppos'd willing to change their State of natural Liberty for that of Subjection," and he also answered in Locke's way the question why and how revolutions take place. The main reason for writing this tract was of course the imminent danger presented by those who rallied to

Jacobitism, who meant to bring in the Pretender and "to overthrow the Revolution."[46]

The quarter of a century that had passed from 1688 to what turned out to be the last year of Queen Anne, finally enabled some writers to view matters in retrospection. One unidentified author, apparently a Whig, pointed out that "This Revolution of State occasion'd likewise a Revolution of some Mens Principles." Another, also a Whig and voicing the views of the Low Churchmen, challenged the official dogma, conveniently stated in the Bill of Rights, that James II had voluntarily abdicated. This allowed him to conclude that "Resistance was the Cause of the Abdication, rather than the Abdication (or as they understood the Word) his withdrawing himself, the Case of the Vacancy of the Throne, and the Revolution."[47] But there was also a new way of looking back at 1688, one surprisingly adopted by Swift. In *The Public Spirit of the Whigs* he engaged thoroughly the opinions advanced by Richard Steele in his famous pamphlet *The Crisis*, though without making a decisive reference to the significance of 1688. Later in 1714, about two months before the queen's death, he wrote *Some Free Thoughts upon the Present State of Affairs*. Here he approached the Revolution from the angle that "the Bulk of those who are now in Action either at Court, in Parliament, or Publick Offices, were then Boys at School or the Universities." A whole new generation had come of age that had not taken part in the unseating of James II nor felt responsible for what had happened. "The Logick of the highest Tories is now, that this was the Establishment they found, as soon as they arrived to a Capacity of Judging." Tories, therefore, no longer really questioned the exclusion of a Catholic prince and the Hanoverian succession. In a way, though Swift did not phrase it so, they had come to accept their own mild version of "Revolution Principles."[48]

Swift expressed these thoughts at the same time as his patron Bolingbroke was working hard to reverse the settlement of 1688. Now in control of the Tory party, Bolingbroke rushed the Schism Act through Parliament in May and June 1714, designed to remove dissenters from the education of children, including their own. This was understood as the first among several measures aimed at weakening the Whigs and rendering the Tories enough power so they could retain the government after the queen's death and perhaps even determine her successor. But Anne died on 1 August 1714, too early for the plan to succeed, and the Tories, with Bolingbroke, saw no other choice at that point but to accept the Hanoverian succession, exactly as Swift had written. There quickly followed the Tories' fall from power, Bolingbroke's flight to France, the failed uprising of the Jacobites in Scotland in the summer of 1715, which tainted the party and the High Church with backing the cause of rebellion, and a very long Whig control of the government afterwards. At this juncture, however, even the Pretender in France could not appreciate the damage done by 1688 to his cause but in terms of the new manner of political discourse. In a manifesto published shortly after the death of Queen Anne he declared right in the opening: "The revolution ruined the English monarchy, laid the foundation of a republican government, and devolved the sovereign power on the people." A year and a few months afterwards, when Parliament was discussing the fate of some nobles who rallied to the side of the Pretender in his failed invasion of July 1715, one member as if denied these views of the Pretender's by repeating a byword he had once heard "that the condemning of the late happy Revolution, could have no other meaning than to make way for another."[49]

On 23 September 1715 Richard Steele dedicated No. 22 of the second series of *The Englishman* to the meaning of 1688. Speaking for the Whig government, he was now even willing to admit: "that the *Revolution* had its Beginning in Force, in Violence, in Injustice, or in Rebellion, it is to us the same Thing." Echoing in his arguments the approach espoused by Swift one year earlier, he asserted that "all Men under forty Years of Age, are Subjects of the Revolution, and cannot by the Laws of God or Man, pay Obedience to, or give Assistance to any other Power but the Legal Descendants of that *Revolution*." In his estimation nine out of ten Englishmen felt that way. The others, who still thought that the unseating of James II had been morally wrong, "may take up Arms if they please, or if they think they did a Criminal Thing in promoting the *Revolution*, let them repent, or expiate their Crimes by themselves; we, who had nothing to do with that Transaction, are on this Side of Time, and are wholly Innocent."[50]

These words would permit perhaps the impression that after 1715 Englishmen simply discarded the debate over 1688 as a forlorn issue. But the matter is more complicated than that. Their long hold on the government, ushered by the Hanoverian succession, allowed the Whigs to impose their own interpretation. As Hugh Trevor-Roper has written: "It became their revolution, almost their monopoly. It was they who trumpeted its glory."[51] This suggests a clue regarding the hidden origins of the epithet "Glorious Revolution." It is quite clear that the expression reflected the Whig victory. We rarely encounter it prior to 1715, but from this date onward the epithet seems to acquire a more commonly understood meaning and is used more frequently (though most eighteenth century authors would continue to write "Revolution," without any adjective).[52] The tendency to "glorify" the revolution was noticeable above all among nonconformists, who understandably come out of the events of 1714-15 with the belief of having been rescued from a great danger, and who saw in 1688 the foundation of their near-equality. Their ministers began shaping up a tradition of preaching on 5 November in praise of the Revolution, the pioneer apparently being Thomas Bradbury, leader of London Congregationalists and famous for his outspokenness with respect to liberty of conscience and the values of political liberty. His sermons on "The Divine Right of the Revolution" were launched perhaps as early as 1707.[53] Yet in due time the notion of a providential quality, which was associated with the early use of "Glorious Revolution," would be converted to a wholly secular idea. From the vantage point of the late eighteenth century the revolution would be deemed "glorious" because it had settled once and for all the conflicts among Englishmen over the constitution and their respective political rights. Finally, with the world witnessing at that stage new examples of revolutions, the gloriousness of 1688 would be appreciated also from a conservative point of view, because it had been accomplished with a minimum of violence and without changing much the old foundations of government. It is this "Glorious Revolution" which Burke would celebrate in his famous essay of 1790.[54]

Already during Walpole's ministry some Whig propagandists adopted the habit of speaking in the name of the "Revolution," while attempting to influence the disposition of the public towards a variety of issues. This manner of use of the term can be seen in *The Independent Whig*, a weekly brochure written by Thomas Gordon and John Trenchard in 1720, and in their *Cato's Letters* (1720-23). The success of these publications was partly due to their merciless attacks on the High Church, but they also displayed an innovative discourse, as expressed in the following fresh dictum, printed on 24 August 1723: "The World is therefore a Foot-Ball; a great Scene of Contentions, Revolutions and Misery."[55] Twelve years later the "Revolution" was enlisted to convince the public that England should enter the War of the Polish Succession on the side of Austria and help maintain the balance of power in Europe. The anonymous author of the tract even saw fit to assume the name of "William Revolution, Esq."[56] Faced with this consummate identification of the Revolution with a new England, now in possession of a worldwide empire, economically powerful and politically self-assured, Bolingbroke, back home following years of exile in France, launched·what was actually a thorough revision of past Tory views of 1688. In his 1730-31 essays in *The Craftsman*, later published as *Remarks on the History of England*, the Revolution became not just the political fact that Tories had come to respect, but a decisive historical event reasserting the liberties of Englishmen as secured by the ancient constitution since Anglo-Saxon times. There was something to gain by this interpretation. It cleared the way for Tories to claim a share not only in the Revolution but in the political world it had created. But Bolingbroke was actually willing to go a step further. Commenting on Machiavelli's view that governments tended over time to degenerate and needed frequent renewals of their constitutions, he singled out England as a polity that had adequately responded to this challenge: "The various revolutions in this kingdom have, in a great measure, answered this end. They have purged off the luxuriances of power; and though few of them have gone so deep as to bring us back to the primitive purity of our constitution, yet they have still preserved us a free people, when liberty is lost in almost every other part of Europe." This passage might be compared to Locke's apologetic defense of revolutions at the end of the second treatise on civil government. Locke, barely venturing to employ the term, went only far enough to allow revolutions as infrequent necessary evils. Bolingbroke, on the other hand, chose to see in them that without which there would be no political freedom.[57]

*   *

As stated at the opening of this chapter, the unseating of James II was to affect the use of "revolution" also in France. It would happen, however, within a different set of circumstances. On the one hand French authors and polemicists were unavoidably bound to reflect the centrality, which the word had newly acquired in English discourse and political debate; on the other hand they faced the need to give the term a somewhat inoffensive meaning, and employ it accordingly, in tune with the norms of French absolutism. That the word was not yet a part of the conventional language in France can easily be gathered from the relevant coverage of events in England as given in the weekly issues of the *Gazette* from mid-November 1688 onwards. William of Orange's landing was termed here "invasion," those who joined him were "séditieux" and "rebelles," and the composite state of England a month later was pictured with the traditional expression "les troubles du Rayaume." Only in the issue of the last day of the year, where there were actually no reports from England because of the closure of all ports in that country, the editors unexpectedly gave the reason for that – "à cause des révolutions qui ont changé toute la face des affaires" ["on account of the revolutions which have changed the situation completely"]. Still, in the issues of the next three months the word was apparently missing, even though they contained detailed analyses on the political options then considered in Parliament.[58] Of course, the *Gazette* was not alone in bypassing "révolution" while handling the events of 1688-89. Other French sources, including two works quickly written by Antoine Arnauld and Denis de Sainte-Marthe, likewise eschewed the term.[59]

Who then instigated the introduction of the term to French discourse in relation to England? Apparently, this was the contribution of the Protestant French exiles, especially the important group of authors residing in Holland. As specified in the previous chapter, both Jurieu and Bayle were employing the term already on the eve of 1688. Right after the event, however, it would appear that the effective diffusion of the term was carried out by the journals of Henri Basnage de Beauval and Jean Leclerc. The first published in Rotterdam, from 1687 on, a monthly review of new books, called *Histoire des Ouvrages des Savants*, a self-declared and worthy successor to Bayle's *Nouvelles de la République des Lettres*. Although employed here and there, it was only during 1689 that "révolution" emerged in this journal as a significant term, especially in its new rapport with England. In the May issue of that year Basnage reviewed an anonymous work that had just been printed in Amsterdam, *Histoire des révolutions d'Angleterre sous le regne de Jacques II jusqu'au couronnement de Guillaume III*. Right in his opening sentence, he hailed the change that had taken place in England as an unforeseen and stupefying event. Those whose plans were upset by "cette révolution si prompte," reacted to it by blackening the image of William of Orange. It was reported that in Paris they were preparing a history of the reign of James II, marked by a sympathetic portrait of the deposed monarch. But Basnage of course rejected their view. Concluding a long factual review of recent English history, he praised the anonymous Amsterdam author for his accuracy in recounting the main occurrences of "this famous revolution which will astonish future generations" ["cette fameuse révolution qui surprendra les siècles à venir"].[60]

This was an entirely new language. Possibly, no one had previously referred in French to a contemporary political event in this manner. We may only guess how Basnage's readers in France reacted to these words. Most of them, although they delighted in reading his monthly collection of reviews, apparently did not share his politics. And yet, this first salvo was continued over the next two years with a more frequent use of the term by Basnage. In September 1689, while reviewing Vertot's work, *Histoire de la conjuration de Portugal*, he called the seventeenth century "un siècle fecond en grandes révolutions." In November 1691, when writing on Raguenet's book on Cromwell, he opened with: "The revolution which led King Charles I to the scaffold and Cromwell to the throne is the most astonishing event of this century." In between he employed the term in reviews of new volumes by Varillas, Vanel and others.[61]

A similar development is noticeable in the language of Jean Leclerc. His *Bibliothèque Universelle et Historique* appeared in Amsterdam in January 1686, and quickly gained wide circulation throughout western Europe. Being more interested in religion and science than in history and politics, Leclerc initially employed "révolution" even less than Basnage. But in 1690 this changed. We first find him using the expression "la révolution d'Angleterre," and then, later in that year, while reviewing a book on fourteenth and fifteenth century English history, suddenly exploding with the following highly polemical statement:[62]

> The Revolution, which happened in England in the year 1688 and the next, and that which still takes place in that Island, are the talk of all of Europe. The peoples who have not completely lost their liberty, praise the conduct of the English and felt sorry for them when they saw them almost giving in to a despotic government. The others, who having been born under absolute Monarchies never tasted the pleasure of being free, find it odd that the English Nation was able to keep what they have lost.
> [La Révolution, qui est arrivée l'année 1688 et la suivante en Angleterre, & ce qui se passe encore dans cette Ile font l'entretient de toute l'Europe. Le peuples, chez qui la liberté n'est pas tout à fait

éteinte, louënt la conduite des Anglois, et les ont plaints, pendant qu'ils les ont vu près de succomber sous le pouvoir despotique. Les autres, qui, étant nez dans des Monarchies absoluës, n'ont jamais goûté le plaisir qu'il y a à être libre, ont trouvé étrange que la Nation Angloise se mit en état de conserver ce qu'ils ont perdu.]

In October 1690 Leclerc published a long favorable review of Locke's *Two Treaties on Civil Government.* Here, at the end, he saw fit to emphasize that "a revolution never happens in a state on account of slight mistakes committed by the government;" more than that, much more, was needed for the people to rise against their rulers. This of course was also Locke's own view; but as we know, although he published it in 1690, Locke wrote in the early 1680s and used the term in the plural form. In Leclerc's phrasing it turned into an indirect defense of 1688. In this way, by their new manner of using the term and by their extolling the events in England as a great gain for political freedom, both he and Basnage actually affected the status of "révolution" in French discourse; and they were not alone. In 1690 Bayle and Jurieu engaged in a heated debate, where the term played an important role. This was an offshoot of the differences that had separated these former friends even before 1688 and that now turned irreconcilable. Jurieu saw in the unseating of James II a partial fulfillment of the "great Revolution" he had spoken of in 1686. He now talked of soon to come other victories for the Protestants, such as the military defeat of Louis XIV, or his conversion, followed by the return of French exiles to their homeland. Disturbed by those eschatological expectations which Jurieu disseminated among the exiles, Bayle published in April 1690 in The Hague a pamphlet (although he never acknowledged his authorship of it) entitled *Avis important aux réfugiez sur leur prochain retour en France.* Jurieu countered this in 1691 with *Examen d'un libelle contre la religion, contre l'état, et contre la révolution d'Angleterre, intitulé Avis Important aux Réfugiez.* He accused Bayle of being part of a secret group headquartered in Geneva, working against Protestant states and religion. Bayle then answered the attack with *La cabale chimérique,* published in Rotterdam in the same year.

All three pamphlets made use of "révolution"; especially Jurieu's which included it fifteen times, eleven of them in the form of "Révolution d'Angleterre."[63] Equally important, however, was the attitude assumed here by Bayle towards revolution as a means to effect political change. He began his *Avis important aux réfugiez* gloating

over the fact that, contrary to predictions, 1689 had ended without
either great crises or "révolutions miraculeuses." He then rejected
Jurieu's principle of sovereignty of the people and warned those who
awaited their opportunity to return to France to first rid themselves of
"a certain republican spirit, which will only introduce anarchy into the
world, the greatest plague of a civil society." Later, he touched
directly on the issue of changing a government by force. In reality, he
argued, it was not the "people" who executed it, but a small group of
individuals, who invariably made up the earliest malcontents and then
went on to spread their anxieties among others, to organize support
for their plans among clergymen and army officers, and so on. This
brought him to a dismal conclusion with regards to the authenticity of
revolutions:[64]

> In a word, these great revolutions, which appear to be the work of all
> the people, when they are carried out in a regular manner are but the
> work of a small number of persons, who strain themselves to the point
> of being willing to act on the first signal out of their own authority and
> without any order of the nation.
> [En un mot, ces grandes révolutions qui semblent être l'ouvrage de tout
> un peuple, quand elles s'exécutent un peu régulierement, ne sont en
> effet que l'ouvrage d'un petit nombres de personnes, qui de leur propre
> autorité, & sans aucun ordre de la Nation ont mis tous les efforts en
> état d'agir au premier signal.]

Considering the date, this criticism of revolution revealed a new
level of perceptiveness. It seemed to accept, though with a grudge, a
modern political scheme and its appropriate designation, while still
maintaining that real political power was always concentrated in a few
hands. Contemporaries, however, could hardly appreciate Bayle's
position. As he wrote in a letter dated 13 May 1697, "they reproach
me even in England that indirectly I condemn the last Revolution and
that I disapprove of the Right of the Peoples in favour of the despotic
authority of Monarchs."[65] But in spite of his critical views on the
people's right to affect a "revolution," or the right of those pretending
to speak for the people, Bayle should be recognized as the French
author who contributed more than any other of his generation to
popularizing the term. This was mainly done through his
Dictionnaire historique et critique (1696-97), the annotated
compendium of biographies, quickly acclaimed by its readers, where
almost every human moral and social value underwent a critical

examination. In various places in this voluminous work Bayle strayed from the theme discussed to give his views on the origins, nature, scope and fate of "revolutions." Suffice it to say that nowhere did he subscribe to the modern revolutionary idea. Revolutions were basically explained by him as great havocs caused by ambitious, power-driven individuals, frequently motivated by imagined petty offenses and resentments. For Bayle these events signified yet another proof of the extent of human folly. When not treating them with a customary sense of irony, he simply admitted that they were unavoidable.[66]

Not all French Protestant exiles adopted the new penchant for the term "revolution." A case in point in Michel Levassor, usually accredited with the authorship of an extreme attack on Louis XIV's despotism, *Les soupirs de la France esclave qui aspire après la liberté*, published in Amsterdam in 1690 (the other candidate for its authorship is Jurieu). The term hardly came into use here, and it was almost omitted in Levassor's preface to his major work, *Histoire de Louis XIII* (1700), where again the absolutist nature of contemporary French government was bitterly censured. On the other hand, an author such as Jean Leclerc returned time and time again to the subject of that "heureuse révolution" of 1688. He did it, for example, in 1705 when writing in his second journal, *Bibliothèque Choisie*, a long eulogy of Locke, whom he had known during his stay in Holland (1682-89). Three years later he dedicated a long review to the three hefty volumes of *A Collection of State Tracts published on occasion of the late Revolution in 1688 and during the Reign of William III* (1705-07). Again in 1715, completing the eulogy of Gilbert Burnet, this time in his third and last journal, *Bibliothèque Ancienne et Moderne*, he explained to his readers that his detractors could never blemish Burnet's reputation, because they were at the same time "the enemies of both the Reformation and the fortunate Revolution, which the arrival of King William produced in Great Britain."[67]

Inside France, the manner to respond to the new visibility of "révolution" was not a simple matter. It turned out to be an insurmountable barrier to such a great polemicist as Bossuet, who in the 1690s continued his debate with French Protestants without touching on the new term. Also Bossuet's rivals within the Catholic camp, Fénelon for instance, by and large kept clear of the term.[68] But French historians, particularly that small group that habitually, and gainfully, ingratiated itself to the monarchy, were better prepared to answer the challenge. To begin with, they had already experimented with the term in the early 1680s. Moreover, Varillas's *Histoire de révolutions en matière de religion*, which began appearing in 1686, had elevated the word to the title of the book, and as such could claim some preparatory responsibility for the epithet "Révolution d'Angleterre." All of this must have been in the mind of the former Jesuit priest, Pierre-Joseph d'Orléans, when he published in Paris in 1689 the first volume of *Histoire des révolutions d'Angleterre depuis la commencement de la monarchie*. He had been an active writer since the early 1670s, authoring mostly lives of Catholic saints. His new work, whose third and last volume came out in 1693, covered English history from the early middle ages to 1691. It aroused interest in England (leading to an English translation in 1711), was reviewed by both Basnage and Leclerc, and was apparently printed three more times in Paris and Amsterdam within twenty-five years. The success of the work encouraged d'Orléans to embark on another one, *Histoire des révolutions d'Espagne*. When he died, however, in 1698, it was not yet complete, and needed others to add the chapters for the fifteenth century, before it was successfully published in Paris and The Hague in 1734.

Compared with Maimbourg and Varillas, d'Orléans handled the term in a more adroit manner, though preferably in the sense of a political disaster. This became apparent, for example, when he described the consequences of the execution of Charles I: "Upon this death England witnessed the most universal and astonishing revolution, which she had ever seen. Everything changed its form, and it was almost impossible to recognize the remains of what she had been for two thousand years. The monarchy, so ancient in that island as the island itself, was entirely destroyed."[69] These dimensions of the term were akin with Varillas's, whose "révolutions" meant political breakdowns brought about by the rebellious spirit of the Reformation. Yet the "révolutions" in the titles of d'Orléans's books were something else. They were not really meant to signify the abandonment of the history of kings in favor of a history of institutions, as seemed to be the opinion of Goulemot.[70] Already Leclerc in his review of 1692 opined that although d'Orléans declared in his preface that he would write on the "revolutions" that had taken place in England, he ended up by giving a rather straightforward history. Leclerc thought that with the title of his book d'Orléans wanted to say that England had always been "the perpetual Theatre of revolutions, the end of one serving as the seed for the beginning of another."[71] But if that could be argued for England, it was hardly a tenable argument to be made for the history of Spain. Therefore, perhaps, d'Orléans might have had in mind another sense of "revolutions." Indeed, he explained it in the opening sentences of his posthumous work: "I write the History of Revolutions of a Monarchy, erected over its own ruins and extended to the point of inspiring glory and fearsome greatness to the rest of the world, and of which the world would have perhaps dreaded much longer, if it had set limits to itself and if it had wasted less its strength in the wish to expand its boundaries. This is the History of Revolutions that happened in the Monarchy of Spain..."[72] Obviously, "revolutions" here meant the entire evolution from smallness to greatness, and then a decline. It amounted to more or less the changing circumstances of a country or a nation throughout history.

In 1689 as well other French historians began to use "révolutions" in the titles of their books. The first, apparently, was Claude Vanel, author of the "revolutions" of the "vast monarchy" of the Turks and of those which had happened in England "during its last reigns."[73] He was followed by the abbé René Vertot, whose three separate books on the "revolutions" of Portugal, Sweden and those that had affected the government of ancient republican Rome, earned a huge success; in fact, they never stopped being reprinted up until the middle of the nineteenth century. Actually, Vertot's first work appeared originally in 1689 as *Histoire de la conjuration de Portugal*. It was translated into English and printed in London in 1700 as *The History of the Revolution in Portugal in the Year 1640*, and entitled *Histoire des Révolutions de Portugal* only with its second enlarged French edition, which also led to its subsequent printing success. But in the meantime, already in 1695, Vertot published the *Histoire des Révolutions de Suéde*, which dealt with Gustavus Vasa's separation of Sweden from Denmark and Sweden's break with Roman Catholicism. This one was immediately translated and had its second edition in London within two years. Vertot's *Histoire de révolutions arrivées dans le gouvernement de la république romaine* came out only in 1719, but received an even warmer welcome.

A new genre of historiography was thus born, of which Vertot might be taken as the erstwhile practitioner. How many titles of "Histoires des Révolutions" by various authors were published in the eighteenth century is difficult to say; perhaps some three dozen. They covered the history of European countries and countries elsewhere, and dealt with both modern and ancient history. By 1738, with French absolutism still going pretty strong, also a *Histoire des révolutions de France* turned up, the work of the Jesuit priest Yves Joseph de la Motte (hiding behind the pen name Mr. De la Hode). Here in the preface the author explained the revolutions he was writing on as "alterations of power and of weakness" that had affected the French government throughout the centuries. He promised his readers that he would stick exactly "to what is understood, and what should be understood by the word Revolution," notwithstanding the fact that all those so-called revolutions had taken place while France continued under the same form of government. No wonder, therefore, that the greatest "revolution" of all was, for him, the consolidation of a strong absolute monarchy under Louis XIV, that enabled France to rival all the other states of Europe, especially the House of Habsburg. But in an apparent contradiction shortly afterwards he hastened to declare: "It is certain that as long as this Monarchy will be governed as it is today, it will have no Revolutions to fear."[74] Some three decades later Claude Renaudot had the idea to cover all of the world's history with a *Révolutions des empires, royaumes, républiques et autres états considerables du monde depuis la création jusqu'à nos jours*. It was, however, a remarkably shallow work, lacking an original point of view. If his "revolutions" had any meaning, they referred to the chronological cycle that corresponded to the growth and decline of any state or empire throughout history.[75]

At their best, the authors of "Histoires des Révolutions" could explain to their readers a revolution as a great, complex event, pertaining to unusual alterations of religion and government. As Vertot wrote in his preface to *The History of the Revolutions in Sweden*, "all the Members of the Society are concern'd in such a *Revolution*; and every Object that appears serves either to alarm their *Conscience*, or to flatter and inflame their *Ambition*." But generally the tendency of the genre was to dilute revolutions of crucial significance. Already Leclerc in 1714, writing a review on a new edition of d'Orléans's *Histoires des Révolutions d'Angleterre*, remarked, contrary to his previous view, that in this manner of writing, revolutions meant "the most beautiful passages of History."[76] The editor of d'Orléans's posthumous *Histoire des révolutions d'Espagne* was of the opinion that what separated the new genre from conventional writing of history was its more lively and stirred up style. A different opinion was voiced by Vertot in the 1722 edition of his work on Portugal, when he explained why its title had been changed from *Conjuration* to *Révolutions*. The change, he claimed, was justified by the addition of earlier and later events to the new edition. Felix Gilbert found this explanation almost frivolous with respect to the author's concept of revolution, and also pointed out the thoughtless use of the term in Dupont-Dutertre's collection of historical anecdotes, *Histoire de conjurations, conspirations et révolutions célèbres, tant anciennes que modernes* (1754-60). Indeed, in these supermarkets of revolutions, the new term tended to be used interchangeably with old terms, and thus lost distinction. Its use in the plural rather than in the singular indirectly helped to impress on the reader the notion that abrupt changes in government were but an expression of inherent instability, which afflicted most countries and which an absolutist government might avoid.[77]

Our appraisal of the "Histoires des "Révolutions" would warrant therefore the judgment that they turned into an indirect yet at least a half-conscious effort to acclaim French absolutism in the face of the new sense that "revolution" had gained in England after 1688. This genre of literature showed no signs of going out of fashion almost until 1789. One of its last examples, as much a best seller as Vertot's work, connected it, however, in a rather surprising way with the beginnings of the late eighteenth century romantic spirit. This was *Les ruines, ou méditations sure les révolutions des empires* by the comte de Volney. It was first published in 1791, although based on impressions gathered by the author during his mid-1780s travels in the Levant. There Volney had savored the experience of meditating in the actual sites of the remains of ancient empires, all of which were brought to an end by "perpetual commotions and successive revolutions." His grasp of the term did not go much beyond the parameters established by the genre of historiography during the eighteenth century, but he was able to invoke a dreamy, almost mystical feeling for the ruins and blend it with his thoughts on past glories and present dejection. France, or perhaps the entire European civilization, he felt, might one day undergo the same "revolution" and fate as the ancient Assyrians, Egyptians, Greeks and Romans. But with all the gloom that the book inspired, it also contained passages where the author gave vent to his belief in progress, improvement and equality for all. Somehow these attitudes combined into a mixture of oriental romanticism, which also hinted at a possible new European colonialist interest in the East.[78]

The semantic perspective that was reflected in the "Histoires des Révolutions," can be seen also in French dictionaries. As Keith Michael Baker has observed, the 1727 edition of Furetière added: "The English call *the Revolution*, the change that took place by the abdication of James II and the crowning of William III, and they see in it the start of a new period" ["Les Anglais appellent *la Révolution*, le changement arrivé par l'abdication de Jacques II, et l'établishment de Guillaume III et ils en font une Epoque"]. But usually French dictionaries stressed the sudden, unpredictable and uncontrollable nature of revolutions, as if they were something that just occurred, in contrast with something that was made by the conscious choice of the people involved.[79] When the *Dictionnaire de l'Académie Française* was finally published in 1694, it gave, like Richelet's and Furetière's works, which had preceded it, two definitions of the term, related to circular motion and change. But now, perhaps more than before, the extemporaneous, dark nature of revolution was stressed. Thus ran the second definition of the *académiciens*:

> Il signifie aussi fig. Vicissitude, grand changement dans la fortune, dans les choses du monde. *Grand, prompte, subite, soudaine, estrange, merveilleuse, estonnante révolution. Le gain ou la perte d'une bataille cause de grandes révolutions dans un Estat. Le temps fait d'estranges révolutions dans les affaires. Les choses de ce monde sont sujettes aux révolutions.*
> [It also means in a figurative manner Vicissitude, a great change in one's fortune, in the things of the world. *A great, prompt, sudden, unexpected, strange, wonderful, amazing revolution. The winning or losing of a battle may cause great revolutions in the State. The age brings forth strange revolutions in the order of things. The matters of this world are subject to revolutions.*]

This bent with regard to the sense of the term was carried even further in the most successful dictionary of the eighteenth century, the so-called *Dictionnaire de Trévoux*, published in the town of that name in 1704 by a group of Jesuit scholars. Its first version in three volumes was to grow with each successive edition, reaching eight volumes by the fifth edition of 1771. To the entry on the word here were added also examples from several seventeenth century authors, but the definition of the political meaning of the word was given a sense of uneasiness and gloom, both in French and in the Latin equivalent:

REVOLUTION, se dit aussi des changements extraordinaires qui arrives dans le monde: des disgraces, des malheurs, de decadences. *Publicae rei commutatio, conversio, calamitas, infortunium, imperii occasus.* Il n'y a point d'Etats qui n'ayent été sujets à de grandes *révolutions.* Les plus grandes Princes ont éprouvé des *révolutions* dans leur fortune. Tous les esprits étoient inquiets, à la veille d'une si grande révolution qui se preparoit.

[REVOLUTION is also used for extraordinary changes that happen in the world: for adversities, misfortunes, declines. *Publicae rei commutatio, conversio, calamitas, infortunium, imperii occasus.* There are no states which had never been subjected to great *revolutions.* The greatest Princes have experienced *revolutions* in their fortune. Everybody was anxious on the eve of such a great revolution which was being made ready.]

These French dictionaries in fact revealed in their definitions a sensitivity to the political meaning of the term that bordered on irritation. In comparison, the great dictionary that was issued between 1726 and 1739 by the Royal Spanish Academy only explained that metaphorically the word meant change, or a new form of government in the state [*Revolución.* Metaphoricamente vale mudanza ò nueva forma en el estado ò gobierno de las cosas.] By way of illustrating the sensitivity towards the word we might close this chapter with an example of its status in France in the early eighteenth century in the sphere of a political public debate. During the ministry of Cardinal Fleury the *parlements,* so submissive under Louis XIV, attempted to champion the Gallican liberties of the church by refusing to register royal edicts that accepted the papal bull Unigenitus (1713), which had decried Jansenism. By now Jansenism as a real movement of reform and piety inside the Roman Catholic church was almost dead. The so-called Jansenists were more than anything the party opposing the Jesuits, who were allied with the royal government. For their part, the *parlements* were not interested at all in Jansenism, but rather exploited the issue of Gallicanism as a means to revive their own political rights against the crown. A number of pamphlets circulated, accusing the government of giving in to the Jesuits and Rome and claiming for the *parlement* the role of an institution representing the people. Finally, the Bishop of Monpellier published a pastoral instruction, where he enumerated the troubles afflicting the French church. He claimed that it was threatened by "a soon to come revolution which would replace the present Church with a new one" ["une prochaine révolution que ferait succéder une Église nouvelle à l'Église present"]. His employment of the term was restricted to a change in the church, not in the government, although the phrasing he used could be compared with the prophecies of the Protestant Jurieu on the eve of 1688. Apparently, this was the first time in the eighteenth century that "révolution" was employed in an inside French debate. In its session of 25 April 1733 the royal council, the highest governing body, condemned the bishop's address, which it found offensive to the church and the king, and tending to stir up emotions and disturb public order. The author of memoirs Mathieu Marais, himself a practicing lawyer at the *parlement* of Paris, wrote to a friend one month afterwards that he too had appreciated the bishop's address, but that the clergyman "had no right to inflate our problems, to speak of 'revolution' or to pray for the Jews." ["mais il ne falloit pas faire le mal si grand, ni parler de *révolution*, ni prier pour les Juifs."][80]

Chapter Seven

The *Philosophes* and the Term

From any angle we look at it there can be no denial that the Enlightenment inherited in the word "revolution" an operative and meaningful political term. In the final analysis it should not be that important whether the political meaning tended towards a "French" sense of a sudden uncontrollable change in government or whether it assume an "English" sense of a change founded on the principle that in certain circumstances the people have the right to intervene in the government. In both senses the word was entirely at the stage of being readily exploitable in the context of political theory. Besides, the most important *philosophes* in France, including Montesquieu, Voltaire and Rousseau, could hardly remain immune to the sense of the term in England during their residence in that country. It would not be far-fetched, therefore, to assume that by the middle of the eighteenth century almost anybody seriously grappling with basic questions of political philosophy in either England or France had a good grasp of the variety of meanings of the term. Pursuing the subject from this point of view, the use of "revolution" in the writings of the *philosophes* becomes an issue of unanticipated significance. It is yet another measure by which to assess the revolutionary aims of the movement on the one hand, or the inhibitions of its leaders in the face of a prospective revolutionary theory on the other hand.

Students of the Enlightenment have usually bypassed this issue, its importance apparently being overshadowed by a predisposition to treat the whole movement as a kind of revolution in ideas and an ancestor of great political revolutions. Indeed, already in 1767 a pioneering work, *Tableau des révolutions de la littérature ancienne et moderne* by the Italian Carlo Denina, was published in Paris in which eighteenth century French letters came close to being interpreted as the last upshot of a series of revolutions throughout Western intellectual history.[1] In much more recent studies one still encounters a view highlighting among the major trends of the Enlightenment a critical "esprit révolutionnaire;" although this comes close to bordering on anachronism since the term "révolutionnaire" is a post-1789 creation.[2] But the basic questions that concern us still have to be addressed: To what extent did the *philosophes* advocate the elimination of the ills of society by recourse to revolution? To what extent did they at least claim revolution to be inevitable? And in what manner did they employ the term "revolution"? As this chapter and the next will attempt to show, until the 1770s the quest for a revolution on the part of the *philosophes* remained essentially subdued on both the ideological and the semantic planes. And although from there on it showed clear signs of being kindled, this trend might have been encouraged, more than by any other factor, by the gaining of independence of the United States.

Before we delve, however, into an inquiry of the use of the term in works of the Enlightenment of a more theoretical nature, it would be useful to introduce some examples demonstrating the use of "revolution" at the time in less exacting forms of discourse. Félix Rocquain gathered a number of these in his masterpiece on the antecedents of 1789, published over a century ago.[3] He cited from the diary and memoirs of the marquis d'Argenson, a friend of Voltaire who was, for a time (1744-47), charged with overseeing French foreign affairs. On 30 July 1743, after the death of Cardinal Fleury, when French public opinion began voicing its resentment of government policies, d'Argenson wrote in his diary: "The Revolution is certain in this situation" ["La Révolution est certaine dans cet État-çi"]. Eight years later, on 1 May 1751, he became more explicatively clear: "Nobody talks but of the need of an early revolution because of the bad state of the internal government" ["On ne parle pas que de la nécessité d'une prochaine révolution par le mauvais état où est le gouvernement du dedans"]. He thought that orderly changes in the French political system were almost impossible, and later that year commented: "All the classes are dissatisfied. Matters are at a rather combustible stage; a riot [une émeute] might turn into a revolt [révolte], and a revolt into a total revolution [une totale révolution], in which true tribunes of the people will be chosen, as well as committees and city councils, and in which the king and the ministers will be deprived of their excessive power to cause harm."

Besides showing his disenchantment with the old system, these words of d'Argenson demonstrate clearly an awareness of the semantic distinction between "émeute," révolte" and "révolution," and also his solid conceptual grasp of the last term. In that same year, on 21 November 1751, he returned to the term and the theme. He now commented that France's enemies might take advantage of "the unpleasant mood of our people, who are tired of the arbitrary government which drives them to misery, by encouraging a revolution in France and by introducing a government controlled by estates-general and provincial estates,..." France's despotic government, he felt, was similar to that of Turkey, and the tendency of the last monarchs to engage in wars had turned her neighbors against her, besides wasting the resources of its people. This was the reason why people were incessantly talking "of this coming revolution in the government" ["de cette prochaine révolution dans le gouvernement"]. And he added a story about an exchange between some men and a monk at the Luxembourg Gardens, where the latter defended the rights of his order, but was answered by his adversaries that "the harshness employed by the government against the clergy would hasten the revolution." Again, on 9 September 1752, he remarked: "Meanwhile public opinion is moving, mounting, growing, which could launch a national revolution" ["Cependant l'opinion chemine, monte, grandit, ce qui pourrait commencer une révolution nationale"].[4]

This rather emphatic manner of using the term in his diary should be matched with d'Argenson's language in a tract on the government of France, published posthumously by his son. Here he justified the need for a political change with an excuse that anyhow circumstances and customs were always on a never ending course of alteration, as underscored by the cliché: "Tout est révolution dans ce Monde." For France he suggested moderate, not extreme reforms, and he ventured an opinion that if the king would ally himself with the people to curb the privileges of the aristocracy, it would not end in "bloody revolutions" ["de révolutions sanglantes"] as had taken place in the history of other nations.[5]

The difference between the use of the term in the diary and the tract suggests an hypothesis that even in the mid-eighteenth century the use of "revolution" in conversation and in writings of private character proceeded with more ease than compared with its use in a formal essay on politics. It is a relevant speculation when we come to examine the term in Montesquieu's *Esprit des lois*, published in 1748, at about the same time that d'Argenson was working on his tract and diary. To begin with, the number of times that Montesquieu employs the term in this vast work is very small, which is a negative evidence on its own. In one place he tells us that "revolutions," aiming at the change of the form of government, cannot be carried out but through endless efforts and that they require good laws to make them last. But his real view of the idea (and the term) is perhaps best revealed in the passage where he praises monarchical government as opposed to despotism. The difference between them, says Montesquieu, is that in the former the people enjoy the protection of the laws and fixed institutions and therefore do not need to go to extremes in order to register their grievances: "Thus all our histories are full of civil wars without revolutions, while the histories of despotic governments abound with revolutions without civil wars."[6]

If this passage is indeed the crucial one, then Montesquieu relegated revolutions to the status of an option mainly suitable in rudimentary, backward polities, unlike his own. This interpretation might be corroborated also through passages in a previous work of his, *Considérations sur les causes de la grandeur des Romains et de leur decadence*, written in 1734. Here too, considering the opportunities, the use of "révolution" is restrictive, especially when compared with the use of "divisions," "séditions" and "désordres." When dealing with the changes which the Roman Empire had undergone in the reigns of Diocletian and Constantine the Great, Montesquieu explains that it is almost always advisable to let a long continuing form of government subsist, because a total change of the political system would necessarily follow theoretical considerations, whereas truly needed practical changes can be discovered only by actual experience. In this passage the term is not used, but it comes towards the end of the essay, when he discusses the frequent changes of dynasties in the Byzantine Empire. Here Montesquieu sums up the process in words that seemingly mean to tell the reader what is his real evaluation of violent, non-constitutional changes in government, and his words are: "The revolutions themselves made revolutions, and the effect became the cause" ["Les révolutions même firent les révolutions, et l'effet devint lui-même la cause"].[7]

The case of Voltaire is much more complicated. First, his overall literary production was immense, comprising an unusually broad range of subjects. Moreover, the span of his creative life, covering some six decades, allowed a use of "revolution" in his later years which had sometimes a definite future oriented sense, when compared with the broad intention of the word in his earlier works. In his early historical essays the meaning of the word was necessarily influenced by the tradition of the "Histoires des Révolutions." When we come to a major work such as the *Essai sur les moeurs*, the evidence is overwhelming. Written in the early 1740s, although first published in 1756, this work used "revolution" over sixty times. In many places, however, Voltaire employs it interchangeably with "changement" in reference to geographical transformations on the face of the earth. This begins already in the second paragraph with the announcement: "It may be that our world has undergone as many changes as the revolutions experienced by states" ["Il peut que notre monde ait subi autant de changements que les États ont éprouvé de révolutions"]. Later he uses the word when dealing with such events as the Sicilian Vespers, the revolt of the Netherlands against Spain, the revolt of Portugal in 1640 and the policies of England in 1650. But his typical use is when the word is carrying the meaning of change in the broadest sense, as in the opening of the last chapter where the whole period of world history covered by the work is termed "ce vaste théatre de révolutions..."

This manner of use is still reflected in his *Annales de l'Empire depuis Charlemagne*, a history of the Holy Roman Empire, written in 1753. In the short dedication to the Duchess of Saxe-Gotha, Voltaire hastens to depict history as a list of the disorders that had engulfed the world, and immediately concludes: "It is important for all the nations of Europe to take lessons from the revolutions of the Empire." The term then returns in the first sentence of the introduction, where in a manner not unlike Maimbourg back in the seventeenth century, he declares the crowning of Charlemagne the only true revolution.[8] In fact, here as elsewhere the term is more often employed to express changes of the broadest sense in contrast to transformations accomplished by previous planning. The recurrent phrases which Voltaire employs are: "toutes les révolutions qui ont changé la face de la terre;" "les révolutions de ce globe;" or "les révolutions qu'éprouva notre globe;" and "tous les peuples ont éprouvé des révolutions."

The last phrase is from the introductory chapter to his masterpiece, *Le siècle de Louis XIV*, first published in 1751. Here Voltaire explained what in his eyes was more significant in human history. He was aiming, he said, at a history of the spirit of an age, not at a history of political and military heroes, neither of revolutions. Louis XIV was merely a symbol of his age, just as the other three ages of extraordinary gains for the human spirit were the ages of Pericles, Caesar and the Medicis, rulers of Renaissance Florence. Further in the work the employment of the term became at best uneven. In chapter two, quickly surveying conditions in the states of Europe, Voltaire mentioned the case of Charles I of England, who had engaged his people in "une guerre civile" and lost everything, including his own life "by an almost unheard-of revolution" ["par une révolution presque inouïe"]. Also the French Fronde was a "guerre civile," although at a certain point the hatred of Mazarin "threatened the court by a revolution." Strangely, however, when he came to the events of the years 1688-90 in England, which absorbed the entire fifteenth chapter, "revolution" almost disappeared. Not that Voltaire played down the significance of the unseating of James II. Indeed, he called it "the age of the true liberty of England," and explained that at that time the English nation, represented by its parliament, finally determined the limits of power in the state, long contested between the king and the people. He also observed that whereas in France William of Orange was considered "usurper of the states of his father-in-law," he was called in England the "liberator of the nation." But somehow, and although he knew very well that in England all these episodes of 1688-90 were dubbed "the Revolution," Voltaire managed to bypass this word. When he finally used it once towards the end of the chapter, it remained unclear whether he meant to refer to the unseating of James II or just to the clashes between the deposed king and William III in Ireland in 1690.

Voltaire's handling of "revolution" is therefore at best indecisive. It is confirmed again in the *Dictionnaire philosophique*, a product of the mid and late 1760s. Arranged alphabetically, this work does not have a separate entry for the term, neither is it employed in articles where one should anticipate its use, such as "Cromwell," "Democratie," "Egalité," "États," "Gouvernement." But in the entry on the English parliament the word is used when he observes the differences in the outcomes of civil wars in England as contrasted with other nations. Among the ancient Romans civil wars produced a shift from republican freedom to an enslaving imperial system of government. In France, adds Voltaire, the civil wars during the reign of Charles VI (1380-1422) were cruel, those of the League were horrible, while the Fronde was simply ridiculous. But in England the long train of internal strife in the seventeenth century yielded liberty; which according to Voltaire may substantiate the view that "that which becomes a revolution in England is nothing more than a sedition in other countries" ["Ce qui devient une révolution en Angleterre, n'est qu'une sédition dans les autres pays"]. Here the term is given a significance almost diametrically opposed to that given to it by Montesquieu, and quite surprisingly stands for political freedom. In the article on Plato on the other hand, Voltaire also mentions "revolution" as the product of civil wars, but restricts himself to the observation that frequently those who begin to undermine a state are just unknowingly paving the road for those who would come after them.[9]

Still, in what should be regarded as an even more unusual use of the term, Voltaire employed it in the context of the effects which he believed the Enlightenment was bound to bring forth. The following example is from his short tract of 1769, *Le cri des nations*, calling for an end to the rights of taxation, which the Roman pontiff still exercised in Catholic countries. He opened with a passage celebrating the expulsion of the Jesuits from France, Portugal and Spain. This, he claimed, could never have been possible a century before, or it would have resulted in excommunications, interdicts and civil wars. But in "le siècle de la raison," when people have become better educated and when Catholic nations were pursuing policies guided by enlightened wisdom, the suppression of the Jesuits ensued as a "heureuse révolution."[10] As Voltaire very well knew, this so-called revolution, made possible by the new climate of ideas, really consisted of arbitrary decisions undertaken by monarchical despots out of considerations not unlinked with internal politics. It is indeed a question whether Voltaire ever conceived of changes, or "revolutions," taking place against the wishes of the established European rulers, with some of whom he was in close touch. But in a letter written on 2 April 1764, he at least dared to consider an option that was absent in his published essays: "All that I look at discharges the seeds of a revolution, which will inevitably take place and which I will not have the pleasure to witness. Frenchmen are late to everything, but finally they arrive. The Enlightenment has slowly spread to the point that it is ready to explode; and then there will be a great uproar. Young people are very lucky; they will see great things."[11]

This last utterance of Voltaire's is a reminder that even great thinkers might say in private more than they are willing to claim in public. In an age when the Bastille was more than just a symbol, caution with the choice of words necessarily led to alternative rhetoric. As we saw before in the case of d'Argenson, it was easier for contemporaries to manage the term in diaries than in essays. Rocquain has given examples from the *Journal* of the gossiping Parisian lawyer Barbier, who at about the same time as Voltaire envisioned a future revolution, and wrote that France faced one of the two choices; either a despotic government (in case the rights of the *parlements* were restricted) or "une révolution générale dans l'État" (in the case that the *parlements* would unite in opposition to the crown). In another place the same diarist told of a priest in Paris who exhorted the parishioners of Saint-Antoine that, in a country where state and church were clashing endlessly, "la révolution" would explode sooner or later.[12]

All this is relevant to the use of the term by Rousseau. Seemingly he was willing to go a step further than Voltaire. In the third book of *Emile* (1762), perhaps his major work, he put in the mouth of the boy's educator the following unambiguous words:

> You assume that the existing order of society will endure, without imagining that that order is subject to inevitable revolutions,... The great becomes small, the rich become poor, the monarch becomes a subject;... We are approaching a state of crisis and a century of revolutions. [And in a note at the bottom of the page Rousseau added] I think it is impossible that the great monarchies of Europe will last much longer; all of them have turned shiny, and every state that shines is about to start its decline. I have more definite reasons for my view than this axiom, but it is not appropriate to tell them, and everybody is aware of them.[13]

The passage is quite significant. On the one hand Rousseau speaks here openly of "revolutions;" on the other hand, he does not hide his uneasiness in discussing such a weighty and sensitive subject. The reluctance to pursue the subject further did not prevent, however, his subsequent fame as a harbinger of revolutions. Once the confrontation with the ancien regime became real, Rousseau, more than any other thinker of the Enlightenment, was declared its foremost ideologist. As early as October 1789 a well argued pamphlet made him responsible for the formulation of the principles that had set three revolutions on fire, that of America, of his own native city Geneva, and of France.

Rousseau was specifically assailed for his upholding of the sanctity of the rights of the citizen, for defending popular sovereignty against that of kings and for claiming that the law was the expression of "la volonté générale;" a dangerous modern principle, contrary to any idea held by political theorists in the past.[14] As a source demonstrating Rousseau's responsibility for the evil theories that had spawned revolutions, the author of the pamphlet referred time and again to the *Contrat social* (1761). But when we examine this famous essay the relative absence of the term "revolution" is easily perceived. It is pretty much the same in his earlier essay, *Discours sur l'origine et les fondaments de l'inégalité parmi les hommes* (1754), although here a cluster of five "revolutions" awaits the reader towards the end of the tract. Four of them have the sense of either changes occurring along the course of time, or they refer to outbursts of violence, typical of despotic governments; only once does the word assume the meaning of a change that would bring a moral benefit to society. This comes in a passage in which Rousseau summarizes the background for the development of inequality, finding that it grew out of the establishing of the right to property, and worsened with the appearance of forms of magistracy and arbitrary power. All of this contributed to creating a worse form of inequality – slavery; and these conditions would stay that way "until new revolutions would dissolve government completely, or would reconcile it with legitimate order" ["jusqu'à ce que de nouvelles révoltuions dissolvent tout à fait le gouvernement, ou le rapprochent de l'institution légitime"]. Here, as later in *Emile*, Rousseau uses the word in a way fitting his ideological position, which postulates a greater political equality among men. But we do not find him repeating this manner of employment in the *Contrat social*, where, in any case, the use of the term is insignificant.[15]

Therefore, there is a strange omission in Rousseau's work. His stress on the theme of inequality in society could have (and perhaps should have) suggested "revolution" as a means of making human existence more conformable with justice. Indeed, there are numerous passages in his essays which anticipate that inference. But somehow he always manages to carry the argument to a not so binding conclusion, or he comes out of the impasse with an evasive utterance such as that it is not for slaves to argue about liberty. In any case we cannot include him among those who advanced the use and meaning of the term. Beside semantic constrictions, his abstaining from exploiting the word probably emanated from an uneasiness lest he transgress the binding norms of political discourse. Even in an age when a new critical essay in an engaging style was avidly sought by the public and read at the court, an author still had to consider the coercive powers of the *parlement* and the church. Rousseau, however, did not share the view of so many other writers of the Enlightenment, who saw in it an age of unbounded moral and social progress. That view seemed to exclude a need for an assertive stand on the part of the governed. For those who held it, but not for Rousseau, "revolution" would have been unnecessary.

Yet another author, who, like Rousseau, doubted whether a mere advancement in ideas was sufficient to achieve social and political progress, was the elusive Morelly. He wrote half a dozen works, the last of which, *Code de la nature*, first published in 1755, meant to justify his utopian vision, called "La Basilade." He too cannot be said to have contributed significantly to the use of "revolution," but at least we find him challenging the conventional notion of the term. In fact, Morelly does that while objecting to Montesquieu's characterization of the different political regimes. What stands at the basis of government, argues Morelly, is "l'intérêt personnel," in other words – "la propriété." Those who are hoping for a perfect government based on the values of liberty tend to overlook the fact that as long as there is private property there will be a clash of interests in society, and any state will one day be destabilized. You cannot attribute, therefore, the "sad revolutions" that demolish empires to the same "blind fatality" that destroys the fortune of a private individual ["C'est en vain que vous attribuez ces tristes révolutions au hasard, à une aveugle fatalité qui cause l'instabilité des empires commes celles de la fortune des particuliers"]. In political life, he explains, chance and fate are but the expressions of conflicts of wills, which are determined by different interests. What other cause then than the "esprit cruel" of property and interest gives the first shake towards revolutions?[16]

Even though Morelly did not elaborate on this theme, his argument was quite impressive. Other essayists hardly made an effort to stray from the conventional use and concept. In *Considérations sur les moeurs de ce siècle*, clearly influence by Voltaire, Duclos spoke of a revolution in national customs of which the ruler was the leader (perhaps bearing in mind Peter the Great of Russia).[17] In yet another work, *L'esprit des nations* by Espiard, the term was used, as in Montesquieu, in contrast to civil wars, with the added qualification however that these two forms of political disturbance were claimed to reflect the spirit of a nation. "Révolutions," therefore, were the lot of England, compared with the French "guerres civiles." This led to a conclusion that in France the respect for political offices and the acknowledgment of the central place of the monarchy united all the spirits and established "the acknowledged impossibility of a revolution" ["l'impossibilité reconnue d'une Révolution"].[18] Helvetius, whose godless *Traité de l'esprit* raised a great controversy when it was first published in 1758, actually avoided the term even when dealing directly with the theme of political change. Baron d'Holbach's *Système de la nature* also had very little to offer on our subject, in spite of its aggressive atheism and materialistic views. This work, circulating in manuscript form and finally published in 1770, was followed six years later by Holbach with *Ethocratie, ou le gouvernement fondé sur la morale.* Here one could verify that the author, for the most part staying aloof from the term, was likewise far from the idea. He mentioned "the terrible and frequent revolutions which test the tyrants of Asia,..." But he believed that reason shed no blood; enlightenment was slow but sure and intelligent men were peaceable.[19]

Passing over from the theorists of the Enlightenment to the historians, the picture changes but mildly. A good early example is the *Nouvelle abregé chronologique de l'histoire de France* by Hénault, which earned a great success in the late 1740s. This author conceded that some events in the modern history of Europe were apt to carry the term "revolution." Among these was the revolt of Portugal against Spain in 1640; yet another was the outcome of the struggle between Charles I and the parliament in England, "a revolution of which there was no precedent." But the Fronde was just a "guerre civile," whereas the events of 1688 in England were labeled "Révolution d'Angleterre."[20] A different use of the term was made in Claude Carloman de Rulhière's account of the coup d'état which made Peter III disappear and placed his wife Catherine II on the Russian throne in 1762. The young author (who in 1787 would become a member of the Académie Française) happened to be in Russia when the events took place, and completed his book shortly afterwards, following his return to France. He regarded the Russian form of government as essentially an oriental despotism, and when he employed "revolution" it had a Montesquieu-like sense of a bloody palace revolt. At one spot he credited the Czarina Elisabeth with an awareness of this endemic situation, namely "with what facility revolution is affected in Russia."[21] Other examples might be gathered in Mailly's extensive study of the Fronde. He was inspired by the new historiography of Voltaire, but in comparison with the latter's view of the Fronde in the *Dictionnaire philosophique*, he refused to see in it anything ridiculous. These "revolutions," he maintained in the introduction, should not only be of interest to all classes of readers, they should also be remembered as a testimony to the weakness of government and the audacity of the subjects during a minority of a king. Therefore, they should merit attention even though they had failed "to be the age of the greatest revolutions," and even though they had not changed the limits of monarchical power and the form of government.[22]

The term "revolution" was perhaps used more freely in French publications appearing outside France; for example, the quasi-journalistic books printed in London between 1774 and 1776 by Pidansat de Mairobert under the title *Journal historique de la révolution operée dans la constitution de la monarchie françoise par M. de Maupeou, Chancelier de France*. They dealt with the substantial changes in the courts of justice effected in 1771 by Maupeou, who had used highhanded measures, such as banishing members of the *parlement* from Paris. But ironically the "revolution" in the title of the publication meant to express the almost despotic manner of the changes rather than to praise or defend them.[23] This "revolution" was therefore a change from the top down rather than from the bottom up.

The term also played a role in the numerous writings of that wandering littérateur, Ange Goudar, whose name (together with that of his pretty English wife Sara) is associated with famous contemporary scandals. In one of his earliest works, a mock "political testament" of a French chief of highwaymen about to be executed, Goudar leveled bitter criticism on the tax collecting system. He made the doomed man speak of a plan for a widely supported uprising. Besides the thousands under his command and influence, the bandit counted on the resentment of the lesser nobility of the south of France. According to his assessment, all that was missing was a foreign war – "and then the revolution would become widespread."[24] Goudar also wrote on the Russian coup d'état of Catherine II, publishing his book in 1763, before Rulhière. He certainly would have subscribed to the latter's view on the despotic nature of the Russian government, and maintained like him that "the despotic empires are exposed to many more revolutions than the other monarchies."[25]   In subsequent writings he criticized almost any aspect of European public life, lamenting the impossibility of real improvement, but arrived at the following conclusion: "Nothing less than a determined conspiracy against all monarchs in general can reinstate the people in their original rights, a remedy worse than the disease; for the anarchy consequent to such a sudden revolution, would be productive of greater evils than any monarchical power, and infallibly destroy what despotism has spared."[26]   Still later, in 1776, Goudar took a look at the recent popular commotions as reflected in disorders in Malta, the Motín de Esquilache in Madrid, the Pugachev peasant revolt in Russia and the bread riots that followed Turgot's new policies of grain circulation in France. He wondered how one was to explain those flare ups in the full age of the Enlightenment and ventured the opinion that turbulences of this kind were more harmful and less productive than uprisings with clear political aims. It brought him to a surprising conclusion: "The political revolutions, which are usually considered the greatest misfortunes, are really less dangerous than these popular plunders."[27]   But Goudar's interest in the idea of revolution apparently lessened afterwards. When his utterances are compared with the examples furnished by other contemporary authors, it is still difficult to determine whether they carried a real innovative slant.

If we make a pause at this point for a midway assessment of the meaning of "revolution" in France during the Enlightenment, the following summary would emerge.[28] The *philosophes* inherited the term after it had come to mean a sudden extraordinary change in the government of a state. Until they started experimenting with it, the word was in most cases used in the plural form, as exemplified by the "Histoires des Révolutions," and conveyed the idea of abrupt ruptures, accomplished without the intervention of human will, experienced rather than acted out. To this general notion Montesquieu added the sense of violent changes which frequently perturbed the stability of despotic regimes. Voltaire, on the other hand, initiated the view of "revolution" as a dynamic process of transformation, essentially the outcome of a change in ideas and beliefs, and the progress of the human spirit that he conceived to be the Enlightenment itself. In addition, both Voltaire and Rousseau had an intimation of great revolutions, apparently political, to take place as a grand finale of the Enlightenment. But they spoke of it in a cryptic manner, which suggested that they regarded the issue as existing at the edge of what one could freely examine. Nowhere in the works of these giants of their age do we find a sustained discussion on the inevitability of revolution, much less on its advisability.

The very short, almost lame, entry on the political meaning of the word in the *Encyclopédie*, published in 1765, is yet another testimony of its relative poverty as an idea or an operative concept. This comes as the first section of a long article, which deals primarily with the meanings of the word in astronomy and mechanics, and it is limited to the following lines:

> REVOLUTION, n.f. means *in the political sense*, an important change that happens in the government of a state. This word comes from the Latin *revolvere*, to turn about. There are no states that have not experienced revolutions, though some more and some less. The abbé Vertot has given us two or three excellent histories of *revolutions* of different countries; namely, the *revolutions* of Sweden, that of the Roman republic, etc.
>
> [RÉVOLUTION, s.f. signifie *en terme de politique*, un changement considérable arrivé dans le gouvernement d'un état. Ce mot vient du latin *revolvere*, rouler. Il n'y a point d'états qui n'aient été sujets à plus ou moins de *révolutions*. L'abbé de Vertot nous a donné deux ou trois histoires excellentes des *révolutions* des différents pays; savoir, les *révolutions* de Suede, celle de la république romaine, etc.]

It is true that this very short note continued with a somewhat longer one on the experience of 1688 in England, an event, according to the writer, to which the English particularly applied the term, although their country had been the stage of many revolutions. But the unseating of James II had been necessitated, it was explained on the authority of Bolingbroke, on account of the king's bad administration and his attachment to Catholicism. Moreover, the problems had really originated during "une révolution precedente" of which Cromwell had been the leading figure and which had started "non sans fondement par rapport à la liberté,..." Only here, in his last sentence, the writer managed to tie the subject at hand with the quest for liberty. But intentionally or not this tie was hatched with the words rebellion and usurpation, and the reader ended up with the impression that revolution was an English aberration, certainly not a French way of conducting politics.

England, as we can see, remained, in French eyes, the mother of revolution. But in England itself attitudes towards 1688 had shifted, and so had the uses given to the political sense of the word once the heated Whig-Tory debate over "Revolution Principles" had become a matter of the past. A good indication of that is found in the famous lexicographical production of the age, *A Dictionary of the English Language* by Samuel Johnson, published in 1755. Four different meanings of "revolution" were given here, relating to movement in a circle, measures of space and time, politics, and rotation in general. To three of his definitions, but not to the political one, Johnson saw fit to add examples from literary sources, mostly from the writings of Milton and Dryden (who had rejected the political sense). The other sense of the word was explained thus: "Change in the fate of a government or a country. It is used among us... for the change produced by the admission of King William and Queen Mary."

Short and almost trivial, Johnson's definition did not reflect the wide consensus which had come to mark the English assessment of 1688, viewing the "Revolution" as a new beginning of national constitutional history. This view was now given support by both parties, and conservative Whigs, holding on to the reigns of government, could actually disclaim any further need of political reform, while maintaining credit for the 1688-89 settlement and the extensive benefits it had brought. This judgment of the revolution was elaborated in yet another famous work, published about the same time as Johnson's dictionary, David Hume's *The History of England from the Invasion of Julius Caesar to the Revolution in 1688.* It quickly gained a wide reading public, replacing *The History of England* (1725-1731), a translation of a work by the French Protestant historian Paul de Rapin-Thoyras, as the standard, relatively comprehensive, record of the national past. It is of interest to note that the first volumes of Hume's work were published in 1754 and dealt with the Stuart period. The rest came later, and in a backward chronological order, the earliest period, covering the Roman centuries, appearing last in 1762. Even more interesting, Hume, writing in a style which meant to be both entertaining and instructive, mostly bypassed the term "revolution." Indeed, in this he may have outdone Rapin-Thoyras, who had used "les Révolutions" for the period immediately following the execution of Charles I.[29] Although when dealing with this particular juncture Hume too made use of the word, he came to it only when asking about the lesson that those "memorable revolutions" carried in historical retrospection. It appeared to him that on the one hand they taught that it was "dangerous for princes to assume more authority than the laws have allowed them," a lesson he believed Charles I himself had absorbed before he died. But there were other lessons there to be learned, "concerning the madness of the people, the furies of fanaticism, and the danger of mercenary armies."[30] He returned again to both the term and the subject in the last chapter, where the climax of 1688 was explained as the end of a continued struggle between the crown and the people along the reigns of four kings. Hume's final words on the event were these:

> The revolution forms a new epoch in the constitution; and was attended with consequences more advantageous to the people, than the barely freeing them from a bad administration. By deciding many important questions in favor of liberty, and establishing a new family, it gave such an ascendant to popular principles, as has put the nature of the English constitution beyond all controversy. And it may justly be affirmed, without any danger of exaggeration, that we, in this island, have ever since enjoyed, if not the best system of government, at least the most entire system of liberty, that ever was known amongst mankind.

On the weight of this passage alone, Hume would appear to be an advocate of revolutions. In fact, his stand on that subject was closer to the opposite side. We can clearly see his real position in a passage, a little further on from the one quoted above, in which he chastised those who maintained the existence of a binding original contract between the ruler and the people. Contrary to their views, claimed Hume, in real societies "great revolutions of government, and new settlements of civil constitutions, are commonly conducted with such violence, tumult, and disorder, that the public voice can scarcely ever be heard; and the opinions of the citizens are at that time less attended to than even in the common course of administration."[31] What Hume meant to say here, and he had argued that point in his philosophical essays since *A Treatise on Human Nature* (1739-40), is that a revolution or a violent uprising could not be the answer to the infringement of a political contract. Revolutions happen as a result of "enormous tyranny and oppression," because governments exist for some mutual benefit, and once the advantage becomes pronouncedly one-sided the obligation of the subjects ceases. He felt that this was not only the case in 1688, and in many other instances throughout history, but that there was at least a common sense authorization for these eruptions and that the right of resistance, which applied to subjects of despotic governments, certainly existed in limited monarchies like England. He did not believe, however, that either law or philosophy could establish when resistance was right. Revolutions were acts of violence that gained legality to the extent that the governments they launched endured. That of 1688 was particularly fortunate in gaining a legal recognition, because the settlement was decided by a freely elected assembly representing the nation. But that one was an exception. Most revolutions failed to accumulate the time, and the resulting consecration as a custom, that gave authority to all forms of government. In an essay addressing the question whether England inclined more to an absolute monarchy or to a republic, Hume, without mentioning either "revolution" or the name of Cromwell, reminded the readers that the country had once undergone a full transformation in the form of regime, but ended up a republic ruled in the manner of an absolute monarchy. If that crucial experience was for Englishmen the foreboding one, then their lesson should be that revolutions endangered liberty.[32]

It would appear that Hume had set the standard, or rather the double-standard, for a whole generation of British essayists of viewing 1688 in contrast with all other revolutions. For example, Robert Wallace, more famous for his treatises on population, wrote in *Characteristics of the Present State of Great Britain* (1758) that "Before the Revolution the nation could place no confidence in its governors."[33] But Adam Ferguson, who got Hume's assistance for his appointment as a professor of philosophy at the University of Edinburgh, showed no particular interest in 1688. In his *Essay on the History of Civil Society* (1766) the term was employed very seldom. When he came to it, the sense was that of a Montesquieu-like "fatal revolution," which transformed a legal authority into a military government and ended up in tyranny.[34] Ferguson distinguished between "rude" and "polished nations," among which England was obviously a model. Somehow, though, he failed to evaluate the contribution of 1688 to England's state of perfection as a civil society. He frequently alluded to the weakness and lack of stability of popular governments, and idealized strong nations, consisting of "vigorous, public spirited and resolute men." In fact, his essay abounded with simplistic, easy generalizations, and while repeating notions such as the "improvement of human nature," it hardly transcended old literary genres extolling the importance of morality. Hume disliked it, but the reading public was apparently captivated by its eloquence. It was quickly translated into German, later into French, and had its seventh English edition in 1814. Yet another Scottish author, John Millar, educated under Adam Smith at Glasgow, similarly avoided "revolution" in his *The Origins of the Distinction of Ranks* (1771). This essay, translated into French in Holland within two years, dealt with the original formation of hierarchies in society. It stressed the process of gathering power by sheer arbitrary acts and even mentioned the usurpation of complete control over the state by monarchs in modern European history. But the author, later on a sympathizer of the French Revolution, had no use for the term at the time he wrote the essay. His former teacher, whose seminal *The Wealth of Nations* came out in 1776, used the term twice in the entire work, and at least once remembered to tie 1688 with his country's economic accomplishments: "That security which the laws in Great Britain give to every man that he shall enjoy the fruits of his own labor, is alone sufficient to make any country flourish,... and this security was perfected by the revolution."[35]

The theme of revolution got more attention in a work of Edward Wortley Montagu, *Reflections of the Rise and Fall of the Ancient Republics adapted to the Present State of Great Britain* (1759). This was the product of a talented but restless mind, who not long afterwards went to the Orient, and later settled in Italy. The book had, however, a measure of success. In 1793, when the third English edition was printed, it also saw the appearance of its second French translation, although the first, published in 1769, had been actually a gross case of plagiarism, concocted by François-Henry Turpin.[36] After he dealt with ancient Greece, Rome and Carthage, Montagu saw fit to dedicate a short chapter to "Revolutions in mixed Governments." He started it with a summary of Polybius's cycle of forms of state, but then worked out a theory on the resolution of conflicts in mixed governments, that is, in states where power is divided among kings, the aristocracy and representatives of the common people. The "revolutions" he discussed were therefore essentially not much more than confrontations in which two political bodies in a mixed government cooperated in an attempt to check the might of the third, not in order to destroy it, however, but to have it contained within its proper political bounds. He brought examples from the history of Denmark and Sweden, but the English experience of 1688 served him as the best case. According to Montagu, this was a joint action by the lords and commons, the two other political bodies, against the third, the king, who wanted to introduce an absolute monarchy. Though 1688 was animated by a verve of patriotism, essentially "the late happy Revolution" was an act "by which the above mentioned crown was restrained within its proper limits, and the government resettled upon its true basis, as nearly as the genius of the times would admit of." But England, according to Montagu, had also gone, on another occasion, through a Polybius-like "circumvolution of Governments," or a cycle of rotation from one form of regime to another. This happened during the "distracted state of Government in this nation from 1648, to the restoration of Charles II." Here, however, Montagu refrained from employing the term "revolution."[37]

The theme of revolution is also found in the short essay of a better known, and more influential contemporary author, Joseph Priestley's *An Essay on the Principles of Government* (1768). Moreover, here the argumentation looks promising from the very start, because, and this is also the subtitle of the work, government is considered in relation to "the nature of political, civil and religious liberty." Priestley indeed goes on to satisfy the reader's expectations. In a strain of arguments, which apparently continue to walk the path first opened by Algernon Sidney a century before him, he paints a hypothetical situation whereby government is abused by those in charge, and instances of oppression and violation of rights become flagrant and universally resented. He then supplies the answer to that state of affairs, and phrases it in no equivocal words: "if, in consequence of these circumstances, it should become manifest, that the risque, which would be run in attempting a revolution would be trifling, and the evils which might be apprehended from it, were far less than these which were actually suffered, and which were daily increasing; in the name of God, I ask what principles are those which ought to restrain an injured and insulted people from asserting their natural rights, and from changing, or even punishing the governors, that is their servants, who had abused their trust; or from altering the whole form of government, if it appeared a structure so liable to abuse?"[38]

This defense of "attempting a revolution" is not merely an endorsement of 1688. Considering Priestley's assertions on the people's "natural rights," their right to punish their governors and to alter the government, what is defended here, although in a veiled manner, is rather the ordeal of 1648-49. In contrast with other political theorists of his time, Priestley rekindled the old seventeenth century English republican tradition. He was aware of course that he would be confronted on that issue with a variety of charges, and so he hastened to advance apologetic explanations. He denied that he was encouraging rebellions, and besides, English history proved that the people rose against their rulers only when there was extreme oppression, going on unabated for a long time (exactly as Locke had maintained). Therefore, rather than be concerned with imaginary dangers to the state or church, which the "court party, or the narrow minded bigots among the inferior clergy" periodically announced in order to serve their own interests, one should recall to what lengths the power of the crown could grow when it was unopposed. And he cited as examples the rule without parliament of Charles II and the almost four years of James II. Also, at present there could be no real danger of rebellion, because "the government of this country is now fixed upon so good and firm basis."[39] These qualifications cast doubt whether Priestley's idea of revolution was at all for local consumption. At the time it was expressed its message might have been more relevant to a branch of the English people across the Atlantic Ocean. Furthermore, very little in his arguments and ideas reflected links with the French Enlightenment. It would seem that in his case the general intellectual effervescence of the time sufficed to rouse old ideas in refurbished words.

Even in Priestley's essay, however, the word "revolution" did not carry a particular weight or resonance. It was used simply to make an argument. Other English authors of those same years could still employ it in a diametrically opposite sense, that is in the sense of a political change for the worse. No other than Edward Gibbon opened the short preface to his immortal masterpiece with a clarification that dealt with "The memorable series of revolutions, which in the course of thirteen centuries, gradually undermined and at length destroyed, the solid fabric of human greatness,...." Employed in this context, the term almost equaled in meaning the words "decline and fall," which featured in the title of the work. This preface was written in 1776, the year that the American colonies declared their independence. A year later, when another great historian, William Robertson, wrote his preface to *The History of America*, he apologized for not including in his narrative the story of English colonization in the northern part of the continent, explaining that he had left it out because of the current dispute between the mother country and the colonials. He added that whatever the outcome of the struggle, it should produce in America a new order of things. But he could not find a better phrase to describe the prevailing situation than "civil war."[40]   Nevertheless, the conflagration in America began to change matters also in England. It helped to convince a small minority that the settlement of 1688-89 had come up far too short in securing the rights of the people and that the Revolution was therefore in need of reassessment.[41] In fact, signs of this new attitude began to form prior to 1776, and Priestley in the aforementioned essay had been among its pioneering voices. Now, however, with the Americans daring to claim what Englishmen could only wish, the issue became timely.

We may gain insight as to how the new circumstances were about to bear on the use of the term "revolution" from an exchange that actually involved two men of conservative leanings. Richard Watson, later Bishop of Llandaff and famous for his *Apology for the Bible* (1796),in which he challenged Thomas Paine, was in 1776 a professor of divinity at Cambridge. On 29 May he preached a sermon there, quickly published as *The Principles of the Revolution Vindicated.* That a man of his outlook would address a largely concurring audience with this subject, just shows how much political values had changed. In fact, Watson went as far as to assert that mankind was made of "equal and independent individuals," that one individual could not have the right to speak for the other, and that no generation of men had the right to establish a form of government which their children would not have the right to change. All of that, and the claim that kings should not run their kingdoms as private estates, was then validated with the utterance: "we are not of those who cannot distinguish between resistance and rebellion; for we venerate the principles of the Revolution,..." Those who apparently failed to make the distinction, though Watson never referred to them by name, were the Americans, who at that point were already engaging the colonial authorities with arms on the battlefield. Indeed, the speaker even went on to criticize the new tyranny of Parliament, but explained that 1688 had been entirely warranted because "the people may conscientiously resist the usurpation of the Crown, even to the altering of the Succession itself."[42]

This sermon, and yet another by Watson preached on 25 October 1776, were answered in an anonymous pamphlet, *The Revolution Vindicated and Constitutional Liberty Asserted.* Its author was William Stevens, treasurer of Queen Anne's Bounty and a friend of members of the Anglican hierarchy. He charged Watson with supporting doctrines that might destroy the constitution, since they grounded all authority in the power of the people. Moreover, he did not fail to tie the sermons of the preacher from Cambridge with the issues at stake in America, claiming that although he did not mean it Watson really backed the "seditious principles" recently advanced by Dr. Richard Price. A friend of Priestley's, Price gained fame in 1776 when he published a long pamphlet, in which he actually defended the rights of the Americans to independence. This conviction was based on his belief in the principles of civil liberty, further strengthened by his judgment that Britain ruled the colonies to her own advantage and that, as she refused to amend her own faulty system of representative government, she had no moral right to impose herself on America. In his reply to Watson, Stevens not only argued a similarity between the latter's ideas and Price's, but actually reproduced a quotation from a sequel pamphlet of Price's, in which he referred to Watson and remarked that those who acknowledged the right of resistance of the people in the final account accepted also their right to change governors and governments. Therefore, argued Stevens, maintaining a right of resistance was admitting Price's system of civil liberty.[43] Throughout this exchange, the term "revolution" was mostly bypassed, except of course when it was employed, with a capital R, in reference to 1688. Interestingly this is also true for Price's *Observations on the Nature of Civil Liberty, the Principles of Government, and the Justice and Policy of the War with America.* There was a "war," or a "civil war," with America, not a "revolution." Only in the final paragraph of his pamphlet did Price allow himself the semantic freedom to announce: "An important revolution in the affairs of this kingdom seems to be approaching."[44] But it was said in connection with needed reforms in the ways Britain was managing her national debt, and perhaps was not even intended to forecast political changes. In any case, Price, the erstwhile defender of the independence of the United States, would need more time, like others, to get used to the epithet the "American Revolution." As we shall see in the next chapter, he will come to it in 1783.

It would seem, therefore, that in England as in France "revolution" really failed to establish itself as a distinctive semantic vehicle for the idea of political change. Aside from the almost universal acknowledgment of the "Revolution" (usually without "Glorious"), authors on politics used it infrequently. If we hold on to the assumption that our findings in both countries are indicative of the general European trends, that leaves us with a rather reserved appreciation of the capacity of the word in the discourse of the Enlightenment, at least prior to 1776. But notwithstanding this general impression, there still remained at the time an opening for some authors to use ideas and phrases that others classified as too daring, offbeat or *outré*. Three such writers, all French, reveal, though in different ways, the inherent revolutionary potential of "revolution" even before any additions accumulated to its meaning in the wake of American independence.

The first of these three is the abbé Mably, Condillac's older brother who had gained experience in the French royal foreign service, before retiring to a life of literary pursuits. Among his many works, the most significant for our purpose is *Des droits et des devoirs du citoyen*. Consisting of a series of dialogues between a Frenchman and an English "milord" of quite obvious republican inclinations, it was apparently written in 1758, but first published only in 1789, four years after the death of the author. This in itself might serve as an indirect indication that our theme and term were simply too risky during the ancien regime, because almost everything in these dialogues revolved on the issue of political liberty and the means to have it established and maintained. Mably first introduces the term in its typical unthreatening sense: "The world is driven by unending revolutions" ["révolutions continuelles"]. But shortly afterwards he employs the word in reference to "une révolution singulière" which had taken place at the first forming of society, when men first took it upon themselves to be citizens, that is, to pursue their private happiness in accordance with some rules and restraints. Further on, in sharp contrast with Montesquieu, he notes that in despotic regimes "no revolution happens nor can any take place," because palace revolts in the manner of Turkey do not produce real change. The Englishman then explains that in a country where the people believe that it is better to obey the law than the caprices of a master, the perspective is different. Here they are continually on the watch to safeguard their liberty, since they realize that otherwise they will end up under an absolute monarchy or some form of an oligarchy. Therefore, he concludes: "I believe then that revolutions are yet possible; a good citizen has therefore to hope, and he is bound, according to his estate, his authority and his capacities, to work for making these revolutions useful for his country."[45]

This concept of revolution, assigning to it the value of a patriotic gesture, was certainly a radical departure from any conventional sense of the term during the Enlightenment. But Mably was only at the beginning. Later in the dialogue the nature of the revolution was spelled out, the Englishman doing most of the talking and the Frenchman gradually being persuaded by his reasoning. It was necessary to aim at controlling the powers of the monarch, including his power to dispose of taxes, make wars, assemble parliaments and enact laws. If these issues were neglected "we will have only unproductive revolutions." Also, it is to be remembered that in order to reform the government, the people need to be won over. In England this had been prepared by the teachings of the Reformation, which had first forged strong commitments to religious freedom, and then transferred them to the realm of politics. But in a country like France it would be better to work slowly. One should base himself on old principles of political traditions and rights, which had been abandoned, and try to revive them. That way the people would not be alarmed by the newness of the suggested reforms, and when the moment comes they would find "their hearts ready for a revolution." One has not to fear revolutions just because they entail violence; a nation amends its vices only when it yearns for change. Much depends on education and on the ability of the people to be on top of the events, rather than to be shaped by them. That way they should be able to launch revolutions and yield something good from them ["...faire des révolutions et produire le bien"]. In France, moreover, the revolution should have a national scope. It cannot be the outcome of regional movements, nor of something in the manner of the Fronde, but must be the fruit of the reborn Estates General, which will be first convoked by the king, but freely elected and afterwards frequently convened. No body but the Estates themselves will have the right to dissolve them, and they will take care of everything, including the matters of the debts of the crown. If they should be controlled by the king, then they would end up just serving the monarchy. If they should be influenced by generals, it might end in a new tyranny; "Cromwell will always have his imitators." Therefore, the reforms should be the work of an independent, national representative assembly. Within these bounds the choices with respect to the work of destroying despotism are clear: "You must choose between a revolution or slavery; there is no middle way."[46]

The ideas and language that served Mably in this tract were echoed in his *Observations sur l'histoire de France*. Probably, the radical thread of arguments that delayed the publication of the former work, affected also the printing of the second. It first appeared in Geneva in 1765 in an incomplete two volume edition. But the full text, continuing up to the reign of Louis XIV, had to wait until 1788 when it was published in Kehl, and in the next year the work made up the first three volumes of Mably's *Oeuvres complètes*, which came out in London. Here too a clear link was made between liberty and revolution. In a separate long chapter discussing the reasons why the government of England assumed a different form from that of France, Mably singled out the Magna Carta of 1215. It balanced the stormy politics of England with something having the status of a fundamental norm and it ensured that "revolutions often begun" would end in some meaningful resolution. France, which never had such a fundamental law, usually terminated each internal conflagration with a compromise reflecting the interests of the moment. This is why in France feudalism gave birth to an absolute monarchy and in England to a free government.[47]

This view of the nature of French political history was carried to its culmination in the last chapter. Mably combined here his critique of French politics as never having a norm of liberty to measure against, with a critique of French society, which always neglected the danger that one group would amass power and wealth on the account of the others. This resulted in empty reforms, uncertain policies, inconstant manners, no respect for the laws and "prolonged revolutions of which our history however never speaks." Since the reign of Louis XIII, he charged, luxury and vices had corrupted the French soul. France became servile, fearing despotism without having the courage to love liberty. He alluded to the Maupeou suppression of the *parlement* in 1771, which first brought public criticism and then a reaction on the part of the government as though there were a real danger to its continued existence. In his mind, all of this was frivolous and childish. Frenchmen had a character that actually conformed with that of their government, which meant that "we do not bear in ourselves any principle of revolution."[48]

This observation was further discussed in a note, but not really explained. Did Mably just mean by it a capacity to rise against oppression, or maybe he had in mind a revolution that would change national politics in a manner suggested in his 1758 essay? Later in the final chapter of the *Observations sur l'histoire de France*, he remarked that French aristocracy had a way of thinking and an influence over the nation that obstructed any chance "à une révolution." Every French bourgeois only dreamt of joining the nobility through the purchase of an appropriate position, the result being that very unusual circumstances were needed to change the "esprit nationale," since "the third estate is nothing in France." It is relevant to note that these kinds of sentiments, let alone the lament on the absence of a revolutionary spirit, were not voiced by Mably in works of his that appeared in the 1770s. A good example is *De la legislation, ou principes de loix*, published in 1776. Here the discourse assumed a more detached tone, and the need for a revolution was either mentioned on behalf of other nations, or expressed with a sigh on opportunities that never materialized because of man's thoughtlessness; "How may revolutions, shaped up by circumstances, miscarry because of our foolishness!" In one place in this work, one of the discussants, a Swede, explained to the other, an Englishman, that in non-despotic monarchies one could still hope that the people, conscious of their rights, would oppose an unfair ruler, just as Englishmen began opposing their monarchs during the reign of James I and the Dutch under Philip II. At bottom, he added, was the political culture of a given society; therefore, "why these national habits could not bring about a revolution?"[49] For one anonymous author who hastened to answer Mably, even this sort of discussion appeared to border on subversion. He countered with a work defending monarchy as the most favorable government to the liberty of the individual, and had it prefaced with a letter of support by Voltaire. Censuring Mably for his republican sentiments, he accused him particularly of supporting a "Révolution générale dans le gouvernement" and of contending that in "moderate monarchies" national political conventions might encourage a revolution against an unapproachable ruler. He rejected strongly that kind of turn of events: "Because this revolution will be fatal; because the example of our neighbors should make us give it up."[50]

The case of Mably and "revolution" is probably unique; that of the abbé Raynal rests on circumstantial evidence. The *Histoire philosophique et politique des établissements et du commerce des Européens dans les deux Indes* was published outside France in 1770. It needed some two years to arouse attention, and by 1774, when the second edition appeared, it was already under attack by clergymen and put on the Index. The height of its influence probably came in 1781, when it was condemned in the *parlement* and burned by the official hangman. This was by far the best known and most frequently reprinted of all the works that assaulted the established political and social status quo prior to 1789. Raynal tackled the vast theme of European discoveries and colonization in Africa, Asia and America. Writing in an unreserved "journalistic" style, as if he were conducting a conversation with the reader, he used his general theme also as a lever to pass criticism on European institutions and customs of his time. This, indeed, was the substance of book nineteen which wound up the work. Though marred by factual mistakes and contradictions, the work still contained a central message – the enduring damage done to man's natural rights and interests, that is to his liberty, by oppressive and predatory despotism. In this sense Raynal's quest was not that different from Mably's, which raises also the question of the meaning and significance with which he endowed the word "revolution."

To begin with, it should be noted that Raynal employs the term dozens of times. It is here, perhaps more than in other works of the Enlightenment, including Voltaire's *Essai sur les moeurs*, that the tendency to invoke the word in allusion to a variety of changes, not necessarily political, becomes patently clear. Some of the best examples come in a digression, while describing the Spanish conquest of Mexico, where Raynal tries to explain why Moctezuma, ruler of a vast empire, meekly surrendered to a few hundred adventurers. It had to do, he writes, with an Aztec superstition based on a legend that people coming from the eastern shores would take command of the land; and he goes on to demonstrate that not just Mexicans are susceptible to superstitions. Our world, he says, had experienced, and still does, the impact of "anciennes révolutions." It is constantly circling and rotating, so that this "grande révolution de toute la masse du globe" is the cause of many regional changes ("petites révolutions"), whereby the sea recedes in one area and covers another. All of this is the reason for those devastating inundations, which had brought endless ruin and human misery, and left their indelible memory among men. The recollections of past catastrophes, he continues, inspire fear of disasters to come. It is the origin of so many legends among different peoples about the end of the world, legends that are also encouraged by fears of volcanic eruptions and earthquakes. These superstitious beliefs, he thinks, are particularly rife in America, where the physical marks of "ces révolutions du globe" are more recent and visible. Generally speaking, man, in his fear, tends to give chance occurrences a status of something that is related to the order of things. And since man is accustomed to believe that the stars above are in control of events below, he ascribes to them the cause of all the misfortune which he cannot explain rationally, and the power over "toutes les révolutions" that result. Since political events, which are so important to men, had always been in their eyes dependent on the movement of the stars, they are continually the theme of false predictions.[51]

This curious theorizing, which perhaps says more about the workings of Raynal's mind than about man's mind, does not bode well for a serious consideration by the author of the term "revolution" as a semantic weapon in his fight against despotism. And indeed when one takes up the long chapter on government in book nineteen it turns out that Raynal employs the word there a few times, but neither in a context that would give it a marked significance, nor in passages that reflect his wish of political change. When he surveys England's political history and constitution "revolution" is missing, although he refers there to the "social agreement" achieved with the crowning of William III, following the "unending storms" under the Stuarts. Later on, when the great issue of how to reform the state comes up, it looks as if Raynal had had a second thought on the whole matter. He suddenly recalls that "the state is a very complicated machine," that a measure favoring the interest of one class might be fatal "à toute la nation;" that these "convulsive movements, which are called coups d'état," might affect for the worse an entire national society for centuries to come. Therefore, any innovation should be carefully considered, and carried out only in response to a clear public demand and after consultation with the "volonté générale." In the next chapter, however, he gives a quick rundown of Europe's political development since the Reformation, and ends with a comparison showing the advantage of republican regimes over absolute monarchies. All absolute sovereigns, he claims, hate popular governments and secretly conspire against them because they fear "l'esprit républicain." But even so, they are not going to prevail. Liberty is about to be born from the bosom of oppression. It is in the hearts of all, and the day of awakening is not far ahead. The instruments of despotism will turn out to be its destroyers, and the enemies of humanity, who at present bear arms against it, will end up fighting on its behalf. This vision of the nearby victory of liberty, full of pathos and phrased in such high rhetoric, is nevertheless devoid of the word "revolution."[52]

With this background, why is Raynal at all to be reckoned with those who advanced the significance of the term? The answer is found in the first and last sentences of the work. At the very beginning, as he tells the reader that the discovery of America and the passage across to the Indian Ocean by sailing below the southern tip of Africa had opened a new age in human history, he does not hesitate to define its meaning thus: "Then began a revolution in commerce, in the strength of nations, in the habits, the manufacturing and the government of all the peoples." As we have seen, French historians since Maimbourg, a full century before Raynal, had used the term in order to introduce to their readers the theme of the work with a rhetorical pitch. But here it is much more than that, because what Raynal's words imply is that since the age of the geographic discoveries human history has had a *revolutionary* nature. And indeed he hastens to underscore this point and raises the question whether the revolutions which are still bound to ensue would just bring more change or change with improvement:

> Everything has changed, and has to change still. But the revolutions of the past, and those that are bound to follow, were they, will they be, useful to human nature? Will man have one day more tranquility, happiness and pleasure? Will his condition be better or only changed?[53]

Apparently, Raynal is not concerned here with political change, but with one of more far ranging consequences, relating to human nature itself. It is to this same kind of expected change that he returns at the very conclusion of the work. He proclaims that he had spoken for all men and that all men are equal in his eyes. He had warned the rulers, bringing to their attention the facts of oppression and of the dishonored rights of the subjects. He does not end, however, with a threat, but with a wish that other writers continue the work that would one day unite all civilized nations and terminate the spreading of vice and oppression among the savages. This yearned for conclusion, the true betterment of man's condition, is now termed "this happy revolution" ["cette heureuse révolution"]. More than wishing for a new political order, it is a dream of a world of justice at the end of days.[54]

As we shall see in the next chapter, Raynal's contributions to the discourse of "revolution" did not stop at that. But before concluding the present one, yet a third example is in order, this time of an author who was using the term prior to the 1780s in a significant propagandistic manner. Simon-Nicolas-Henri Linguet, born in Rheims in 1736, had been making a name for himself in Paris since the mid-1760s, both as an author of historical and political essays and as a trial lawyer who handled a number of sensational cases. In both capacities he managed, intentionally, to alienate men of established rank. Some of his ideas, such as his outrageous defense of slavery in Asian despotic governments, brought upon him the enmity of that renowned group of French economists – the Physiocrats; whereas the explosive language he employed in his legal practice pitted him against his colleagues, who by 1775 had him barred from the order of advocates. After serving for some time as editor of a periodical financed by the publisher Pancouke, he left in 1776 to London and started his own journal, the *Annales politiques, civiles et littéraires du dix-huitième siècle*. It quickly became influential all over western Europe, and was also admitted to France, where the king became fond of reading it, in spite of formal official restrictions on its circulation. Several times interrupted, once from September 1780 to May 1782 on account of Linguet's imprisonment in the Bastille, it continued to appear irregularly until 1792. [55]

Linguet had touched the term "revolution" already in one of his earliest works, *Histoire des révolutions de l'empire romain* (1766). But when one examines his theory of civil laws, or "fundamental principles of society," which came out in 1767, it is easily discovered that the term is rarely employed. Moreover, there are no signs that he is earnestly interested in extensive political change as a goal. When he uses the term "revolution," it is in a Montesquieu-like sense of an insurrection in a despotic government; "ce qu'on appelle des révolutions." Also in another work, comparing Asian political systems with those of Europe, when Linguet finally mentions "des révolutions," it is in the context of Asian despotism.[56] But the use is strikingly different in the programmatic introductory essay to the *Annales*, which came out in March-April 1777. Here he launched an overall review of Europe's politics, society, economy and culture in which he also gave attention to the significance of the newly proclaimed independence of the United States. The Americans, he thought, enjoyed the vigor of a young and prosperous people. Having bypassed stages of development which other nations usually needed to go through, their splendor was "the fruit of a swift revolution." He also dared to imagine that one day America would overpower Europe: "The hour of this revolution is uncertain; but it is inevitable as long as America becomes free and prosperous."[57]

These and other instances where he employs the term, hardly prepare the reader for the last part of the introduction, entitled: "Of the society in general: Singular revolution by which Europe is threatened." In contrast with Mably, who had drawn a theoretical model of a political revolution, and with Raynal, who had spoken of a revolution in terms of a great change in human affairs in some distant future, Linguet evokes an almost tangible specter of a menacing insurrection which awaits Europe in a very short time. This revolution would be a result of the despotic character of government and the vast imbalances in the social make-up of Europe. The continent is heading towards "une subversion totale" in a manner resembling the great slave revolts in ancient Rome. Although on the surface everything exudes affluence, writes Linguet, underneath the peasant and the agricultural laborer are agonizing, subordinated to a regime of military oppression and exploitation. He reminds his readers of the fourteenth century Jacquerie in France, and similar violent peasant revolts in England and Germany, all suppressed by the nobility. In the eighteenth century, he goes on, despite the contraction of serfdom, exploitation of the agricultural journeyman continues, and in even a larger scale than before, and it is aggravated by faulty financial arrangements favoring the money lenders. Since governments everywhere back up this socio-economic structure with a repressive military apparatus, it all works to hasten "the hour of the great revolution that I proclaimed at the beginning of this chapter." He sees indications of the coming explosion in instances of ferment among peasants of different countries such as Italy, Bohemia and even France. The immediate future is therefore bound to produce one of two scenarios; either progressive and ever hardening repression by state organized military forces, which would leave Europe covered with skeletons, or a wide scale insurrection, led by a new Spartacus, who would lead his comrades to true liberty by effecting a thorough division of agricultural lands. One or the other of these two calamities is inevitable, proclaims Linguet, and he announces his intention to follow them up in his journal as they come closer to take concrete shape day by day.[58]

As Keith Michael Baker maintains, the actual content of Linguet's diagnosis and predictions was perhaps less important than the tone of urgency with which they were delivered. But there are also other questions to consider here. Given the fact that when they finally gathered momentum the waves of rebellion seemed to respond more to the ideas and impulses of the Enlightenment than to the accumulated rages of an exploited proletariat, it would appear that Linguet not only failed to perceive the goals of the revolution but completely misjudged its circumstances. It is true that he consistently propounded the peasants and wage earners as the truly exploited European classes. Still, one wonders to what extent we are not facing here, once again, his habitual tendency to stir up emotions by saying the opposite of almost everybody else. As we have seen, if they spoke of "revolution" al all, the *philosophes* liked to tie it to the compelling forces of the new ideas and values. Linguet, on the contrary, wanted to link it with a state of undisturbed coercion and lack of material benefits. In this connection it is relevant to add that he displayed a lukewarm attitude toward the insurgents in America. Moreover, by the mid-1780s he appeared more intent on ingratiating himself with the French monarchy than committed to the prospect of revolution.[59] But finally, he too employed the term in the context of change accomplished by the force of ideas. This comes in a passage of an essay which he published in 1788 on Voltaire, in which he considered the influence of the writings of that great *philosophe* on education, law, justice and government. Although he had no power to effect real reforms, Linguet wrote there, Voltaire "had an influence on the general state of mind [l'esprit général] which produced them in the long run, and he made a true revolution in this state of mind." He thought that before Voltaire arbitrary acts of government never raised the least objection or protest. After him, no government could disregard the public voice and its outcry on behalf of reason and justice.[60]

With this concession of Linguet's to the power of ideas, we might conclude the survey of the place of "revolution" in the writings of the *philosophes* prior to the molding of the epithet the "American

Revolution." The balance does not show a clear preference for the term. Although they left us an overwhelming evidence of their acute awareness that ideas could stimulate real change, only on rare occasions do we come across point-blank assertions in their writings that the Enlightenment was bound to end up with a "revolution." Voltaire and Rousseau intimated cryptically to that effect, and Raynal in an even more open manner, but hardly spelling out the full extent of his vision. Mably, on the other hand, did not (or could not) publish the works in which he pursued this subject, whereas Linguet spoke from England of an imminent "revolution," but of one that was not the product of a change in ideas. If this summary indeed reflects the general tenor of the writings of the *philosophes*, then it would also mean that up to about the late 1770s "revolution" was not an issue seriously discussed in the intellectual circles. Neither can we say that it was considered at that stage a political concept to be acted upon, nor can we argue that the *philosophes* endowed it with a definite sense of a world-wide historic transformation of human affairs. In the next two chapters we will try to sort out how exactly these two new attributes of "revolution" gathered wider credibility in the wake of American independence and its repercussions.

Chapter Eight

From "Independence" to "Revolution" in America

When relating to the events of the years 1776 to 1783 many, perhaps most works on the early history of the United States, indiscriminately employ the terms American Revolution and American Independence (or American War of Independence). Still, the meaning of the terms is substantially different. The second denotes a struggle through which the thirteen English colonies on the Atlantic seaboard acquired a status of a sovereign nation; but the first suggests more than that. It implies as well the advent of a new political order, fulfilling ideas of individual liberty and democracy and suggesting itself as a model of a modern plan of government to be followed elsewhere. Indeed, this meaning of the term is almost undeniable in light of the significance that the word "revolution" has taken in the past two hundred years. Therefore, we should be interested to know how and when the term "revolution" joined "independence" in reference to the events surrounding the launching of the first modern republic. Moreover, as we shall see in the next chapter, this semantic development impelled a much tighter link between "revolution" and the idea of political change.

Ideas exchanged much later between Thomas Jefferson and John Adams may serve us as a point of departure. In a letter written on 10 August 1815, Jefferson addressed himself to "the subject of the American Revolution." He doubted whether "the life and soul of history" of this great theme could ever be written, since most of the discussions in the Continental Congress, leading to important decisions, had been held behind closed doors, and no notes or records were ever taken of them. In his often quoted answer, dated 24 August 1815, Adams espoused a different view:

As to the history of the revolution, my ideas may be peculiar, perhaps singular. What do I mean by the revolution? The war? That was no part of the revolution; it was only an effect and consequence of it. The revolution was in the minds of the people, and this was effected from 1760 to 1775, in the course of fifteen years, before a drop of blood was drawn at Lexington. The records of thirteen legislatures, the pamphlets, newspapers, in all the colonies ought to be consulted during that period, to ascertain the steps by which the public opinion was enlightened and informed concerning the authority of parliament over the colonies.[1]

Clearly, in Adams's view of 1815, the revolution actually consisted of the change in American political consciousness, brought about during the long propaganda campaign which preceded the opening of hostilities in April 1775. However, the term "revolution" was rarely employed then, and it is generally absent from the pamphlets, manifestoes, proclamations or newspaper articles throughout the years leading to 4 July 1776. To be sure, it is not absent altogether. For example, in an article published in the *Boston Gazette* of 19 December 1768, Samuel Adams could mention "the glorious revolution by William the third" to substantiate his claim that since that event a standing army could be raised in time of peace only with the consent of parliament.[2] But neither he nor, it would seem, anybody else used the term "revolution" in relation to the aspirations or aims of the then ongoing colonial opposition to the British government.

This absence of the term in the 1760s is not devoid of a certain irony. It appears that the generation about to embark on political independence was unaware of the fact that the colonies, so to speak, had already experienced one "revolution." The event in question consisted of a series of uprisings against the colonial authorities in April 1689, as soon as news arrived from England of the unseating of James II by William of Orange. In Boston the governor of the Dominion of New England, Sir Edmund Andros, was arrested, charged with enacting "laws destructive of the Liberty of the People," and sent to England to stand trial; there however he was released and after three years returned to America as governor of Virginia. In 1691 a short tract, *The Revolution in New England Justified* by Edward Rawson appeared in Boston. It opened with the following announcement: "The Doctrine of *Passive Obedience* and *Non*

Resistance, which a sort of men did of late when they thought the World would never change, cry up a Divine Truth, is by means of the happy *Revolution* in these Nations, exploded, and the Assertors of it become ridiculous."[3] The author then explained that the "revolution" in New England had been undertaken in compliance with that in the mother country, and because the Americans considered the officials appointed by King James as usurpers who deprived the inhabitants of their old charter of government. It would seem, however, that in addition to gathering courage for the uprising upon receiving news of the events in England, the use of the new term reflected a certain artificial trendiness on the other side of the Atlantic. Nevertheless, it did not enter the political discourse of the Americans to the extent of becoming an expression to be used on the eve of their separation from England.

This can easily be confirmed. We have it from Jefferson himself that until February 1776, when people first became acquainted with Thomas Paine's *Common Sense*, nobody even dared openly to use the word "independence," let alone "revolution."[4] As for Paine himself, throughout his epoch making lengthy pamphlet, with its repeated insistence on "independence" and use of terms such as "separation," "civil war," "natural rights" and "continental form of government," the word "revolution" is employed only once, and not in reference to the situation in America. This is especially significant because there are some passages where Paine actually endows the colonial struggle with aims going much further than just the attainment of self-government. He claims that the Americans have "every opportunity, and every encouragement before us to form the noblest, purest constitution, on the face of the earth. We have it in our power to begin the world over again."[5] But in this clear expression of revolutionary fervor and consciousness he completely refrains from using the term "revolution."

When he does mention "revolution" Paine obviously has in mind the events of 1688 in England. It is used as he refutes the notion that a monarchy of hereditary succession is the best guarantee against civil wars. "The whole history of England," says Paine, "disowns the fact. Thirty kings and two minors have reigned in that distracted kingdom since the Conquest; in which time there have been (including the Revolution), no less than eight civil wars and nineteen rebellions."[6] Actually, this single employment of the term (with a capital R) in *Common Sense* points towards explaining why the word was generally absent from the pre-1776 political vocabulary. In America, as in England, the word had become attached to 1688 in the sense of an extraordinary occurrence, while at the same time the usual meaning of the term conveyed the impression of sudden, violent political ruptures, rather unplanned and full of disorder.

No wonder, therefore, that that standard piece of revolutionary literature, the Declaration of Independence, has no trace of the term. Likewise, the immediate reaction to the event by contemporaries who took part in it revealed at least a reluctance to use the term. Thus, of the twelve letters of members of the Continental Congress who reported on the debates and the framing of the declaration, only one, sent by John Adams to his wife Abigail on 3 July 1776, employed the word. "You will see in a few days," wrote Adams, "a Declaration setting forth the causes which have impelled us to this mighty revolution, and the reasons which will justify it in the sight of God and man."[7] Also Samuel Adams, in a letter of 27 July 1776, associated the notion of revolution to the Declaration of Independence: "Was there ever a Revolution brot [sic] about, especially so important as this without great internal Tumults & Violent Convulsions!"[8] In both cases, however, particularly in the second, the use of the term still echoed the then current negative attitude toward revolutions.

Furthermore, it is not to be assumed that these early associations of "revolutions" with independence were anything more than incidental expressions. In the case of John Adams it is possible to track his perception of the concept during the next years as revealed in his diary. He rarely used the term, and when he did it was in an almost slighting manner, or in circumstances which implied that he was merely citing the words of others. As late as 17 June 1783, when he was in Versailles at the negotiations for the peace treaty, Adams still reiterated the old view which saw revolution as a fatal occurrence. He described a casual exchange on the subject with the Spanish ambassador, Count Aranda: "He said Tout, en ce monde, a été Révolution. I said true – universal History was but a Series of Revolutions. Nature delighted in Changes, and the World was but a String of them. But one Revolution was quite enough for the Life of a Man. I hoped, never to have to do with another."[9]

Reading early attempts to clarify the historical meaning of 4 July 1776, one is impressed again by the almost complete absence of the term "revolution." A case in point is the "Oration on the Advantages of American Independence," the first public address of its kind, delivered in Charleston, South Carolina by David Ramsay to commemorate the second birthday of the United States. Ramsay, the future historian of the revolution, is already hailing the new nation as "the first people in the world, who have had it in their power to choose their own form of government." He is confident that "the cause of America is the cause of Human Nature," and believes that the American experience is not only going to inspire other people to extirpate tyranny, but "teach mankind to plough, sow, plant, build and improve the rough of Nature." Nevertheless, he lacks an epithet that would cover this great idea other than "American Independence"; although in one place he employs the phrase "the fruits of our glorious revolution."[10] Benjamin Rush, the famous physician and Ramsay's former teacher at the College of Philadelphia, who corresponded on 10 December 1778, with the historian William Gordon, longed to see America becoming an asylum for "the persecuted and the oppressed of all countries."[11] For him 4 July 1776 amounted to a first step in the establishment of liberty. At that point Rush too had no use for the term "revolution."

This near absence of the term "revolution" in the immediate years following independence receives a final corroboration when we survey the writings of Paine. In December 1776, he wrote the first of a series of fourteen political pamphlets called "The American Crisis," the last of which appeared in December 1783. These were well distributed and helped sustain Americans' belief in the righteousness of their cause throughout the war. Paine, who signed the pamphlets as "Common Sense," frequently used combative language, charged with invectives against the British government and its commanding generals. Time and again he praised and defended American "independence," but (except in the final pamphlet) nowhere employed the term "revolution" as a possible label for either the separation from Britain or the ongoing struggle to preserve that act. The word that Paine used was "crisis," which in itself indicated a decision on his part in the choice of terminology, since the employment of the word "revolution" would have fitted better what he had in mind (at least from the point of view of the modern reader). In one passage, where he did employ the word "revolution," it was in the context of toying with an idea of instigating a rebellion against George III in England, following a landing of an American force.[12]

But while Paine's series of pamphlets was in progress the term "American Revolution" appeared, possibly for the first time, at the head of an official publication sponsored by the United States government. It was printed in February 1779 by way of reply to the British Commission on Conciliation, which had come over from England in the previous year. When the commission published, in October 1778, an offer of pardon to all Americans who would accept conciliation, the Continental Congress appointed a three man committee to deal with the matter. Its long text of rebuttal, compiled by Gouverneur Morris, the young talented member from New York, was printed at the expense of the Congress in an edition of 1,300 copies. It was entitled *Observations on the American Revolution.*[13]

Morris was an unlikely personality to launch such a weighty epithet as the "American Revolution." Although he acted at the time as the foremost publicist among the members of the Congress, he was rather conservative by inclination and conviction, and more interested in financial, military and diplomatic affairs than in ideology. In a paper dealing mainly with issues of taxation, which he had written in 1774, Morris summarized his own conservative outlook with the words: "I think government should be founded on stationary and not on revolutionary principles."[14] Therefore, perhaps his coining of a new phrase was not unrelated to what James Madison later described as a "fondness for saying things and advancing doctrines that no one else would." Indeed, there is something more to that. In January 1779, about a month before the publication *Observations on the American Revolution*, Morris succeeded in convincing the Congress to dismiss Paine from his position as secretary to the committee of foreign affairs, a move that came as an off-shoot of the Deane-Lee scandal. In a speech in the Congress he called Paine this "mere Adventurer from England, without fortune, without family or connections, ignorant even of Grammer."[15] Clearly, Morris was not about to borrow Paine's epithet of "American Crisis." He must have felt a need to choose his own.

When we turn to the work itself, actually a long pamphlet of just over one-hundred and twenty pages, it is quickly discovered that the use of the new label is somewhat restrained. To begin with, much of the text consists of long citations from official proclamations, addresses, letters and manifestoes arguing the legitimacy of the American position. All of this material is devoid of the word "revolution." Except as part of the title of the work, it is used by

Morris (without "American") apparently just three times at the beginning and the very end of the tract.[16]   In the first instance, discussing the conditions of "the British colonies before the revolution," the word more or less signifies independence.   Morris claims here that North America grew up politically from settlements of talented Europeans, weary of the lack of freedom in the old world, who, out of necessity and habit, subjected themselves to the king of England upon his promise to afford them protection.   In his view the Americans were tied to a prince, not to England and her parliament. As free people they never relinquished their right to independence once the crown should violate its contract with them.   The action taken by the Americans on 4 July 1776 is thus compared by him to that of the English people themselves against their king in 1688; "that right exercised in the revolution of England, demonstrated since, and generally admitted, must draw with it the right to independence, which is above stated."   Only on the last page did he allow himself to place the term within the context of a visionary expression of faith in the future of America, and even here the manner of his use of the word was rhetorically stale.   This whole passage stands in contrast to the polemical character of the work.   Having reiterated his opinion that independence was practically secured, Morris ends with proclaiming America the future "asylum of mankind," the home of the poor and the oppressed, and also the great new center of the world's commerce and industry.   For all that had happened, and that which is in store for them, Americans should thank "the Universal Parent – that God of the heavens and of earth, whose infinite majesty, for providential favor during the last revolution, almighty power in our preservation from impending ruin,... we cannot cease with gratitude and with deep humility to praise, to reverence and adore."

It is not clear whether the new label in the title of Morris's work had an immediate influence.   Paine certainly abstained initially from using it, although in his case the enmity toward Morris may explain the reason.   For the next three years Paine would stick to his own vocabulary, and although he finally adopted the term "revolution" it was instigated by a wholly different source.   But to follow this development, it is necessary to cross the ocean to France.   What was intricate and challenging to the Americans, accustomed to the view that revolutions were a murky business (except that of 1688), could not be more natural when observed from the other side of the Atlantic. To the French the confrontation between the colonials and the British government, escalating into violence, gave the impression of a "revolution" even before the declaration of independence.[17] Thus when Raynal completed his survey of the still continuing conflict in North America, he had no hesitation about its title. As it happened, the manuscript was taken to England, where it was published in March 1781 simultaneously in French and English.[18]

For our purpose here it is appropriate to refer to the English version, entitled *The Revolution of America*. Raynal dealt therein with a variety of themes. He gave a factual account of the conflict, which obviously was loaded with mistakes. He analyzed the motives behind the policies adopted by England and France, not overlooking the contradictions in the position assumed by his own country. But he also touched upon the subject of revolutions; what are the general causes of a revolutionary upheaval and what are the specific causes in the case of America. His premise was clear: "There is no society but which has the same right to change, as their ancestors had to adopt, their form of government. Upon this point, it is with societies as if they were at the first moment of their civilization." Furthermore, nobody is obliged to live under a tyranny, a form of government which is abominable to God, who "has imprinted on the heart of man the sacred love of liberty." Therefore, those who rise up in the name of liberty are as if undertaking the cause of the whole human race. Onlookers, who are being oppressed in their turn, feel as if their own chains are becoming lighter. "These great revolutions of liberty, moreover, admonish despots. They warn them... not to trust to impunity without end."

Was that too the case of America? Raynal had some reservations. In his words: "None of those energetic causes, which have produced so many revolutions upon the globe, existed in North America." There the British government upheld the laws, was tolerant in matters of religion and respected the customs of the people. Nor could it be charged with the careless use of arbitrary power, committing outrages and the like. The whole question, in Raynal's opinion, "was reduced to the knowing whether the mother country had or had not, the right to lay, directly or indirectly, a slight tax upon the colonies." He found it an "almost metaphysical question... scarcely of sufficient importance to cause the multitude to rise."[19]

It must have taken some time before Raynal's book reached America, because the *Letter Addressed to the Abbé Raynal on the Affairs of North-America; In which the Mistakes in the Abbé's*

Account of the Revolution of America are Corrected and Cleared Up, was completed by Paine only in August 1782. Paine found it necessary to write yet another lengthy pamphlet to expose the "misconceived and misstated" causes which Raynal suggested for the rupture between England and her colonies. He especially objected to Raynal's views on the missing "energetic causes of the revolution." Raynal erred, wrote Paine, because he had been observing America from far away and could not perceive the changes effected there between 1763 and 1776. This led him to declare to the world, according to Paine, "that there was no real cause for the revolution."

Paine criticized Raynal for not appreciating correctly the "usurpation of the Americans' most precious and sacred rights" by such measures as the Stamp Act of 1764 or the Declaratory Act of 1766. He then advanced his strongest argument: "Had the Abbé said that the causes which produced the revolution in America were originally *different* from those which produced revolutions in other parts of the globe, he had been right. Here the value and quality of liberty, the nature of government, and the dignity of man, were known and understood; and the attachment of the Americans to these principles produced a revolution as a natural and almost unavoidable consequence." This is why, claimed Paine, the American revolution had an unprecedented significance, effecting a profound change in the manner of government. "Those of other nations are, in general, little more than the history of their quarrels."

Paine's arguments were not devoid of exaggerations and one-sidedness. But the contrast between his view of revolution and Raynal's should not be overlooked. To the latter's concept of peoples' ephemeral right to vindicate their liberty, Paine substituted the view of revolution as a solid acquisition of a more just system of government. On the other hand, it is also crucial to observe that while he took issue with Raynal's ideas, Paine borrowed from him the term "revolution," a word he had seldom used before and never in the same context. Now it acquired relevance to the conflict between the thirteen North American colonies and their mother country, and to its outcome. Moreover, in Paine's new use of the term it was now given meanings such as an accelerated process of change, as can be seen from the phrasing: "Our style and manner of thinking have undergone a revolution more extraordinary than the political revolution of the country."[20]

It is almost certain that the combined effect of Raynal's book and Paine's reply gave currency to the phrase "American Revolution." Besides the 1781 edition in French, published in London as well as in Dublin and Stockholm, Raynal had a second English version by another printer which appeared in London in the same year. This last was reprinted in 1782 in Edinburgh, London, Norwich (Connecticut), Philadelphia and Salem. Paine's *Letter*, which first came out in Philadelphia in September 1782, was reprinted in Dublin, London and Trenton (New Jersey) before the end of that year, and the Philadelphia edition went through three printings by 1783. On 7 September 1782 Paine wrote to General Washington, presenting him with fifty copies of the *Letter* to be distributed to the army. In his reply of 18 September, Washington acknowledged the gift. He too then adopted the new term. In his appeal to the nation of 8 June 1783 he used the term twice: first as he doubted "whether the Revolution must ultimately be considered as a blessing or a curse: a blessing or a curse not to the present age alone, for with our fate will the destiny of unborn Millions by involved." Later on in the same document he called for measures to strengthen the ties among the states under one "Sovereign Authority" so that "the fruits of the Revolution" would be preserved.[21] As for Paine, the switch over to the new term was reaffirmed in his last pamphlet of the "American Crisis," which came out in December 1783. Right in the opening sentence he declared "the greatest and completest revolution the world ever knew, gloriously and happily accomplished."[22]

In 1784 the new term was bolstered by yet another work. This was the *Observation on the Importance of the American Revolution and the Means of Making it a Benefit to the World* by Richard Price, whose earlier work has been already discussed in the previous chapter. As we have noted, in February 1776 a long pamphlet of his appeared in London, in which he expressed sympathy for the Americans and championed their rights.[23] The tract included passages which resembled ideas of the Declaration of Independence. It ran through numerous editions and reprints in England and America, and started a wave of polemics in England, where most opinions were against Price. In recognition the Continental Congress in October 1778 offered Price United States citizenship and asked for his help in matters of finances. Although he declined to leave England, Price later mentioned in a letter to Benjamin Rush that because of his support of America and opposition to the war "I have gone thro' much abuse and some danger in this country."

Price corresponded with several prominent Americans, among them Benjamin Franklin. In his letter to Rush dated 26 June 1783, he noted that "The struggle has been glorious on the part of America; and it has now issued just as I wished it to issue; in the emancipation of the American States and the establishment of their independence... I think it one of the important revolutions that has ever taken place in the world. It makes a new opening in human affairs, which may prove an introduction to time of more light and liberty and virtue than have been yet known."[24]

The line of thinking expressed in this letter to Rush, was expanded and further developed in Price's essay which was published in the following year. This was a mature work, written almost as an intellectual testament. Price considered the changes effected in America as means to form a society of new values; commitment to peace, to individual liberties, to education, even to the just distribution of wealth (his tract was somewhat rejected in the South because of the author's criticism of slavery). America's was singled out as a model for future revolutions.[25]

Price's *Observations on the Importance of the American Revolution* appeared in English in 1784 both in London and Boston, and had a French translation, published in London by the comte de Mirabeau in the same year. Another London edition in English came out in 1785, and yet others in Dublin, New Haven, Philadelphia and Trenton; it was published in Charleston in 1786. The work therefore enjoyed the widest circulation. It thus completed the trend toward establishing the term "American Revolution" as a standard label for the coming into being of the United States, with its distinct meaning and claim.

From here on, men who had not used the term before also made it their own, although the transition was not rapid and smooth in every case. Benjamin Rush, who wrote to Price on 25 May 1786, easily adopted the term "American Revolution," which fitted well with his thoughts about the challenges facing the new nation;[26] as did David Ramsay, whose *History of the Revolution of South Carolina from a British Province to an Independent State* was published in Trenton in 1785. Ramsay took steps to have his work translated into French. He wrote to Thomas Jefferson, then serving as American minister to France. In his reply of 31 August 1785 from Paris Jefferson remarked: "I am much pleased to see a commencement of those special histories of the late revolution which must be written first before a good general one can be expected."[27] Jefferson's employment of "the late revolution" would perhaps indicate that the equation of "revolution" with "independence" was then not entirely acceptable to him. But whatever doubts he and others may have had about the use of the term, the die was cast. By 1789, when Ramsay's major work, *The History of the American Revolution*, appeared in Philadelphia, the new terminology had already gained a wide diffusion.

As we have seen, the term "American Revolution" postdates the Declaration of Independence by several years. Though it appeared in Gouverneur Morris' pamphlet of 1779, there are good reasons to believe that the most decisive contribution to the new formula came only in 1781 and 1782 with Raynal's *Revolution of America* and Paine's *Letter*. This exchange not only got wide public attention, it led to an altered meaning of the term "revolution," when Paine substituted the older notion of change of government through violence and turmoil with the concept of a revolution as a step toward a worthier, more deserving political system. Price's tract of 1784 gave more substance to this new concept of revolution, and at the same time added a final measure of legitimacy to the phrase "American Revolution." No doubt, by the mid-1780s, as the young nation became conscious of the fact that its struggle for independence had been won, a need was felt for a communicable idiom that would express its self-awareness of its recent formative experience. The term "American Revolution" also answered that need.

We can see a clear response to this need in the "third part" of the *Grammatical Institute of the English Language* by the famous lexicographer and educator Noah Webster, first published in 1785. The purpose of this "third part" was to familiarize American youth with the geography, history and system of government of the United States. In the preface to the third edition, signed October 1787, Webster complained that until then books generally used in the schools neglected "the writings that marked the revolution, which are not inferior in any respect to the orations of Cicero and Demosthenes,..." He inserted therefore into his primer not only data on geography and history, but also sketches of important battles of the War of Independence and letters and declarations of leaders of the new nation, which in his view could kindle patriotic feelings in the young students. In various places he saw fit to educate the readers on the importance and meaning of the revolution. Political independence was not everything: "A revolution in the form of government is but a revolution in name; unless attended with a change of principles and manners, which are the springs of government." Therefore, "A fundamental mistake of the Americans has been, that they considered the revolution as completed, when it was just begun." In Webster's opinion the change in the American ways of life, as a legacy of the revolution which had yet to be fulfilled, was of the widest implications. Even American women had a role to play – for instance, once they decided to stop imitating foreign styles and say: "we will *give* the laws of fashion to our *own nation*, instead of *receiving* them from *another*; we will perform our part of the revolution." Finally, he gave the students a reasoned explanation of "the immediate and necessary consequences of the American revolution." An event of that magnitude, "detaching millions of people from their parent nation, could not have been effected without the operation of powerful causes." But rather than enumerating the causes, he went on to stress the collective mental process that stood at the bottom of modern revolutions: "A change of sentiment prepares the way for a change of government, and when that change of sentiment had become general in America, nothing could have prevented a revolution."[28]

Chapter Nine

French (and English) Radicals and the "American Revolution"

The consequential effect of the American Revolution in shaping the climate of opinion in France of the 1780s is a well documented theme; the most detailed survey is perhaps still a veteran work by Bernard Faÿ, written in a vivid style.[1] As Talleyrand later wrote in his memoirs, recalling the years just prior to 1789: "We talked of nothing but America."[2] As we shall see, some of the most outstanding French political writers of those years, among them Turgot, Mably, Condorcet and Mirabeau, saw fit to examine the transformation that had taken place in America with the clear intent of gleaning from it moral and practical lessons for Europe, and particularly for France. They were impressed with the ability of the Americans to write constitutions and form governments in a deliberate manner, through a procedure relying on representative assemblies embodying the principle of the sovereignty of the people. They also observed with interest the methods employed in America to define the functions and offices of government, to maintain norms of equality before the law, and prevent the abuse of power. In the light of what was to ensue, those inspired by the American experience who yearned for changes at home, might be looked upon as the pre-1789 radicals. It is true that the term "radical" was not used in France in a political sense before the Restoration of 1815, but it was beginning to be heard in England in the 1780s in reference to reforms in the system of parliamentary representation.[3] Therefore, by applying it to French authors making a stand on behalf of political reforms, we are not tainting them with an entirely anachronistic label.

Within the wider theme of the impact of American independence, what should be of foremost interest to us here is the role played by the

term "American Revolution," and as a sequel to that the new status
which the word "revolution" now attained in European political
discourse. As we have seen, the phrase "American Revolution" was
really a new ideological formula, which quickly emerged in the early
1780s. It would appear therefore quite safe to assume that this phrase
was indeed the lever that finally propelled "revolution" upward,
endowing it with a sense of urgency, and with the meaning of a code
word standing for a whole program. However, as plausible as this
inference appears from the nature of the discussion in this study, it
still has to be stressed, given the absence of a clear judgment on this
issue elsewhere. For example, an author of one comprehensive study
on the modern ideas of revolution argued not long ago that the term
might have been brought to France in the late 1780s from Germany,
where the person who had begun to propagate its use had supposedly
been none other than the King of Prussia, Frederick II.[4] That an
interpretation of this mold should be seriously maintained only proves
that a detailed survey of the circumstances of "revolution" in the
1780s is still in order.

As early as 1777 Jeanne Manon Philipon, soon to become Mme
Roland, wrote to a friend: "I am very glad to share with you the
thought about the importance of this revolution; I follow it with
interest, and I desire the liberty of America as a just revenge over so
many manners of violation of natural right..."[5] But these were the
words of an articulate young woman in her early twenties. They
should not be taken to mean more than that from the very start the
term linked itself, here and there, to an exchange of views over
America. A corroboration is gained from an examination of the
Affaires de l'Angleterre et de l'Amérique, the semi-clandestine
journal published in Paris (although it gave the place of publication as
"Anvers") from the spring of 1776 to the autumn of 1779. Its author
was Edmé-Jacques Genêt, who apparently received financial support
from the minister of foreign affairs, the comte de Vergennes.
Throughout the three years of the journal's existence Genêt did much
to spread information about America and make its cause popular with
the French public. He published a translation of the Declaration of
Independence less than two months after it was proclaimed, and
afterwards added the texts of the constitutions of the individual states,
in addition to news about the conduct of the war, opinions in England
and the policies adopted by France. He also got in touch and was
helped by the American envoys to France, Benjamin Franklin and

John Adams. All of this was undertaken, of course, in an effort to counteract the propaganda of newspapers supporting the British side, and in order to accomplish the task Genêt even printed a full translation of Richard Price's long pamphlet of 1776 which had defended the right of the Americans to a separate government. However, although the journal employed the word "révolution" a few times, it was done in a perfunctory and almost purposeless manner. The expression used most was "guerre d'Amérique."[6]

But even before the journal ended its existence, the first French book on the conflict on the other side of the Atlantic came out with "revolution" in its title. This was the *Abrégé de la révolution de l'Amérique angloise* by Pierre Ulric Dubuisson, which was published in Paris late in 1778. On the top of all the pages inside, a short title hovered with an even more promising phrasing – "Révolution des États-Unis d'Amérique." The author was a native of Saint Domingue, who had collected his material chiefly from newspapers. Coming to France earlier that same year, he hastily put together a detailed account of events since 1774, clearly intended to quench the thirst of the public for information on the subject. Although here the term appeared in the text as well with some frequency, it was handled in a manner still far from using it as a symbol for a great historic transformation. In the preface one came upon a statement assuring the reader that the recent recognition of the United States by France gave respectability to "a revolution, which will one day change the political interests of all the nations of the one and the other hemispheres," but apparently the preface was not written by the author.[7] Two years later, Antoine Marie Cerisier, a secretary at the French embassy in The Hague, published a collection of nine dialogues where *Le destin de l'Amérique* was discussed. Most of the fictitious speakers here represented English political personalities, who were obviously opposed to the Americans. Only in the last dialogue, where the main speaker was a philosopher, the idea that England should give liberty to the Americans and help to end all vestiges of colonialism elsewhere, was finally developed. Lord North then branded the philosopher a traitor, but subsequently came to appreciate the nobility of the idea. And yet, it is remarkable that even the philosopher failed to use "revolution."

Michel René Hilliard d'Auberteuil, who had visited New England in 1777-78, added a new outlook to the discussion. His *Essais historiques et politiques sur les Anglo-Americains*, published in

Brussels in two volumes in 1781-82, put some stress on the global significance of "the revolution, the history of which I am the first to undertake." He listed the names of some sixty military officers, headed by the marquis de La Fayette, who had volunteered to fight for American independence even before France concluded a formal treaty with the United States. But his views on the wider impact of the events contained a strange forewarning. He saw American independence possibly leading to an entire change of the political system of Europe, as well as to many inevitable wars, which might continue for a whole century and cause the downfall of several nations. Even so, at the end of his work he emphatically rejected the notion "that the revolution could not be considered complete as long as England persisted in sending over more military units." He assured his readers that the vastness of the United States, its resources, population and the character of its government, which secured the civilian authority against an attempt of a military takeover, would prove an adequate guarantee to its continued independence.[8] When this work was republished in Paris in 1783, its title changed to *Essais historiques et politiques sur la révolution de l'Amérique septentrionale*. This was a shift of no small relevance, since it combined with other indications. In the same year Cerisier published in Brussels and Amsterdam a French translation of Thomas Paine's letter to the abbé Raynal. As we remember, in that pamphlet the latter's unappreciative view of the revolution in his *Révolution de l'Amérique* of 1781 was strongly combated, though the new term got endorsed.

The stage was being set for a more serious debate over the significance of the "American Revolution." But before we delve into the French segment of it, we should take note of the language that was used at that time in the works of an English author. Thomas Pownall had spent seven years in America, returning to England in 1760 after having served as governor of South Carolina. As much as Edmund Burke, who criticized the imprudence of the policy towards the colonies, he too became conspicuous during the debates in Parliament over America. In 1780 he introduced a bill designed to hasten the making of peace. That same year John Almon published Pownall's long pamphlet, *A Memorial most humbly addressed to the Sovereigns of Europe on the present State of Affairs between the Old and New World*. Although the name of the author was missing, his identity was hinted at in Almon's preface. The main idea, and Pownall put it forward forcefully, announced that "The independence of America is fixed as fate; she is mistress of her own fortune." In fact, Pownall saw America as a coming power which would soon affect the European balance of states. He argued that England's war against France and Spain could not alter the realities on the other side of the Atlantic, and predicted an eventual wave of insurrections in South America. In addition, he went on to consider the newborn political entity in America as a novel experiment in the history of mankind. Pownall praised the inquisitiveness and sense of practicality of the Americans, their ability to apply themselves to almost any kind of human endeavor, and their manner of acquiring, disseminating and making good use of information. These traits, together with the huge resources at their disposal, he claimed, would certainly ensure that America would become a great empire. Significantly, however, Pownall declined to use the word "revolution." This term took over only when the pamphlet appeared in 1781 in Amsterdam in an abridged and faulty French translation, entitled *Pensées sur la révolution de l'Amérique Unie.* Its publication might have been encouraged by John Adams, who was then in The Hague. The new preface, containing phrases which echoed the language of Raynal, referred to the importance of Pownall's essay "at a time when this Revolution has captured the attention of both the old World and the new," and employed the epithet "la Révolution Américaine." This was of course the terminology of the French editor, because two years later, when Pownall issued a further pamphlet on the theme of American independence, this time with his name of the title page, his use of the word "revolution" was still noticeably hesitant.[9]

If Raynal had nothing to do with the preface of the 1781 French translation of Pownall's tract, he nevertheless wielded in that year a great deal of influence in European intellectual circles with respect to America. Together with the publication of his *Révolution de l'Amérique*, Raynal announced the setting up of a prize of 1,200 livres to be awarded by the Academy of Lyons for a tract addressing the question whether the discovery of America had been useful or harmful to mankind. It was to be bestowed by 1783, but was never given, because the answers were not deemed satisfactory (according to Raynal and members of the Academy). Of the tracts submitted, four were subsequently printed, including two by the abbé Louis Genty and the marquis de Chastellux.[10] They both viewed the discovery of the New World as an event not devoid of a certain misfortune for mankind, since it rekindled a large scale use of slavery. But they also touched upon the issue of the recent American struggle for freedom, and acclaimed it as the threshold of a new era. Genty, designated on the title page of his tract as royal censor (among other ranks), even termed the independence of the Anglo-Americans "the event the most likely to hasten the revolution which should restore happiness on earth."[11] It should be observed, however, that in this case "revolution" was not an epithet for the sum of changes that had taken place in North America; it was rather an expression of faith in the march of history towards an age of greater equality among men, exactly as Raynal had seen it back in the early 1770s at the end of his *Histoire philosophique et politique.*

The choice of Genty not to term American independence a "revolution" is matched by Chastellux. He too, in a short and truly insignificant tract, apparently written in 1783, lauded the new political structure erected by Franklin, Washington, Hancock and the Adamses, yet bypassed the word "revolution."[12] Indeed, here the omission comes as a great surprise. Chastellux had visited the United States in the years 1780 to 1782, meeting almost all the important personalities of the struggle for independence. He even published there an early version of his travel-diary, whose completed and reworked text appeared in Paris in 1786. In several places in this work the word "revolution" is employed, but the impression is that in doing so Chastellux might have reiterated words of his American interlocutors. This is especially plausible with regard to his account of a conversation with Samuel Adams in Philadelphia on 8 December 1780, where the expression is: "The revolution has been accomplished, and now the Republic is beginning; it is like a newborn child, which must be nourished and reared."[13] In a short essay on arts and sciences in America, which he wrote on the eve of his return to France, it might be observed that he could also handle the term on his own. He writes there of the two principles that guided the Americans "in the present revolution"; a positive principle consisting of the exercise of reason in choosing a government best suited for their needs, and a negative one, expressed in the actions they took in defying Britain.[14] But as mentioned, the term does not occur in the essay which Chastellux entered for the competition at the Academy of Lyons (if indeed that essay belonged to him).

The Academy of Toulouse also set up an essay prize competition, of which two tracts subsequently appeared in print, authored by

Chevalier Deslandes and Jean Baptiste Mailhe. Here the subject was not the discovery of America and its significance, but rather "the greatness and the importance of the revolution which happened to take place in North America." The phrasing displayed, however, a certain ambivalence. While referring to its greatness and importance, it still regarded the revolution to be an event of an almost accidental nature ("qui vient de s'opérer"). Mailhe, the winner of this contest in 1784, perhaps aided by his being an advocate of the *parlement* of Toulouse, actually composed a short address in high rhetoric. He called America's "the greatest and the most important of the revolutions," but quickly added that the greatness was partly due to the courage of French volunteers. While conceding that the revolution had an importance that transcended its own time and place, he made it clear that he did not regard America as a model for France. The same irresolute attitude was reflected when he came to deal with "revolutions" in historical perspective. "It is during revolutions that great quality is formed," he wrote, and he cited as examples the violent crises that preceded the achievements of Augustus, Pope Leo X and Louis XIV. But shortly afterwards he felt compelled to remind his readers that "it was observed how peoples, following a revolution, passed suddenly from a state of vital energy to one of absolute carelessness."[15] Evidently, the experience of a revolution was not trustworthy enough to be recommended to his own countrymen.

There was no dearth of books in the 1780s whose titles featured the word "revolution"; but the use of the term did not reflect the new perception in every case.[16] Furthermore, works that dealt with American independence as the outcome of local and international military conflicts, like those by the abbé Pierre de Longchamps and D.J. Leboucher, had very little bearing on the new semantics and the ideas they stood for.[17] As late as 1787 François Soulès could publish a four volume survey of the political-military conflict of Great Britain and her former American colonies and call it, in a seventeenth century fashion, *Histoire des troubles de l'Amérique anglaise*. That the meaning of "revolution," with regard to what had happened in America, was not yet unequivocal, can be gleaned from the reading of one of the most valuable works that were published during those years: Crèvecoeur's *Letters from an American Farmer*. Here was an unusual case of a Frenchman, who had settled in America and resided close to New York for many years, and who had actually opposed independence almost until his return to France. His *Letters*, which he began composing in the early 1770s, were written in English and contained vivid descriptions of nature, customs and work habits in America. The first edition, published in London in 1782, conveyed an impression that the author's notion of "revolution" was, if anything, close to the sense of the word "catastrophe." Correspondingly, the term was missing from the dedication, which he addressed to Raynal. By then, however, Crèvecoeur had reached France, where he was quickly befriended by a number of influential persons. In fact, the reception he was given in Paris was so congenial that by the end of 1783 he could sail back to New York, this time as the consul for France. Back in France he left a translation of his work into French with some additions. It came out in Paris in 1785 in two volumes with a new dedication, this time to the marquis de La Fayette. While the translation retained the uses of the term in the older sense ["le choc des factions et des révolutions"], it revealed, in a passage obviously written in France, a new appreciation for the efforts, sufferings and deaths which had been sustained on behalf of American independence. Now Crèvecoeur announced that "such an auspicious and invaluable revolution will mend all our wrongs and will cure all our wounds" ["une révolution si heureuse, si inappreciable réparera tous nos maux, et guérira toutes nos blessures"][18]

That Crèvecoeur might have discovered the American "revolution" in France, should not come, however, as a great surprise to us. By the time he arrived in France, the initial interest in the struggle of the former thirteen colonies was transformed into an acute concern over their future. The *philosophes* now tended to consider the brand new United States as their choice place, where reason could realize for man what had been only dreamt of before. In 1782, when John Adams came to Paris as a member of the American team of negotiators for peace, he met Mably, who told him that he intended to write "sur la Révolution Américaine." In October of that year Adams addressed, therefore, a detailed letter to Mably which he had a friend translate into French, surveying the main sources available for writing a history of the revolution, and the nature of the problems that would be encountered in doing this.[19]

As we remember, Mably had been exploring a "révolution" for France since the late 1750s. Both the term and the idea had a place in his *Principes de morale*, an essay apparently completed in 1781, though published three years later. Here, for example, he saw the banishing of King Tarquin by the people of Rome as a "revolution" that had gained for the people both civic virtue and enlightenment, thus laying a basis for a greater equality among the citizens. In another place he pointed to Cromwell as a prototype of those persons destined "to make revolutions and throw societies into confusion" ["à faire de révolutions et bouleverser les societés"].[20] Following his contact with Adams he wrote four letters, where the issues that the United States had to face in the writing of the constitution were discussed. They were printed in 1784 and had an English translation in the next year, the year Mably died. Right at the beginning of the first letter he explained the reason why America was so important. At a time when "almost every European nation remains plunged in ignorance respecting the constitutive principles of society," the former thirteen colonies in America, now a republic, have discovered "the real dignity of man" and were about "to draw from the sources of the most enlightened philosophy those humane principles on which they mean to build their forms of government." This new development for the entire human race, he told the Americans, had been made possible following their becoming "the authors of your fortunate revolution." And later on, speaking to the people of Georgia, he declared with vivid emotion: "My brethren! my friends! let us return thanks to Providence for having conducted America to that happy revolution by which she is secured in possession of her independency."[21] Mably was concerned, however, lest the Americans would make mistakes. He warned them "not to employ democracy in a republic, but with extreme precaution." The model they should follow, he thought, was that of ancient Sparta, which had combined a strong government with a sense of morality. In an unmitigated democracy, he felt, one group would soon aspire to impose a tyranny, and then "The only system of politics becomes revenge. Revolutions follow each other, and fortune alone decides concerning the fate of the republic."[22]

A comparable approach was displayed in the same year by a relatively new voice, the comte de Mirabeau. A prolific writer since his youth, in the mid-1770s Mirabeau had authored a tract against despotism, in which he styled himself, "citizen of the world, brother to all men," making also known his opinion that "Europe, the slavish Europe, will never lack despots." His conception of "revolution" in this tract tended to follow the views of Montesquieu, who, as we noted, had related revolutions to the nature of despotic government in Asia. But since Mirabeau now denounced despotism in Europe as well, at one spot he awarded Louis XIV the distinction of having prepared France for "une révolution." It was to happen as a result of that king's wasteful expenditures and highhanded policies, and was delayed only because of the exhaustion of the French people and their cowardice. In yet another place he used, however, a somewhat inflated phrase; "absolute revolutions with true national titles." It was meant to describe the series of changes in Europe which saw political power shifting from the hands of the feudal knights to those of the highest nobles, then to those of the king's favorites, ministers, and finally his financiers.[23]

His *Considérations sur l'Ordre de Cincinnatus*, which appeared in London in September 1784 revealed an entirely different orientation. Like Mably, Mirabeau was now impressed by America and also worried lest the Americans should lose the political virtues that elevated them above the European morass of tyranny and oppression. In the first part of this work he dealt, therefore, with the controversial issue of making the descendants of officers in the War of Independence members in the Society of the Cincinnati. He was concerned that the hereditary clause of the Society would make of it eventually an aristocratic military nobility, which in his mind contradicted the aims of the revolution; "the most amazing revolution, the only one perhaps which philosophy would admit" ["la révolution la plus étonnante, la seule peut-être qu'avoue la philosophie"]. In order to show the true nature of the revolution, he followed his own *Considérations* with a letter sent to Richard Price by Turgot, the former French comptroller of finance (1774-76), and then with a complete French translation of Price's *Observations on the Importance of the American Revolution*, accompanied by Mirabeau's own "reflexions" and notes. Thus the entire volume really turned into a piece of propaganda, explaining, recommending and eulogizing the revolution. That it reached a fourth edition by 1788, demonstrates that it also came close to accomplishing the author's aims. And Mirabeau, who opened it with an attack on the idea of hereditary right, ended it fittingly with a plea to the Americans, exhorting them to continue their work for the sake of all of mankind:

> It is a giant step that you have taken... Complete your work. Fashion men by education; shape up, above all by example and by the influence of symbols, the only effective and durable way, a generation worthy of the times of the Revolution, a race of men, who, trained daily by the principles of prudence, loves justice and moderation, detests the scourge of ambition and war, and is capable finally of demonstrating to

the world the rare sight of a union between enlightenment and morality, peace and liberty. Let the tyrants tremble upon merely hearing the name of your happy country! Let the oppressed find there an always open asylum! And let a kind of good luck leap out from the bosom of this new land upon our nations, which might at least sweeten the misfortunes of the old world.[24]

Although the language that Mirabeau used was highly rhetorical, the message, thinly veiled, was a radical one. That he dared to do so at all, can only be explained by the fact that he wrote his work and published it in England. His imprisonment, two years later, in the dungeons of the infamous castle of Vincennes, was perhaps related to this.[25] Inside France the use of this kind of rhetoric remained almost impossible. But we have indications that, even so, around 1780 the word "revolution" was becoming more conspicuous in French discourse, and it is quite significant that the trend was reflected in a conservative and reserved forum such as the speeches of reception of new members of the Académie. Condorcet particularly made use of the term in his address of 21 February 1782, telling his distinguished listeners that the effects of the present times were inevitably bound to bring "both auspicious revolutions and great discoveries."[26] Indeed, Condorcet might be taken as a test case of the new pivotal importance of "revolution" in the 1780s. As a matter of fact, the term and the idea would become central to his thought from here until his death.

Known as a brilliant mathematician since his youth, Condorcet gradually shifted his attention to economics, and then to social and political subjects. The intellectual road he traveled had to do with his friendship with Turgot, with whom he corresponded throughout the 1770s. Little of their exchange indicated, however, an interest in America or in "revolution."[27] The first of the two to touch on the subject of America was apparently Turgot, who in 1778, after he had been forced to resign his ministerial post in the government, wrote on this theme to Richard Price. Turgot opined that an independent America could serve the hope of mankind, but he had reservations with regards to the structure of government that the Americans were about to adopt. Obviously, he had no use for the term "revolution."

Following Turgot's death in 1781, Condorcet wrote his biography, which was published in London in 1786. Here he lamented the failure of his friend to save France by instituting necessary financial and legal reforms. He also mentioned Turgot's intellectual links after his retirement, his exchange of letters with Adam Smith, and with Price on "les moyens de rendre la révolution de l'Amérique utile à l'Europe."[28] This was, however, an entirely new phrasing, in line with what Condorcet was writing in the mid-1780s rather than with what Turgot had in mind in 1778. In 1783 Condorcet began to compose a draft for the prize competition sponsored by Raynal and the Academy of Lyons. He never submitted it, however, and subsequently changed the subject and wrote not on the usefulness of the discovery of America, but on the influence of the American Revolution on Europe. His *De l'influence de la révolution d'Amérique sur l'Europe* appeared in 1786 in the form of a pamphlet under the pseudonym P.B. Godard. In a few dozen pages it attempted to assess the significance of the new political being across the Atlantic in a broad historical perspective. Condorcet's ideas resembled some of Price's views in his tract of 1784, and, like Price, he deplored the retention of slavery by the United States. But otherwise, he felt, so much had been done for the advancement of the rights of man, that one could say that America made concrete the moral, legal and political values which Montesquieu and Voltaire retrieved for humanity in their books. Respect for the liberties of the individual, religious tolerance, unrestricted access to work and commerce, freedom of the press – all of that was yet for Europe to learn from America, and implement. He thought that one obvious effect of American independence would have to be the lessening of competition among European sea powers, and that "the revolution itself should make wars more uncommon in Europe." He observed that in America the commitment to peace had been taken by the state itself in its pledge to avoid aggrandizement by conquest; there no king was surrounded by groups of warring courtiers. In sum, the American Revolution contained a great promise for the future of humanity; it would encourage enlightenment, moral progress and material gains. France particularly had much to learn from it and to emulate.[29]

This warm espousal of the American Revolution by influential writers such as Mably, Mirabeau and Condorcet, should not compel us, however, to conclude that at this stage either the idea, the concept, or the use of the term "revolution," had gained a final victory. France of the mid-1780s was still a society where the vast majority of members in the intellectual community remained tied to the monarchy. In these circles the apparent vogue, headed by a number of enthusiasts, of importing "revolution" to France, must have given, if anything, a reason for concern. One could not deny anymore the existence of "revolution," but one could still try to manage the term in a manner that would possibly restrain its implied threat. Something of this attitude can be seen in the *Essai sur les États-Unis*, published in 1786 by Jean-Nicolas Démeunier. He was a royal censor and also a secretary to the brother of the king, the future Louis XVIII. His work, concentrating on the emergence of the United States as a political body, opened of course with a section entitled: "What were the causes of the revolution, and a historical summary of this revolution." But as a matter of fact, much of what Démeunier had to say on the revolution was borrowed from Raynal, sometimes in long quotations, including Raynal's opinion that the whole question at the bottom of the friction between the colonies and the mother country was little more than an altercation over the right to impose a certain tax. In addition, he chastised those, like Turgot and Mably, who saw in the political system of the United States an example to be followed.[30]

A similar polemical attitude could be found in Soulès's work of 1787, where at the end of the fourth and last volume the author launched an offensive against those who were blinded by "the noble cause that had produced the revolution." They tended naively to conceive of the inhabitants of North America as virtuous, enlightened and highminded individuals, forgetting that the real number of educated persons in the colonies was small in comparison with those who were ignorant, or who had something to gain by independence. Soulès also thought that the quality of the political leadership in the United States was deteriorating, showing that "la Philosophie" had not made real progress there, or that the electorate was as corrupt as that of Europe. He reminded his readers that the Europeans had introduced their vices and bigotries to America already before the onset of "cette fameuse révolution."[31]

The aforementioned essay of Démeunier's on the United States actually consisted of a separate issue of the very long article which he contributed to the *Encyclopédie méthodique* (1784-88), a general compendium on politics in four volumes, of which he was also the editor. It is of interest to note that this survey included distinct entries on the terms "état," "démocratie," "gouvernement," "liberté politique," "monarchie absolue," "souveraineté" – but not on the term "révolution." It did have, however, entries on "décadence des états," "dissolution des états" and "sédition." There Démeunier made use of the word "révolution," but it was done in the context of emphasizing the monarchist point of view, namely that every attempt to force a change in government should be responded to with the strongest repressive measures. Nevertheless, in "décadence des états" he also made an effort to equate this kind of occurrence particularly with revolution, suggesting the following definition:

> If the changes act upon great things; if kingdoms or empires are dismembered, weakened, destroyed; if nations become extinct, and if the face of the universe, so to speak, is thrown into confusion – it is called *revolutions*.

Clearly, in this definition revolution was not just change; it was change on a grand scale and of far-reaching significance in the political sphere and beyond. But other than that, Démeunier remained bound to the tradition that saw "revolution" as an event that man had to accept passively, and not as a means to accomplish an ideal plan. As he went on, elaborating on the differences between various political revolutions, he finally indicated the sources of difficulties inside the state that might cause crises of government. Among these he listed a faulty constitution, despotic rule, corrupt ministers, a continuous fall of either agricultural or industrial production, indebtedness or insolvency of the state, relaxation of military discipline and decline in the mores of a people. Whereas in monarchies a revolution might ensue from intrigues among ministers and generals, in republics the cause might be resentment over the policies pursued by the chief executives, or it might emanate from a division between the upper class and the common people. Démeunier bypassed, however, the new concept of revolution as an attempt for a new order of things, aiming at a more equitable system of government.[32]

The ongoing debate among French writers on the character of the American Revolution (and the new concept of revolution that extended from there), attracted the attention and subsequently the intervention of Americans then in France. Filippo Mazzei, the Italian horticulturist who became a resident of Virginia and an envoy of her government in Europe during the struggle for independence, published in Paris in 1788 a substantial work in four volumes, engaging and refuting the arguments of some of the main French contenders. His whole third volume consisted of a critique of the views of Raynal, and the second contained a rejection of those of Mably, but at the end of the fourth he inserted the text of Condorcet's *De l'influence de la révolution d'Amérique*.[33] As reflected in his diary, John Adams had been impressed by the keen interest of the *philosophes* in America since his first arrival in France in 1778. But he was equally offended by their false notions and their condescending attitude when assessing the innovations of the Americans in the form and structure of government. Early in 1787, when he was serving as envoy to Britain, Adams published *A Defence of the Constitutions of Government of the United States of America.* Right in the preface to this work, he touched on the issue of the necessary equilibrium in the structure of government, as carried out by means of separation of powers. This new system, he contended, had not been known to ancient democracies, and should be recognized as a useful method to keep a government stable for a prolonged time. And he added this:

> Human nature is as incapable now of going through revolutions with temper and sobriety, with patience, and prudence, or without fury and madness, as it was among the Greeks so long ago. The latest revolution that we read of was conducted, at least on the one side, in the Grecian style, with laconic energy; and with little attic salt; at least, without too much patience, foresight, and prudence, on the other. Without three orders, and an effective balance between them, in every American constitution, it must be destined to frequent unavoidable revolutions: if they are delayed a few years, they must come in time.

Evidently, Adams was not interested in exporting the American Revolution. Very clearly, he employed the term "revolution" as a caveat, defending only the way that the Americans were going about framing their own form of republican government. But at this point, many of his European readers might have been won over to the terminology as well as to the idea. Before we turn, however, to observe how this outlook came to be reflected in France on the eve of the calling up of the Estates General, notice should be taken of a parallel trend in England, where "revolution" now suddenly evinced unmistakable signs of revival. The following example is pertinent particularly because of the implied shift at the level of rhetoric. Throughout the eighteenth century English political authors and pamphleteers reserved "Revolution" for reference to 1688. But in April 1782, when the ministry headed by Lord North was finally replaced by that of the Marquis of Rockingham, John Almon, the Whig journalist and bookseller, published a short tract, hailing the change, entitled *The Revolution in MDCCLXXXII Impartially Considered.* The term was employed here in a rather liberal manner, and the author, seemingly conscious of this, saw fit to explain the reason: "This important and critical change of Ministers, may, with great propriety, be called a *Revolution*. There is no other word in our language which so fully and properly expresses the force, and extent of the late total defeat of Corruption and Usurpation. It is no less a Revolution of system and government than that of 1688." Still, in spite of the comparison, it is doubtful whether the terminology employed by Almon in 1782 was inspired by that of 1688. We should not exclude the possibility that it reflected the nascent epithet that was then being attached to the uprising and separation of the American colonies. Lord North, who had mishandled the dispute with the Americans, and was thus responsible for their "revolution," deserved going down by yet another one at home. Almon charged him and his ministers with bringing Britain to the point that "To persevere was Ruin – to save must be Revolution."[34]

One wonders whether the title of Almon's tract did not influence that of Richard Price's *Observations on the Importance of the American Revolution*, which came out in 1784. We dealt with this decisive work in the preceding chapter in the context of the consolidation of the term "American Revolution." We might recall that it had a quick impact in France through the translation made by Mirabeau. Indeed, in a very real sense this contribution helped bridge the gap between the ideals of the Enlightenment and the idea of revolution. That revolution was now considered by Price and his circle as a most valuable accomplishment, comes through clearly from words written by Adams in his diary on 16 July 1786. Recording a conversation in London with Price's nephew, Adams cited the views of the latter, which reflected of course those of his uncle; "that a Revolution of Government, successfully conducted and completed, is the strongest Proof, that can be given, by a People of their Virtue and good Sense. An Interprize of so much difficulty can never be planned and carried on without Abilities, and a People without Principle cannot have confidence in each other."[35]

These kinds of sentiments were probably the real motivation behind the launching of the Society for Commemorating the Glorious Revolution, commonly known as the Revolution Society. In a subsequent publication the reason for its founding was given as the obvious wish to celebrate the completion of one full century since the events of 1688, which had established the "principles of Civil and Religious Liberty." It was further claimed that the Society had been originally set up soon after 1688, and supposedly met annually without interruption from that time onward. But as the founders very well must have known, discounting the annual preaching on 5 November of some nonconformist divines during the early part of the eighteenth century, there was no trace of the existence of a political body associated with the Glorious Revolution. In fact, the Revolution Society was meant as the successor to the Society for Constitutional Information, a body committed to political reform, founded in 1780, which lost some of its fervor after a few years. In that body, as in the new one, were such men as Major John Cartwright, the "father of reform," who advocated universal male suffrage and who had supported American independence since before 1776. The chairman of the Revolution Society was Earl Stanhope, a veteran member of the House of Commons, where he had opposed the war with the Americans; he was related by marriage to the younger William Pitt. The first name on the list of the twenty member organizing committee was that of Richard Price, and there were four other dissenting pastors and members of Parliament. In sum, the Revolution Society was an offshoot of the radical movement, clamoring for political reforms, that had been making headway in England since the 1770s. Although the Bill of Rights of 1689 (from which "revolution" was missing) had stated the great achievements of William III as "delivering this Kingdom from Popery and arbitrary Power," the new centennial organization of 1788 affirmed its belief in the following principles:

I. That all civil and political authority is derived from the people;
II. That the abuse of power justifies resistance;
III. That the right of private judgment, liberty of conscience, trial by jury, the freedom of the press, and the freedom of election, ought ever to be held sacred and inviolable.

The name of the Revolution Society might have been linked to 1688, but its principles reverberated with the sounds of 1776. However, both were timely; indeed, so timely that within a year after its founding these principles would allow the casting of suspicion over the new body, namely that its true aim was not reform but subversion.[36]

The rediscovery of "revolution" within the radicalizing English politics of the 1780s could not resound with these same echoes in France, where political representation was anyway non-existent. But also across the channel unmistakable signs appeared at that point, confirming the startling surge of the idea, of the use of the term, and of the linkage of both with America. As mentioned at the end of the introduction, Arthur Young, then traveling in France, commented already in October 1787 on a conversation, apparently among Frenchmen of upper class background, where America (as a source of inspiration) and "revolution" (as the means) were spiritedly discussed. The French author who came closest to reflecting this mood in his writing was unquestionably Jacques Pierre Brissot de Warville. A number of years younger than either Condorcet or Mirabeau, Brissot was more of a professional writer than a *philosophe*. Moreover, in the ten years after he came to Paris in 1774, for the most part he handled political matters in a circumspect manner. The attitude can still be seen in his essay *De la verité* of 1782. Even though he praised Milton, Sidney and Locke as great champions of free speech, and even though he defended liberty of the press as the foundation of a true spirit of philosophical inquiry, he could not yet bring himself to seriously discuss the issue of truth and public opinion when confronted with despotism and oppression.[37] Brissot really turned against the existing regime following his two month imprisonment in the Bastille on the basis of a *lettre de cachet* issued on false evidence, supplied by a personal enemy in the spring of 1784. His *De la France et des États-Unis, ou de l'importance de la Révolution de l'Amérique pour la bonheur de la France* was completed in Paris early in 1787 and came out in London later that year; in 1788 it had an English translation. The work also carried the name of his Genevan friend, Étienne Clavière. But the long introduction, containing Brissot's more daring ideas, was signed by him alone.[38]

Since the body of the work dealt mostly with commercial matters, such as the different goods that could be traded between France and America, the separate political, or ideological aim of the introduction seemed doubly confirmed. Brissot referred here to the writings of Raynal, Mably and Mirabeau on the American Revolution, and to Paine's letter of rebuke to Raynal. Just prior to this he announced that in a manner similar to the ancients, who had been accustomed to giving their children names that were intended to evoke a sense of moral excellence, he was about to address the people of the United States as "Américains libres," because the new order of things brought about by "la révolution d'Amérique" demanded a new nomenclature. Here in fact was a clue to the difference between Brissot and French authors that preceded him. They too appreciated the importance of the American Revolution, but they still wrote about it, especially Raynal, from the standpoint of ultimate European superiority. For his part, Brissot now used the revolution, and the unquestioned benefits it had brought, in his judgment, to the American people, in order to impress upon the Europeans, Frenchmen particularly, the conviction that at this moment of human history they had been left behind. In this sense, although superficially complying with the restraints imposed by the old regime, Brissot's tone of writing was essentially propagandistic. He declared that he was not going to tire the reader with arguments on how the revolution had assured liberty in the United States; neither was he about to speak of the physical and moral regeneration of man in America, nor of the impossibility that despotism would go on existing there side by side with liberty – all that he considered a foregone conclusion. His interest, he wrote, was restricted to the question of the benefits that Europe, and especially France, were about to gain from the revolution. The most important of these appeared to him to be the welcomed influence of the revolution on human knowledge, contributing to a lessening of prejudices and intolerance. Enlightened by this revolution, the governments of Europe would be obliged to end the abuse of the rights of their subjects, who being tired of bearing the weight, might decide to take refuge in the asylum offered in the United States. It meant to him that from within the states of Europe there must come a "revolution favorable to the people." Summarizing his views, and hinting that he was not at liberty to reveal all that was on his mind, he did not forget, of course, to take pride in the fact that France had contributed to the victory of the American Revolution.[39]

In 1788, despairing of the absence of changes at home, Brissot sailed to the United States, intending a long stay. But when he learned of the rising tension in France and the decision to convoke the Estates General, he hastened to return, arriving in Paris before the end of that year. That he found time during the next two years to prepare his American travel diary for publication, attests to his conviction that the United States remained relevant to France; it was printed in April 1791 and had an English translation in 1792. As soon as he returned, Brissot became active in the anti-slavery league, *Société des Amis des Noirs*. He was joined there by Mirabeau, Condorcet, Volney, and other men who would shortly rise to prominence in French politics, including Pétion and La Fayette. In reality, the activity of the league was meant to accelerate political change inside France. For that reason, Thomas Jefferson, then American minister to France (and a slave owner), was invited to attend the meetings, which he, however, declined.[40] Yet Jefferson and La Fayette were close friends, and the latter, as well as others, consulted the renowned author of the draft of the American Declaration of Independence with regard to the proceedings at the Estates General. The feeling in late 1788 and early 1789 among many members of the French privileged classes, including part of the aristocracy, was that much could be accomplished by imitating the Americans and accepting their revolution as a model. Condorcet had begun, already in 1787, the writing of a series of pamphlets, in which, behind the guise of "un citoyen des États-Unis," he discussed constitutional issues such as the division of powers, a legislature representing the entire nation, equal political rights and free speech.[41] Though the terms "révolution" or "révolution d'Amérique" did not weigh much in these short tracts, the ideas they contained were clearly linked to the views he had maintained in his seminal contribution of 1786.

When was the term "revolution" adopted to embrace the sum of ongoing events in France? Even a seemingly trivial question such as this should not be evaded. Not long ago, it was the opinion of one authority that at the end of 1789 the word "revolution" gained a new sense, associating it with the idea of a general uprising. This might be a correct observation, but it is impossible to admit the view of the same author that in the spring of 1789 men could not yet conceive of a revolution in the modern sense because they had no grasp of it.[42] That some Frenchmen keenly felt that they were involved in a revolution is revealed in that often repeated anecdote about an exchange between Louis XVI and the Duke of Liancourt upon hearing the news of the assault on the Bastille. To the king's question: "Est-ce donc une émeute?" the duke replied, "Non, Sire, c'est une révolution."[43] Apparently, both knew it was a "revolution." The king simply wished it to be something less; perhaps a riot, a commotion, a revolt. The duke merely designated realities with the appropriate semantics. But contemporaries did not have to experience the fourteenth of July to fall upon the term. On 27 June 1789, after the king reversed his earlier stand and ordered the clergy and the nobles to join the third estate in one national assembly, Arthur Young wrote: "The whole business now seems over, and the revolution complete."[44] Of course, the revolution was only beginning; the point is, however, that Young had no hesitation about selecting his term. Even before that, on 9

February 1789, Brissot spoke in the *Société des Amis des Noirs* on the "universal agitation" in favor of liberty, which might encourage the blacks in America to take arms "upon the news of this revolution."[45] In the same month Philippe-Antoine Grouvelle, until then a poet who found employment as secretary to some nobles, published his first political tract, *De l'autorité de Montesquieu dans la révolution présente*. And Rulhière, apparently writing in the last months of 1788, spoke for himself and for many others: "This is a bright and dangerous hour, which many people regard as the time of a revolution."[46] The Parisian journal *Révolutions de Paris*, which began appearing as a brochure on 18 July 1789, actually used for its title the older, or traditional expression; in the plural "révolutions" still meant occurrences, the run of events during the cycle of time. But here too, the plural in the title, having no particular political reference, was quickly joined by the use of the word in the singular in the texts – "une révolution," "l'étonnante révolution," "cette révolution à jamais mémorable dans les fastes de notre histoire," and by January 1790 – "la Révolution de 1789." In a short while it would be given the final phrasing – "la Révolution française."[47]

The new semantics, and the fact that in contrast with the Americans the French employed "revolution" from the very start, are connected with that peculiar development, namely the early, indeed premature, eruption of a debate over the admissibility of the French Revolution. As we know, this debate began in earnest much before the terror of 1793-94, the horrible September 1792 massacres which led to the proclamation of the republic, or even the enactment of the still monarchical constitution of September 1791. This might indicate that at least in part the debate derived from the question whether "revolution" was allowed at all. But to follow the essentials of the controversy we have to move over to England. The organizers of the Revolution Society, who celebrated late in 1788 the centennial of the Glorious Revolution, could have dismantled it at that point. Instead, goaded by the mercurial events in France during the summer of 1789, they scheduled another general meeting of the Society for 4 November 1789. There Richard Price moved for the sending of a congratulatory letter to the National Assembly "on the Revolution in that country, and on the Prospect it gives to the two first Kingdoms in the World, of a common participation in the blessings of Civil and Religious Liberty." Furthermore, it was hoped that the example of France would encourage other nations to assert "the *unalienable* rights of

Mankind, and thereby to introduce a general reformation in the governments of Europe, and to make the world free and Happy." This letter, signed by the chairman, Earl Stanhope, began a long correspondence between the Society and distinguished personalities in France, among them the Duke of Liancourt and Condorcet, as well as with French regional societies "for liberty."[48]

Equally important was the lecture which Price delivered in this second meeting. It was soon published as *Discourse on the Love of Our Country*, and reprinted six times in the early months of 1790. But with all due regard to Price's patriotism, the more outspoken passages in his lecture gave testimony of his love of something of a political nature and of a much broader scope. The following sentences, phrased in a manner of a personal political credo, have also a momentous significance for the emergence of the modern revolutionary tradition, because of Price's pioneering attempt to draw a straight connecting line between the Glorious, the American and the French revolutions:

> I have lived to see the rights of men better understood than ever; and nations panting for liberty which seemed to have lost the idea of it. I have lived to see thirty millions of people, indignant and resolute, spurning at slavery and demanding liberty with and irresistible voice; their king led in triumph, and an arbitrary monarchy surrendering himself to his subjects. After sharing in the benefits of one Revolution, I have been spared to be a witness of two other Revolutions, both glorious. And now, methinks, I see the ardor for liberty catching and spreading; a general amendment beginning in human affairs; the dominion of kings changed for the dominion of laws, and the dominion of priests giving way to the dominion of reason and conscience.[49]

A careful examination of Price's words might show that he regarded the French Revolution as done. Following the destruction of the Bastille and the march of the women to Versailles (5-6 October 1789), which had forced the monarchy to bow to the power of the people, and in the wake of the king's acceding to the principles of political equality and popular sovereignty as enshrined in the Declaration of the Rights of Man (26 August 1789), most of what Price hoped for appeared sustainable. But to Edmund Burke the activities of the Revolution Society and Price's *Discourse* looked rather than expressions of thanks for past revolutions, a call for new ones, in England as well. His famous *Reflections on the Revolution in France* was written very quickly as a long diatribe, although it also contained pages of inspiring literary beauty. Printed still in 1790, its immediate huge success showed that British opinion was really sharply divided, the vast majority of the reading public probably concurring with Burke's scorn of "political theologians and theological politicians, both at home and abroad." One of his main points of argument with Price concerned the interpretation of 1688. As we saw, for the latter the Glorious Revolution attested that in England all political authority derived from the people. Burke denied of course any basis for such an interpretation, which in his mind awarded the people "fictitious rights." Price and his followers, he charged, "in all their reasoning on the Revolution of 1688, have a revolution which happened in England about forty years before, and the late French revolution, so much before their eyes, and their hearts, that they are constantly confounding all the three together." To Burke 1688 demonstrated the exact opposite. The omission of a principle of a king of popular choice in the Bill of Rights, meant for him that the idea was rejected by Parliament even at the time most appropriate for its adoption. Therefore, the acceptance of William of Orange as king was "an act of *necessity* in the strictest moral sense in which necessity can be taken." The alternative to that was recalling James II or civil war. 1688 was "glorious" because it involved only "a small and a temporary deviation from the strict order of a regular hereditary succession."[50]

In contrast with the circumspection of 1688, which he hailed, the conduct of the French since 1789 was in Burke's eyes bold, unrestrained, and for that reason careless. It is indeed to his credit that his diagnosis of the French Revolution in 1790 would be sustained by the character and nature of the events in the next four years. But although the historic facts which would furnish him with a basis for vindicating his own brand of political moralism were yet to come, Burke hastened to assail those at home, like Price, who played rashly with "these politics of revolution." They proceeded, he claimed, to excite their audience, filling their minds with the most unrealistic ideas: "This sort of people are so taken up with their theories about the rights of man, that they have totally forgot his nature." Price's sermon of 4 November 1789, charged Burke, contained such a wild, enticing message, that in the wake of it "plots, massacres, assassinations, seem to some people a trivial price to obtain a revolution." The objective of Price, he intimated, was England itself, though he had chosen an indirect path to get near it, exploiting an ongoing political drama in another country: "There must be a great change of scene; there must be a magnificent stage effect; there must be a grand spectacle to rouse the imagination, grown torpid with the lazy enjoyment of sixty years security, and the still unanimating repose of public prosperity. The Preacher found them all in the French revolution."[51]

One important reply to Burke came immediately from Joseph Priestley. He struck a personal note, reminding Burke of their political cooperation of many years, and he also pointed at the latter's apparent change of heart: "That an avowed friend of the American revolution should be an enemy of that of the French, which arose from the same general principles, and in great measure sprung from it, is to me unaccountable." How could Burke pass judgment on the French, he asked, before it was even known whether they succeeded or failed? And he observed in this connection a new linguistic development: "Thus every successful revolt is termed a revolution and every unsuccessful one a rebellion." He then chided Burke for resorting to distortions, such as his play on words calling the members of the Revolution Society "the gentlemen of the *society for revolutions.*" But Priestley also rejected Burke's interpretation of 1688, maintaining that on the background of that event the principle that power in any state derived from the people had been already accepted by such authorities as Lord Somers, Bishop Hoadley and John Locke. Particularly, however, he protested Burke's treatment of Price, which in his mind tainted the latter unfairly with the excesses and outrages committed in France. Truly, claimed Priestley, Price lamented the atrocities in France more sincerely than Burke: "He wishes to recommend the revolution, and therefore is sorry for every thing that disgraces it; whereas you wish to discredit it, and are evidently not displeased with any circumstance that favours your purpose."[52]

But Burke's attack on Price and the Revolution Society turned out to be a decisive one. Moreover, it aided the consolidation of a conservative trend within the English political establishment, which was abetted ironically by the tendency of the Society itself to flaunt its support of the radicals in France. By 1791 even Earl Stanhope showed his reservations, declining to attend a banquet, foolishly scheduled to be held in London on 14 July. Price's death in that year was another reason why the Society quickly disappeared. Burke, however, was soon answered from an unanticipated side. Late in 1791 and early in 1792 Thomas Paine's *Rights of Man* appeared in two parts, the first part of which carried the subtitle "Being an answer to Mr. Burke's Attack on the French Revolution." In England since 1787 (and soon in France), Paine accused Burke of sowing the seeds of conflict between France and England on behalf of persons who stood to profit in the event of a war. More important perhaps, in contrast with Priestley, Paine, an American citizen, did not bother to use 1688 as a fig leaf to conceal a belief in the sovereignty of the people. At the end of the first part he said it aloud: "As it is not hard to perceive, from the enlightened state of mankind, that hereditary governments are verging to their decline, and that revolutions, on the broad basis of national sovereignty, and government by representation, are making their way in Europe, it would be an act of wisdom to anticipate their approach, and produce revolutions by reason and accommodation, rather than commit them to the issue of convulsions... It is an age of revolutions, in which everything may be looked for."[53]

In the context of the present study, what meets the eye more than anything in the *Rights of Man* is the free and effective manner in which Paine handles the term "revolution." This is particularly indicative when we remember the absence of the word in *Common Sense* (1776) and in all except the last issue of the series *The Crisis* (1776-83). Now, however, the term comes into its own as Paine exploits the epithets "American Revolution" and "French Revolution" to argue that a global trend, ushering fundamental changes in the system of government, is advancing from west to east, promising progress to nations and "a new era to the human race." At one place he even calls this trend a "counter revolution," since it is about to recover for man the rights of which he had been dispossessed at some early periods through acts of tyranny. But it is hard to agree with Hannah Arendt that Paine too, no less than Burke, felt that absolute novelty would be an argument against, not for, the authenticity and legitimacy of the rights of man. Almost everything else in Paine's arguments underscores the character of the newness in the ongoing trend of revolutions. Indeed, on this issue he repeats the same point of view that he had already expressed in *Common Sense*, even before the new term entered his discourse, namely that "we have it in our power to begin the world again." Also, the expression "counter revolution" was not Paine's own minting, but rather a combination of words that he must have borrowed from the French, where it entered political language about 1790.[54]

The main ideas of the *Rights of Man* bear similarity to those expressed by Condorcet in his *Esquisse d'un tableau historique des progrès de l'esprit humain*. Condorcet wrote this essay in 1793, the year before he committed suicide to avoid the guillotine; it was first printed in 1795, both in French and in English. In this, his best known work, he traced the development of the human spirit through ten epochs, or stages, of which the last was said to carry man to his ultimate perfection. Interestingly, according to Condorcet human progress came in a gradual way, seeing man passing in succession from living in groups organized as hordes to communities based on pastoral and agricultural activities, and then to societies forming states, where writing was invented, and later on printing. The upshot came at the point when science and philosophy threw off the yoke of religious authority, thus opening the doors to the ninth epoch, which extended from Descartes to the formation of the republic in France. Here, however, gradual progress changed to progress by means of revolution:

> Every thing tells us that we are approaching the era of one of the grand revolutions of the human race. What can better enlighten us as to what we may expect, what can be a surer guide to us, amidst its commotions, than the picture of the revolutions that have preceded and prepared the way for it? The present state of knowledge assures us that it will be happy.[55]

The "surer guide" to the last, happy, ultimate epoch of human perfection were of course the American and French revolutions. It is quite ironic that Condorcet, soon to depart from this world as a consequence of fears, suspicions and political rivalries unleashed by the French Revolution, chose to embrace "revolution" as a means to secure for man an everlasting happiness. But it is also important to emphasize that both the ideas and the semantics he now used were relatively new to him. As we remember, the term "revolution" hardly entered his writing in this sense until the early 1780s, whereas his subscribing to republican principles was even more recent, perhaps as late as 1791. And yet the term is handled in this famous work in such a "natural" way, and Condorcet's claim that the *philosophes* had prepared the world for revolution follows so obviously from his reasoning, that one wonders whether this essay had not misled later generations to take for granted the "revolutionary" character of the French Enlightenment. However, in his complete assimilation of the new semantics Condorcet merely approximates the development of Paine. He also agrees with Paine that the French Revolution received its original impulse from the independence of America. In his view, the creation of the United States and its war with England opened a great debate in Europe over the rights of man. Even in "the most enslaved countries" people began to discuss the nature of the political rights that belonged to them, and "In this state of things it could not be long before the transatlantic revolution must find its imitators in the European quarter of the world." Because of her attachment to the ideas spread by the *philosophes* on the one hand, and her retarded system of government on the other, France became the inevitable choice for the beginning of the revolution on the European continent. It was also inevitable that in France the revolution would assume a different character than in America. Here it had to be more thorough and more violent, because unlike the Americans the French had to eradicate a corrupt system of taxation, remnants of feudal tyrannies, hereditary distinctions, privileges of the rich and of powerful corporations, and religious intolerance. As for the changes that were about to affect the European states, Condorcet believed they were inevitable and that they could be summarized as a revolution of either one or another type:

> [E]ither the people themselves would establish a system of policy upon those principles of nature and reason, which philosophy had rendered so dear to their hearts; or government might hasten to supersede this event, by reforming its vices, and governing its conduct by public opinion. One of these revolutions would be more speedy, more radical, but also more tempestuous; the other less rapid, less complete, but more tranquil: in the one, liberty and happiness would be purchased at the expense of transient evils; in the other, these evils would be avoided; but a part of the enjoyments necessary to a state of perfect freedom, would be retarded in its progress, perhaps for a considerable period, though it would be impossible in the end it should not arrive.[56]

Apparently, Condorcet viewed the prospects of "revolution" with unbounded confidence. In yet another writing of that time he spoke in terms of either change or revolution. A people needed to know that it could always get rid of a law or institution that disturbed its existence. Only that knowledge would bring it to respect legal authority; otherwise, "toute société tend continuellement à des révolutions nouvelles..."[57] But it is also to his credit that he did not lose sight of the problem of political terms and their shifting meanings, or as he put it, that the change of the senses of words indicated a change in reality itself. The observation comes at the end of a short paper, "Sur le sens du mot révolutionnaire," which appeared on 1 June 1793, the day before Condorcet's party, the Brissotins, was smashed by Robespierre and the Montagnards. He opened with the observation that "révolutionnaire" applied to anything connected with a political revolution, and that the adjective was first fashioned during France's own revolution, which saw the country turning in a few years from a despotic polity to the only republic where liberty was based on complete equality of rights. Therefore, concluded Condorcet, the word "révolutionnaire" should properly apply only to revolutions which aimed at the extension of liberty. This, however, was just his preliminary characterization. By mid-1793 Condorcet was keenly aware that "revolutionary" carried a sense of emergency, or that a measure so called was actually a coercive or a repressive one. He explained that this sense of the word resulted from the dynamics of a great revolution on the march. During its course there would always appear those who would attempt a change in the other direction, namely a "contre-révolution." The freedom of action of an opposition within the main body of a citizenry involved in a revolution, could endanger the gains made on behalf of the majority and sanctioned therefore the passage of necessary repressive laws. Hence his plea at the end of the paper to adopt "revolutionary" measures not in order to prolong the revolution, or contaminate it with blood, but with the aim of bringing it to completion in the quickest manner.[58]

Unfortunately, at about the time this plea was made the French Revolution entered its most hectic phase. The man who took charge of France's destiny during the next year was apparently less concerned than Condorcet that "revolution," and "revolutionary," would be enlisted by the rhetoric of dictatorship and suppression. Both these terms star in the seminal speech which Robespierre made to the Convention on behalf of the Committee of Public Safety on 25 November 1793 [5 Nivôse of the second year of the Republic]. Still, Robespierre too felt that these two words needed definitions, and he began by underscoring the confusion surrounding their new meaning:

> The doctrine of revolutionary government ["gouvernement révolutionnaire"] is as new as the revolution which brought it forth. One should not look for it in the books of political writers, who never anticipated this revolution, nor in the laws issued by tyrants, who,

willingly abusing their power, are little preoccupied with searching for its legitimacy. Likewise, this word is but a reason for fear or a subject for slander to the aristocracy; it is a matter of shock to tyrants; to most people – an enigma; it must be explained to all, so as to rally at least the good citizens around the principles of the public interest.[59]

Revolutionary government, explained Robespierre, was the type of regime inevitably adopted by the French republic at its birth, while it was engaged in a struggle for survival. A revolutionary government could not be restricted by the legal subtleties of a constitution. It needed extraordinary powers to deal with unforeseen situations and ever new and pressing dangers. During times of peace constitutional government could concern itself with civil liberties and individual freedom; but at times of war, under a "régime révolutionnaire," it was public authority itself that had to be defended against all who were attacking it. Robespierre was clearly referring here to internal not external enemies, and he added this threatening warning: "The revolutionary government owes to the good citizens all the national support; it owes to the enemies of the people nothing but death."

He then went on to deny that "revolutionary" had anything to do with arbitrariness or tyranny. Those who claimed so were either stupid wranglers or would be traitors who meant to lead the people astray and return the old regime. Yet even though revolutionary government was constitutionally less restricted, it had no less legitimacy than an ordinary government, because it was supported by the most sacred of all the laws – "le salut du peuple." In contrast with Condorcet, Robespierre cared little about the duration of a revolutionary government. The real important issue was that power should be held by sincere and trusted leaders.

> Upon indicating the duties of the revolutionary government, we have marked its dangers. The greater its power, the more its activity is free and fast, the more it has to be steered in good faith. The day it will fall in tainted or treacherous hands, freedom will be lost; its name will then turn to be the pretext and the excuse of the very counter-revolution; its energy will be that of a violent poison.[60]

Thus associated with purity of heart, this concept of revolutionary leadership brings to mind the images of other sponsors of revolution in more recent times; men who used the same motto, either insincerely, like Stalin, or sincerely, like Ernesto "Che" Guevara. But as we might recall, Cromwell already in his speech of January 1655 had amazingly given the term essentially a similar bearing, when he alluded to "the revolutions of Christ himself." Fittingly, an American author, writing in 1794 against the excesses of the French Revolution, charged that its leaders "with a grimace of a Cromwell, they deprive every man who will not go all the lengths of their rash measures, of both *liberty* and life." The writer was Noah Webster, whose long pamphlet got the approbation of both houses of Congress. It expressed the shift of opinion in the United States, from an early stand of sympathizing with the French revolutionaries, when it looked as if they were reenacting the American experience, to a critical view of dismay, when it turned out that the French repudiated the old form of religion, violated churches, massacred clergymen, put thousands to death without caring for due process of law, practiced direct (rather than representative) democracy at times of crisis, and pretended to turn their revolution into a war of all peoples against all kings. To Webster, France as ruled by the Jacobins was experiencing "a despotism so severe and bloody" as she had not seen in any previous age. He was confident, however, that civil war and much bloodshed would finally "compel the nation to renounce the idle theories of upstart philosophers" and resume a government guided by wisdom and plain political principles. But his was not a Burkean rejection of revolution in favor of gradual reform. He stressed the view that "a revolution was affected before the Jacobins had formed themselves into a constituent body, and assumed a sovereign sway."[61] The French erred, however, when they did not maintain their first revolution, the one that defended the rights of man against tyranny (and admitted an American inspiration). The implications of this criticism were inescapable. Webster was actually suggesting that there were two alternative methods of a modern revolution, one competing against the other. The French might have owed much to the American in its earlier stages, but it ended up as something else, and with an epithet that evoked quite different notions and resonance.

Conclusion

Having charted it in some detail along the course of this book, the road to glory of the term "revolution" might now be quickly sketched again within the following broad lines: The twin Italian words, *rivoluzione* and *rivolgimento*, attained a meaning of an extraordinary change, alteration of government by force, popular uprising or commotion, in the current speech of Florence, sometime during the early part of the fourteenth century. This sense of the words apparently developed spontaneously, in addition to the other better known sense, that of a circling movement, which the two words had held as the Italian equivalent of the Latin *revolutio*. Because the political meaning of *rivoluzione* had a status of popular slang, it was used very seldom by humanist authors in the fifteenth and sixteenth centuries. But during the second half of the sixteenth century the word benefited somewhat from the linguistic trend which came to appreciate the vernacular of the age of Dante, Petrarch and Boccaccio. Therefore, when the *Vocabolario della Crusca* was published in 1612, it stressed the political meaning of *rivoluzione*, duly illustrating this sense of the word with appropriate quotations from the chronicles of the Villani brothers.

The next and crucial stage came with the general European political crisis of 1640-60. First, enterprising Italian authors such as Assarino and Giraffi, selected *rivoluzioni* for the titles of their accounts of the revolts against Spain in Catalonia and Naples. Then other well known Italian political commentators such as Gualdo Priorato imitated the innovation, or employed the term in conspicuous passages where they discussed the European situation, as did

Bisaccioni. The Fronde in France and the replacement of Charles I's monarchy by the Commonwealth in England, signaled the entrance of the word to the political discourse of these two countries. Though it turned out to be a very partial entrance, arousing from the start unmistakable signs of objection, there are enough examples demonstrating the new presence of the word in the works of diverse authors such as Mezeray and Salmonet in France, or Ascham and Howell in England. These writers, and others, now employed it rhetorically to express various arguments within the debate on the most pressing issue of those years, namely the issue of change of government by violent means. Further evidence of its importance is supplied in the letters of Mazarin and the speeches of Cromwell. The role played by "revolution" in royal documents associated with the English Restoration of 1660, also confirms the view that in the twelve years following 1648 the new term gained a measure of exposure and use in western Europe.

Then came long years when "revolution" was seemingly denied any progress at all. As argued here, this cannot be explained just by claiming that the new meaning needed a period of gestation. As it is impossible for us today to wipe from our minds the connotations given to words in current use, so it was for people in the second half of the seventeenth century. Great authors such as Hobbes, Locke and Dryden in England, or Mme de Sévigné, Bossuet and Molière in France, who used "revolution" rarely, or not at all, should lead us to believe that after about 1660 the new meaning of the 1650s quickly became unacceptable, or rather "politically incorrect." The initial disposition to use it fizzled out when faced with the absolutist norms of politics which held sway during the next three decades. Still, at the same time some writers, particularly William Temple, Cardinal Retz and the comte de Modène, left us proof that they did not consider the political sense of "revolution" either outdated or irrelevant. In time, as the political and religious tensions again escalated, the term found more users, and in 1688 it re-entered the public domain, this time to stay.

More than the contribution of ponderous political thinkers, however, the entrenchment of "revolution" after 1688 was the work of partisan pamphleteers such as Bishop Burnet, the author of *The Judgment of Whole Kingdoms and Nations* and Jonathan Swift. This reflects of course the development in England, where "revolution" now supplied a convenient term for William of Orange's unseating of James II, and where it was eventually joined with the final sanctifying adjective – "glorious." In France the word became at the same time part of political discourse as well, but in contrast with English authors French writers attempted to endow it with the sense of something beyond man's control, fatal and consequently negative. This outlook was well mirrored in the numerous "Histoires des Révolutions."

With the exception of the peculiar attachment of Englishmen to their "Revolution," the Enlightenment inherited in the word a meaningful political term, though one not yet semantically tuned to transmit a yearning for political change. Still, in the final reckoning the failing of the *philosophes* to exploit the word was perhaps their own shortcoming, particularly in the case of Rousseau. Though at the end we find the term put to use in the writings of several French eighteenth century authors, among them Mably and Raynal, this was not enough to imprint "revolution" in the minds of their avid readers across the Atlantic Ocean, namely the founding fathers of the United States. As we saw, on the whole the actors of 1776 refrained from employing the term. Only gradually, after the struggle against Britain had been practically won, and when the passage of some years allowed a retrospective look at the events and their significance, did "revolution" join "independence" as an epithet for the emergence of the first modern republic.

This took place in the early 1780s, and the epithet was rather quickly seized upon by European political authors, especially French and English, and converted into a terminological weapon, conveying (direct or indirect) demands to enact in their own societies changes of a political nature similar to those effected by the "American Revolution." As a result, the French Revolution had the word in use from the very beginning, which in turn quickly allowed the appearance of related terms such as "revolutionary" and "counter-revolution." But the immediate effect was not just limited to a reordering of political discourse. The joining of "revolution" to 1688, 1776 and now 1789, soon allowed a suggestive ideological reevaluation of the past (and the future) in the sense of linking these three historical landmarks together, and hammering out of their pretended interconnection an early version of the modern revolutionary idea. As we saw, the idea occurred to Richard Price in a memorable speech of 1789. It was soon further elaborated on by Paine in *The Rights of Man*, and by Condorcet in *Esquisse d'un tableau historique des progrès de l'esprit humain*. Indeed, the notion that "revolution" was the embodiment of a great idea on the march began to sprout even before. It must have been on the mind of Mirabeau in 1784 when he called America's "the most amazing revolution, the only one perhaps which philosophy would admit."

The early formula of the modern idea of revolution had to do with personal political freedoms, civil liberties, equality before the law, that is to say the norms governing the function of a democratic society. It is precisely this aspect which makes it an "early" version. Soon it would be revised and restated in terms of social rather than just political change. In fact, this shift of the modern idea of revolution happened so fast that it is appropriate to remind ourselves that it began long before the publication of the Communist Manifesto in 1848. As early as 1794 Babeuf posed the question: "What is, generally speaking, a political revolution? What is, in particular, the French Revolution?" To which he gave the answer: "An open war between patricians and plebeians, between the rich and the poor."[1]

The quick "socialization" of the modern revolutionary idea severed it from the early political version, and from the events that allowed its erstwhile formulation. Of the three "revolutions," 1688, 1776 and 1789, the first two at least had very little to contribute to the goal of social change (and the third really got nearer to social issues only in its later stages). This is why the American Revolution, so avidly discussed in the years just prior to the outburst in France, lost its relevance as a model as soon as European society felt the social consequences of industrialization. Throughout the nineteenth century the American model of revolution carried weight only in Latin America, and there, unfortunately, real accomplishments were pretty dismal. On the other hand, in Europe even liberal revolutionaries, backed by the middle classes, tended to believe that revolution as a purely political idea was off the mark since it failed to address the question of collective identity in an age of nationalism. In the twentieth century the early modern version almost turned obsolete. New models of revolution, the Russian, the Chinese or the Cuban, attracted the attention of peoples about to gain political independence. But history being a sort of game with no predictable result, it turns out that at present, following the demise of the Soviet Union, the relevance of the early modern version is again on the rise. The current skepticism about revolution as an attempt to remake society at one violent, furious moment, somehow redeems the value of the idea of revolution as an answer to political repression.

But with these notes on the idea of revolution in our world today we have gone a considerable distance beyond the boundaries of the mere entrance of the term into Western political discourse. Rather than forcing a connection between the semantic development and our own political culture, let us turn back in time and ask – what does the history of the term "revolution" teach us about the nature of political values and beliefs in the seventeenth and eighteenth centuries? The guiding supposition behind this question is that "revolution" took an inordinately long time to be accepted. Does this not reflect an overall profoundly conservative disposition, particularly within the ruling and intellectual circles, and among political thinkers? Does it not purport to tell us that the system of government by monarchy was rooted in the minds of Englishmen and Frenchmen of those times more deeply than historians are nowadays usually willing to admit? Thus, by either rejecting "revolution" for a considerable length of time, or by admitting it in a partial and restricted sense, contemporary political authors were actually giving indirect testimonies of their inability to conceive of a change from monarchism.

Of course, the case was not that simple. It has been recently claimed that the widespread movements of rebellion, civil wars and disturbances associated with the general crisis of 1640-60 were not just revolts of a regional or even "national" character, but that they actually amounted to a series of events signaling a new European level of political awareness. In contrast with the sixteenth century *religious* revolts caused by the Reformation, those of the mid-seventeenth century had a clear *political* orientation. Moreover, despite the many traditional attitudes that they expressed, the separate movements of 1640-60 communicated a continental sense of political breakdown, chiefly exemplified by the wide resonance given to the *rivoluzioni* of Naples of 1647.[2] And yet, with all the interest generated by the revolts practically nowhere can we find authors undertaking a sustained defense of the rebels and their aims (unless the support is given on grounds of obvious self-interest). As we have seen, in Italy, where a widely read group of political commentators quickly produced written chronicles of the events, no publication favored the revolts.[3] But it was in these inhospitable circumstances that the term "revolution" really opened its discursive and political career, propelled to the forefront on the one hand by the obvious need of writers to come out with a fresh word, and one that could be effectively used rhetorically, rejected on the one hand by the overwhelming ingrained distrust of revolts and rebellions, which the new word was suspected to condone.

Perhaps the greatest irony related to the difficult entrance of the new term is that its seminal potential would not be recognized even by those very few who consciously opted for major political change. Here the case of Milton is particularly outstanding. In his *The Tenure of Kings and Magistrates* (1649), which appeared soon after the setting up of the Commonwealth, Milton went much further than the principle of the subjects' right to resist tyranny, adding that freedom was mankind's "natural birthright," and that a people were authorized to retain or depose a ruler whether a tyrant or not, "merely by the liberty and right of free born men to be governed as seems to them best." But as we have seen, Milton avoided the brand new term with which, through the work of Ascham, he was unquestionably familiar. He could not conceive (on the lexical plane) of the "right of revolution." With one exception, the same limitation hampered the language of James Harrington. In his autobiography, Burnet told of Harrington's and Henry Neville's attempt of 1659 to set up a model of an elective democratic government. Considered in the standards of our present political culture, this could be described as an effort by *intellectuals* to preserve the Commonwealth after Cromwell's death. But Burnet writes that the attempt became "a matter of diversion and scorn," and that the mere endeavor of some "enthusiasts" to involve themselves in such a plan, helped convince onlookers that it was time to return the monarchy.[4]

This anecdote sheds light on the peculiar entanglement of the new semantics, backed by a nascent wish for political change and disavowed by the old craving for customary monarchism. As we have seen, the years 1659-60 witnessed the new term "revolution" used in England more frequently than before in reference to abrupt changes in government, commotions or civil war. But it was still difficult for those few committed to the replacement of the monarchy with a republic, to verbalize their idea with "revolution." One reason for that might be that essentially the idea was to them a legacy of ancient Rome, transmitted to the seventeenth century also by Renaissance humanist authors, especially Machiavelli. Yet "revolution" was at this stage a very new word, and one apparently smacking of sensationalism. Presumably, it could only contaminate the purity of the pristine idea.

The attending fusion between "revolution" and the idea of fundamental political change, was to be therefore the true test of the new term. As we saw, before 1688 some authors tried if not to delegitimize the political sense, at least to blacken it, as did Nalson and Varillas. On the other hand, right after 1688 Burnet saw fit to promote the term with the aim of defending a case of a transfer of government by force. But these, and other uses of the word in political discourse, equally failed to accomplish the fusion of "revolution" and the revolutionary idea. In essence, this lack of alliance continued throughout most of the Enlightenment, and it might suggest that the conservative biases of European political thinkers were eroding slower than we would like to believe. When the modern vision of revolution was finally proclaimed in America in 1776, it still had to wait some half a dozen years for the term to join the idea. But from this point on (disregarding our habitual careless anachronism of covering with the term breakdowns of government throughout history), there is no revolution without "revolution." John Evelyn and the Duke of Liancourt might have used similar expressions. But there was a great difference between what the first meant when he wrote in 1688 "it looks like a Revolution," and what the second meant in 1789, when he corrected Louis XVI with "Non, Sire, c'est une révolution." In the second case the fusion of the word with the idea gave it an altered intent.

Notes

Introduction

1.   See F. Brunot, "Un mot transfiguré: Révolution" in his *Histoire de la langue française des origines à 1900* (Paris, 1937), IX, pp. 617-22.

2.   G. Savile, "The Anatomy of an Equivalent," *The Complete Works*, ed. W. Raleigh (Oxford, 1912), p. 104.

3.   Or still another example. In the mid-1990s, during President Clinton's first term, the Congressional majority in the United States talked much of the "Republican Revolution," a phrase which apparently carried the promise to drastically reduce the burden on the American taxpayer.

4.   R. Chateaubriand, *Oeuvres* (Paris, 1978), p. 48. This and all other translated passages in the present study, unless otherwise indicated, were done by the author.

5.   M. I. Finley, "Revolution in Antiquity" in *Revolution in History*, eds. R. Porter and M. Teich (Cambridge, 1986), pp. 49-50. P. A. Howell, "The Greek Experience and Aristotle's Analysis of Revolution" in *Revolution: A History of the Idea*, eds. D. Close and C. Bridge (Totawa, New Jersey, 1985), pp. 15-31.

6.   Certainly not as new as Thomas More's ingenious invention *utopia*, but relatively new when compared with Latin and Latinized words that made up the basic political vocabulary of the early modern political thinkers, such as *civilis, dominium, libertas, nobilitas, politicus, virtus.*

7.   *De civitate dei*, lib. XII, cap. 14; lib. XXII, cap. 12.

8.   F. Guicciardini, *Opere,* ed. R. Palmarocchi (Bari, 1932), VII, p. 222.

9.   G. Savonarola, *Prediche del reverendo padre fra Gieronimo da Ferrara per tutto il anno* [1496] *nuovamente con somma diligentia ricordette* (Venice, 1540), p. 227.

10. Vespasiano da Bisticci, *Vite di uomini illustri*, ed. L. Frati, 3 vols. (Bologna, 1892-93), I, pp. 266, 334, 337. For an extended discussion of *stato* in the language of the Renaissance see A. Tenenti, *Stato: un'idea, una logica; dal comune italiano all'assolutismo francese* (Bologna, 1987), pp. 53-97.

11. G. Dati, *Istoria di Firenze dall'anno MCCCLXXX all'anno MCCCCV* (Florence, 1735), pp. 112-13.

12. *Cronica volgare di anonimo fiorentino dall'anno 1385 al 1409*, ed. E. Bellondi, *Rerum Italicarum Scriptores*, Tomo XXVII, Parte ii (Bologna, 1917), pp. 20, 176, 235.

13. For example, while discussing the destruction of Jerusalem by emperor Vespasian and his son Titus, Giovanni Villani explained it as God's punishment of the Jews for the death of Christ, so that "mai poi non ebero I Giudei stato ne recetto di loro signoria." G. Villani, *Cronica*, ed. F. Gherardi Dragomanni, 4 vols. (Florence, 1844-45), III, p. 214.

14. P. Charron, *De la sagesse*, dernière edition, revues, corrigées et augmentées (Paris, 1635), p. 173.

15. E. Fournier, *L'esprit dans l'histoire; recherches et curiosités sur les mots historiques* (Paris, 1882), pp. 263-66.

16. R. W. Carlyle and A. J. Carlyle, *A History of Mediaeval Political Theory in the West*, 6 vols. (Edinburgh, 1962), VI, p. 373.

17. B. Latini, *Li livres dou trésor*, ed. F. J. Carmody (Berkeley, 1948), pp. 32, 49, 120, 392.

18. Christine de Pisan, *Le livre des fais et bonnes meurs du sage Roy Charles V*, ed. S. Solente, 2 vols. (Paris, 1936), II, pp. 159-60.

19. M. Mendle, "Parliamentary Sovereignty: a very English Absolutism" in *Political Discourse in Early Modern Britain*, eds. N. Phillipson and Q. Skinner (Cambridge, 1993), p. 98.

20. A. Pagden, ed., *The Languages of Political Theory in Early Modern Europe* (Cambridge, 1987). "Revolution" is also missing from M. Viroli's *From Politics to Reason of State* (Cambridge, 1992). In this case the absence is justified, since the work is limited to the theme of the acquisition and transformation of the language of politics from 1250 to 1600.

21. R. G. Collingwood, *The New Leviathan, or Man, Society, Civilization and Barbarism* (Oxford, 1942), p. 199.

22. K. Griewank, *Der neuzeitliche Revolutionsbegriff; Entstehung und Entwicklung*. The author died in 1953. The book was published two years later by his students and friends from drafts he had left. I have used the second edition (Frankfurt a. M.: Europäische Verlagsanstalt, 1969). Before he died Griewank had summarized his main views on the subject in "Staatsumwälzung und Revolution in der Auffassung der Renaissance und Barockzeit," *Wissenschaftliche Zeitschrift der Friedrich Schiller Universität Jena* (1952-53), Heft I. Yet another comprehensive study in German, apparently never published, is the Ph.D. dissertation of Franz W. Seidler, *Die Geschichte des Wortes Revolution: Ein Beitrag zur Revolutionsforschung*

(Ludwig Maximilians Universität, Munich, 1955). M. J. Lasky's *Utopia and Revolution* (Chicago, 1976) is a vast, thoroughly researched work, that contains considerable quantities of information on the history of the term "revolution." But the scope of this book is much wider. It really deals with the hold that the revolutionary idea had on Western intellectuals over the past 500 years.

23. H. Arendt, *On Revolution* (New York, 1963), pp. 27-36 and *passim*. Compare also P. Zagorin, *The Court and the Country; The Beginning of the English Revolution* (London, 1969), pp. 10-16. Griewank's interpretation was also disseminated in English through translations of excerpts of his work. See H. Lubasz, ed., *Revolution in Modern European History* (New York, 1966), pp. 55-61. Emphasis on the astronomy/astrology derivation of the term "revolution" was made in the works of Eugen Rosenstock-Hussey, actually published prior to those of Griewank. See his "Revolution als politischer Begriff in der Neuzeit," *Festgabe... für Paul Heilborn (Abhandlungen der Schlesischen Gesellschaft für Vaterländisch Kultur, Geisteswiss. Reihe)*, Heft 5 (1931), which the present author unfortunately has not been able to locate. Rosenstock's views, however, are repeated in his *Out of Revolution* (New York, 1938), *passim* and in his *Die europäischen Revolutionen* (Stuttgart, 1951), pp. 3-5. Echoes of these views sometimes resound even in the writing of scholars whose knowledge of the original sources should have counseled them caution. See for example Eugenio Garin, *Rinascite e rivoluzioni* (Rome, 1975), p. 300.

24. A. Hatto, "'Revolution': An Inquiry into the Usefulness of an Historical Term," *Mind*, LVIII (1949), pp. 495-517.

25. This observation would also be relevant to a work which attempted to uncover the origins of the early modern revolutionary spirit such as M. Walzer's *The Revolution of the Saints* (Cambridge, Mass., 1965). Throughout the entire book the author never bothered to consider the background or status of the term "revolution," evidently because it was clear to him that until well after the outbreak of the English civil war (1642-48) this word had no bearing on the language of the men contended by him to have conveyed the new reformist ("revolutionary") awareness.

26. F. Gilbert, "Revolution," *Dictionary of the History of Ideas*, ed. P. P. Wiener (1973), IV, pp. 153-54.

27. A. Young, *Travels in France during the Years 1787, 1788, 1789*, ed. M. Betham-Edwards (London, 1913), pp. 97-98.

Chapter One

1.   The *Historia antica di Ricordano Malispini dall'edificazione di Fiorenza per insino l'anno 1281 con l'aggiunta di Giachetto suo nipote dal detto anno per insino al 1286*, first published by Giunti in Florence in 1568,

has been considered of doubtful authenticity ever since. At present it is viewed as a concoction of early sources with passages from later chronicles. Compagni's *Cronica* covers the history of Florence from 1280 to 1312. It too is sometimes claimed to consist of a late fifteenth century refashioning. But as for the terminology that these two works employ to express political change, they both are within the bounds found in chronicles of uncontested authenticity of the next three generations. Cf. J. Larner, *Italy at the Age of Dante and Petrarch, 1216-1380* (London, 1980), pp. 10, 15.

2.   Among Florentine authors, *romore* (also spelled *rumore*), *novità* (also written *novitade*) and *trattato* are commonly employed by the Villani brothers, by Marchionne Stefani, whose *Cronica fiorentina* goes to 1385, and by Nado da Montecatini, who covers Florentine affairs from 1374 to 1398. This terminology also proliferates in several contemporary chronicles and memoirs of the 1378 Ciompi revolt, collected in *Il tumulto dei Ciompi; cronache e memorie*, ed. G. Scaramella, *Rerum Italicarum Scriptores* [hereafter *RIS*], Tomo XVIII, Parte iii (Bologna, 1917), and in the *Cronica volgare di anonimo fiorentino*, ed. E. Bellondi, *RIS*, XXVII, ii (Bologna, 1917), formerly attributed to Piero Minerbetti, which covers the years 1385 to 1409. The same terms can also be found in important fourteenth century chronicles of other Tuscan towns: *Istorie pistorese* [1300-1348], ed. S. A. Barbi, *RIS*, XI, v (Città di Castello, 1927); *Cronica senese attribuita ad Agnolo di Tura del Grasso, detta Cronica Maggiore*, eds. A. Lisini and F. Giacometti, *RIS*, XV, vi (Bologna, 1933), which belongs to the third quarter of the fourteenth century; Ranieri Sardo, *Cronaca di Pisa*, ed. O. Banti (Rome, 1963), going to 1399; and Giovanni Sercambi, *Le croniche*, ed. S. Bongi, 3 vols. (Lucca, 1892), covering the history of Lucca, where, however, terms such as "discordia," "divisione," "scandalo" are used more by the author than "novità."

3.   The use of the term by Matteo Villani has been pointed out by Hatto, "'Revolution': An Inquiry into the Usefulness of an Historical Term," p. 502; and see also K. Griewank, "Staatsumwälzung und Revolution in der Auffassung der Renaissance und Barockzeit," p. 13.

4.   G. Villani, *Cronica*, lib. 9, cap. 219; II, p. 282.

5.   *Ibid.*, lib. 12, caps. 1, 19 and 32; IV, pp. 5, 41 and 59, where he terms a "revolution" the expulsion from Florence of the *condottiere* Walter of Brienne, Duke of Athens, in 1343 ["alla rivoluzione della cacciata del duca e di sua signoria"].

6.   This expression is found in one of Cola's few proclamations that were given at the time an Italian translation. See Cola di Rienzo, *Epistolario*, ed. A. Gabrielli (Rome, 1890), p. 239.

7.   *Istorie di Matteo Villani cittadino fiorentino* (Florence, 1581) lib. 4, cap. 89, lib. 5, cap. 19, lib. 9, cap. 34; pp. 270, 284, 526. In reference to France, Matteo Villani has "il Reame di Francia in tanta rivoluzione e traverse."

8. For example, G. Villani, *Cronica*, lib. 11, cap. 138; III, p. 375; M. Villani, *Istorie*, lib. 3, cap. 22, lib. 6, cap. 17, lib. 7, cap. 40; pp. 55, 153, 333, 393-94.

9. Hatto, pp. 510-11.

10. Pierre Duhem, *Le système du monde*, 10 vols. (Paris, 1954), IV, p. 187; see also Lynn Thorndyke, *A History of Magic and Experimental Science*, 8 vols. (New York, 1923-58), II, p. 834.

11. *Guidonis Bonati foroliviensis mathematici de astronomia tractatus X* (Basel, 1550), cols. 489, 563-64, 612-13.

12. *Abrahe Avenaris judei astrologi peritissimi in re iudiciali opera, ab excellentissimo philosopho Petro de Abano post accuratam castigationem in latinum traducta* (Venice, 1507). See also L. Thorndyke, "Peter de Abano: A Medieval Scientist," *Annual Report of the American Historical Association* (1919), I, pp. 317-26.

13. Salimbene de Adam, *Cronica*, ed. G. Scala, 2 vols. (Bari, 1966), II, pp. 755, 847.

14. Latini, *Li livres dou trésor*, pp. 80-81, 95, 391.

15. Ristoro d'Arezzo, *Della composizione del mondo* (Milan, 1864), pp. 46-50, 266, 312.

16. *Ibid.*, pp. 240-41, 245.

17. Cf. G. Siebzehner-Vivanti, *Dizionario della Divina Commedia* (Florence, 1954) and *Enciclopedia Dantesca* (Rome, 1973), IV, p. 900.

18. See Cecco d'Ascoli's "In spheram mundi enarratio" in *The 'Sphere' of Sacrobosco and its Commentators*, ed. L. Thorndike (Chicago, 1949), pp. 344-411; in this tract the phrase "revolutio(nes) annorum mundi" occurs four times, pp. 375, 386 and 400 (twice). The passage where he first uses the phrase runs thus: "Et secundum quod in revolutione annorum mundi impeditur vel exaltatur in circulo planeta qui dominatur provincie, sic fortunia et infortunia apparent in una provincia et non in alia."

19. Cecco d'Ascoli, *L'Acerba*, ed. P. Rosario (Lanciano, 1926), pp. 44, 52, 58, 108.

20. G. Villani, lib. 12, cap. 4; IV, pp. 71-73.

21. *Ibid.*, lib. 10, cap. 86; III, p. 81. My translation of "disasseroccato" is tentative. The word is spelled "disasroccato" in the 1537 edition of Giovanni Villani, and "disarrocato" in the passage illustrating the entry *Revoluzione* in the *Vocabolario della Crusca* (1612). The *Cronica senese*, p. 478, a late fourteenth century compilation which copied heavily from Villani, gives the whole passage, but has "vedrete di sasseronchato." Machiavelli, in his biography of Castruccio, put in the mouth of the dying man an entirely different and longer speech.

22. G. Villani, lib. 9, cap. 284; II, p. 318. And see also lib. 9, cap. 219; II, p. 283, where the expression is: "perché si volgesse stato nella città."

23. M. Villani, lib. 5, cap. 13; p. 282.

24. Francesco Alunno [real name Francesco del Bailo], *Le ricchezze della lingua volgare sopra il Boccaccio* (Venice, 1557). Under the entry AVOLGIMENTO the author adds: "RIVOLGIMENTO. Rivoluzione. In Rivolgimenti delli stati communi habbiano adoperato etc. EP."

25. See the "Cronichetta d'incerto" in *Cronichette antiche di varii scrittori del buon secolo della lingua toscana*, ed. D. M. Manni (Florence, 1733), pp. 173-217. In 1368, writes the anonymous author, the nobles "volsono lo stato di Siena." But he is more inclined to use "mutamenti di Stati;" see pp. 181, 188, 191.

26. M. Stefani, *Cronica fiorentina*, ed. N. Rodolico, *RIS*, XXX, i (Città del Castello, 1903), p. 425.

27. In *Croniche fiorentine*, ed. F. Ildefonso di San Luigi (Florence, 1784), pp. 74-75, Nado da Montecatini writes: "Siena si levò dentro a romore per temenza, che lo stato del popolo minuto,... non rivolgesse lo stato." And see *Cronica volgare*, pp. 69, 176. At about the same time the term was strangely introduced into the *Chronica Urbevetana*, a short survey of events of fourteenth century Orvieto, written in Latin, but heavily invaded with vernacular colloquialisms. The expression here is "in multis revolutionibus status civitatis." It refers to the long years of civil strife that marked the internal life of Orvieto after the death of Count Ermanno Monaldeschi in 1337. See "Le antiche cronache di Orvieto," *Archivio Storico Italiano*, serie V, III (1889), p. 44.

28. B. Castiglione, *Il cortegiano*, lib. 1, cap. 36. On Dante, see R. Waswo, *Language and Meaning in the Renaissance* (Princeton, 1987), p. 52.

29. F. Villani, *Le vite d'uomini illustri fiorentini*, ed. F. Gherardi Dragomanni (Florence, 1847), pp. 18, 54.

30. Poggio's work was translated by his son Jacopo and printed in Florence in 1492 as *Historia fiorentina*. The terms employed there in reference to political breakdowns include "sedizioni civili," "sedizioni domestiche," "discordie civili," "tumulto," as well as "ribellione" and "romore."

31. Hans Baron, *The Crisis of the Early Italian Renaissance*, rev. ed. (Princeton, 1966), pp. 168-172.

32. G. Cavalcanti, *Istorie fiorentine*, 2 vols. (Florence, 1838-39), I, p. 32. The full phrase is: "Mentre la fortuna accordava le sue ire col mal volere dei nostri malvagi oumini, a tanti rivolgimenti di Romagna, e a si malvagi abassamenti di republica, quanti ne seguì nella Città di Firenze..."

33. F. Rinuccini, *Ricordi storici dal 1282 al 1460 colla continuazione di Alamanno e Neri suoi figli fino al 1506*, ed. G. Aiazzi (Florence, 1840). Here the uprising that had brought the Ciompi to power in 1378, and the one that brought them down, are both termed "romore" (pp. xxxvi, xxxviii). But the Pazzi conspiracy of 1478 is said to have intended "grande novità e mutazione" (p. cxxviii).

34. M. Palmieri, "Della vita civile" in *La letteratura italiana; storia e testi*, Vol. 14, *Prosatori volgari del quattrocento*, ed. C. Varese (Milan, 1955), p. 395; L. B. Alberti, *I libri della famiglia*, eds. R. Romano and A. Tenenti (Turin, 1972), p. 353. On the political terminology of the fifteenth century see also Nancy S. Struever, *The Language of History in the Renaissance* (Princeton, 1970).

35. Bernardino da Siena, *Prediche volgari sul campo di Siena, 1427*, ed. C. Delcorno (Milan, 1989), pp. 397, 401, 411, 494.

36. C. Landino, *Commento sopra la Commedia di Dante Alighieri* (Venice, 1484), at his comments to Canto 3 of the Inferno.

37. I. Landucci, *Diario fiorentino del 1450 al 1516*, ed. I. Del Badia (Florence, 1883); B. Masi, *Ricordanze (dal 1478 al 1526)*, ed. G. O. Corazzini (Florence, 1906).

38. Vespasiano's expressions are: "Istando la città in tante revoluzioni" and "istando le cose in queste rivoluzioni." See his *Vite di uomini illustri*, III, p. 24.

39. "Compendio delle rivelazioni" in *Scelta di prediche e scritti di Fra Girolamo Savonarola*, ed. P. Villari and E. Casanova (Florence, 1898), pp. 354-67. Savonarola's words on page 360 are: "Ma io le dissi a certi miei famigliari, come fu il tempo determinato della morte di Innocenzo VIII e di Lorenzo de' Medici, la rivoluzione dello Stato di Firenze, la quale dissi che sarebbe quando il Re di Francia sarebbe in Pisa;" and shortly afterwards, "Appropinquandosi poi il Re di Francia e la rivoluzione dello Stato fiorentino."

40. *Ibid.*, p. 367.

41. *Ibid.*, p. 100, and see also his expression on page 240 "tante mercanzie, tante rivoluzioni."

42. "Epistola di Girolamo Benivieni, cittadino fiorentino, mandata a Papa Clemente VII a dì primo di Novembre [1530]" in Benedetto Varchi, *Storia fiorentina*, ed. G. Milanesi, 3 vols. (Florence, 1857), III, pp. 314-15.

43. Additional proof is supplied, for example, in minutes taken at the deliberations of Florence's council of state, where on 14 March 1495 one of the speakers referred to Savonarola's sermons "ne' tempi della revolutione dello stato." See C. Lupi, "Nuovi documenti intorno a Fra Girolamo Savonarola," *Archivio Storico Italiano*, serie terza, III, i (1866), p. 36. In his description of the chasing out of Florence of Piero de' Medici in November 1494, Tibaldo de' Rossi, an eye witness, refers to the events twice as a "rivolgimento delo stato." See his "Ricordanze" in *Delizie degli eruditi toscani* (Florence, 1786), XXIII, pp. 296-98. Yet another term that was used during the 1494 banishment of the Medicis is "garbuglio," carrying the sense of a popular insurrection, disturbance or turmoil. It held on in popular speech during the next decades, and was later used in reference to events in Florence in 1527-30. Eventually it penetrated Spanish, French and English. See the

documents published in *Archivio Storico Italiano*, appendice, VII (1849), pp. 140, 263 and nuova serie, XVIII, parte seconda (1863), p. 7.

44. K. Griewank, *Der neuzeitliche Revolutionsbegriff*, pp. 115-19.

45. The most recent English translation converted Guicciardini's first *rivoluzione* to "disturbances," accepted his second as "a revolution" and rendered his third as a "revolt." See *The History of Florence*, trans. M. Domandi (New York, 1970), pp. 4, 20, 226. The Italian text I have used is that edited by A. Greco (Novara, 1970). It should be acknowledged, however, that even in this work of Guicciardini's "alterazione dello stato" and "mutazione dello stato" by far outnumber "rivoluzione."

46. Felix Gilbert, *Machiavelli and Guicciardini* (Princeton, 1965), pp. 273-74.

47. F. Guicciardini, *Le cose fiorentine*, ed. R. Ridolfi (Florence, 1945), p. 17.

48. "Discorso di Messer Niccolo Guicciardini del modo del procedere della famiglia de' Medici in Firenze et del fine che poteva havere lo Stato di quella famiglia" in R. von Albertini, *Das florentinische Staatsbewustsein in Übergang von der Republik zum Prinzipat* (Bern, 1955), p. 352; "Discorso di Alessandro de' Pazzi, al Cardinale Giulio de' Medici. Anno 1522," *Archivio Storico Italiano*, I (1842), p. 420. I. Nardi, *Istorie della città di Firenze*, ed. L. Arbib, 2 vols. (Florence, 1842), I, p. 27, II, p. 11.

49. Varchi, *Storia fiorentina*, I, pp. 161, 200; A. Caro, *Lettere famigliari*, ed. A. Greco, 3 vols. (Florence, 1957-61), II, p. 24.

50. D. Giannotti, "Discorso sopra il riordinare la repubblica di Siena" in *Opere politiche e letterarie*, ed. F.-L. Polidori, 2 vols. (Florence, 1850), I, pp. 341-42.

51. *Trattato de' governi di Aristotile*, tradotto da Bernardo Segni (Milan, 1864), p. 283.

52. It came out again in Venice in 1571, and once more in 1591 together with the works on the Venetian government by Contarini and Giannotti.

53. Erizzo, "Discorso dei governi civili" in Contarini, *Della repubblica et magistrati di Venetia* (Venice, 1591), pp. 230-31, 233, 242-43.

54. *I dialoghi del Platone*, tradotti da S. Erizzo (Venice, 1574), p. 320a.

55. L. Guicciardini, *Commentarii delle cose più memorabili seguite in Europa* (Venice, 1565), p. 57.

56. G. B. Adriani, *Istoria de' suoi tempi* (Venice, 1587), pp. 1, 5-6.

57. G. Botero, *Delle relazioni universali* (Brescia, 1595), p. 84.

58. See P. Sarpi [Pietro Soave], *Historia del concilio tridentino*, 2nd ed. ([Venice], 1629), pp. 279, 430, 732; H. C. Davila, *Historia delle guerre civili di Francia* (Venice, 1630), pp. 1, 145-46.

59. P. Paruta, *Della perfezione della vita politica* (Venice, 1599), p. 461.

60. F. Figliucci, *De la politica, overo scienza civile, secondo la dottrina d'Aristotile, libri otto* (Venice, 1583); G. A. Palazzo, *Ragion di stato* ([?], 1604); L. Zuccolo, *Considerazioni politiche e morali* (Venice, 1621); L. Settala, *Della ragion di stato libri sette* (Milano, 1627); F. Albergati, *La republica regia* (Bologna, 1627); and see also the various excerpts in B. Croce and S. Caramella, eds., *Politici e moralisti del seicento* (Bari, 1930).

61. C. Spontone, *Dodici libri del governo di stato* (Verona, 1600), pp. 32, 253.

62. T. Campanella, *Aforismi politici*, ed. L. Firpo (Turin, 1941), pp. 125-39; T. Campanella, *Del senso delle cose e della magia*, ed. A. Bruers (Bari, 1925), pp. 315-16, 317-18, 320-21.

63. See "rivoluzione" in M. Ciliberto, *Lessico di Giordano Bruno*, 2 vols. (Rome, 1979).

64. For example, it appears in Cherubino Ghirardacci's *Della historia di Bologna, parte terza*, first published 1598; see the modern edition, *RIS*, XXXIII, ii (Città di Castello, 1915), p. 369. The use of the term in a political sense by Conestaggio in his *Dell'unione del regno di Portogallo* (1585), was translated in 1600 by E. Blount to English in the same word and sense; see Hatto, p. 504. Alessandro Sozzini entitled the manuscript he completed in 1587 on the history of Siena, "Il successo delle rivoluzioni della città di Siena." See the text in *Archivio Storico Italiano*, II (1842), pp. 1-434; Raffaello Roncini's "Delle istorie pisane libri XVI" of the late sixteenth century has the term at least twice; see *Archivio Storico Italiano*, VI, parte prima (1844), pp. 790, 854. Angelo di Constanzo (1507-91), author of a history of Naples, might have borrowed the term from the Villani brothers to whom he refers. He uses it when describing the Sicilian Vespers of 1283, calling the event: "Questa grande, e cosi repentina mutazione e rivoluzione,..." See his *Storia del regno di Napoli* (Napoli, 1839), pp. 1, 116, 134.

65. O. Malavolti, *De l'historia di Siena* (Venice, 1599), I, pp. 40a, II, 109b, III, 132b-133a. A similar addition of "revoluzioni" by a printer is found in the posthumous book of the Florentine scholar Pierfrancesco Giambullari. He had died in 1555 and his *Historia dell'Europa*, published in Venice in 1566, has the term in the index and on the margin of page 56a, but not in Giambullari's text. In the *Historia fiorentina di M. Piero Buoninsegni* (Florence, 1581), the index has an entry referring to a "Trattato di rivolgimento di Stato in Firenze," yet the term is not to be found in the indicated text.

66. Cited by Lasky, *Utopia and Revolution*, p. 242.

67. A. Campiglia, *Delle turbolenze della Francia in vita del Re Henrico il Grande* (Venice, 1617), p. 94.

68. Neither "rivolgimento" nor "rivoluzione" are used, however, in the text of this work, and it might well be that the title was fashioned by the printer, Olivier Alberti.

69. A. Mascardi, *La congiura del Conte Gio. Luigi de' Fieschi* (Milan, 1629), p. 52.

70. A. Goracci, "Breve istoria dell'origine e fondazione de città del Borgo di San Sepolcro," in F. Villani, *Le vite d'uomini illustri fiorentini*, pp. 192-95, 202-03.

71. M. Bisaccioni, *Sensi civili sopra il Perfetto Capitano di H. D. R. e sopra la Tactica di Leone Imperatore* (Venice, 1642), p. 20; A. Zilioli, *Delle historie memorabili de' suoi tempi*, 3 vols. (Venice, 1642-46), II, pp. 59, 262, 273, 285.

Chapter Two

1. It should be made clear that there is no intention to deal here with the controversy surrounding the causes of the mid-seventeenth century "general crisis." For salient works touching upon that subject consult: *Crisis in Europe, 1560-1660*, ed. T. Aston (1965); *Preconditions of Revolution in Early Modern Europe*, eds. R. Forster and J. P. Greene (Baltimore, 1970); T. K. Rabb, *The Struggle for Stability in Early Modern Europe* (New York, 1975); *The General Crisis of the 17th Century*, eds. G. Parker and L. M. Smith (1978); P. Zagorin, *Rebels and Rulers, 1500-1660* 2 vols. (Cambridge, 1982).

2. Benedetto Croce, *Storia dell'età barocca in Italia* (Bari, 1929), pp. 99-108, still retains illuminating observations on Italian historiography of that period.

3. A. Zilioli, *Delle historie memorabili*, II, pp. 59, 262, 273, 285, III, 179. V. Siri, *Il Mercurio: overo historia de' correnti tempi*, 15 vols. (Casale, 1644-82), I, pp. 44, 345.

4. G. B. Birago Avogadro, *Turbolenze di Europa* (Venice, 1654), p. 617.

5. It is not out of order to emphasize that Assarino was indeed the first to use *rivoluzioni*. In his *The revolt of the Catalans* (Cambridge, 1963), p. 593, J. H. Elliott gave the date of printing of Assarino's work as 1648 in Bologna, an error that was repeated in his paper, "Revolts in the Spanish Monarchy" in Forster and Greene, *Preconditions*, p. 110. This incorrect date was retained by C. Vivanti in *Storia d'Italia*, eds. R. Romano and C. Vivanti, 6 vols. (Torino, 1972-76), II, p. 417.

6. See Domenico Cerniglia, *Saggio su Luca Assarino, storico e letterato del secolo XVII* (1969); and the biographical article by A. Asor-Rosa in *Dizionario Biografico degli Italiani*, IV (1962), pp. 430-33.

7. L. Assarino, *Delle rivoluzioni di Catalogna...dove pienamente si narrano le origini, e le cagioni di tutte le turbulenze in quella Provinzia succedute dal principio del Regnare de Filippo IV* [where the origins and the

reasons of all the disorders that have taken place in that province since the beginning of the reign of Philip IV are fully told] (Genoa, 1644), p. 32.

8. On Melo see E. Prestage, *Francisco Manuel de Melo* (Oxford, 1922); also the biographical notes of the editor to the edition of Melo's *Politica militar en avisos de generales* (Buenos Aires, 1943).

9. F. M. de Melo [pseu. Clemente Libertino], *Historia de los movimientos y separación de Cataluña* (São Vicente, 1645), pp. 24b, 27a. This book was reprinted in Portugal in 1692 and 1696, and had several later editions with modernized spelling ("rebolución" being turned into "revolución"), starting with that of Madrid of 1808.

10. A. Giraffi, *Le rivoluzioni di Napoli* (Venice, 1647), pp. 8, 11.

11. P. Reina [pseu. Andrea Pocili], *Delle rivoluzioni della città di Palermo avvenute l'anno 1648* (Verona, 1649), pp. 151, 170-71, 177.

12. Contemporary sources are listed in H. G. Koenigsberger, "The revolt of Palermo in 1647," *Cambridge Historical Journal*, VIII (1946), pp. 129-44.

13. P. Reina [pseu. Idoplare Copa], *L'Idra dicapitata* (Vicenza, 1662), pp. 249-304.

14. I have used the edition published by A. Altamura in Naples, apparently in 1970. See especially pp. 254-70, 305.

15. G. Tontoli, *Il Mas'Aniello, overo discorsi narrativi la sollevazione di Napoli* (Naples, 1648); see the *Nota* to the reader, the introduction, and p. 113.

16. A. Nicolai, *Historia ...dell'ultime rivoluzioni della città e regno di Napoli* (Amsterdam, 1660), pp. 43, 83, 101.

17. See V. Conti, *Le legge di una rivoluzione; i bandi della repubblica napoletana dall'Ottobre 1647 all'Aprile 1648* (Napoli, 1983).

18. Nicolai, p. 184.

19. "Documenti sulla storia economica e civile del regno, cavati dal carteggio degli agenti del granduca di Toscana in Napoli, dall'anno 1512 sino al 1648" in *Archivio Storico Italiano*, IX (1846), pp. 347-48, 351 and 387. Pages 376-78 of this volume contain an abbreviation of a seemingly fictional exchange between the Pope and the Spanish ambassador to Rome with interesting uses of the term. But this text has been apparently edited. For a recent account of the Neapolitan revolution of 1647-48, including a reasoned survey of the sources, see R. Villari, *The Revolt of Naples*, trans. J. Newell (Cambridge, 1993).

20. A. Inveges, *Annali della felice città di Palermo* 3 vols. (Palermo, 1649-51), I, p. 3.

21. V. Siri, *Bollo di Vittorio Siri nel Mercurio Veridico del Sig. Dottore Birago* (Modona, 1653); Birago's work and his stature as an historian is assessed by V. Castronovo, *Dizionario Biografico degli Italiani*, X (1968), pp. 620-23.

22. G. B. Birago Avogadaro *Historia africana della divisione dell' imperio degli arabi* (Venice, 1651), p. 440.

23. Translation from the Italian of *Ristretto delli moti moderni d'Inghilterra*, tradotto del latino in italiano dal Dottor Gio. Batt. Birago Avogadaro (Venice, 1652), p. 3.

24. Translation from the Italian of G. B. Birago Avogadaro, *Delle historie memorabili che contiene le sollevazioni di stato de' nostri tempi*, p. 129.

25. G. Gualdo Priorato, *Historia delle guerre di Ferdinando Secondo e Ferdinando Terzo Imperatori e del Re Filippo Quarto di Spagna contro Gustavo Adolfo re di Suetia e Luigi XIII re di Francia*, 4 vols. (Venice, 1648-54); in IV, pp. 159-67 he employs for the 1647 Palermo revolt mainly "sollevazione" and "tumulto." Later on, p. 207, he introduces the Masaniello revolt with these same terms. On Gualdo's stature as a historian see G. Toso Rodinis, *G. Gualdo Priorato, un moralista veneto alla corte di Luigi XIV* (Florence, 1967).

26. G. Gualdo Priorato, *Historia delle revoluzioni di Francia sotto il regno di Luigi XIV e regenza d'Anna d'Austria* (Venice, 1655); the English translation begun by Henry Carey, Earl of Monmouth (died 1661), and completed by William Brent, appeared in London in 1676. But the term "revolutions" was dropped from the title, which was rendered as "The history of France..."

27. Translation from the Italian. Cf. C. Vivanti, *Storia d'Italia*, II, pp. 416-17, who saw the passage important enough to quote it at length.

28. This seems to be Bisaccioni's major goal in the writing of political history. See V. Castronovo in *Dizionario Bigrafico degli Italiani*, X (1968), p. 641.

29. M. Bisaccioni, *Historia delle guerre civili di questi ultimi tempi* 2nd ed. (Bologna, 1653), pp. 215-16, 397, 509, 727. Bisaccioni's ideas are not in conflict with views expounded by some modern historians as L. Stone, *The Causes of the English Revolution, 1529-1642* (1972). In fact, ideas contending a similar causality of revolutionary upheavals (without yet employing the term "revolution") are to be found already in Francis Bacon's essay "Of Seditions and Troubles."

30. *Opere scelte di Ferrante Pallavicino* (Amsterdam, 1673), second part, pp. 269-316. The date of composition of this tract is 1643.

31. *Ibid.*, pp. 562-63, 564, 567.

32. Article by G. De Caro, *Dizionario Biografico degli Italiani*, XIV (1972), pp. 712-20.

33. G. Brusoni, *Varie osservazioni sopra le Relationi Universali di Giovanni Botero* (Venice, 1659), pp. 53, 82, 141, 147. Brusoni's claim that Cromwell's government was even more authoritarian than the royal tyranny it replaced was also voiced by English contemporaries.

34. Cf. G. Brusoni, *Dell'historia d'Italia dall'anno 1625 sino al 1660* (Venice, 1661), pp. 489, 543, 645; G. Brusoni, *Historia dell'ultima guerra tra Veneziani e Turchi*, 2 vols. (Venice, 1673), I, pp. 192-93.

35. B. Nanni, *Historia della Repubblica Veneta* 2 vols. (Venice, 1662-86), I, pp. 623, 630-33, II, pp. 124, 258.

36. G. Leti, *Dialoghi politici, o vero la politica che usano in questi tempi i prencipi e repubbliche Italiane per conservare i loro stati e signorie* (Geneva, 1666), pp. 95, 261, 283, 285; G. Leti, *Il nipotismo de Roma*, 2 vols. (Amsterdam, 1667), I, p. 220, II, pp. 420, 422; A bibliographical list of Leti's works published during his 12 years of residence in Geneva (1661-72) is given in L. Fasso, *Avventurieri della penna del seicento* (Florence, 1924), pp. 26-32.

37. Leti, *Dialoghi politici*, pp. 247, 854-55.

38. For example, the Neapolitan abbot Vincenzo d'Onofrio, who completed, about 1670, a work on the history of Naples in the wake of the suppression of the 1647-48 revolt, mentioned in his address to the reader the preceding *rivoluzioni*, but neglected to use the term in the main body of his text. See V. d'Onofrio [pseu. Innocenzo Fuidoro], *Successi del governo de Conte d'Oñatte (1648-1653)*, ed. A. Parente (Naples, 1932); the word is not used in any appreciable degree in Bernardo Giustiniani's *Historia generale della monarchia spagnuola antica e moderna* (Venice, 1674), nor in Andrea Valerio's *Historia della guerra di Candia* (Venice, 1679). Having failed to retain an important place in the language of historians, *rivoluzione* also remained extraneous to late seventeenth century Italian political thought. See, for example, the discourse of Gianlorenzo Lucchesini, *Saggio della sciocchezza di Nicolo Machiavelli* (Rome, 1697).

Chapter Three

1. J. M. Goulemot, "Le mot révolution et la formation du concept de révolution politique (fin XVIIe siècle)," *Annales historiques de la Révolution Française*, XXXIX, No. 190 (1967), pp. 417-44.

2. *Ibid.*, p. 418, note 2. In a later work, *Discours, histoire et révolutions* (Paris, 1975), p. 36, Goulemot gave more evidence on the use of the term during the Fronde.

3. K. M. Baker, "Revolution," *The French Revolution and the Creation of Modern Political Culture*, eds. K. M. Baker, F. Furet and C. Lucas, 3 vols. (Oxford, 1987-89), II, pp. 41-62.

4. C. Jouhaud, *Mazarinades; la Fronde des mots* (Paris, 1985); H. Carrier, *La presse de la Fronde* (1648-1653): *les Mazarinades; la conquête de l'opinion* (Geneva, 1989).

5. F. de la Noue, *Discours politiques et militaires*, ed. F. E. Sutcliffe (Geneva, 1967), pp. 19-22, 34-36.

6. *Les oeuvres d'Estienne Pacquier* (Amsterdam, 1723), I, p. 90.

7. Michel de Montaigne, *Essais*, liv. III, chap. 9.

8.   See P. Robert, *Dictionnaire alphabétique et analogique de la langue française* (Paris, 1981), VI, pp. 18-19; and E. Huguet, *Dictionnaire de la langue française du seizième siècle* (Paris, 1962), p. 589.

9.   P. de L'Estoile, *Memoires-Journaux*, eds. Brunet, Champollion, Halphen et al., 12 vols. (Paris, 1888-96), III, p. 289; V, p. 231.

10.   M. de Nostredame, *Les Oracles*, ed. A. le Pelletier, 2 vols. (Paris, 1867), II, pp. 10, 15, 17-18, 157.

11.   [P. de L'Estoile], *Memoires pour servir à l'histoire de France*, 2 vols. (Cologne, 1719), I, p. 263.

12.   L. Le Roy, *Des troubles et differents advenans entre les hommes par la diversité de religions* (Paris, 1569), p. 25.

13.   L. Le Roy, *De l'excellence du gouvernement royal* (Paris, 1575), pp. 2a, 43a, 73b.

14.   I use here the contemporary English translation; *Aristotle's Politiques, or Discourses of Government*, translated out of Greek into French, with expositions... by Loys Le Roy (London, 1598), pp. 334-35.

15.   L. Le Roy, *De la vicissitude ou variété des choses en l'universe*, texte revu par Philippe Desan (Paris, 1988), pp. 23, 51, 68. The text follows the first French edition. This book had French reprints in 1576, 1577, 1583 and 1584; it was published twice in Italian in 1582 and 1585, and was translated into English in 1594.

16.   Charron, *De la sagesse*, liv. III, pp. 34, 45-59.

17.   C. Le Bret, *De la souveraineté du roy* (Paris, 1632), p. 9. Le Bret's expression is: "Toutesfois depuis que la fortune s'est meslée des affaires humaines, elle a par ses continuelles révolutions tellement perverty l'ordre des grandeurs & des puissances de la terre, qu'il est maintenant bien difficile de cognoistre qui sont celles que l'on peut dire proprement souveraines." See also Henri de Campion's essay on history and politics, originally written in 1641, in his *Mémoires*, ed. M. Fumaroli (Paris, 1967), pp. 254, 280.

18.   P. Monet, *Inventaire des deus langues, française et latine* (Lyon, 1636), p. 769.

19.   Naudé, *Considérations politiques sur les coups d'estat*, pp. 65, 143, 149, 164, 200. The term is apparently missing, however, from Naudé's massive *Jugement de tout ce qui a esté imprimé contre le cardinal Mazarin, depuis le sixième Janvier, jusques à la declaration du premier Avril mil six cens quarante-neuf* (n. p., [1649]). This work, cast in a dialogue, is also known, after the name of its main speaker, as Le Mascurat.

20.   F. E. de Mezeray, *Histoire de France dupuis Faramond jusqu'à maintenant*, 3 vols. (Paris, 1643-51), I, pp. iii, 47, 402; II, pp. 48, 241.

21.   J.-L. Guez de Balzac, *Les oeuvres diverses* (Paris, 1659); the bulk of the nineteen "discours" were composed during the 1630s. V. Voiture, *Les oeuvres*, 2 vols. (Paris, 1677); the first volume and the first seventy pages of the second contain his letters, first published in 1649. The word "revolution"

is also missing from Vaugelas's posthumous work (he died in 1650), *Nouvelles remarques sur la langue française* (Paris, 1690).

22. G. Ménage, *Les origines de la langue française* (Paris, 1650), pp. 332-33, and see p. 483 for his discussion of the word "Mutin."

23. *Les oeuvres de Monsieur Sarasin*, 2 vols. (Paris, 1685); this is the second printing, which in it first volume, pp. 164-219, has his incomplete essay on the conspiracy of Wallenstein.

24. J. Vallier, *Journal (1648-1657)*, eds. H. Courteault and P. de Vaissiere, 5 vols. (Paris, 1902-18), I, p. 3.

25. *Gazette de France*, No. 1 (January 1648), p. 1; No. 22 (8 February 1648), p. 190; No. 48 (19 April 1652), pp. 385-86.

26. *Mémoires du Duc de Guise* in *Nouvelle collection des mémoires pour servir à l'histoire de France*, 3ième serie, VII (Paris, 1839), p. 32.

27. *Lettres du Cardinal Mazarin*, ed. M. A. Chéruel, 9 vols. (Paris, 1872-1906), II, pp. 524-26. *Recueil des instructions données aux ambassadeurs et ministres de France*, X, *Naples et Parme*, ed. J. Reinach (Paris, 1893), pp. 16, 33; *Mémoires de Du Plessis-Besançon*, ed. Horric de Beaucaire (Paris, 1892), p. 304.

28. R. Kerviler and E. de Barthelémy, *Valentin Conrart, premier secrétaire perpetuel de l'Académie Française, sa vie et sa correspondance* (Paris, 1881), pp. 475, 496.

29. J. Chapelain, *Soixante-dix-sept lettres inédites à Nicolas Heinsius (1649-1658)*, ed. B. Bray (The Hague, 1966), pp. 136, 160.

30. *Mémoires de Omer Talon* in *Nouvelle collection des mémoires pour servir à l'histoire de France*, 3ième série, VI (Paris, 1839), pp. 297, 354, 411, 443.

31. The following presentation is based on findings in four hundred and eighty four *Mazarinades*, inspected at the New York Public Library, the Library of Congress and the Folger Shakespeare Library in Washington, in addition to the representative selection of one hundred *Mazarinades* edited almost a century and a half ago by Celestin Moreau, and the fifty-two published in facsimile by Hubert Carrier in 1982.

32. *Remontrance de la Reine d'Angleterre à la Reine Regente touchant la mort de son mary à l'estat present* (A Paris: chez Robert Feuge, 1649), p. 4.

33. *Le procès verbale de la canonisation du bienhereux Jules Mazarin, faite dans le consistoire des partisans, par Catalan et Tabouret, séant Emery antipape. Apothéose ironique* (A Paris: chez Claude Boudeville, 1649), p. 3.

34. *La politique burlesque dedié à Amaranthe*, par S. T. F. S. L. S. D. T. (A Paris, 1649), p. 33.

35. *Choix de Mazarinades*, ed. C. Moreau, 2 vols. (Paris, 1853), I, pp. 294-95. The French texts of these two passages run thus: "Il semble, Madame, que le ciel, dupuis trente ans, ait conjuré la ruine de toutes les Monarchies. C'est pourquoy il faut éviter soigneusement ce qui peut donner

lieu a de révolutions si funestes." And again: "crainte que les peuples affamez ne perdent legitimement le respect qu'ils doivent a Vostre Majesté; et crainte aussi que ces révolutions si merveilleuses et si prejudiciables à tant de Royaumes n'achevent leur cours au préjudice du vostre, si vous ne luy donnez bien tost la paix, en mettant fin à toutes ces guerres tant domestiques qu'estrangeres."

36. *Ibid.*, II, p. 202; H. Carrier, ed., *La Fronde, contestation démocratique et misère paysanne; 52 Mazarinades*, 2 vols. (Paris, 1982), Tract No. 36, p. 29.

37. Moreau, II, pp. 230-31, 233; Carrier, Tract No. 23, p. 12.

38. *Le coup d'estat de la Guyenne presenté à Monseigneur le Prince de Condé, & à Messieurs de Bordeaux* (A Paris: chez Gilles Dubois, 1651), p. 5.

39. *Le Royal au Mazarin, luy faisant voir par la raison et par l'histoire* [1652], p. 5.

40. *La declaration de Monseigneur le duc de Guise, faicte à Bordeaux le troisième du mois courant, sur la jonction de ces interests avec ceux de Messieurs les Princes; avec toutes la particularitez de sa sortie* (A Paris: chez Guillaume de la Court, 1652), p. 8.

41. Kerviler and de Barthelémy, p. 522; *Correspondance de Jacques Dupuy et de Nicolas Heinsius (1646-1656)*, ed. H. Bots (The Hague, 1971), p. 125; Philip A. Knachal, *England and the Fronde* (Ithaca, 1967), pp. 86-87.

42. R. Mentet de Salmonet, *Histoire de troubles de la Grand' Bretagne*, 2 vols. (Paris, 1661), II, pp. 367-69; R. Mentet de Salmonet, *The History of the Troubles of Great Britain*, trans. J. Ogilvie (London, 1735), pp. 517-18.

43. [R. Mentet de Salmonet], *Remonstrance très-humble, faite au serenissime Prince Charles II, Roy de la Grand' Bretagne, &c. sur la conjonture presente des affaires de sa Majesté* (A Paris: chez Antoine Vitré, 1652), p. 3.

44. Mezeray, *Histoire de France*, III, p. 1013; and see also his use of the word on pp. 942 and 1134.

45. *Ibid.*, p. 601; "les principaux autheurs de cette grande révolution ne sembloient pas estre disposer a se soumettre à un Duc, après avoir secoué le joug d'un Roy, mais s'imaginoient pouvoir former une Democratie sur le moule de celle de Suisses, qu'ils appelloient le plus heureux peuple de la Chrestienté."

46. *Ibid.*, p. 604; "le souslevement de tant de villes ne se devoit point appeller rébellion, mais révolution; qu'il estoit juste contre un Roy perfide et hypocrite, et que le destin mesme sembloit l'authoriser."

47. La Noue, p. 34.

48. In his *Dictionnaire* entry on Bodin, Pierre Bayle repeated the story of Bodin's speech to the inhabitants of Laôn, ascribing to him almost the same words. This was written, however, some fifty years after Mezeray. Bayle's source is a work by Ménage.

49. J.-F. Battail, *L'avocat philosophe; Geraud de Cordemoy (1626-1684)*, (The Hague, 1973).

50. *Mémoires* in *Oeuvres du Cardinal de Retz*, ed. A. Feille et al., 10 vols. (Paris, 1870-96), II, pp. 94-95.

51. [Cardinal de Retz], *La conjuration du comte Jean-Louis de Fiesque* (Paris, 1665), p. 105; see also the critical edition edited by D. A. Watts (Oxford, 1967), p. 34, and Mascardi, *La congiura del Conte Gio. Luigi de' Fieschi*, pp. 51-52, where the expression is "una turbulenta rivolutione." In Retz's sermon of 1646 it is "les désordres qui accompagnent la révolution des États;" see his *Oeuvres*, IX, p. 85.

52. Retz, *Oeuvres*, V, p. 312. The authorship of this pamphlet, written for the sole purpose of annoying Mazarin, was also claimed by Guy Joly, Retz's secretary, who did not use, however, the term much in his own writing. See his *Mémoires* (Paris, 1825), p. 426.

53. Retz, *Oeuvres*, VI, p. 61; "Apologie des Frondeurs" (May 1650) in Moreau, *Choix de Mazarinades*, II, p. 186. The French text of this passage is: "il n'y a point d'exemples de révolution qui l'on ne doive appréhender d'un peuple si cruellement *Foulé*." Foulé, notes Moreau, was the name of a hated intendant.

54. *Recueil des instructions données aux ambassadeurs et ministres de France*, XXIV, *Angleterre*, ed. J. J. Jusserand (Paris, 1929), pp. 35-38.

55. *Lettres du Cardinal Mazarin à la Reine* (1651-1652), ed. M. Ravenel (Paris, 1836), pp. 5-6.

56. *Lettres du Cardinal Mazarin*, III, pp. 284, 642, IV, p. 96, V, p. 584, VII, pp. 115, 174, 209, IX, 278, 428.

57. *A Collection of the State Papers of John Thurloe*, 7 vols. (London, 1742), III, p. 163.

58. *Correspondance de Jacques Dupuy et de Nicolas Heinsius (1646-1656)*, ed. H. Bots (The Hague, 1971), p. 121.

59. The word "revolutions" appeared in 1652 in the subtitle of another book translated to French, Thomas Hobbes's *Le corps politique*, translated by Samuel Sorbière. It actually repeated the full title of the 1650 English edition with which, however, Hobbes had nothing to do.

60. See the letters in the appendix to F. Guizot, *Monk; chute de la république et l'établissement de la monarchie en Angleterre en 1660* (Brussels and Leipzig, 1851), pp. 165, 186, 243, 259, 276, 279-80.

61. Saint-Evremont, *Oeuvres en prose*, ed. R. Ternois, 4 vols. (Paris, 1962-69), I, p. 141.

62. *Mémoires de Louis XIV*, ed. J. Lognon (Paris, 1927), p. 126.

Chapter Four

1. See, for example, M. G. Finlayson, *Historians, Puritanism and the English Revolution* (Toronto, 1983), pp. 20-21; also R. C. Letham, "English Revolutionary Thought, 1640-1660," *History*, XXX (1945), pp. 38-39.

2. *Harleian Miscellany* (London, 1808-11), V, pp. 217, 446.

3. [J. Howell], *A Trance: or News from Hell, brought fresh to Towne by Mercurius Acheronticus* (London, 1649), p. 9. This short tract was written months before its publication. Howell's allegorical essay on the different European states, entitled *Dendrologia*, was first printed in 1640 and quickly translated into French. See the third edition (Cambridge, 1645), to which are attached his *England's Tear for the Present Wars* and *The Pre-eminence and Pedigree of Parliament*, the term "revolution" is absent throughout.

4. V. F. Snow, "The Concept of Revolution in Seventeenth Century England," *The Historical Journal*, V, (1962), pp. 167-74; M. Lasky, "The Birth of a Metaphor; on the Origins of Utopia and Revolution," *Encounter* (Feb., 1970), pp. 35-45 and (Mar., 1970), pp. 30-42, and later in his *Utopia and Revolution* (Chicago, 1976); C. Hill, "The Word 'Revolution'," in his *A Nation of Change and Novelty* (London, 1990), pp. 82-101.

5. Lasky, *Encounter* (Mar., 1970), p. 34.

6. *The Works of Sir Thomas Browne*, Ed. C. Sayle, 3 vols. (Edinburgh, 1912), I, p. 28.

7. Hill, pp. 88-89. See also I. Rachum, "The Term 'Revolution' in Seventeenth Century English Astrology," *History of European Ideas*, XVIII, No. 6 (1994), pp. 869-83.

8. Snow, p. 170; Lasky, *Encounter* (Mar., 1970), p. 31; Hill, p. 87.

9. P. D., *Severall Politique and Militarie Observations upon the Civill and Militarie Governments* (London, 1648), pp. 46, 50, 64, 69-70.

10. Cf. P. Zagorin, *A History of Political Thought in the English Revolution* (London, 1954), p. 66; I. Coltman, *Private Men and Public Causes; Philosophy and Politics in the English Civil War* (London, 1962), p. 205.

11. Ascham's 1648 edition was printed by H. Moseley, and the expanded 1649 edition by W. Wilson. In 1689 the work was reprinted again, though without Ascham's name, and the title changed, to suit the circumstances, to *A Seasonable Discourse, Wherein is Examined what is Lawful during the Confusions and Revolutions of Government; Especially in the Case of a King Deserting his Kingdom.*

12. Ascham, *A Discourse* (1648), pp. 2-3, 25, 93; *Of the Confusions and Revolutions* (1649), pp. 34-38, 70-73, 131-33.

13. See Barker cited in Hill, p. 88, and "Declaration of the Commission of the General Assembly," 9 October 1648, in J. Thurloe, *State Papers*, I, p. 105.

14. [R. Sanderson], *A Resolution of Conscience in Answer to a Letter sent with Mr. Ascham's Book, Treating how far it may be Lawful to Submit to an Usurped Power* (1649), pp. 5-6; H. Hammond, *A Vindication of Dr.*

Hammond's Address from the Exceptions of Eutactus Philodemius (London, 1649); A. Ascham, *A Reply to a Paper of Dr. Sanderson's, Containing a Censure of Mr. A. A. his Book of the Confusions and Revolutions of Government* (London, 1650); [A. Ascham], *An Answer to the Vindication of Doctor Hammond against the Exceptions of Eutactus Philodemius* (London, 1650), pp. 5-6.

15. Wren's tract was published only later, in J. Gutch's *Collectanea Curiosa* (Oxford, 1781), I, pp. 228-53. Its title, "Of the Origins and Progress of the Revolution in England," could have been added by the editor. See Snow, p. 170; Hill, p. 92.

16. "The Process and Pleading in the Court of Spain, Upon the Death of Anthony Ascham" (London, 1651) in *Harleian Miscellany*, VI, pp. 236-47; See also P. B. Marriman, *Six Contemporaneous Revolutions* (Oxford, 1938), pp. 108-10.

17. Clarendon, E. Hyde, Earl of, *A Brief View and Survey of the Dangerous and Pernicious Errors to Church and State in Mr. Hobbes's book entitled Leviathan* (Oxford, 1676), pp. 7-8; Coltman, pp. 208-10, 223.

18. *Patriarcha and Other Political Works of Sir Robert Filmer*, ed. P. Laslett (Oxford, 1949), pp. 188, 279.

19. G. P. Gooch, *English Democratic Ideas in the Seventeenth Century*, 2nd ed. (Cambridge, 1927), pp. 159-62; Zagorin, pp. 121-27.

20. M. Nedham, "A short History of the English Rebellion" (1648); the poem was reprinted in 1661, when Nedham, for obvious reasons, strove to give testimony of his royalist past. See *Harleian Miscellany*, VII, pp. 185-208. "Revolution" does not appear in Nedham's *The Case of the Kingdom Stated* (London, 1647), which is a short and rather objective analysis of the aims of the main political parties; neither in Nedham's short pro-royalist play, *The Second Part of Crafty Cromwell, or Oliver his Glory as King* (London, 1648).

21. M. Nedham, *The Case of the Commonwealth of England stated* (London, 1650), pp. 1-2, 6, 80-94.

22. *Mercurius Politicus*, No. 25 (21-28 November 1650), p. 407; No. 66 (4-11 September 1651), p. 1046; No. 67 (11-18 September 1651), p. 1061; No. 70 (2-9 October 1651), p. 1109. In the last two places the meaning of the word is actually more related to time than to politics.

23. J. Selden, *Of the Dominion or Ownership of the Sea, two Books* (London, 1652); Hill, p. 90.

24. M. Nedham, *A True State of the Case of the Commonwealth of England, Scotland and Ireland* (London, 1654), pp. 2, 4.

25. Hill, pp. 89-92.

26. [W. Sancroft], *Modern Policies Taken from Machiavel, Borgia and other choice Authors*, 4th ed. (London, 1653); first edition of this tract came out in July 1652. See his "Principle VI."

27. *Great Brittain's Post*, 14-21 December 1653.

28. *The Politique Informer*, 23-30 January 1654. In comparison, the *Mercurius Politicus* had no "revolution" when reporting on the setting up of the Protectorate. Only in No. 222 (7-14 September 1654), p. 3761, one falls upon a rare use of the term ("an Account of a new Revolution this day") to describe Cromwell's intervention in the debate of Parliament over the form of government.

29. *The Letters and Speeches of Oliver Cromwell*, ed. T. Carlyle, 3 vols. (London, 1904), II, pp. 274-75.

30. *Ibid.*, II, pp. 419, 426, 428. This speech of Cromwell's was given a wide distribution, having been printed both in London and Edinburgh. See *His Highness Speech to the Parliament in the painted Chamber at their Dissolution*, upon Monday the 22d of January 1654 [1655], pp. 14, 19, 20, 21.

31. Lasky, *Encounter* (March 1970), pp. 31-32; Snow, p. 169; Hill, p. 87.

32. J. Howell, *Epistolae Ho-Eliane; Familiar Letters Domestic and Forren*, 2nd ed. (London, 1650), III, p. 2. The first edition of the *Epistolae* appeared in 1645. The second edition was enlarged "with divers supplements, and the dates annexed which were wanting in the first, with an addition of a third volume of new letters." Howell had discussed the revolts of Catalonia and Portugal against Spain already in a letter of the 1645 edition, but he did not use there the word "revolution."

33. See J. Howell, *Lexicon Tetraglotton, an English-French-Italian-Spanish Dictionary* (London, 1660). Here "revolution" was given the equivalence of "révolution, rappel" in French, "rivocazione" in Italian and "revocación, rebuelta" in Spanish.

34. J. Howell, *Some Sober Inspections made into the Carriage and Consults of the Late-long Parliament* (London, 1655), pp. 4, 9.

35. R. L'Estrange, *A Modest Plea both for the Caveat and the Author of it, with some notes upon Mr. James Howell and his Sober Inspections* (London, 1661).

36. M. Nedham, *The Excellencie of a Free-state* (London, 1656), pp. 37, 77, 79-80, 135. A similar use of the term ("in a Revolution or Rotation of their Assemblies") appears in Nedham's article in *Mercurius Politicus*, No. 354 (19-24 March 1657), p. 7674.

37. Cf. Lasky, *Encounter* (March 1970), pp. 34-35; *The Complete Works of John Milton* (New Haven, 1971), V, pp. 1, 403.

38. Hobbes's last sentence of the postscript goes thus: "And although in the revolution of states, there can be no very good constellation for truths of this nature to be born under (as having an angry aspect from the dissolvers of an old government, and seeing out the backs of them that erect a new), yet I cannot think it will be condemned at this time, either by the public judge of doctrine, or by any that desires the continuance of public peace."

39. *The Political Works of James Harrington*, ed. J. G. A. Pocock (Cambridge, 1977), pp. 228, 820.

40. *Ibid.*, pp. 405-06; See the interpretations of this passage in Snow, p. 171, and Hill, p. 93.

41. *Mercurius Politicus*, No. 432 (2-9 September 1658), p. 803.

42. "An Account of the Fall of the Protector, Richard Cromwell, in a Letter from Nehemiah Bourne," *The Clarke Papers*, ed. C. H. Firth (London, 1899), III, p. 217.

43. *Mercurius Politicus*, No. 60 (20 December 1659 – 5 January 1660), p. 989.

44. Cited by Lasky, *Encounter* (Mar., 1970), p. 35.

45. C. Harvey, *Atheniastes, or the Right Rebel* (London, 1661), pp. 149-50.

46. G. Torriani, *A Dictionary Italian and English formerly compiled by John Florio* (London, 1659); E. Phillips, *The New World of English Words* (London, 1658).

47. W. Lilly, *Merlini Anglici Ephemeris* (London, 1658), pp. 1, 23.

48. W. Andrews, *De Rebus Caelestibus* (London, 1659).

49. Given by Lasky, *Encounter* (Feb., 1970), p. 42.

50. *The Works of the most Excellent Philosopher and Astronomer Sir George Wharton* (London, 1683), p. 387.

51. "Democritus turned Statesman; or Twenty Queries between Jest and Earnest, proposed to all true-hearted Englishmen," *Harleian Miscellany*, VII, pp. 82-86.

52. *A Collection of Several Letters and Declarations sent by General Monck* (London, 1660), p. 15.

53. Monck's speech is given at length in D. Riordan de Muscry, *Relation des véritables causes, et de conjonctures favorables, qui ont contribué au rétablissement du Roy de la Grande Bretagne* (Paris, 1661), pp. 117-33. The French wording is: "Vous estes tesmoins, Messieurs, que dans cette funeste révolution de nos Royaumes, les actions les plus injustes, les plus noires et les plus violentes, ont esté authorisées par la fureur Epidémique d'une multitude insensé."

54. *A Collection of His Magesties gracious Letters, Speeches, Messages and Declarations since April 4/14 1660* (London, 1660), pp. 9, 11, 23, 26-27.

55. W. Wylde, *A Speech Spoken to his most Sacred Majesty, Charles the Second in his passage from the Tower to Whitehall* (London, 1661).

56. The last of these twelve treatises, dated by Howell 12 March, 1659, is a call to restore the monarchy. Only there we find: "The Ile of Great Britain hath been always a Royall Island... although she had four or five Revolutions and changes of Masters," pp. 408-409. See also Howell's preface to *Florus Hungaricus, or the History of Hungaria and Transylvania* (London, 1664).

57. R. L'Estrange, *A Memento Treating of the Rise, Progress and Remedies of Seditions, with some Historical Reflections upon the Series of our Late Troubles*, 2nd ed. (London, 1682), p. 17.

Chapter Five

1.   Cf. S. N. Zwicker, *Politics and Language in Dryden's Poetry; The Arts of Disguise* (Princeton, 1984), p. 33.

2.   Apparently, the only book to deviate from this rule is François Bernier's *The History of the Late Revolution of the Empire of the Great Mogol* (London, 1671). The French original of this work, describing the author's travels in India from 1658 to 1668, came out in Paris in 1670 and earned a great success. Permission to print the English translation was not given by the licenser Roger L'Estrange, but by John Trevor, Charles II's "principal Secretary of State." As mentioned in chapter 2, note 26, Gualdo Priorato's *Historia delle rivoluzioni di Francia* (1655) was translated to English and printed in 1676 as *The history of France.* Thus, if we add Howell's *Twelve Several Treaties of the Late Revolutions of These Three Kingdoms* (1661), published before the Licensing Act of 1663, the number is two.

3.   Thomas Blount's *Glossographia; or a Dictionary Interpreting the Hard Words... in our Refined English Tongue* came out first in 1656. Its third edition, printed in 1670, still had: "Revolution (*revolutio*) a returning back to the first place or point, the accomplishment of a circular course." Elisha Cole's, *An English Dictionary* (London, 1676), had: *"Revolution,* a turning round to the first point." Thomas Holyoke's English-Latin dictionary, printed in 1677, translated *revolutio* as "A turning back to the first place or point: a revolution of the celestial spheres." Adam Littleton's Latin dictionary, also first printed in 1677, had: *"A revolution or turning about."* Only Guy Miège, a Frenchman residing in England, paid attention to the changing meaning. His dictionary, printed in London by Basset in 1684, translated the word from English to French as "révolution, vicissitude," and from French to English – "revolution, change, alteration."

4.   *A Collection of His Majesties Gracious Letters*, pp. 70-71.

5.   Clarendon, *A Brief View and Survey of the Dangerous and Pernicious Errors to Church and State*; and his *History of the Rebellion*, Bk. xi, sec. 207 [Vol. IV, p. 467]. Here he writes that members of Parliament, excluded in December 1648 after Pride's Purge, "forbore coming any more to the House for many years, and not before the revolution." Clearly, in this case the "revolution" means the Restoration.

6.   J. Gadbury, *Collectio geniturarum* (London, 1679), pp. 147, 155-56; H. Coley, *Nuntius Coelestis, or Urania's Messenger of 1679* (London, 1679), and also his *Nuntius Coelestis* of 1682; J. Partridge, *Mercurius Coelestis* (London, 1680), and his *Merlinus Redivivus* of 1684, 1685 and 1686; W. Lilly, *Astrological Judgments* (1681), where there is a use

in the political sense: "War and other mischief attends some of our neighbour Nations; as also many Alterations, Changes and Revolutions;" J. Holwell, *A New Prophecy; or a Prophetical Discourse of the Blazing Star that Appeared, April the 23rd 1677* (London, 1679); J. Gadbury, *Ephemeris or a Diary Astronomical, Astrological, Meteorological for the Year of Our Lord 1688* (London, 1688). And see also I. Rachum, "The Term 'Revolution' in Seventeenth Century English Astrology."

7.   Hill, "The Word 'Revolution'," pp. 94-95.

8.   I have used the first French edition – E. Chamberlayne, *L'estat présent de l'Angleterre* (Amsterdam, 1669), p. 85. Here the text goes thus: "...c'est pourquoy lors que pendant les dernières révolutions & bouleversements, le diable & les hommes ont employé toute leur industrie imaginable, pour tascher de changer cette Monarchie en Democratie, & le Royaume en République,..."

9.   W. Temple, *Works*, 4 vols. (Edinburgh, 1754), II, pp. 30, 53, 55, 56, 360-62, 370, 374-75.

10.   *The Works of the Famous Nicholas Machiavel*, trans. H. Neville, 3rd ed. (London, 1720), pp. 253, 534; see also F. Raab, *The English Faces of Machiavelli* (London, 1965), pp. 219-220, and M. Goldie, "The Civil Religion of James Harrington" in A. Pagden, ed., *The Languages of Political Theory*, pp. 197-222.

11.   [H. Neville], *Plato Redivivus: or a Dialogue Concerning Government* (London, 1681); or the modern edition by C. Robbins, *Two English Republican Tracts* (Cambridge, 1969), p. 182.

12.   [A. Marvell], *An Account of the Growth of Popery and Arbitrary Government in England* (Amsterdam, 1677), p. 14; and cf. Hill, p. 95.

13.   J. Locke, *Two Treaties of Civil Government*, Bk. ii, chap. xix, secs. 223, 225.

14.   A. Sidney, *Discourses Concerning Government*, 2nd ed. (London, 1704), pp. 103, 129, 256, 400. It is indeed odd that Sidney, who was acutely aware of the negative rhetorical ring of words such as "sedition" and "rebellion," could not bring himself to a freer experimentation with the new political sense of "revolution." Cf. S. A. Nelson, *The 'Discourses' of Algernon Sidney* (Cranbury, N. J., 1993), pp. 122-26.

15.   But right after his death in Holland appeared a short and fierce denunciation of his personality entitled: *Memoires of the Life of Anthony late Earle of Shaftesbury; with a Speech of the English Consul in Amsterdam concerning him and a Letter from a Burgher there about his Death, offered to the Consideration of the Protestant Dissenters* (London, 1683). Here, on the first page, Shaftesbury and his followers were accused of "obstinacy against the Laws, and their Lawful Governours, by the expectation of a revolution in the Government it self, which they have and do with their utmost art and industry endeavour to undermine and overthrow."

16. H. Foulis, *The History of the Wicked Plots and Conspiracies of our Pretended Saints* (London, 1662), pp. 23-24. Foulis supposedly translated and cited here from the Jesuit author Adam Contzenus, whose *Politicorum libri decem* appeared in Mainz in 1617.

17. *The Observator*, III, No. 1 (11 February 1685).

18. "The Judgment and Decree of the University of Oxford, passed in their Convocation, July 21, 1683, against certain pernicious Books, and damnable Doctrines destructive to the Sacred Persons of Princes, their State and Government, and of all human Society," in *Somers' Tracts*, 4 vols. (London, 1748), III, pp. 223-27.

19. "The Trial of Lord William Russell at the Old Bailey, London for High Treason, July 13, 1683" in *Letters of Lady Rachel Russell*, 4th ed. (Dublin, 1774); "An Account of what passed at the Execution of the late Duke of Monmouth" in *Somers' Tracts*, I, pp. 216-20.

20. In his bulky *De jure naturae et gentium*, first published in Lund in 1672, Pufendorf mentioned several times Bernier's *Histoire de la dernière révolution des États du Grand Mogul* (Paris, 1670), which he rendered into Latin as *De nuperis motibus in imperio Magnis Mogolis*. Thus the resounding French "révolution des États" was exchanged for the somewhat trifling "motus," which is closer to signifying a commotion or uprising.

21. *Oraisons funèbres et panégyriques par Bossuet* (Paris, 1870), p. 3; J. B. Bossuet, *Discours sur l'histoire universelle*, 3rd ed. (Paris, 1700), pp. 466, 474. In fact, the word comes at the heads of chapters one and two of the third part, which deals with empires, and is not employed in the text. In the *Histoire de variations des eglises protestantes* Bossuet used "guerre civile," "rébellions" and some other terms, in addition to "variations" which he applied mainly to changes in doctrine and ritual.

22. E. Sommer, *Lexique de la langue de madame de Sévigné*, 2 vols. (Paris, 1866), has no entry for "révolution," though it does have for "désordre," "émotion" and others.

23. J. F. Senault, *Le monarque, ou les devoirs du souverain* (Paris, 1661), p. 215; P. Hay, *Traité de la politique de France* (Cologne, 1669), p. 187; P. Lemoyne, *De l'art de régner* (Paris, 1665), p. 598.

24. This is taken from the English translation; F. de Motteville, *Memoirs for the History of Anne of Austria*, 5 vols. (London, 1725), I, p. xvi. It came out just two years after the first French edition.

25. Goulemot, "Le mot révolution," p. 418, found the word ten times in the first 300 pages of Retz' memoirs, whereas "guerre civile" appeared there 25, and "émotion" 16 times.

26. Cardinal de Retz, *Memoirs*, 4 vols. (London, 1723), I, p. 118.

27. *Lettres de Cardinal Mazarin*, II, pp. 526, 561. The references of Mazarin to Modène are made in two letters to Fontenoy, the French ambassador in Rome, dated 25 November and 21 December 1647. A

different evaluation of Modène, his character and qualities, appears in Nicolai's *Delle rivoluzioni di Napoli* (1660), pp. 395-96.

28. [Modène, Esprit de Raimond de Marmoiron, comte de], *Mémoires de comte de Modène sur la révolution de Naples de 1647*, ed. J.-B. Mielle, 3rd ed., 2 vols. (Paris, 1827), I, pp. 1-3, 53.

29. *Ibid.*, I, pp. 121-29.

30. *Ibid.*, II, pp. 493-95.

31. *Journal des Savants*, 3 May 1666, p. 216.

32. "Révolution" is not used by Galardi in *Traité politique concernant l'importance du choix exact d'ambassadeurs habiles* (Brussels, 1666); but it becomes a part of his language in his *Raisons d'estat et réflexions politiques sur l'histoire et vies des roys de Portugal* (Liège, 1670), pp. 1, 6, 27, 180. In yet another short work by Galardi, *La tyrannie heureuse ou Cromwell politique* (Leiden, 1671), the word is used in the "Épistre," and in pp. 6, 74, 90 and 104 (where he gives Lemoyne's *Art de régner* as his source).

33. Other accounts of Molière's life, however, have him joining in 1643, at the age of twenty three, the Béjart theatre family troupe and marrying the youngest sister of Madeleine, Armande, born around 1645.

34. La Fayette, Marie Madeleine Pioche de la Vergne, comtesse de, *Vie de la princesse d'Angleterre*, ed. M.-T. Hipp (Geneva, 1967), pp. 24, 25.

35. R. Simon, *Histoire critique du vieux testament* (Paris, 1680).

36. J. de La Bruyère, *Oeuvres complètes*, ed. J. Benda (Paris: Gallimard, 1951), p. 396.

37. See G. Ménage, *Observations sur la langue françoise*, 2 vols. (Paris, 1675-76); D. Bouhours, *Remarques nouvelles sur la langue françoise* (Paris, 1675), and his *Suite de remarques nouvelles sur la langue françoise* (Paris, 1693); N. Andry de Boisregard, *Réflexions sur l'usage présent de la langue françoise* (Paris, 1689), and his *Suite de réflexions critiques sur l'usage présent de la langue françoise* (Paris, 1693); and Morvan de Belleregarde, *Réflexions sur l'élégance et la politesse du style* (Paris, 1695).

38. A. Furetière, *Dictionnaire universel contenant généralement tous les mots français tant vieux que modernes*, 3 vols. (The Hague and Rotterdam, 1690); P. A. de la Place, ed., *Pièces interessantes et peu connues pour servir à l'histoire et à la litterature*, 8 vols. (Brussels, 1784-90), V, pp. 239-41.

39. L. Maimbourg, *Histoire des croisades pour la deliverance de la Terre Sainte*, 2nd ed., 4 vols. (Paris, 1676), I, p. 1; L. Maimbourg, *Histoire de lutheranisme* (Paris, 1680), p. 3. In his *Histoire de la décadence de l'empire après Charlemagne*, first published in 1679, Maimbourg referred right at the beginning to "les terribles révolutions" of the Roman empire in the West after the death of Constantine, and later to "tant d'estranges révolutions" in Italy; see the Paris edition of 1686, pp. 1, 58. The word is used once in a similar sense also in the opening of his *Histoire de la Ligue*.

40. P. Bayle, *Oeuvres diverses*, 4 vols. (The Hague, 1727), II, p. 56.

41. P. Bayle, "Pensées diverses à l'occasion d'une comète" in *Oeuvres diverses*, III, pp. 66, 144, 146.

42. The references here are to the reprinted edition, consisting of the entire first volume of the *Oeuvres diverses* (1727). See Article IV (April 1684), p. 32; Article I (May 1685), p. 280; Article VI (November 1685), pp. 416-19, where he writes on the "trois grandes révolutions" of England in the years 1547-59, while reviewing a French translation of Burnet's work on the English Reformation; and in Article VIII (April 1686), p. 541, the term is applied to the revocation of the Edict of Nantes.

43. A. de Varillas, *Histoire des révolutions arrivées dans l'Europe en matière de religion*, 4 vols. (Paris, 1686-87), I, p. 1 (of the "Avertissement"); *Nouvelles de la république de lettres*, Article IV (March 1686), p. 510.

44. G. Burnet, *Reflections on Mr. Varillas's History of the Revolutions that have happened in Europe in Matters of Religion* (Amsterdam, 1686), pp. 51-52. This work of Burnet's was reviewed by Bayle in the *Nouvelles de la république des lettres*, Article IX (October 1686), pp. 673-74. Also Jean LeClerc, editor since 1686 of the *Bibliothèque universelle et historique*, gave attention to the Varillas-Burnet exchange. Cf. G. Ascoli, *La Grande-Bretagne devant l'opinion française au XVIIe siècle*, 2 vols. (Paris, 1930), II, pp. 236-38.

45. P. Jurieu, *L'accomplissement des prophéties, ou la deliverance prochaine de l'Eglise* (Rotterdam, 1686); the passage given here is taken from the English translation, *The Accomplishment of the Scripture Prophecies* (London, 1687), p. vi. See also P. Hazard, *The European Mind, 1680-1715* (Harmondsworth, 1964), pp. 127-29, 315.

46. E. Merlat, *Traité de pouvoir absolu des souverains* (Amsterdam, 1685), pp. 160-61; *Nouvelles de la république des lettres*, Article VII (August 1685) and Article VI (March 1686), P. Bayle, *Oeuvres diverses*, IV, pp. 632-33.

47. *The Works of Aphra Behn*, ed. M. Summers, 6 vols. (London, 1915), I, p. 338.

48. L. Maimbourg, *The History of the League*, trans J. Dryden (London, 1684), pp. 3-4; and see also "The Postscript," pp. 4-5, where Dryden lumps together the years of 1640-60 in almost the same way that Hobbes did at the end of *Behemoth*, but without the use of "revolution." Later on in the postscript, Dryden develops ideas on the link between the Reformation and the rise of political rebelliousness in western Europe. Actually, his view anticipates by two years Varillas's thesis on the supposed aim of the religious reformers to incite "revolutions" in all the countries of Europe. For further details on Dryden's translation see A. Roper, "A Critic's Apology for Editing Dryden's *The History of the League*," *The Editor as Critic and the Critic as Editor*, papers read at a Clark Library seminar, 13 November 1971 (University of California, Los Angeles, 1973), pp. 41-72.

49. L'Estrange's letters to Nalson, dated 23 August, 27 September and 4 October 1677, are reproduced in J. Nichols, *Illustrations of the Literary History of the Eighteenth Century*, 8 vols. (London, 1822), IV, pp. 68-70.

50. J. Nalson, *The Common Interest of King and People* (London, 1677), p. 65.

51. J. Nalson, *An Impartial Collection of the Great Affairs of State* (London, 1682), I, pp. ii, iii-iv, lvii, lxxix.

52. *Ibid.*, II, pp. i, ii, iv, xi.

53. "Revolution" is missing in *The Present Interest of England* (London, 1683) and in yet another short pamphlet ascribed to Nalson, *Reflections upon Collonel Sidney's Arcadia* (London, 1684). In another pamphlet, *Toleration and Liberty of Conscience Considered* (London, 1685), pp. 29-30, written shortly after the accession of James II, Nalson explains that Louis XIV is persecuting the Protestants in France, possibly because he wants to prevent in his own kingdom "the terror of the Revolutions which have happened to his Neighbours."

54. "To the most Reverend Father in God, William Lord Archbishop of Canterbury,…and John Lord Archbishop of York" (5 March 1685), in *Somers' Tracts* (1748), II, pp. 355-58.

55. Savile, *The Complete Works*, pp. 60, 139-40.

56. *Revolution Politicks*, Being a Complete Collection of all the Reports, Lyes and Stories, which were the Fore-runners of the Great Revolution in 1688 (London, 1733), Part V, pp. 18-19.

57. G. Burnet, *A Collection of Eighteen Papers, Relating to the Affairs of Church and State during the Reign of James the Second* (London, 1689), pp. 83, 86; *A Supplement to Burnet's History of My Own Time*, ed. H. C. Foxcroft (Oxford, 1902), pp. 522-28.

58. *The Diary of John Evelyn*, ed. E. S. Beer, 6 vols. (Oxford, 1955), IV, p. 609; and also see Hill, p. 96.

Chapter Six

1. It was the unequivocal opinion of J. M. Goulemot that although the term belonged to French political vocabulary prior to the unseating of James II, the accession of William of Orange to the English throne modified its manners of use and gave it definition. See his "le mot révolution," pp. 417, 435-43.

2. *A Compleat Collection of Papers, in Twelve Parts, relating to the great Revolutions in England and Scotland, from the time of the seven bishops petitioning K. James II against the dispensing power, June 8, 1688, to the coronation of King William and Queen Mary, April 11, 1689* (London, 1689).

3. *A Collection of State Tracts, published on occasion the late Revolution in 1688 and during the reign of King William III*, 3 vols. (London, 1705-07), I, pp. 108, 149, 285, 430, 466, II, p. 1, III, p. 731. This collection contains some 180 tracts of which about a third belong to the year 1689.

4. J. Welwood, *Indication of the present Great Revolution in England;* W. Kennett, *A Dialogue between two Friends occasioned by the late Revolution of Affairs and the Oath of Allegiance*; E. Stephens, *Important Questions of State, Law, Injustice and Prudence, both civil and religious, upon the late Revolutions and present state of these Nations*; A. Ascham, *A Seasonable Discourse wherein is Examined what is Lawful during the Confusions and Revolutions of Government; especially in the Case of a King deserting his Kingdom*; all published in London in 1689.

5. W. A. Speck, *Reluctant Revolutionaries; Englishmen and the Revolution of 1688* (Oxford, 1988), pp. 1, 241-42. And see also Hill, "The Word 'Revolution'," p. 96, expressing disagreement with J. P. Kenyon's notion of the meaning of the term on the eve of 1688.

6. "Reflections upon the late great Revolution, written by a Lay-hand in the Country for the Satisfaction of some Neighbours," *A Collection of State Tracts* (1705), I, p. 264. In other tracts the "revolution" is spoken of as a development that secured the existence of Protestantism in England and other states in Europe, or as "a departure from the former Constitution." Also, there is a reference to William of Orange as "being descended of those who by Revolutions had sav'd Europe more than once." See I, pp. 274, 276, 411; III, p. 728.

7. *Essays of John Dryden*, ed. W. P. Ker, 2 vols. (Oxford, 1926), II, pp. 38, 241.

8. See particularly the essay "Of Liberty" in J. Collier, *Essays upon Several Moral Subjects*, 4 vols. (London, 1698-1709).

9. T. Clayton, *William III and the Godly Revolution* (Cambridge, 1996), especially pp. 28-52. Clayton's interpretation clashes with J. P. Kenyon's, who called the view that the revolution had been heavenly inspired "a devotional platitude." See his *Revolution Principles; the Politics of Party, 1689-1720* (Cambridge, 1977), pp. 24-25.

10. [G. Burnet], *An Enquiry into the Measures of Submission to the Supreme Authority* [1688]. This is an 8 pp. leaflet, printed in Holland, lacking any indication as to place and date of publication.

11. G. Burnet, "A Sermon Preached in the Chappel of St. James's before His Highness the Prince of Orange, the 23rd of December, 1688" in his *A Second Collection of Several Tracts* (London, 1689), pp. 1, 2, 15, 22-23.

12. G. Burnet, *A Sermon Preached before the House of Commons, on the 31st of January 1688[9]* (London, 1689), pp. 30, 31.

13. *A Pastoral Letter writ by Gilbert [Burnet], Lord Bishop of Sarum, to the Clergy of his Diocess, Concerning the Oaths of Allegiance and Supremacy to K. William and Q. Mary* (London, 1689), pp. 6, 8, 10-13. The

same issue had been examined already in March 1689 in an anonymous *The Case of Allegiance in our Present Circumstances Considered*. Here too the new term was employed several times, pp. 2-3. The author maintained that it was necessary for Englishmen to get rid of "false Principles about Government and Obedience" and "if we find such Principles do rather inslave than oblige our Consciences, and are as inconsistent with Truth, as they are with the present Revolution, we must take the honest courage, to break of these bands, and assert our Liberty."

14. *Vindication of the present Great Revolution in England in Five Letters pass'd betwixt James Welwood, M.D. and Mr. John March, Vicar of Newcastle upon Tyne* (London, 1689), pp. 2, 6, 25.

15. W. Sherlock, *The Case of the Allegiance due to Soveraign Powers* (London, 1691), pp. 4, 50. See also Kenyon, pp. 26-29.

16. T. Wilson, *God, the King, and the Country, united in the Justification of this present Revolution* (London, 1691), pp. 15, 19.

17. *The Works of the late Reverend Mr. Samuel Johnson* (London, 1710), pp. 216, 264, 272; [S. Johnson], *Remarks upon Dr. Sherlock's Case of Allegiance* (n.p., n.d.), p. 17.

18. Bayle, *Oeuvres diverses*, IV, p. 650.

19. J. Tyrell, *Bibliotheca Politica: or an Inquiry into the Ancient Constitution of the English Government, ...* wherein all chief arguments, as well against, as for the late Revolution, are impartially represented, and considered, in thirteen dialogues (London, 1694). And see Kenyon, pp. 36-37.

20. *A Collection of State Tracts*, II, pp. 112, 159, 438,458.

21. *Ibid.*, II, pp. 253, 268, 271, 525.

22. See, for example, *The Revolution Justified, from Principles of Reason and Scripture* (London, 1697).

23. The tract was apparently first published in 1707 in *A Collection of State Tracts*, III, pp. 694-728. See especially pp. 695, 697-98, and cf. Kenyon, pp. 43-45, 219.

24. "A Memorial drawn by King William's special Direction, intended to be given in at the Treaty of Ryswick: justifying the REVOLUTION, and the Course of his Government," *Somers' Tracts* (1748), I, pp. 400-409. In addition to Kenyon, M. J. Lasky, *Utopia and Revolution*, pp. 449-51, commented on these passages.

25. "The Dangers of Mercenary Parliaments" and "Considerations on the Nature of Parliaments," are both in *A Collection of State Tracts*, III, pp. 638-50. See pp. 640 and 645.

26. *A Collection of State Tracts*, III, pp. 70-71, 81, 225-26, 301, 353. And see also [J. Whittel], *A Short Review of the Remarkable Providences attending our gracious Sovereign William the IIIrd* (London, 1699), where the "Divine Providence" exegesis is mingled with sound political and historical arguments.

27. It was printed by W. Onley for John Sturton without the name of the author. In 1706 another play, *The Revolution of Sweden: A Tragedy*, the work of Catherine Cockburn, concentrated on Gustavus Vasa, who had gained independence from Denmark in the sixteenth century.

28. J. Evelyn, *Diary*, V, p. 623.

29. J. Swift, *Bickerstaff Papers and Pamphlets on the Church*, ed. H. Davis (Oxford, 1957), p. 149.

30. Yet another short outline is H. T. Dickinson, "The Eighteenth Century Debate on the 'Glorious Revolution,'" *History*, LXI (1976), pp. 28-45.

31. Cited by Kenyon, pp. 103-108; Dickinson, p. 33.

32. B. Hoadly, *The Foundation of the present Government defended* (London, 1709), pp. 22-24.

33. *The Revolution no Rebellion* (London, 1709), pp. 11-12.

34. *The True, Genuine, Tory-Address, to which is added an Explanation of some Hard Terms now in use* (London, 1710). That same year Hoadly published an expanded exposition of his views on issues such as rebellion, passive obedience and "patriarchal scheme of government," entitled *The Original and Institution of Civil Government* (London, 1710).

35. H. Sacheverell, *The Perils of False Brethren, both in Church and State* (London, 1709), p. 12-13.

36. *The Answer of Henry Sacheverell, D.D. to the Articles of Impeachment exhibited against him by the Honourable House of Commons* (London, 1710), p. 3; and see also Appendix A in the work of G. Holmes, *The Trial of Doctor Sacheverell* (London, 1973), pp. 279-82.

37. Cited by Dickinson, pp. 34-35.

38. Kenyon, pp. 134-35.

39. *The Bishop of Salisbury his Speech in the House of Lords on the First Article of the Impeachment of Dr. Henry Sacheverell* (London, 1710), p. 16; Kenyon, pp. 140-41.

40. *Ibid.*, p. 138.

41. "An Essay towards the History of the last Ministry and Parliament, containing seasonable Reflections on Favourites, Ministers of States, Parties, Parliaments and Publick Credit" in *Somers' Tracts* (1748), II, p. 250.

42. The reprint published in London in 1771 was labeled the tenth edition and followed by one in Philadelphia (1773) and another in Newport, R.I. (1774), called the eleventh and twelfth editions respectively. Kenyon was inclined to give the authorship to Thomas Harrison, publisher of the 1709-10 edition, or somebody backed by him, perhaps even Burnet. See his Appendix A, pp. 209-10.

43. *The Judgment of whole Kingdoms and Nations*, 3rd ed. (London, 1710), p. 46.

44. Cited by Lasky, *Utopia and Revolution*, p. 450 and Kenyon, p. 165.

45. J. Swift, *The Examiner and Other Pieces Written in 1710-1711*, ed. H. Davis (Oxford, 1957), p. 147.

46. *The Revolution and Anti-Revolution Principles Stated and Compar'd* (London, 1714), pp. 4, 9, 14-15, 44.

47. *The Liberties of England asserted in Opposition to Popery, Slavery and Modern Innovation* (London, 1714), p. 21; *Revolution Principles fairly Represented and Defended* (London, 1714), p. 37.

48. J. Swift, *Political Tracts, 1713-1719*, eds. H. Davis and I. Ehrenpreis (Oxford, 1953), p. 92.

49. *The Parliamentary History of England* (London, 1811), VII, pp. 21, 228.

50. R. Steele, *The Englishman*, ed. R. Blanchard (Oxford, 1955), pp. 339-40.

51. H. Trevor-Roper, *From Counter-Reformation to Glorious Revolution* (Chicago, 1992), p. 231.

52. Defoe, for example, defended "the late glorious Revolution" in the *Review* of January 1710, during the Sacheverell trial, maintaining that its foremost achievements were to secure the crown in the hands of the Protestants and to assert the right of the people, assembled in parliament, to dispose of the crown. See *An English Garner*, VII, pp. 460-64.

53. Bradbury's list of sermons in the British Library Catalog, given annually on 5 November and touching the subject of 1688, ranges from 1705 to 1746. See also John Newman, *The Character and Blessings of a Good Government*, a Sermon preached at Salters-Hall, November 5th 1716 (London, 1716), p. 6; Jonathan Gyles, *The Welcome; or Great Britain's Happiness in the Hanoverian Succession* (London, 1717), p. 1.

54. Dickinson, pp. 43-44.

55. *Cato's Letters: or Essays on Liberty, Civil and Religious, and Other Important Subjects*, 4 vols., 5th ed. (London, 1748), IV, p. 293.

56. [William Revolution], *The Real Crisis; or the Necessity of Giving Immediate and Powerful Succor to the Emperor Against France* (London, 1735), pp. 5-7.

57. *The Works of Lord Bolingbroke*, 4 vols. (London, 1844), I, pp. 218, 308-09, 510, II, pp. 9-10, 27, 98-99. See also I. Kramnick's remarks in the introduction to his edition of Bolingbroke's *Historical Writings* (Chicago, 1972), pp. *xl-xlv*, and Dickinson, pp. 37-38.

58. *Gazette de France*, No. 55 (24 December 1688), pp. 689-92; No. 56 (31 December 1688), p. 704; No. 5 (5 February 1689), pp. 55-56.

59. Goulemot, "Le mot révolution," pp. 426-27, 436-37.

60. *Histoire des Ouvrages des Savants*, V (May 1689), pp. 268-75.

61. *Ibid.*, V (June 1689), p. 351; VI (September 1689), p. 26; VI (October 1689), p. 65; VI (November 1689), p. 107; VI (February 1690), p. 263; VIII (November 1691), p. 101.

62. *Bibliothèque Universelle et Historique*, XVI (1690), pp. 30-31, 203, 213; XIX (1690), pp. 589-90. I have used the Amsterdam re-edition (1702-18).

63. . Goulemot, "Le mot révolution," pp. 428-29.

64. P. Bayle, *Oeuvres diverses* (1727), II, pp. 583, 602.

65. *Ibid.*, (1731), IV, p. 735.

66. See the articles "Drusus," note D; "Edward IV," note O; "Pontus de la Gardie," note C; "Mucia," "Vespasian," note E.

67. *Bibliothèque Choisie*, VI (1705), pp. 377, 381; XV (1708), pp. 1-109. *Bibliothèque Ancienne et Moderne*, III (1715), p. 431.

68. In Fénelon's "Examen de conscience sur les devoirs de la royauté," originally written around 1700, the term is employed once, and even that passage might be a later paraphrase of the words of the author. See *Oeuvres diverses de Fénelon* (Paris, 1824), p. 272.

69. J. d'Orléans, *Histoire des révolutions d'Angleterre*, 6 vols. (Paris, 1795), III, p. 434.

70. Goulemot, *Discours, histoire et révolutions*, p. 184.

71. *Bibliothèque Universelle et Historique*, XXII (1692), p. 31.

72. J. d'Orléans, *Histoire des révolutions d'Espagne*, 4 vols. (The Hague, 1734), I, p.1.

73. C. Vanel, *Abrégé nouveau de l'histoire générale de Turcs, où sont décrits les événements et les révolutions arrivées dans cette vast monarchie* (Paris 1689); and *Abrégé mouveau de l'histoire générale d'Angleterre, ... avec les révolutions qui y sont arrivées sous les derniers règnes* (Paris, 1689). In an earlier work Vanel had used a traditional term – *Histoire des troubles de Hongrie* (Paris-Amsterdam, 1686).

74. [Y. J. de La Motte], *Histoire des révolutions de France*, 4 vols. (The Hague, 1738), II, pp. 575-76.

75. C. Renaudot, *Révolutions des empires, royaumes, républiques*, 2 vols. (Paris, 1769), II, pp. 1-2.

76. *Bibliothèque Ancienne et Moderne*, (1714), II, p. 227.

77. F. Gilbert, "Revolution," *Dictionary of the History of Ideas*, IV, p. 154; K. M. Baker, "Revolution," in *The French Revolution and the Creation of Modern Political Culture* (Oxford, 1988), II, pp. 43-44.

78. C. F. Volney, *The Ruins; or a Survey of the Revolutions of Empires* (Philadelphia, 1799), especially pp. 76-96.

79. Baker, "Revolution," pp. 42-43.

80. M. Marais, *Journal et mémoires sur la régence et le règne de Louis XV (1715-1737)*, 4 vols. (Paris, 1863-68), IV, p. 489.

Chapter Seven

1.   Denina, a professor of humanities in Turin, had his work first published in Italian in 1763, in Glasgow of all places. It had an English translation in 1771.

2.   See I. O. Wade, *The Structure and Form of the French Enlightenment*, 2 vols. (Princeton, 1977), II, pp. 251-416.

3.   F. Rocquain, *L'esprit révolutionnaire avant la Révolution, 1715-1789* (Paris, 1878).

4.   *Journal et mémoires du marquis d'Argenson*, 9 vols. (Paris, 1845), IV, p. 83, VI, pp. 404, 464, VII, pp. 22-23, 295; Rocquain, pp. 145-47.

5.   R. L. d'Argenson, *Considérations sur le gouvernement ancien et présente de la France* (Liege, 1787), pp. 12, 189-91.

6.   *Esprit de lois*, Book V, Chaps. 7 and 11; I used the text of the second volume of the *Oeuvres complètes* of Gallimard's Bibliothèque de la Pléiade (Paris, 1951).

7.   *Ibid.*, pp. 151, 168, 193.

8.   *Oeuvres complètes de Voltaire*, 70 vols. (Basle, 1784-90), XXV, pp. 29, 31.

9.   *Ibid.*, XLII, pp. 255-57, 322.

10. *Ibid.*, XXIX, p. 127.

11. Cited by Rocquain, p. 245.

12. *Ibid.*, pp. 240-43.

13. J. J. Rousseau, *Oeuvres complètes*, 4 vols. Bibliothèque de la Pléiade (Paris, 1959-69), IV, p. 468. *Emile ou de l'education* was ordered burned by the *parlement* of Paris as soon as it appeared in 1762.

14. A. N. Isnard, *Observations sur le principe qui a produit les révolutions de France, de Geneve et de l'Amérique dans le dix-huitième siècle* (Evreux, 1789), pp. 4-5, 46-49, 54-55, 61.

15. Rousseau, *Oeuvres complètes*, III, pp. 187, 190-91, 416. For an interpretation with a different emphasis see Griewank, pp. 165-68.

16. *Code de la nature par Morelly*, edited by Villegardelle (Paris, 1841), pp. 100, 104.

17. [C. P. Duclos], *Considérations sur les moeurs de ce siècle* (n. p., 1751), p. 237.

18. [F. I. D'Espiard], *L'esprit des nations* (The Hague, 1752), pp. 240, 242, 248.

19. [P. H. D. baron d'Holbach], *Ethocratie, ou le gouvernement fondé sur la morale* (Amsterdam, 1776), p. 283.

20. C. J. F. Hénault, *Nouvel abregé chronologique de l'histoire de France*, 3rd ed. (Paris, 1749), pp. 444, 446, 550.

21. C. C. Rulhière, *The History, or Anecdotes, of the Revolution in Russia in the Year 1762* (London, 1797), pp. xi, 8.

22. J. B. Mailly, *L'esprit de la Fronde*, 5 vols. (Paris, 1772-73), I, pp. 64-65, V, p. 816.

23. See J. Popkin, "The Prerevolutionary Origins of Political Journalism" in *The French Revolution and the Creation of Modern Political Culture* (Oxford, 1987), I, pp. 212-15.

24. [A. Goudar], *Testament politique de Louis Mandrin, généralissime de troupes de contrebandiers, écrit par lui-même dans sa prison* (Geneva, 1755), p. 5.

25. [A. Goudar], *Mémoires pour servir a l'histoire de Pierre III, empereur de Russie* (Frankfurt, 1763), p. 34.

26. [A. Goudar], *The Chinese Spy; or Emissary from the Court of Pekin, Commissioned to Examine into the Present State of Europe*, 6 vols. (London, 1765), VI, p. 230.

27. Cited from Goudar's *Réflexions sur la dernière émeute de Malte* (Amsterdam, 1776) by C. Baudi di Vesme, *Le primi manifestazioni della rivoluzione d'occidente in Francia e nelle repubbliche oligarchiche, 1748-75* (Turin, 1972), pp. 11-12.

28. With some change of nuances, I rephrase here the view of K. M. Baker; see his "Revolution" in *The French Revolution and the Creation of Modern Political Culture* (Oxford, 1988), II, pp. 41-43, 50-51.

29. P. de Rapin-Thoyrat, *Abregé de l'histoire d'Angleterre*, 3 vols. (The Hague, 1730), III, p. 271. On his stature as an historian see H. Trevor-Roper, "Our First Whig Historian: Paul de Rapin-Thoyrat" in his *From Counter-Reformation to Glorious Revolution*, pp. 249-65.

30. D. Hume, *The History of England from the Invasion of Julius Caesar to the Revolution in 1688*, "a new edition," 8 vols. (London, 1767), VII, p. 157.

31. *Ibid.*, VIII, pp. 307, 310. In yet another passage, actually written after the two that were cited, Hume expresses the opinion that revolutions can be either good or bad. It comes as he recounts the story of the dethronement of Richard II in 1399: "All the circumstances of this event, compared to those which attended the late revolution of 1688, show the difference between a great and civilized nation, deliberately vindicating its established privileges, and a turbulent and barbarous aristocracy, plunging headlong from the extremes of one faction into those of another." *Ibid.*, III, pp. 49-50.

32. D. Hume, *A treatise of Human Nature*, Book III, "Of Morals," Part I, section 10, "Of the Objects of Allegiance." I have used the text of *The Philosophical Works*, eds. T. H. Green and T. H. Grose (London, 1886), II, p. 325; D. Hume, *Essays; Moral, Political and Literary* (London, 1903), pp. 52-53. See also N. Philipson, "Propriety, Property and Prudence: David Hume and the Defense of the Revolution" in *Political Discourse in Early modern Britain*, pp. 302-20.

33. Cited by Dickinson, "The Eighteenth-Century Debate on the Glorious Revolution," pp. 39-40.

34. A. Ferguson, *An Essay on the History of Civil Society*, 2nd ed. (London, 1768), pp. 110-11, 249-50, 398, 419.

35. A. Smith, *An Inquiry into the Nature and Causes of the Wealth of Nations*, eds. R. H. Campbell, A. S. Skinner and W. B. Todd, 2 vols. (Oxford, 1976), p. 540.

36. F.-H. Turpin, *Histoire du gouvernement des anciennes républiques, où l'on découvre les causes de leur élévation et de leur dépérissement* (Paris, 1769). Nowhere does Turpin mention the name of the true author. Also in the second French translation Montagu's name is missing. See *De la naissance et de la chute de ancienne république*, traduit de l'anglais par le citoyen Cantwel (Paris, 1793).

37. E. W. Montagu, *Reflections of the Rise and Fall of the Ancient Republics* (Basle, 1793), pp. 336-38.

38. J. Priestley, *An Essay on the Principles of Government* (London, 1768), pp. 24-25.

39. *Ibid.*, pp. 30-31, 33-35.

40. I have used the first French translation; W. Robertson, *L'histoire de l'Amérique*, 4 vols. (Paris, 1778).

41. See Dickinson, pp. 40-41.

42. R. Watson, *The Principles of the Revolution Vindicated, in a Sermon Preached before the University of Cambridge on Wednesday, May 29, 1776* (Cambridge, 1776), pp. 5, 6, 8.

43. [W. Stevens], *The Revolution Vindicated and Constitutional Liberty Asserted* (Cambridge, 1777), pp. 15-16. See also J. A. Park, *Memoirs of William Stevens Esq.* (London, 1812), pp. 113-14.

44. R. Price, *Observations on the Nature of Civil Liberty*, 2nd ed. (London, 1776), p. 109.

45. Mably, *Des droits et des devoirs du citoyen* (Paris, 1876), pp. 6, 8, 30-31; and see the thorough discussion in Baker's "Revolution," pp. 45-49.

46. Mably, *Des droits*, pp. 35, 42, 106-106, 122-24.

47. *Observations sur l'histoire de France* in *Collection complète des oeuvres de l'abbé de Mably* (Paris, 1794-95), II, p. 283.

48. *Ibid.*, III, pp. 300-301, 306, 313, 542.

49. Mably, *De la législation, ou principes de loix*, 2 vols. (Amsterdam, 1776), I, pp. 188, 191, II, pp. 43-44.

50. *Les vrais principes du gouvernement françois*, (Geneva, 1780), pp. 107, 128.

51. G. T. F. Raynal, *Histoire philosophique et politique des établissemens et du commerce des Européens dans les deux Indes*, 3rd edition, 3 vols. (Geneva, 1775), I, pp. 652-54. This edition is said to have been watched over by Raynal himself, and has his name on the title page and his picture in profile.

52. *Ibid.*, III, pp. 459, 465, 470-72, 475, 482, 484, 496.

53. *Ibid.*, I, pp. 1-2. This concept of revolution might be compared with his note at the bottom of page 18 in reference to the sixteenth century: "Le siècle des révolutions avançoit à grandes pas. La nature humaine alloit

connoître de nouvelles lumieres et la liberté; mais il devoit lui couter des guerres et des crimes."

54. *Ibid.*, III, p. 583.

55. Incurring difficulties in my attempts to locate Darlene Gay Levy's *The Ideas and Careers of Simon-Nicolas-Henry Linguet* (Urbana, 1980), I have used Benjamin Paskoff's *Linguet; Eighteenth Century Intellectual Heretic in France* (New York, 1983), which is a posthumous publication of a Ph.D. dissertation written in the 1940s. See also Popkin, *art. cit.*, pp. 216-18, and Baker, *art. cit.*, pp. 53-54.

56. S. N. H. Linguet, *Théorie de loix civiles, ou principes fondamentaux de la société*, 2 vols. (London, 1767), I, pp. 74-75, 82; Linguet, *Du plus heureux gouvernement, ou parallele de constitutions politiques de l'Asie avec celles de l'Europe*, 2 vols. (London, 1774), I, p. 28.

57. Linguet, *Annales politiques,...* [Geneva: Slatkine reprint, 1970], I, pp. 5-6, 11-13, 15.

58. *Ibid.*, I, pp. 83-84, 94-98, 101-103.

59. See the *Mémoire au roi, par M. Linguet, concernant ses réclamations, actuellement pendantes au parlement de Paris* (London, 1786); Paskoff, pp. 78-82.

60. Linguet, *Examen raisonné des ouvrages de Voltaire*, 2nd ed. (Paris, 1817), p. 215. First edition of this work came out in Brussels in 1788.

Chapter Eight

1. *Correspondence of John Adams and Thomas Jefferson (1812-1826)*, ed. P. Wilstach (Indianapolis, 1925), pp. 114-16.

2. *The Writings of Samuel Adams*, ed. H. A. Cushing (New York, 1904), I, p. 269. Also Jefferson in his "Summary View of the Rights of British America" of August 1774 employed "revolution" only in this context: "Since the establishment, however, of the British constitution at the glorious Revolution, on its free and ancient principles,..."

3. [E. Rawson], *The Revolution in New England Justified, and the People There Vindicated from the Aspersions Cast upon them by Mr. John Palmer* (Boston: Printed for Joseph Brunning, 1691), p. 1.

4. Jefferson's remarks to this effect are in his *Notes on Virginia*, written in 1781-82 and first printed in Paris in 1784. The term "revolution" is absent from Jefferson's vocabulary even at this comparatively late date. See *The Writings of Thomas Jefferson*, ed. A. A. Lipscomb (Washington, D.C., 1903), II, pp. 165-66.

5. *The Political Works of Thomas Paine* (London, 1844), pp. 33-34.

6. *Ibid.*, p. 12.

7. *Letters of Members of the Continental Congress*, ed. E. C. Burnett, 7 vols. (Washington, D.C.: Carnegie Institution, 1921-1934), I, p. 526. Of the

twelve letters mentioned three are by John Adams, but only in that of 3 July, 1776 does he call independence a "mighty revolution." The term is similarly absent from letters written in the two weeks following the Declaration and from the announcements of the president of the Congress, John Hancock, to the New Jersey Convention and to General Washington. Cf. *Ibid.*, II, pp. 1-23.

8.   *The Writings of Samuel Adams*, III, p. 304.

9.   On 23 June, 1779 he referred thus to Benjamin Franklin: "It is universally believed in France, England and all Europe that his Electric Wand has accomplished all this Revolution but nothing is more groundless." *Diary and Autobiography of John Adams*, ed. L. H. Butterfield, 4 vols. (Cambridge, Mass., 1961), II, pp. 391, 408, III, p. 138.

10.   The Oration is in "David Ramsay, 1749-1815; Selections from his Writings," ed. R. L. Brunhouse, *Transactions of the American Philosophical Society*, New Series, Vol. 55, Part 4 (1965), pp. 183-90.

11.   *Letters of Benjamin Rush*, ed. L. H. Butterfield (Princeton, 1952), pp. 221-22.

12.   "The American Crisis," No. 2, 13 January 1777, *The Political Works of Thomas Paine*, p. 55.

13.   *Journals of the Continental Congress, 1774-1789*, ed. W. C. Ford, 34 vols. (Washington, D.C., 1904-1937), XII, pp. 1013, 1063, XIII, pp. 421, 1452. See also *Letters of Members of the Continental Congress*, IV, pp. 59, 83.

14.   J. Sparks, *The Life of Gouverneur Morris*, with selections from his correspondence and miscellaneous papers, 3 vols. (Boston, 1832), I, p. 27.

15.   Cited by Max M. Mintz, *Gouverneur Morris and the American Revolution* (Norman, 1970), p. 121.

16.   [G. Morris], *Observations on the American Revolution* (Philadelphia: Printed for Styner and Cist, 1779), pp. 1, 4, 122.

17.   For example, the periodical *Affaires de l'Angleterre et de l'Amérique*, actually sponsored by the French foreign ministry from 1776 to 1779, mistakenly reported in its first issue "M. Adams" as the author of the pamphlet *Common Sense* and "un des premiers pivots de la révolution." See the quotation in a note in *Diary and Autobiography of John Adams*, II, p. 352.

18.   Guillaume Thomas François Raynal, *Révolution de l'Amérique*, (London, 1781), 183 pp. This and the English translation in just two pages less, were both printed by Lockyer Davis, Holburn. Raynal was perhaps not entirely pleased with the London publication because two years later he published an enlarged version in French, *Tableau et révolutions des colonies angloises dans l'Amérique septentrionale*, 2 vols. (Paris, 1783).

19.   Raynal, *The Revolution of America*, pp. 40, 126-27, 173.

20.   *The Political Works of Thomas Paine*, pp. 186, 188, 204.

21.   *The Writings of George Washington from the Original Manuscript Sources, 1745-1799*, ed. J. C. Fitzpatrick (Washington, D.C., 1938), XXVI,

pp. 486-88; and see also vol. XXVII, pp. 52, 268, where on two different occasions, 8 July and 13 December 1783, he mentioned the "History of the Revolution," and "May the Revolution prove extensively propitious to the cause of Literature."

22. *The Political Works of Thomas Paine*, p. 151.

23. See also Carl B. Cone, *Torchbearer of Freedom; The Influence of Richard Price on Eighteenth Century Thought* (Lexington, 1952), pp. 76-82. Also D. O. Thomas, *The Honest Mind; The Thought and Work of Richard Price* (Oxford, 1977), pp. 148-51.

24. Cited by Cone, p. 107.

25. R. Price, *Observations on the Importance of the American Revolution* (London, 1784), especially pp. 1-2, 68-73, 83-84; Thomas, pp. 263-68; Henri Laboucheix, *Richard Price, théoriien de la révolution américaine* (Paris: Didier, 1970), pp. 41-42, 162.

26. "Most of the *distresses* of our country and of the *mistakes* which Europeans have formed of us, have arisen from the belief that the American Revolution is *over*. This is so far from being the case that we have only finished the first act of the great drama. We have changed our forms of government but it remains yet to effect a revolution in our principles, opinions and manners so as to accommodate them to the forms of government we have adopted." *Letters of Benjamin Rush*, p. 388.

27. "David Ramsay, 1749-1815; Selections from his Writings," p. 92. Ramsay and Jefferson continued to correspond until 1813.

28. N. Webster, *An American Selection of Lessons in Reading and Speaking*, 3rd ed. (Philadelphia, 1787), pp. 5-6, 214, 216-17, 222.

Chapter Nine

1. B. Faÿ, *L'esprit révolutionnaire en France et aux États-Unis à la fin du XVIIIe siècle* (Paris, 1925); I have used the English translation, *The Revolutionary Spirit in France and America; A Study of Moral and Intellectual Relations between France and the United States at the End of the Eighteenth Century* (New York: Cooper Square, 1966).

2. Cited in *The New Cambridge Modern History* (Cambridge, 1965), VIII, p. 440; see also the views there on the impact of American independence on Europe in the chapter written by R. R. Palmer.

3. Compare the entries on the word "radical" in the *Oxford English Dictionary* against the French *Le Robert*.

4. J. H. Billington, *Fire in the Minds of Men; Origins of the Revolutionary Faith* (New York: Basic Books, 1980), p. 19.

5. Cited by L. M. Gidney, *L'influence des États-Unis d'Amérique sur Brissot, Condorcet et Mme Roland* (Paris, 1930), p. 16.

6.　*Affaires de l'Angleterre et de l'Amérique*, IV, p. ccxx, XVII, p. clvii; and see G. B. Watts, *Les Affaires de l'Angleterre et de l'Amérique and John Adams* (Charlotte, N. C.: Heritage Printers, 1965).

7.　[P. U. Dubuisson], *Abrégé de la révolution de l'Amérique angloise* (Paris, 1778), pp. 1, 3, 4, 6, 16, 338, 394, 430.

8.　M. R. Hilliard d'Auberteuil, *Essais historiques et politiques sur les Anglo-Américains*, 2 vols. (Brussels, 1781-82), I, pp. 9-10, II, pp. 389-90, 400.

9.　[T. Pownall], *Pensées sur la révolution de l'Amérique Unie* (Amsterdam, 1781), p. iv; T. Pownall, *A Memorial Addressed to the Sovereigns of America* (London, 1783), pp. 12, 85. "Revolution" is entirely missing in tracts published in 1780 in London by Joseph Galloway, a renegade native American, born in Maryland, who changed sides in 1777 and subsequently left for England.

10.　Faÿ, *The Revolutionary Spirit*, pp. 196-98.

11.　L. Genty, *L'influence de la découverte de l'Amérique sur le bonheur du genre humain* (Paris, 1788), p. 317.

12.　[F.-J., marquis de Chastellux], *Discours sur les avantages ou les désavantages qui résultent pour l'Europe de la découverte de l'Amérique* (London, 1787), p. 68.

13.　F.-J. Chastellux, *Travels in North America in the Years 1780, 1781 and 1782*, trans. H. C. Rice Jr., 2 vols. (Chapel Hill, 1963), I, pp. 135-36, II, p. 391.

14.　*Ibid.*, II, pp. 533-34.

15.　J. B. Mailhe, *Discours qui a remporté le prix à l'Académie de Jeux Floraux en 1784 sur la grandeur et l'importance de la révolution qui vient de s'opérer dans l'Amérique septentrionale* (Toulouse, 1784), pp. 4, 20-22.

16.　A case in point is Francis d'Ivernois, *An Historical and Political View of the Constitution and Revolutions of Geneva in the Eighteenth Century*, trans. J. Farell (Dublin, 1784), of which the original French edition came out in 1782. In 1789 the same author published in London a work entitled *Tableau historique et politique de deux dernières révolutions de Genève*.

17.　P. de Longchamps, *Histoire imparciale des événements politiques et militaires de la dernière guerre* (Amsterdam, 1785); [D. J. Leboucher], *Histoire de la dernière guerre entre la Grande-Bretagne et les États-Unis de l'Amérique, la France, l'Espagne et la Hollande* (Paris, 1787).

18.　[J. Hector St. John de Crèvecoeur], *Lettres d'un cultivateur américain, écrites a W. S. Ecuyer, depuis l'année 1770 jusqu'à 1781*, 2 vols. (Paris, 1785), I, pp. 18, 52, 289, 419.

19.　The letter was printed by Adams in 1787 at the end of the first volume of his *A Defence of the Constitutions of Government of the United States of America*; see especially pp. 384, 388.

20.　Mably, *Principes de morale* (Paris, 1784), pp. 225, 337.

21. Mably, *Remarks Concerning the Government and the Laws of the United States of America* (Dublin, 1785), pp. 2, 5, 94.

22. *Ibid.*, pp. 28, 38.

23. [H. G. Riquetti, comte de Mirabeau], *Essai sur le despotisme*, 2nd edition (London, 1776), pp. vii, 80, 121, 154, 287, 299.

24. Mirabeau, *Considérations sur l'Ordre de Cincinnatus* (London, 1784), pp. 1, 7, 328.

25. Mirabeau, *Enquiries Concerning Lettres de Cachet, the Consequences of Arbitrary Imprisonment and the History of the Inconveniences, Distresses and Sufferings of State Prisoners*, 2 vols. (London, 1787).

26. J. Starobinski, "Éloquence antique, éloquence future: aspects d'un lieu commun d'ancien régime," *The French Revolution and the Creation of Modern Political Culture*, I, especially pp. 317-20; also A. B. Spitzer, "In the Beginning was the Word: The French Revolution," *Journal of Interdisciplinary History*, XIX, No. 4 (1989), pp. 621-33. Even Rulhière had "révolution" twice in his "discours de reception" of 4 June 1787; see *Oeuvres de Rulhière*, 6 vols. (Paris, 1819), II, pp. 15, 27.

27. *Correspondence inédite de Condorcet et de Turgot (1770-1779)*, (Paris, 1883).

28. Condorcet, *Vie de M. Turgot* (London, 1786), pp. 196-97, 202.

29. "De l'influence de la révolution d'Amérique sur l'Europe" in *Oeuvres de Condorcet*, 12 vols. (Paris, 1847), VIII, pp. 11, 25, 28-30. See also the translated excerpts in Condorcet, *Selected Writings*, ed. K. M. Baker (Indianapolis, 1976), pp. 71-83, and M. M. Mintz, "Condorcet's Reconsideration of America as a Model for Europe," *Journal of the Early Republic*, XI, No. 4 (1991), pp. 493-506.

30. *Encyclopédie méthodique*, 4 vols. (Paris, 1784-88), II, pp. 349-57.

31. Soulès, *Histoire des troubles*, IV, pp. 263-65.

32. *Encyclopédie méthodique*, II, pp. 28-33.

33. [F. Mazzei], *Recherches historiques et politiques sur les États-Unis de l'Amérique septentrionale*, 4 vols. (Paris, 1788).

34. [J. Almon], *The Revolution in MDCCLXXXII Impartially Considered* (London, 1782), pp. 5-6.

35. *Diary and Autobiography of John Adams*, III, p. 194.

36. *An Abstract of the History and Proceedings of the Revolution Society in London* (London, 1789), pp. 5-7, 14-15; E. C. Black, *The Association; British Extra-parliamentary Political Organizations, 1769-1793* (Cambridge, Mass., 1963), pp. 214-15.

37. J. P. Brissot, *De la verité, ou meditations sur les moyens de parvenir à la verité dans toutes les connoissances humaines* (Neuchâtel, 1782), pp. 250-58.

38. For a short survey of Brissot's ideological development see the introduction by M. Soceanu Vamos and D. Echeverria to the new translation of his *New Travels in the United States of America, 1788* (Cambridge, Mass., 1964).

39. E. Claviere and J. P. Brissot de Warville, *De la France et des États-Unis* (London, 1787), pp. ix-x, xxx-xxxiii; compare the parallel passages in the English translation, *Considerations on the Relative Situation of France and the United States of America, Shewing the Importance of the American Revolution to the Welfare of France* (London, 1788).

40. Faÿ, *The Revolutionary Spirit*, pp. 234-44.

41. *Oeuvres de Condorcet*, IX, pp. 1-143; and Faÿ, pp. 255-60.

42. D. M. G. Sutherland, *Révolution et contre-révolution en France, 1789-1815* (Paris, 1991), p. 103.

43. F. Brunot, *Histoire de la langue française*, IX, p. 617; J. A. Goldstone, *Revolution and Rebellion in the Early Modern World* (Berkeley, 1991), p. xxi.

44. Young, *Travels*, p. 182.

45. J. P. Brissot, *Mémoire sur les noirs de l'Amérique septentrionale lu à l'Assemblée de la Société des Amis des Noirs, le 9 Fevrier 1789* (Paris, 1789), p. 53.

46. *Oeuvres de Rulhière*, II, p. 133.

47. Cited by Baker, "Revolution," pp. 55-58.

48. See the texts of all of these letters in *The Correspondence of the Revolution Society in London with the National Assembly and with various Societies of the Friends of Liberty in France and England* (London, 1792).

49. R. Price, *Discourse on the Love of Our Country* (London, 1790), pp. 49-50; and see Black, *The Association*, p. 216.

50. E. Burke, *Reflections on the Revolution in France*, "The Seventh Edition" (London, 1790), pp. 2, 13, 21, 23-24.

51. *Ibid.*, pp. 95-96.

52. J. Priestley, *Letters to the Right Honourable Edmund Burke, Occasioned by His Reflections on the Revolution in France* (Birmingham, 1791), pp. iv, vii, 21-22, 23, 37, 39-40.

53. *The Political Works of Thomas Paine* (1844), pp. 280, 347.

54. *Ibid.*, pp. 356-57; Arndt, *On Revolution*, p. 38.

55. Condorcet, *Outlines of an Historical View of the Progress of the Human Mind* (London, 1795), pp. 19, 230-31.

56. *Ibid.*, pp. 261, 265-67.

57. *Oeuvres de Condorcet*, X, p. 608. This comes from a short tract of November 1792, "De la nature des pouvoirs politiques dans une nation libre."

58. *Ibid.*, XII, pp. 615, 619, 623.

59. *Rapport sur les principes du gouvernement révolutionnaire*, fait au nom du Comité de Salut Public par Maximilien Robespierre, imprimé par

ordre de la Convention, le 5 Nivôse de l'an second de la République une et indivisible, p. 2.

60. *Ibid.*, pp. 3, 5; and see, for example, the discussion of this speech in M. J. Sydenham, *The French Revolution* (New York, 1965), pp. 206-207.

61. [N. Webster], *The Revolution in France Considered in Respect to its Progress and Effects* (New York, 1794), pp. 37-38, 69-72.

Conclusion

1. As cited by *Le Robert*, VI, p. 18.
2. R. Villari, *The Revolt of Naples* (1993), pp. 171-74.
3. *Ibid.*, p. 178.
4. Burnet, *History of My Own Time*, I, pp. 150-51.

INDEX

Note: Since the word/term "revolution" appears throughout the book, it is omitted from the Index.

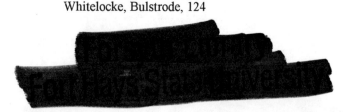

"REVOLUTION"

The Entrance of a New Word Into Western Political Discourse

Ilan Rachum

University Press of America,® Inc.
Lanham • New York • Oxford

Copyright © 1999 by
University Press of America,® Inc.
4720 Boston Way
Lanham, Maryland 20706

12 Hid's Copse Rd.
Cumnor Hill, Oxford OX2 9JJ

Library of Congress Cataloging-in-Publication Data

Rachum Ilan.
"Revolution" : the entrance of a new word into Western political
discourse / Ilan Rachum.

Includes index.
Discourse analysis—Political aspects—History. 2. Rhetoric—
Political aspects—History. 3. Revolutions. I. Title.
P302.77.R33   1999   320'.01'4—dc21   99—41524 CIP

ISBN 0-7618-1503-1 (cloth: alk. ppr.)
ISBN 0-7618-1504-X (pbk: alk. ppr.)

㊉™The paper used in this publication meets the minimum
requirements of American National Standard for Information
Sciences—Permanence of Paper for Printed Library Materials,
ANSI Z39.48—1984

To Stephanie

On the Threshold of Our
Sixth Seven-Years Revolution